THE A TO Z GUIDE TO

BIBLE
SIGNS and
SYMBOLS

Understanding Their Meaning and Significance

Neil Wilson and
Nancy Ryken Taylor

BakerBooks

a division of Baker Publishing Group
Grand Rapids, Michigan

Published by Baker Books
a division of Baker Publishing Group
P.O. Box 6287, Grand Rapids, MI 49516-6287
www.bakerbooks.com

Printed in the United States of America

Library of Congress Cataloging-in-Publication Data
Wilson, Neil S., 1950–
    The A to Z guide to Bible signs and symbols / Neil Wilson and Nancy Ryken Taylor.
        pages cm
    ISBN 978-0-8010-1479-6 (pbk.)
    1. Symbolism in the Bible—Dictionaries. I. Taylor, Nancy Ryken. II. Title.
    BS477.W48 2015
    220.6′403—dc23   2014027149

Developed by Livingstone, the publishing services division of Barton-Veerman Company. Contributing staff included: Rick Ezell, Nancy Ryken Taylor, Katherine Wilson, Neil Wilson, Larry Taylor, Tom Shumaker, and Dave Veerman.

15   16   17   18   19   20   21   7   6   5   4   3   2

THE A TO Z GUIDE TO

BIBLE
SIGNS and
SYMBOLS

The A to Z Guide to Bible Signs and Symbols is dedicated to all those who eagerly read the figurative language of God's Word, appreciate the literary scope of God's amazing written revelation, apply the truth presented in creative ways, and will immediately note with delight the many signs and symbols we didn't have room to include. Biblical signs and symbols can be described the same way the apostle John summarized the signs of Christ he chose for his Gospel:

> *Jesus performed many other miracles that his disciples saw. Those miracles are not written in this book. But these miracles have been written so that you will believe that Jesus is the Messiah, the Son of God, and so that you will have life by believing in him.*
>
> *(John 20:30–31)*

Contents

Introduction   10

A   Altar   16
Ark   18
Arm   20

B   Babylon   22
Baptism   24
Beast   26
Bethlehem   28
Birth   30
Black   32
Blood   34
Body   36
Book/Scroll   38
Branch   40
Bread   42
Bride   44
Bridegroom   46
Brimstone   48
Building   50
Bull/Calf   52

C   Camel   54
Canaan   56
Candlestick/Lamp
  Stand   58
Circumcision   60
Clear/Crystal/
  Transparent   62
Clothing   64
Cornerstone   66
Cross/Crucifixion   68
Crown   70

D   Darkness   72
Day   74
Deer   76
Donkey   78
Door/Doorpost   80
Dove/Wild Pigeon   82

E   Eagle/Vulture   84
Eden   86

Egypt   88
Eye   90

F   Father   92
Feast/Banquet   94
Feet   96
Fire   98
Fish   100
Five   102
Flowers   104
Forty   106
Four   108

G   Gate   110
Goat   112
Gold   114
Graft   116
Grapes   118

H   Hand   120
Head   122
Heaven   124
Honey   126
Horn   128
Horse   130

I   Incense   132

J   Jar/Pottery/Vessel   134
Jonah in the Great
Fish   136
Jordan River   138

K   Key   140
Kingdom   142

L   Lamb/Sheep   144
Lamp   146
Leprosy   148
Light   150
Lion   152
Locust   154
Lord's Supper/Last Supper/
Lord's Table   156

M   Mark/Seal   158
Marriage   160
Meal   162
Mirror   164
Mountain/Hill   166
Mount Moriah   168
Mount Sinai   170

N   Nineveh   172

O   Oil   174
One   176
One Hundred Forty-Four
Thousand   178

P   Passover   180
Pigs   182
Precious Stones   184
Purim   186
Purple   188

Q | Quail   190

R | Rainbow   192
Raven/Crow   194
Red/Scarlet   196
Ring   198
Rome   200
Root   202

S | Sabbath   204
Sacrifice/Offering   206
Salt   208
Sea of Galilee   210
Seed   212
Serpent on a Pole   214
Serpent/Dragon   216
Seven   218
Ship/Boat   220
Silver   222
Six Hundred Sixty-Six   224
Sodom   226
Son   228
Stone/Rock   230
Sword   232

T | Tabernacle   234
Temple   236
Thousand   238
Three   240
Threshing Floor   242
Throne   244

Tower   246
Tree   248
Trumpet/Shofar   250
Twelve   252
Two   254

U | Unleavened Bread/
Yeast   256

V | Veil/Curtain   258
Vine   260

W | Water   262
White   264
Wilderness   266
Wind   268
Wine   270

X | Xerxes the Great
(and Other Significant
Rulers)   272

Y | Yoke   274

Z | Zion/Jerusalem   276

Image Credits   279

Introduction

W e want a sign!" The demand was issued in a threatening tone that left unspoken the "or else!" that was part of the tense moment. Jesus had just cleared the temple court in Jerusalem that had been turned into a kind of farmers' market / money exchange under the permission of the religious people in charge. They were not happy with Jesus, and decided the best way to get rid of him and bring back the merchants was to challenge his right to intervene. They demanded his credentials. "Show us you have the right to order us around! Do a miracle! You claim to speak for God? Prove it!" John 2:13–22 gives us a glimpse of the significance of signs and symbols in the Bible. When his opponents demanded proof, Jesus said, "Tear down this temple, and I'll rebuild it in three days" (John 2:19). His hearers thought he was referring to the impressive buildings surrounding them, but John explains Jesus was using the temple as a symbol: "But the temple Jesus spoke about was his own body. After he came back to life, his disciples remembered that he had said this. So they believed the Scripture and this statement that Jesus had made" (John 2:21–22).

Before Jesus is actually recorded as having performed any miracles, he faced a similar challenge: "If you are the Son of God, tell these stones to become loaves of bread!" (Matt. 4:3). Satan taunted him, "Prove you're the Son of God. Show me a sign; whip up a miracle." The exchange that follows between Satan and Jesus during the wilderness temptation (Matt. 4:1–11) is one of the places in the Bible that emphasizes the significance of signs and symbols in understanding what God tells us in his Word.

Bible Signs and Symbols

Maybe your first question in opening this book is, what are signs and symbols and what is the difference between them? Good question. Signs point or draw attention; symbols represent. Signs are clues; symbols are pictures that denote an object, purpose, or concept. Public bathrooms around the world display recognizable symbols (usually on the door) that indicate male and female facilities. In some cases, signs and symbols work together. Walk through an airport in a foreign place and you will see signs displaying a plate and utensils, indicating a place to eat in the direction of the arrow. Signs are like calling cards, passports, and deeds—not necessarily related directly to an object, they confirm or prove a claim. The signs that you own a car or home are the keys in your hand and the title in your possession with your signature (itself a sign) on the correct line. Signs don't have to be documents; they can be unconnected events or circumstances whose occurrence indicates the truth of a different claim.

In the English Bible, the word *sign* translates the Greek word *semeion*, which is used in a passage like Luke 2:12, "This is how you will recognize him" (or as the King James translation puts it, "And this shall be a sign"): "You will find an infant wrapped in strips of cloth and lying in a manger." Literally, the angel said, "And this will be to you the sign that what I just said is true about the Savior, who is Christ the Lord, born to you this day in the city of David." Signs serve as X that marks the spot. When we find or see a sign, we expect to find what we were told we would find.

The word *symbol* is used rarely in any translation of the Bible. God's Word, for example, uses the term twice (Ps. 74:4; Isa. 8:18). But the term is often used by students of the Bible to describe the teaching style of the Scriptures. Biblical writers often substituted a trait or quality in one familiar object to highlight a similar or parallel trait they were explaining. Symbols often allowed Bible people to talk about one thing while actually describing something else.

The word *sign*, in comparison, is used many times throughout the Bible. The Greek word *semeion* is often translated *miracle* because that usually is the primary idea. To those eager to confront Jesus, a miracle on command might demonstrate that he had some special powers from God, but it would also demonstrate he was vulnerable to manipulation. If he'd felt it necessary to "prove" himself, he would actually be revealing a lack of confidence in his own identity. Jesus didn't fall for Satan's challenges in the wilderness—"If you are the Son of God" (Matt. 4:3, 6)—because in "proving" who he was he would be yielding control to Satan. The sign-miracles Jesus performed were in response to genuine need rather than a need on his part to demonstrate to doubters who he was. Even the miracle of walking on the water wasn't done by Jesus "on command" or because the disciples expected/demanded it, but to give them an indelible lesson.

Perhaps you are one of those people who is already thoroughly confused about Bible signs and symbols and is just looking for an introduction to shed some light on the strange, unusual, and surprising aspects of this book we often refer to as the Word of God. One of the surprises may be that when you understand the way signs and symbols are used, you will figure out many of them for yourself. Whether it was *signs*, *symbols*, or *Bible* that caught your attention, we trust that *The A to Z Guide to Bible Signs and Symbols* will deliver some helpful insights and answers as you explore the Scriptures on your own.

Rules for Signs and Symbols

The Bible itself is self-conscious about its symbolic nature. One of the most important interpretive questions to ask when studying an apparent Bible sign or symbol is, does this imagery or idea appear elsewhere in Scripture? The Bible often explains itself quite clearly and discourages our efforts to find symbolism or signs where there are none. See, for example, Luke 11:29–32, where Jesus addresses the lack of signs because people are evil and won't even benefit from the sign God *does* offer. But God's Word has plenty of interesting symbols for us to understand.

By way of caution, here are several easy errors that affect our quest and understanding of signs and symbols in Scripture:

- *Background blindness.* Sometimes we read into the Bible the current meanings of words that were not intended by the original writer. One of the reasons we study the culture and history that surrounds the Bible is to be aware of how this "background" informs the words and pictures we find in Scripture. If our early reading of the Bible takes us to a verse like 1 Corinthians 5:7 ("Remove the old yeast of sin so that you may be a new batch of dough, since you don't actually have the yeast of sin. Christ, our Passover lamb, has been sacrificed"), our understanding of Paul's message will depend on our awareness of Old Testament Passover history and traditions, the place of Passover in Jesus' ministry, and the role of yeast in the

Passover preparations. The background isn't stated in the verse but it is scattered throughout Scripture.

Taking the time to understand the cultural context of events and statements in Scripture often deepens their meaning or sharpens their impact on our lives. For example, it could be said that the climax of Jesus' teaching occurred during that last week of his ministry when he was asked an honest question about the most significant aspect of life. Although Matthew (22:34–40) doesn't really distinguish the following interaction from the rest of the hostile questioning Jesus faced, Mark makes the point that one of the listening scribes "saw how well Jesus answered" (Mark 12:28), so he asked a genuine question: "Which commandment is the most important of them all?" (v. 28). Jesus answered directly with what everyone listening to him that day immediately recognized as the Shema, the summary commandment of Deuteronomy 6:4–5. The scribe enthusiastically agreed with Jesus (vv. 32–33). After all, he had probably uttered that commandment several times that day already! Jesus wasn't telling him something his listeners didn't already know. He quoted Old Testament words that were as familiar to them as their own names. He wasn't creating a new teaching; he was holding his audience deeply accountable to what God had already said. Yet note that despite the scribe's wholehearted agreement with Jesus on what was the most important commandment of all, Jesus gently told him, "You're not too far from the kingdom of God" (v. 34). Conversations about this passage in a secular, pluralistic society like ours can easily miss the impact Jesus' words made in a rampantly religious society. His last comment informed his questioner and the rest of the audience that even knowing what was the most important expectation from God, and perhaps repeating it often in prayer, at best left someone "not too far from the kingdom of God."

- *Literal insensitivity.* Here we find two sides to the issue. The first one is presented in a question like, "Do you believe the Bible is literally true?" This is usually a trick question designed to attack the reliability, truth, and inerrancy of Scripture. If a believer says yes, he or she is likely to hear, "So when Jesus calls Herod a fox, he meant that the king had four paws and a tail? 'Cause that would be the literal meaning of his statement, right?" But if the believer says no, the likely accusation is, "So, you don't really believe the Bible is true?" The whole idea that we can identify and describe Bible signs and symbols depends on our understanding that the Bible can communicate when truth is being presented figuratively and when it is being presented literally. And sometimes there is a place for both figurative and literal interpretation, for as we have already pointed out, understanding what the Bible says is the first step in seeking to understand what it means.

Another side of the "literal" question arises when both parties are claiming to take the Bible seriously, but one is being *too* literal. In a recent article ("Seven Deadly Sins of Bible Study"), author Jack Kuhatschek describes one such encounter: "Several years ago the cult expert Walter Martin [author of the outstanding book *Kingdom of the Cults*] was giving a lecture on Mormonism. A few Mormons heard about the lecture and decided to attend. About halfway through the meeting, one of them stood up and began arguing that God the Father has a physical body like ours. He 'proved' his point by quoting passages that refer to God's 'right arm,' 'hand,' 'eyes,' and so on.

"Martin told the person to read aloud Psalm 17:8, 'Hide me in the shadow of your wings,' and asked whether that meant God also has feathers and wings. 'But that's simply a figure of speech,' protested the Mormon. 'Exactly!' replied Martin."

Kuhatschek goes on to comment, "In order to avoid a wooden kind of literalism, we need to realize that the biblical authors communicated in a variety of ways—through metaphors, similes, and symbols—and through a variety of literary genres, such as history, proverbs, parables, letters, poems, and prophecy. We must identify the type of language and literature an author is using in order to interpret his meaning correctly. If we assume, for example, that an author is speaking literally when he is speaking metaphorically (the mistake made by the Mormon), we end up with nonsense."

- *Anchorless texting.* Another mistake is to take a word or phrase that serves in a symbolic way in one part of Scripture and assume that it serves the same way elsewhere, when it may not. Look at the first few chapters of the Gospel of John, where the word *water* is used in at least four very different ways: plain water; baptismal water; physical birth; and living, spiritual water. If we try to force one meaning on *water* in every circumstance, without taking the context into account, we will end up confused. (See the entry for *water* for more on this.)

- *Linguistic handicap.* If we are reading an older translation of the Bible, such as the King James Version, the grandeur and richness of the language should not lull us into unawareness that words from the Elizabethan English culture of 1611 may mean something different today. Consider, for example, something as simple as the word *want* as used in the familiar phrase, "The LORD is my shepherd; I shall not want" (Ps. 23:1 KJV). As used today, the verb means "to desire," but as used in

the KJV, the word means "lack" or "need." Understanding that term affects our expectations from God's role as Shepherd (does he promise to give me what I want or what I need?) and it significantly colors all the figurative language derived from a sheep's life and relationship with its shepherd that fills this psalm.

As a reflection of the character of God, the Bible is rich in imagery, style, and variety in communication. God's authorship ensures a single guiding hand and mind while God's use of human writers spread over one and a half millennia ensures a scope unequaled in literature.

The Bible demands much from language and gives a lot back. It has been translated into more languages than any other book, and there is intense interest in making it available in every active language on the face of the earth. In a sense, the story of the division of human speech that is recorded in Genesis won't come full circle until every person has the opportunity to read God's Word in their mother tongue. The Bible is a translatable book, demonstrating a unique character that seems to fit a language in the same way God fits into a life. Living languages that express the human experience and adapt to reflect both its constants and changes find their greatest purpose in conveying God's Word.

Bible Signs and Symbols Today

The wide impact of the Bible on thought and language can be partly seen in the ongoing use of signs and symbols in common language. We can even see this illustrated in the book itself, since its various parts were written over a millennium and a half. The scope of Scripture allows for not only the introduction of signs and symbols, but also a development in their use as succeeding generations discovered that an effective picture of truth can expand to reflect a greater understanding of that truth. Consider, for example, a word such as *light,* introduced in Genesis 1:3. Reading the first chapter in the

Bible, we discover that light was present *before* those objects we usually think of as sources of light. God said "Let there be light" in verse 3 and didn't say "Let there be lights" until verse 14. From its introduction on the first page of Scripture to its appearance in the last chapter of Revelation (22:5), the word *light* develops a portfolio of meaning worth exploring—as do all the entries in the sampling included in *The A to Z Guide to Bible Signs and Symbols*.

Those familiar with Scripture will probably discover one or two of the favorite signs and symbols have been overlooked or not given enough attention. Any claim to provide much more than an introductory exposure to the range and significance of biblical signs and symbols would fly in the face of our experience with the Bible, which demonstrates on its own a remarkable capacity for speaking with fresh symbolic language into contemporary life. So, for example, people introduced today to the original languages of the Bible (Hebrew, Aramaic, and Greek) are somewhat surprised to discover that text messaging originated long before modern times. The written form of the Hebrew language includes no vowels, making the entire Old Testament a collection of God's text messages to us!

So enjoy *The A to Z Guide to Bible Signs and Symbols* with your Bible open. The specific sign and symbol words for this volume are derived from the GOD's WORD translation of the Bible, so if you are using a different translation, you may find variation in English words on occasion. These will generally be synonyms, not completely different terms.

May this book expand your palate for the bread of life and living water. May it sharpen your awareness of the lamp God has provided for your feet and the light it can be for your path. And may you discover that though God's Word has been written, published, and closed, it remains a living and powerful tool that can transform your life today and prepare you for eternal living with the Author of the Book.

Bible Signs and Symbols in Prophecy

The Bible speaks into life at any and every moment in history. Because it is timelessly true, a special connection exists between Scripture and the idea of prophecy. Every writer God used in publishing his Word was writing for his own day as well as for the future—in ways the writers could only dimly understand, if at all. Peter notes this in his first letter:

> The prophets carefully researched and investigated this salvation. Long ago they spoke about God's kindness that would come to you. So they tried to find out what time or situation the Spirit of Christ kept referring to whenever he predicted Christ's sufferings and the glory that would follow. God revealed to the prophets that the things they had spoken were not for their own benefit but for yours. What the prophets had spoken, the Holy Spirit, who was sent from heaven, has now made known to you by those who spread the Good News among you. These are things that even the angels want to look into. (1 Pet. 1:10–12)

So, in the sense that it is timeless, all Scripture is prophetic. When 2 Timothy 3:16–17 makes the claim for the divine inspiration of the Bible, it also addresses the usefulness or profitability of Scripture for "teaching, pointing out errors, correcting people, and training them for a life that has God's approval." This usefulness is declared without time constraints. What was true then is true now. The Bible continues to be *useful* for all these purposes.

Many of the signs and symbols in Scripture have been employed fully or partially to convey prophecy. But a word used even extensively in a prophecy section doesn't cease to have its regular meaning elsewhere. Paul, for example, asked Timothy to bring certain scrolls to Rome (2 Tim. 4:13), and in his vision in Revelation John saw symbolic scrolls that will be unsealed at the end of the age. Paul's scrolls were made of velum and intended to be unrolled and read; John's symbolized huge records of history to be unfurled in a vision. Because of the connection between signs, symbols, and prophecy, the articles in *The A to Z Guide to Bible Signs and Symbols* will attempt to give appropriate attention to that aspect of biblical language usage. The usage often comes in layers, so we find in the pages of Scripture real horses, symbolic horses like the ones God mentioned to Jeremiah ("If you have raced against others on foot, and they have tired you out, how can you compete with horses?" [Jer. 12:5a]), and prophetic horses like the ones seen by John in Revelation.

Our understanding and appreciation of symbolic and prophetic language will always rely on our understanding of common, daily language. The first builds on the second. If we have no concept of birth and its wonder and limitations, how can we understand the "second birth" or "being born from above" (John 3:3)? If we don't grasp the reality of heaven and earth as a creation of Almighty God, how can we engage with the pictures of the new heaven and the new earth?

God gave us his book to reveal himself. It was meant for us to understand, though some parts are difficult to understand. It's always better to admit we don't understand some part of Scripture than to simply make something up out of thin air. This is particularly true of prophetic passages. G. K. Chesterton offered one of the best descriptions of what occurs when people insist on being able to interpret all of Revelation: "And though St. John the Evangelist saw many strange monsters in his vision, he saw no creature so wild as one of his own commentators" (*Orthodoxy* [Wheaton: Shaw, 1994], 13). *So we approach the signs and symbols in the Bible with humble interest and reasonable caution.*

Bible signs and symbols enrich our lives by showing us how God uses what's common to prepare us for what has depth and meaning. The prophetic side of biblical signs and symbols reminds us that God is working out his plan everywhere, in everything, at all times. The value of signs, symbols, and prophecy is partly in their capacity to provoke our curiosity, but they come to their full significance when we remember that they all point to God and our never-ending need to understand and respond to him more fully.

Peruse and use *The A to Z Guide to Bible Signs and Symbols*, remembering that these brief studies of biblical terms and ideas are meant to accomplish more than the increase of knowledge. They invite us into deeper intimacy with the Author of these ideas. As you discover more about God and his unique Book, may you pass through fearful moments when you realize that the God who authored the Bible knows you in exquisite detail, and then move on to the ever-expanding delights of knowing God as he allows us to know him.

Altar

In the Old Testament, the object erected time and time again to communicate the presence and power of God was an altar. The altar could be a single rock or a loosely organized arrangement of large stones, so people were never far from an altar or could build one in a few moments. Nothing was more prominent as a biblical image for worship and allegiance to God than the altar. It is no exaggeration to say that the most visible sign of one's devotion to the true God in the worship of the old covenant was the building of altars or traveling to them for acts of sacrifice or offering.

Usually constructed with stones that had not been fashioned with tools, the altar was a raised platform on which a fire was kindled. Its form suggested a table or brazier. Altars would be placed beneath the open sky where their smoke could ascend to the heavens. Later, when the altars were constructed for tabernacle worship in the wilderness and for the temple in Jerusalem, they were cast or covered in metal, and the four corners rose, forming points called *horns*.

Altars in the Old Testament

Noah was the first man in the Bible to build an altar, and he did so as an expression of thanksgiving for God's protection during the flood. Abraham, the next altar builder, constructed several as he wandered through the desert. His altar at Shechem was a symbol of his entrance into the Promised Land (Gen. 12:7). He also sacrificed animals and called on the name of the Lord at altars he had built at Bethel, Ai, and Hebron (Gen. 12:8; 13:18). Isaac and Jacob followed his example and built altars in connection with the renewal and expansion of God's covenant.

The tabernacle had two prominent altars: the altar of burnt offering (Exod. 27:1–8) and the altar of incense (Exod. 30:1–10). The altar of burnt offering was located near the front entrance of the tabernacle and was used for the daily burnt offering and meal offering. It symbolized the need for daily cleansing from sin and the necessity of having sin atoned for before one could enter the presence of God. The altar of incense was in front of the veil that separated the most holy place from the rest of the tabernacle. Priests burned incense here, offering up an aroma that was symbolic of prayer and praise rising up to God. In later years the temple had these same basic altars, albeit in a more permanent form.

Altars were sometimes built in Bible times as a commemoration of an event. In Joshua 22 Reuben, Gad, and the half tribe of Manasseh built an altar east of the Jordan River with no intention to use it for sacrifices but as a symbol of solidarity with the rest of Israel.

From Daily Sacrifice to Once-for-All Atonement

An altar was a place of slaughter. In fact, the Hebrew word for *altar* comes from the word that is often translated "slaughter." The altar would be stained with blood, for its central purpose was blood sacrifice. Helpless live animals came squealing to the altar, and their necks were placed on the unhewn stones and sliced open. The blood would flow as the animal was placed on the open flame. The stench was strong, the sight grotesque, and the sounds horrifying. The fire—a symbol of God's presence—would consume the animal. As the sacrifice was made on the altar, God appeared to his people and a holy interchange occurred.

The blood from the animal was either sprinkled against the altar or smeared on its horns, and it was the blood that atoned for the sins of

Jacob knelt before an altar to commemorate the expansion of the covenant.

the people (Heb. 9:22). God declared, "Blood contains life. I have given this blood to you to make peace with me on the altar. Blood is needed to make peace with me" (Lev. 17:11). The sacrifice symbolized our need for a savior. The sacrificial animal stands in our place; the animal dies instead of us.

When we reach the New Testament, the blood running down the sides of the altar reminds us of God's atoning work. Where animal sacrifices permeate the Old Testament, the New Testament is filled with references to Jesus as the ultimate atoning sacrifice. Jesus died on the cross as the Lamb of God, shedding his blood for the sins of humankind. And throughout the Christian era continuing to the present day, when the church gathers at the communion table to celebrate the Eucharist, Christians drink from a cup that symbolizes the blood of Jesus. In the end, the altar reminds us of Jesus' sacrifice and God's provision. Because of the once-for-all sacrifice of Jesus on the cross, we no longer use altars in worship. Sometimes the front of a church is called an altar, but the symbol that has replaced the altar in the worship of Jesus is the table where we meet Christ and share in communion.

Key Verse

The priests slaughtered the goats and made their blood an offering for sin at the altar to make peace with the LORD for Israel. (2 Chron. 29:24)

In addition to the altars to the one true God, throughout the Old Testament we see references to altars built to false gods. Because these were both a practical element involved in the worship of these gods and a symbolic representation of allegiance to them, pagan altars had to be torn down as the Israelites conquered the Promised Land (Deut. 12:2–3). Whether or not a king adhered to this directive determined how he would be remembered—as a follower of God or a follower of false gods. Indeed, we are all remembered for our worship, whether or not we build altars in our hearts to God and continually tear down altars to the false idols of self, prestige, or false religion.

Top, this altar from a Neolithic Tarxien temple dated 3000 BC is an example of a primitive altar.

17

Ark

The term *ark* in Scripture has two main meanings: one is a large boat built by Noah, and the other is the ark of the covenant that was housed in the tabernacle and later in the temple. Both of these images encapsulate important spiritual truths related to salvation.

Noah's Ark

The ark (also translated "boat" or "ship") in Genesis 6–8 was, quite literally, a huge undertaking. With no modern tools, Noah built a three-story boat that was 450 feet long and 75 feet wide. The gopher wood from which it was constructed was covered with waterproof pitch. The final touches included a roof, a window, and internal walls to make rooms. This floating home became a refuge that guaranteed the continuance of the human race and the animal

Noah's ark came to rest on Mount Ararat.

kingdom. It separated the chosen survivors from those who perished in the flood.

The ark was a symbol of salvation and preservation. In contrast to those who suffered under God's judgment and were destroyed in the flood, those in the ark were saved from death and punishment. God "remembered" these chosen ones

and showed them mercy (Gen. 8:1; 1 Pet. 1:3). The rebirth aspect of salvation is symbolized by the ark as well: after the flood, Noah and his sons rebirthed the human race as a sort of second Adam (Gen. 9:2–3). God's charge for them to be fruitful and multiply echoes the original creation mandate in Genesis 1. The Hebrew word translated as "ark" in the story of Noah is used in one other place in Scripture—the story of Moses being placed in a basket or "ark" on the Nile River when his life was in danger from Pharaoh's death edict against Hebrew boys. Here also God's chosen man was saved from a watery death and carried safely in the ark through his providential care. The scope of the story could not be more different—a tiny basket for one baby versus a giant ark for an entire family and a pair of every animal on earth—but the symbol of salvation and preservation is the same.

The presence of an ark in both of these stories is no coincidence. Noah and Moses have many similarities in terms of their significance to Israel. Each man stood at a turning point in Israel's history and saved the nation from annihilation. They both fulfilled the covenant promise that God would protect Israel. In both of their stories, the ark served as a physical instrument of preservation and a symbol of salvation—a guarantee of the continuance of the nation of Israel at a time when all hope seemed to be lost. But it was also a symbol of the possibility of salvation, God's intent to save sinful humankind even as he executes judgment against civilizations that are opposed to him.

In the New Testament, Peter further emphasizes the ark as a symbol of salvation when he draws a parallel between the flood of Noah's day and the waters of baptism: "They are like those who disobeyed long ago in the days of Noah when God waited patiently while Noah

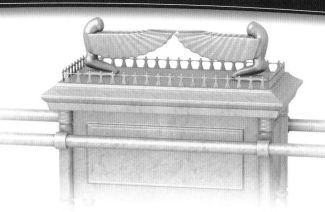

built the ship. In this ship a few people—eight in all—were saved by water. Baptism, which is like that water, now saves you" (1 Pet. 3:20–21a). Believers are saved from death and given new life just like Noah and his family, and later Moses, were saved from death and birthed a new era in Israel's history. But they had to go through the water. The water that signified judgment in Noah's day has been transformed through the work of Jesus into the waters of death, cleansing, and resurrection as believers are reconciled to God and declared righteous before him. In all these cases God in his mercy reaches down and rescues believers from death and they are reborn (John 3:5). The ark is a sign of the salvation from death and rebirth to new life that is the gospel.

The Ark of the Covenant

The ark of the covenant was the most sacred possession of the Israelites, built at the same time as the tabernacle. It was a box about 45 by 27 by 27 inches in size, made of acacia wood overlaid with gold. On each corner was a gold ring, and through these rings poles were placed for carrying. Inside the ark of the covenant were the stone tablets on which were written the Ten Commandments, a golden pot of manna, and Aaron's rod. These were all reminders of God's covenant with Israel and his faithfulness to them.

The most important feature of the ark of the covenant was the mercy seat, which was a piece of gold that sat on top of the ark, resting between two gold statues of cherubim that faced each other with outstretched wings. Each

year on the Day of Atonement, the blood of a sacrificial animal was smeared on the "throne of mercy" as a sign of God's mercy to forgive sin. This "throne of mercy" was the symbolic throne of God, indicating that he lived among his people (Lev. 16:2; Num. 7:89).

The sacred ark of the covenant was a symbol of God's mercy—mercy to live among his people and mercy to forgive their sin. Each time they moved camp during the wilderness wanderings, God led them with the tangible symbol of the ark of the covenant. The ark of the covenant is a visible sign of the truth that God mercifully comes to his people, forgiving and guiding them in their daily life on earth, and leading them safely to the Promised Land.

Key Verse

Faith led Noah to listen when God warned him about the things in the future that he could not see. He obeyed God and built a ship to save his family. Through faith Noah condemned the world and received God's approval that comes through faith. (Heb. 11:7)

Dutchman Johan Huibers has built a full-scale replica of Noah's ark that can be toured by up to three thousand visitors per day. He has filled it with a mix of life-size reproductions and some live animals so guests can get a feel for what it was like to live on the ark. The boat is moored in the city of Dordrecht, just south of Rotterdam.

Top, a replica of the ark of the covenant, viewed from the side.

19

Arm

Aside from its physical definition, *arm* is used in Scripture as a symbol of power in action—either divine or human. The context will of course determine whether the word is meant literally or figuratively, and whether its figurative sense is power used for good or for evil.

God's Mighty Arm

The most common function in Scripture for the symbol of a powerful arm is to describe the mighty actions and purposes of God. The biblical writers often referred to his "mighty arm": "Your arm is mighty. Your hand is strong. Your right hand is lifted high" (Ps. 89:13). The idea behind this symbolic picture is so obvious that modern translations often convey the meaning directly. For example, GOD'S WORD translates Psalm 77:15 as, "With your might [literally *arm*] you have defended your people, the descendants of Jacob and Joseph."

One of the frequent contexts for the use of *arm* in referring to God also communicates his willingness to intervene powerfully in the affairs of this world. He instructed Moses, "Tell the Israelites, 'I am the LORD. I will bring you out from under the oppression of the Egyptians, and I will free you from slavery. I will rescue you with my powerful arm and with mighty acts of judgment'" (Exod. 6:6). The word *powerful* translates a Hebrew expression for "outstretched or reaching action" on God's part. God is not just powerful at a distance; he is fully able to judge, defend, and act on behalf of those he wants to protect or correct. This is the idea in Deuteronomy 3:34; 5:15; 1 Kings 8:24; 2 Kings 17:36; Psalm 136:12; and Jeremiah 21:5.

God's Compassionate Arms

Isaiah refers to God's arm more often than any other biblical book (fourteen times). Among these is a prophetic picture of God's compassionate care for his people, even after he has had to correct them severely: "Like a shepherd he takes care of his flock. He gathers the lambs in his arms. He carries them in his arms. He gently helps the sheep and their lambs" (Isa. 40:11). Fitting in with this meaning of the symbol, we think of his "arms" supporting us in times of

An arm is a symbol of strength.

God's power is portrayed as an arm raised in victory.

need and sorrow. Scriptures such as Deuteronomy 33:27 are poignant reminders of God's tender care: "The eternal God is your shelter, and his everlasting arms support you." Many hymns, such as "Leaning on the Everlasting Arms," reflect that sentiment.

The comforting aspects of God's enveloping arms can be seen most clearly when God puts on human flesh. In the New Testament we see God with flesh-and-blood arms, and he doesn't hesitate to use them. "Jesus put his arms around the children and blessed them by placing his hands on them" (Mark 10:16). Both Mary the mother of Jesus (Luke 1:51) and John (John 12:38) saw in Jesus the revelation of God's power/might that was anticipated in Isaiah 53:1: "Who has believed our message? To whom has the LORD's power [arm] been revealed?" The mode of Jesus' death leaves us with a powerful picture of how far God went to show us his love. Romans 5:8 declares, "Christ died for us while we were still sinners. This demonstrates God's love for us." God was willing to open his arms in love to us, even if that meant being nailed to a cross.

The Arm of Judgment

While God's powerful arm is usually portrayed as working to redeem and protect his people, it is occasionally meant as a symbol of judgment. When his people committed idolatry, God declared that he would allow the Babylonians to conquer them, saying, "I will fight you in anger, fury, and rage with my powerful hand and my mighty arm" (Jer. 21:5). The same powerful arm that redeemed the Israelites from slavery in Egypt (Deut. 4:34) now sided with Babylon to bring about her defeat.

Occasionally in Scripture arms are used to symbolize human agency, usually for evil. When the psalmist prays, "Break the arm of the wicked and evil person. Punish his wickedness until you find no more" (Ps. 10:15), he is referring not to the literal breaking of arms but to the figurative breaking of the power of evil people and the hold they have on the powerless. He is in effect asking God's arm of judgment to be raised against the forces of evil in the world.

God's arm as a symbol for his power at work in the world can be an image of both comfort and fearsome judgment. For the believer, the image need not cause fear—God works on our behalf, both defending the causes of righteousness with his strength and bearing us up in the face of our troubles. But those who wield their power to work evil and injustice, opposing God's work in the world, should fear the arm of the Lord that has the power to bring them down.

Key Verse

Almighty LORD, you made heaven and earth by your great strength and powerful arm. Nothing is too hard for you. (Jer. 32:17)

What have I to dread, what have I to fear,
Leaning on the everlasting arms?
I have blessed peace with my Lord so near,
Leaning on the everlasting arms.

Leaning, leaning, safe and secure from all alarms;
Leaning, leaning, leaning on the everlasting arms.

"Leaning on the Everlasting Arms" by
Anthony J. Showalter and Elisha Hoffman, 1887

Babylon

When Satan attempts to establish his visible kingdom on earth at the end of the age, we already know what he will designate as his capital—Babylon. That city name shows up throughout Scripture in several different ways, but all point to that ultimate culmination of the evil city that sets itself up against God at the end of human history.

The Historical Babylon

In Bible history, Babylon is tied to ancient Babel, mentioned in Genesis 11 as the place where people decided to build a tower and declare themselves godlike. The result of that fruitless effort was the division of languages throughout the world. Babylon became one of the greatest cities in the ancient world, both in size and splendor.

For ancient Israel, Babylon represented humiliation and destruction. Babylon was one of God's tools of punishment. The Babylonians destroyed Jerusalem, including Solomon's great temple, in 586 BC and deported large numbers of Jews into exile. The most famous of the Jewish exiles to live in Babylon was Daniel. Babylon is a constant presence in the accounts of 2 Kings and 2 Chronicles. All the Major Prophets (Isaiah, Jeremiah, Ezekiel, and Daniel) mention the city, though Isaiah's prophecies anticipate the disaster coming and Jeremiah records the effects of the Babylonian conquest.

The Symbolic Babylon

Symbolically, Babylon represents the archenemy of all God's people. It is the dreaded symbol of a mighty world power that is opposed to God and that crushes its enemies and oppresses them. The genealogy of Jesus in Matthew 1 mentions the exile in Babylon several times, reminding us that God's sovereign plan cannot be thwarted by terrible events. But the remainder of New Testament references to Babylon make use of the name as a symbol of a wicked and powerful city rather than the actual ancient city.

The Babylon for early Christians was Rome. Not only did the empire represent the kind of domination that paralleled the Babylonian epoch, but the death of Christ and the persecution of believers also occurred under the authority of Rome. So when Peter writes, "Your sister church in Babylon, chosen by God, and my son Mark send you greetings" (1 Pet. 5:13), he is almost certainly referring to Rome. Babylon is mentioned six times by John in Revelation (14:8; 16:19; 17:5; 18:2, 10, 21). While some interpret these references to mean an actual reconstructed city in modern Iraq, other details seem to indicate that Rome was the city in mind. In Revelation 17 the angel explains that the woman Babylon is a city that sits on "seven mountains" (v. 9)—a geographic figure that fits Rome much better than Babylon. When the original readers are considered, only Rome fits as the identity of Babylon. For the early Christians, suffering under Rome was endured because of ongoing reminders that the appearance of invincibility meant nothing compared to God's plan and power.

The figurative Babylon of the book of Revelation is not only a city that opposes God but a city that is full of every kind of abuse of power. The arrogance of opposing God meets its logical end in murder of the martyrs, exploitation of the weak, and every imaginable type of debauchery. In Revelation 17, Babylon is described as "the Mother of Prostitutes and Detestable Things of the Earth. . . . The woman was drunk with the

blood of God's holy people and of those who testify about Jesus" (vv. 5–6).

As a prophetic book with application to the closing chapter of history itself, Revelation uses Babylon to stand for whatever seat of power represents the final rebellion of Satan against the kingdom of God. It is the symbol representing the gathered multitude of humanity that insists on making its last stand against God. Revelation captures the hopelessness of that resistance, the tragedy of lost humanity, and the amazing fact that God has rescued a remnant from every tribe, tongue, and nation who will dwell with him for all eternity in the New Jerusalem, the city that is everything Babylon could never be.

Of course, God gets the last word. Once God has finished using her as a tool of judgment, Babylon will be thrown down and God will triumph. Jeremiah prophesied about this at length, and the book of Revelation ends with accounts of her downfall. "Frightened by her torture, they will stand far away and say, 'How horrible, how horrible it is for that important city, the powerful city Babylon! In one moment judgment has come to it!'" (Rev. 18:10). God will never allow evil to prevail but at the end of history will rule in justice and throw down everything that opposes him. His rule of peace is where Christians place their hope, and the downfall of all the wickedness that is symbolized by Babylon is good news indeed.

Key Verse

You destructive people of Babylon,
blessed is the one who pays you back
with the same treatment you gave us.
(Ps. 137:8)

Symbols Used for Babylon

Babylon is the city that became a symbol for a mighty pagan power, but many images are also used to represent it as God's hand of judgment: a tenant farmer placing a heavy yoke on other nations (Isa. 47:6; Jer. 27:1–12; 28:1–17); a war club (Jer. 51:20–23); a golden cup full of God's wrath, poised to inebriate the nations (Jer. 51:7); a zookeeper controlling the lion of Judah (Ezek. 19:9); a prostitute's spurned lover (Ezek. 23:11–35); a fire under the kettle of Jerusalem, boiling out her impurities (Ezek. 24:1–14); Israel's captor (Ps. 137:1, 8). These images for Babylon flesh out the picture of what Babylon as a symbol meant to the people of God: she was a fearsome tool of God's judgment. The prophecies of her downfall were messages of hope to them.

Top, Babylon was an advanced ancient city that left behind many archaeological treasures, such as this relief of protective spirits.

23

Baptism

Purification rituals involving water were common in ancient religions, so baptism would not have seemed like a practice that was peculiar to the early Christian church. For them, however, it was a once-for-all ritual washing rather than a repeated act. It is now a symbolic washing away of sins upon conversion to faith in Christ. John the Baptist called it a "baptism of repentance" (Mark 1:4). It is an outward sign of an internal purification from sins, enacted when a person chooses to be a part of God's kingdom. The sacredness of this transaction is intimated by the fact that we call baptism a *sacrament*, which means "holy action."

Spiritual Symbol

First, baptism is a symbolic joining with Christ in his death and resurrection. When the action of baptism is explained, as it is in Romans 6, the

John the Baptist contrasted baptism of the Spirit with baptism of the fire of judgment.

sequence is set against Jesus' death and resurrection: "Don't you know that all of us who were baptized into Christ Jesus were baptized into his

death? When we were baptized into his death, we were placed into the tomb with him. As Christ was brought back from death to life by the glorious power of the Father, so we, too, should live a new kind of life" (Rom. 6:3–4). Baptism is an identification with the crucifixion so that the believer can benefit from the redemption it brings.

Baptism is also a symbol for the empowering of the Holy Spirit (Acts 11:16). It represents a spiritual transaction that cannot be seen—the Holy Spirit's baptism of a believer into the body of Christ upon conversion. Peter made the connection between baptism of the body and baptism by the Holy Spirit: "Peter answered them, 'All of you must turn to God and change the way you think and act, and each of you must be baptized in the name of Jesus Christ so that your sins will be forgiven. Then you will receive the Holy Spirit as a gift'" (Acts 2:38). He is not saying that the Holy Spirit's presence is contingent on baptism but rather that both of those events are part of the process of coming to faith in Christ.

In the church, the method of baptism has historically become a point of contention. When and how it is done is up for debate. But Paul makes a significant point when he writes in Ephesians 4:4–6, "There is one body and one Spirit. In the same way you were called to share one hope. There is one Lord, one faith, *one baptism*, one God and Father of all, who is over everything, through everything, and in everything" (italics added). Paul wasn't speaking of a certain way of baptizing; he was speaking of the one spiritual transaction that baptism symbolizes—a person being in Christ and Christ's Spirit being in a person. This is what unifies us as believers.

The public profession of faith is also often associated with baptism. Conversion in the book of Acts is always followed by baptism (2:41; 8:12, 13, 16, 36; 9:18; 10:48; 16:15, 33; 18:8;

19:5; 22:16). In this case baptism becomes an outward and public sign of faith, similar to baptism's precursor in the Jewish faith: circumcision. The physical mark of circumcision was a sign of faith in the Old Testament and identification with God's covenant community, Israel. But in the New Testament, baptism is the outward sign of faith and identification with the Christian community (Rom. 4:11; Col. 2:11–12).

Physical Symbol

Apart from its spiritual symbolism, baptism is also used in Scripture to portray being overwhelmed by something. John the Baptist contrasted baptism of the Spirit with baptism of the fire of judgment (Matt. 3:10–12; Luke 3:9, 16–17). Jesus himself compared the pain and anguish of his last days to a type of baptism (Mark 10:38; Luke 12:50). Even today we use the term "baptism by fire" to symbolize an experience that we are thrown into without being properly prepared, often referring to difficult circumstances or troubles. This symbolism for baptism is not very far removed from the baptism of new believers. When Christians are baptized, they are overwhelmed by the grace of God and the cleansing that he freely offers them, and often they are overwhelmed by the ministry of the Holy Spirit in their lives.

Key Verse

By one Spirit we were all baptized into one body. Whether we are Jewish or Greek, slave or free, God gave all of us one Spirit to drink. (1 Cor. 12:13)

The early translators of the Bible into English decided not to translate the Greek word *baptizo* and related words but to simply borrow them through transliteration. This practice of borrowing words was already in place as early as Jerome's Vulgate translation into Latin in about AD 400. Our English Bibles are filled with borrowed words (*angel, amen, hosanna, hallelujah,* and so forth) that have been lifted from Greek and Hebrew. In the case of *baptism,* this decision was likely made because by that time, several traditions regarding the manner of baptism were already in place (sprinkling, pouring, and immersing), and leaving the original word alone allowed the traditions to also stand. At the time the New Testament was written, the word *baptizo* and related words were almost exclusively used to describe dipping, immersing, and putting things into and under water.

Top, this baptism site in the country of Jordan is typical of those found in the Middle East.

25

Beast

In a few places in the Bible, the term *beast* is used in its modern descriptive sense of a menacing or mindless animal whose behavior is somewhat unpredictable. Jacob compared his son Issachar to a donkey or beast of burden (Gen. 49:14), creating a picture of capacity and stubbornness as strong traits in his ninth born. Many biblical monsters seem to be mythical, or

Beasts of burden were an important part of life in the ancient world.

at least are symbolic of threats to God's order and authority in the world. But unlike the monstrous beasts of surrounding cultures and religions, God retains power over all the beasts and chaos in the world, and will ultimately defeat them.

Beast (or *animal* in God's Word) takes on a particular prophetic role in Daniel 7 where four nightmarish creatures appear, each made up of combined features from familiar animals and representing future kingdoms that will rise to control the world. This vision of Daniel parallels the prophetic sequence in Nebuchadnezzar's dream of the gigantic statue in Daniel 2; but whereas the earlier vision pictures the political rise and fall of the nations, this vision of beasts centers on the moral decay that dooms each of these kingdoms.

Behemoth and Leviathan

In God's extended monologue with Job (Job 40:15–24) a creature called Behemoth is described at length. The term is the transliterated Hebrew word for "beast," sometimes also translated "dragon." Although this animal is not clearly identified, its somewhat nonaggressive nature and herbivore diet appear to be that of a hippopotamus. God uses this animal as a reminder to Job that God created such impressive creatures that humans cannot tame, much less invent. Behemoth symbolizes God's unique creative power that we reflect as creatures made in God's image but that we cannot duplicate.

Job then describes a sea creature called Leviathan (41:1–34). This twisting serpent of the water is a literal creature, but seems to be described hyperbolically rather than scientifically. Despite the terror this creature elicits, Psalm 104:25–26 uses Leviathan as an example of God's creative power: "The sea is so big and wide with countless creatures, living things both large and small. Ships sail on it, and Leviathan, which you made, plays in it." Like Behemoth, this giant beast is a symbol for God's creativity and his power over creation.

The Beasts of Revelation

The book of Revelation uses the term *beast* more than the rest of Scripture. More than forty times John refers to certain participants in the final rebellion against God as beasts, or "the beast." In biblical language, the primary beast of Revelation is also known as the Antichrist (see 1 John 2:18–19). Two beasts figure prominently in Revelation. One is introduced in 13:1 as a beast from the sea, displaying many of the characteristics of Daniel's four beasts. In

an obscene mockery of the great idea that we are made in the image of God (Gen. 1:27), the first beast appears to be made in the image of the dragon/serpent Satan, from whom he gets his power and authority. This beast (the Antichrist) also becomes the object of worship by much of humanity (Rev. 13:3–4). He is a symbol of all that is opposed to God. The second beast arises from the earth and functions as the enforcer for the first beast (see Rev. 13:11–14). Both beasts appear to symbolize humans who operate under the control of Satan. Like the beasts of Daniel, they are heads of systems of power, but they function under the evil authority of Satan who can only exercise as much power as God allows.

The first beast represents the fact that governing leadership and authority can be twisted into the service of evil: "The serpent gave its power, kingdom, and far-reaching authority to the beast" (Rev. 13:2b). When Jesus was tempted in the wilderness, this was the final offer made by the tempter: "Once more the devil took him to a very high mountain and showed him all the kingdoms in the world and their glory. The devil said to him, 'I will give you all this if you will bow down and worship me'" (Matt. 4:8–9). What Jesus rejected Satan eventually finds someone to accept. The dragon/serpent/Satan of Revelation 12 and the two beasts form an obvious and offensive trinity in their determined efforts to resist and overthrow God. Their fate is sealed and made apparent in Revelation 19:19–20 when the Word of God, Jesus, arrives with the armies of heaven and defeats Satan and his armies.

Key Verse

Then I saw what looked like a sea of glass mixed with fire. Those who had won the victory over the beast, its statue, and the number of its name were standing on the glassy sea. They were holding God's harps. (Rev. 15:2)

Can we or will we be able to identify the beasts when they appear on the scene of history? For John in writing Revelation, Rome under the leadership of Nero certainly matched many of the traits of a world under the control of Satan and his beasts. Many succeeding generations of Christians have been able to see in their circumstances possible candidates for the roles of the two beasts on the stage. Attempts to identify the beasts with specific leaders or even to limit John's prophecy as a message for the first-century church all appear to ultimately miss the main point—that John was given the vision as an ever-present reminder to all believers of the real temptation to settle our hopes in this world and on the systems of the world to the disregard of God's ultimate plan and purpose.

Bethlehem

The very name *Bethlehem* immediately awakens thoughts of carol lyrics and the story of Christmas. Yet the tale of that little town reaches far back into history, when the Promised Land was just a promise. The village is first mentioned, almost as a sad footnote, in the itinerary of Jacob's trip back from Haran with his growing family, only to have his beloved Rachel go into labor just outside Ephrath (Gen. 35:16) and die while giving birth to the youngest of the patriarch's sons, Benjamin. Her burial place is identified as Bethlehem (Gen. 35:19).

Fast-forward five hundred years and Bethlehem was the hometown of Elimelech, who became the father-in-law of Ruth the Moabitess. Widowed, she eventually married Boaz and they produced Obed. Ruth and Boaz were the great-grandparents of David of Bethlehem, the youngest son of Jesse and the eventual great king of Israel (Ruth 4:11–22). In this chapter of the town's story lies the reason why Joseph of Nazareth and Mary (both with family ties to David's lineage) had to journey back to Bethlehem for the census ordered by the Roman conquerors, which placed Mary in the town when Jesus was born (Luke 2:1–7).

In geographic terms, Bethlehem is situated in hill country five miles southwest of Jerusalem. Its name means "house [*beth*] of bread [*lehem*]." The village was also called Bethlehem Ephrathah (Mic. 5:2), Bethlehem-Judah (1 Sam. 17:12), and "the city of David" (Luke 2:4 KJV). It is mentioned about forty-five times in the Old Testament and eight times in the New Testament (all in the Gospels).

Small but Significant

Bethlehem symbolizes how God can use what is seemingly unimportant to make a lasting impact. Never confuse size with significance. Bethlehem's location is insignificant, just off the major road leading to the Negev. But the events that have happened there changed history. David was born there and anointed as

This street scene from Bethlehem helps us imagine what it may have looked like when Joseph and Mary were there.

Bethlehem was the place where the Son of God entered into human history as a helpless baby.

king of Israel (1 Sam. 16:4–13); thus it is known as the city of David. Most importantly, Bethlehem is the place where Jesus was born (Matt. 2:6; Luke 2:6–7). Jesus arrived, not in the holy city of Jerusalem, not in the major cultural center of Athens, not in Rome, the seat of government, but in the tiny hamlet called Bethlehem.

God had promised that David would always have a descendent on the throne. Before Jesus

came that promise seemed impossible. Being born in Bethlehem, Jesus fulfilled the prophecy of Micah that a ruler of Israel would come from there (Mic. 5:2). Jesus was then the newborn and long-awaited King and Messiah. David put Bethlehem on the map, and Jesus made sure it would never be forgotten. The "house of bread" became the place of sustenance first for the Jews with David's birth and then for all people with Jesus' birth.

Birth and Death

Bethlehem was often associated with death in the Bible. Its first appearance was mentioned in Rachel's death. Upon hearing of the birth of Jesus (the King of the Jews), Herod the Great ordered the killing of all the male children age two and under in the town and surrounding areas. Yet Jesus' escape from death was only temporary. The prophecy given by the angel to Joseph would eventually be fulfilled: "She will give birth to a son, and you will name him Jesus [He Saves], because he will save his people from their sins" (Matt. 1:21). Too often we focus on the baby in the manger, the happy hope that Bethlehem offered, and fail to properly recognize the significance of his death on the cross. The manger led to the cross. We cannot have Christmas without Easter, Bethlehem without Golgotha. Jesus was born to die. But because of

his death salvation is made available. Jesus, the Bread of Life, was born in the house of bread so that we might have spiritual bread—eternal life.

Key Verse

You, Bethlehem Ephrathah,
are too small to be included among
Judah's cities.
Yet, from you Israel's future ruler will
come for me.
His origins go back to the distant
past, to days long ago. (Mic. 5:2)

The words to the famous hymn "O Little Town of Bethlehem" were penned by Phillips Brooks after a trip to the Holy Land in 1868. They emphasize both the smallness of the town itself and the significance of what took place there for all of human history.

O little town of Bethlehem,
how still we see thee lie;
above thy deep and dreamless sleep
the silent stars go by.
Yet in thy dark streets shineth
the everlasting light;
the hopes and fears of all the years
are met in thee tonight.

Birth

Birth is our universal means of arrival in life. We can't begin to experience all that life has to offer until we have passed through the moment of birth. Life has a formative phase in the womb that the psalmist describes beautifully:

> You alone created my inner being.
>> You knitted me together inside my
>>> mother.
> I will give thanks to you
>> because I have been so amazingly and
>>> miraculously made.
>> Your works are miraculous, and my
>>> soul is fully aware of this.
>> My bones were not hidden
>>> from you
>> when I was being made in secret,
> when I was being skillfully woven in an
>> underground workshop.
> Your eyes saw me when I was only a fetus.
>> Every day of my life was recorded in your
>>> book
>> before one of them had taken place.
>> (Ps. 139:13–16)

Scripture repeatedly reminds us that birth, whether physical or spiritual, is an act of God (Deut. 32:18). Ultimately, no life exists apart from God's sovereign will. Scripture records many instances of barren women giving birth to remind us of this truth: Sarah (Isaac), Rebekah (Jacob), Manoah's wife (Samson), Hannah (Samuel), and Elizabeth (John the Baptist). And of course the virgin birth of Christ is the prime example of birth being a supernatural event.

Birth and Pain

Birth is first mentioned in Scripture in connection with the fall of humankind. One of the results of sin entering the world was an increase in pain connected with birth (Gen. 3:16). For this reason, childbirth is a symbol for pain that comes with a hopeful conclusion in mind. Just as a mother anxiously awaits the birth of her child, Paul tells us that all of creation eagerly awaits redemption: "We know that all creation has been groaning with the pains of childbirth up to the present time" (Rom. 8:22). And Jesus talked about the anguish of waiting for his appearance as the hopeful pains at the end of a woman's pregnancy (John 16:21–22). He looked not only to the relatively brief agony the disciples would suffer during his crucifixion and death—followed by his astounding resurrection—but also to the joyous redemption it would bring.

Birth and Timing

Closely related to the pain of birth is the fact that one never knows when the moment of birth will occur. So childbirth is also a symbol for an event that is expected but will begin at an unknown moment—we know it will come and are even eager for it to begin, but we don't quite know when it will happen. That is why Paul describes God's amazing and priceless offer of eternal life as a wonder just as unexpected as birth pangs for a woman who cannot bear children (Gal. 4:27). And when Jesus describes the terrible events that will occur as the world lives its final days, he equates the early troubles to birth pangs: "Nation will fight against nation and kingdom against kingdom. There will be earthquakes and famines in various places. These are only the beginning pains of the end" (Mark 13:8). The pain of these events and their unknown timing make childbirth a perfect metaphor.

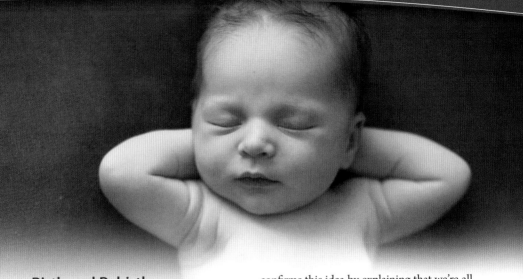

Birth and Rebirth

Personal discoveries and enlightening experiences are often described with the phrase "I felt like I was born again." Those who know the Bible immediately think of a specific use of that phrase in Jesus' life (John 3:1–16). The idea of birth or rebirth in a spiritual sense was not entirely new among the people to whom Jesus was speaking (Ezek. 36:25–27; Joel 2:28–29), but it did not make sense to Nicodemus until Jesus explained that God himself is intimately involved not only in our physical birth but also in our spiritual birth. In the Gospel of John, this connection is made early, speaking of Jesus:

> He went to his own people, and his own people didn't accept him. However, he gave the right to become God's children to everyone who believed in him. These people didn't become God's children in a physical way—from a human impulse or from a husband's desire to have a child. They were born from God. (1:11–13)

Just as physical birth is a gift of God, so is spiritual birth. It is like the wind, unable to be controlled by human beings. It is also a new beginning that initiates a natural process of growth. That's why birth is such a fitting symbol for salvation.

When Jesus said, "No one can see the kingdom of God without being born from above" (John 3:3), he was declaring that people can live their entire lives without being born in the way that ultimately matters. The apostle Paul confirms this idea by explaining that we're all stillborn spiritually: "You were once dead because of your failures and sins" (Eph. 2:1). John has already clearly stated that the birth being discussed cannot be achieved by our own desires or the desire of any other human (John 1:11–13). It's up to God and his grace. "But God is rich in mercy because of his great love for us. We were dead because of our failures, but he made us alive together with Christ. (It is God's kindness that saved you.) God has brought us back to life together with Christ Jesus and has given us a position in heaven with him" (Eph. 2:4–6).

Key Verse

Praise the God and Father of our Lord Jesus Christ! God has given us a new birth because of his great mercy. We have been born into a new life that has a confidence which is alive because Jesus Christ has come back to life. (1 Pet. 1:3)

The word "sorrows" in [Matthew 24 KJV] verse 8 is from the Greek term *odin*, which speaks of the travail and pain of childbirth. The afflictions Christ lists here are like birth pangs. At first they are relatively mild and infrequent, but then they come in relentless waves, faster and harder as the time approaches.

John MacArthur, *The Second Coming*
(Wheaton: Crossway, 1999), 89

Top, both physical and spiritual birth are miraculous acts of God.

Black

The color mentioned most often in the Bible is not really a color at all—it is the absence of color. Objects that absorb light rather than reflect all or part of it look dark or black to us. Several Hebrew words are typically translated "black," since there are shades of darkness. These words are sometimes translated as "darkness" or "gloom." Because black is the absence of light, to use it as a symbol for evil or something that is terrifying makes sense.

Fear

Darkness is frightening because one cannot see approaching dangers. When Joel records the effects of a future event that he calls "the Day of the Lord," he includes the fact that "the sun and the moon turn dark" (Joel 2:10). Part of the terror of that day is the darkness—an absence of the light of God in a figurative sense and the literal light that makes one able to see.

Death and Decay

Other uses of *black* in Scripture point to a pattern symbolizing decay and death. Dead skin is black (Lam. 4:8). In his complaint to God, Job described the effect of his disease as making his skin dark/black before it peeled away (Job 30:30). Black is also the color of moral decay. Micah connects darkness with God's judgment when he rails against false prophets who will "have nights without visions . . . darkness without revelations. The sun will set on the prophets, and the day will turn dark for them" (Mic. 3:6). This is closely related to the themes of darkness and light that we see particularly in John's writings.

Evil

The fact that black is a symbol for evil is evident in the fact that the dark arts are called "black magic" (Deut. 18:10, 14; Josh. 13:22; 1 Sam. 15:23). These practices are expressly forbidden in Scripture and are associated with evil: "They practiced black magic and cast evil spells. They sold themselves by doing what the Lord considered evil" (2 Kings 17:17). These things are done in the dark and believers flee from

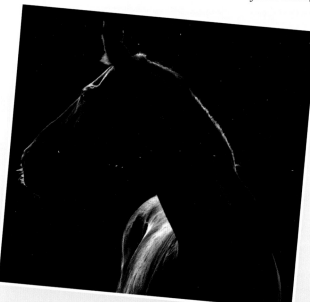

The black horse in Revelation is a harbinger of death and destruction.

them as they live in God's light. We are told, "Have nothing to do with the useless works that darkness produces. Instead, expose them for what they are" (Eph. 5:11).

Judgment

Black is a color that symbolizes God's terrifying judgment. In Revelation 6:1–8, a black horse appears along with three other horses (white, red, and pale). These are known as the four horsemen of the Apocalypse. They are released on earth as a result of one of the opened seals of judgment. The rider on the black horse carries a scale that will measure the distorted value of food in a time of terrible famine. In Revelation 6:12, the sun goes black as a result of a terrible earthquake: "I watched as the lamb opened the sixth seal. A powerful earthquake struck. The sun turned as black as sackcloth made of hair. The full moon turned as red as blood." Apparently the dust storm created by the earthquake darkened the sun and reminded John of black hair woven into sackcloth. The appearance of black in prophetic passages in the Bible, even when they describe God's actions, is related to judgment and distress. Indeed, hell itself is called "blackest darkness" (2 Pet. 2:17; Jude 1:13 NIV).

Key Verse

The earth will mourn, and the sky will grow black.
I have spoken, and I have planned it.
I won't change my plans, and I won't turn back. (Jer. 4:28)

Suppose one reads a story of filthy atrocities in the paper. Then suppose that something turns up suggesting that the story might not be quite true, or not quite so bad as it was made out. Is one's first feeling, "Thank God, even they aren't quite so bad as that," or is it a feeling of disappointment, and even a determination to cling to the first story for the sheer pleasure of thinking your enemies are as bad as possible? If it is the second then it is, I am afraid, the first step in a process which, if followed to the end, will make us into devils. You see, one is beginning to wish that black was a little blacker. If we give that wish its head, later on we shall wish to see grey as black, and then to see white itself as black. Finally we shall insist on seeing everything—God and our friends and ourselves included—as bad, and not be able to stop doing it: we shall be fixed for ever in a universe of pure hatred.

C. S. Lewis, *Mere Christianity*
(1952; repr., San Francisco: Harper, 2009), 118

Blood

Like water, blood is a fluid that is essential for life. When we donate blood, we help save lives. Those who lose too much blood risk death. For biblical authors, blood was a powerful symbol for humanity itself. God's blessing of Noah and his sons included the following warning: "Whoever sheds human blood, by humans his blood will be shed, because in the image of God, God made humans" (Gen. 9:6). Blood also stands for the impermanence of our human bodies. The "flesh and blood" of our earthly bodies is contrasted with our future heavenly bodies, which will not decay (Gen. 6:3; 1 Cor. 15:50).

Blood as an Omen

Because blood indicates some type of injury, it was thought of as a bad omen. The Nile River turned to blood—an unnatural and fearsome omen of things to come (Exod. 4:9; 7:17). The water in Moab looked like blood and helped bring about Israelite victory (2 Kings 3:22). Apocalyptic imagery refers to blood in the sky and water (Rev. 16:4; Joel 2:30–31). Peter concurs that this is a sign of the day of the Lord (Acts 2:19).

Blood and Guilt

We often describe a murderer as someone who has "blood on their hands," and some passages in Scripture attribute blood with personal guilt. Taking a life is, of course, the ultimate act of violence and is sin, but the symbol repeatedly used to point out the guilt incurred by such actions is blood. After being murdered by his brother Cain, Abel's blood "cried out" to God from the ground (see Gen. 4:10). Israel, guilty of much violence, had "bloody footprints" (Hosea 6:8) and "hands . . . covered with blood" (Isa. 1:15). Violent people are called "bloodthirsty" (Ps. 139:19). And the land where violence occurred was considered "polluted with blood" (Ps. 106:38). Hands stained with blood are also "stained with sin" (Isa. 59:3). Even here there is hope of redemption, for in Hebrews 10:22, the symbolic act of being sprinkled with Christ's blood frees us from a guilty conscience.

Blood and Impurity

The presence of blood signifies some type of rupture in creation—either injury or illness. Thus it is symbolic of uncleanness or defilement (Lam. 4:14). An issue of blood ("chronic bleeding") made a person unclean and unable to participate in the Jewish community (Lev. 12; Luke 8:43). In comparison to God's holiness, man's attempt at righteousness is compared to menstrual rags (Isa. 64:6). The Old Testament law is filled with specific instructions on the handling of blood, and the commandment "never eat any fat or blood" (Lev. 3:17) informs today's Jewish dietary (kosher) laws.

Blood and Salvation

Foreshadowing the sacrifice of Christ, blood in the Old Testament was a key component in the system of atonement instituted by God. The lifeblood of a sacrificial animal symbolically represented the life of the individual. Leviticus explains that the life is in the blood: "Blood contains life. I have given this blood to you to make peace with me on the altar. Blood is needed to make peace with me" (Lev. 17:11; see also v. 14). The Old Testament standard of life for life was satisfied through the sacrifice

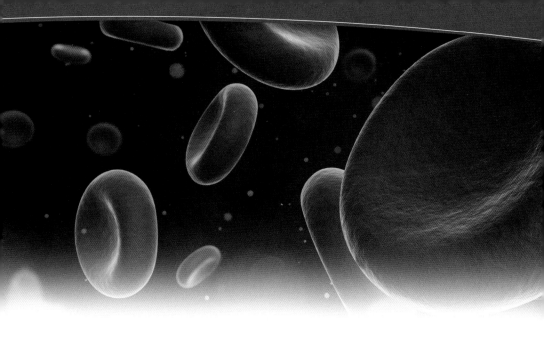

of animals—human guilt was assuaged by the taking of animal life. In the New Testament we discover that the ultimate once-for-all shedding of blood was the willingly shed blood of Christ, the perfect sacrifice: "God was also pleased to bring everything on earth and in heaven back to himself through Christ. He did this by making peace through Christ's blood sacrificed on the cross" (Col. 1:20). Old Testament sacrifices were a sign of the final sacrifice of the spotless Lamb. The price for all sin had been paid, and shedding of blood was no longer necessary. Just as the sacrificial blood of animals was used to seal the covenant between God and Abram (Gen. 15), the shedding of Jesus' blood on the cross instituted a new covenant between God and humanity.

Blood features prominently in the celebration of Passover. Exodus 12 explains how the Israelites were spared the judgment of God by sprinkling lamb's blood on their doorposts. The blood stood as a sign that they were the chosen people, and the angel of the Lord "passed over" the homes of the Israelites during their captivity in Egypt. Christ dramatically reinterpreted the blood symbolism of Passover during the last meal he celebrated with his disciples. Taking the cup of wine, Jesus said, "This is my blood, the blood of the promise. It is poured out for many people so that sins are forgiven" (Matt. 26:28). As one of the elements of communion, blood is often associated with Christ's suffering. Yet, the blood in the Passover represents the sacrifice of Christ's life itself, rather than merely his experience of physical pain. The wine of communion is a sign that represents the lifeblood of Christ, poured out on our behalf and of which we become partakers.

Key Verse

He said, "Here is the blood that seals the promise God has made to you." In the same way, Moses sprinkled blood on the tent and on everything used in worship. As Moses' Teachings tell us, blood was used to cleanse almost everything, because if no blood is shed, no sins can be forgiven. (Heb. 9:20–22)

> The blood of Christ stands not simply for the sting of sin on God but the scourge of God on sin, not simply for God's sorrow over sin, but for God's wrath on sin.
>
> P. T. Forsyth, *The Cruciality of the Cross* (London: Hodder and Stoughton, 1909), 208

Top, blood is essential to life, and therefore a necessary part of atonement.

Body

Throughout Scripture we find the wonder and mystery of the human body, designed by God (Ps. 139:13–15). Jesus created a body for himself, and Adam was the prototype. Paul described Jesus as "the image of the invisible God, the firstborn of all creation" (Col. 1:15). Jesus chose the human body as the form or image he would live in while on his earth mission. Our bodies become symbolic reminders that we were designed with a purpose, shaped to be the aware and obedient servants of God, the Maker of heaven and earth. Furthermore, the fact that Jesus took on human flesh shows that though the body is dust and is wasting away (Gen. 3:19; 2 Cor. 4:16), it is good and useful, part of what makes us human beings in the image of God.

Body and Soul

The Old Testament view of the body doesn't usually emphasize components like flesh, spirit, or soul, but instead sees the human as a created unit. Job said to God, "My throat would rather be choked. My body would prefer death to these dreams" (Job 7:15). But among the Psalms and Proverbs we can also find a distinction between the body and the soul: "That is why my heart is glad and my soul rejoices. My body rests securely" (Ps. 16:9; see 31:9). Proverbs weighs in with "Pleasant words are like honey from a honeycomb—sweet to the spirit and healthy for the body" (16:24). So we see a gradual understanding that in the body resides the eternal soul, which continues after the body has died.

The Body as a Symbol of Spiritual Well-Being

The Bible gives the understanding that our bodies are affected by sin. Biblical writers seemed to understand what scientists are now proving: our state of mind affects our health. We are told that "a tranquil heart makes for a healthy body, but jealousy is like bone cancer" (Prov. 14:30). Psalm 38 says, "No healthy spot is left on my body because of your rage. There is no peace in my bones because of my sin" (v. 3), and then proceeds to list all the effects of sin on the physical body. These were not primarily literal aches and pains but more the symbolic connection between body and spirit. The outward condition of the body symbolizes what is going on inside the soul.

The Bible also uses the body as a symbol of circumstances. The wealthy are portrayed as fat (Job 15:27), and the poor as wasting away (Isa. 17:4). The wicked are sleek and fat (Ps. 73:4–17), while the oppressed are emaciated. The body is an external dwelling that reveals a person's status and lifestyle.

The Body Redeemed

By the time we enter the world of the New Testament, widespread Greek thought regarded the body as evil. However, the Scriptures never portray the body itself as evil. It is marred by sin and is mortal as part of the curse, but the body is also part of us that God wants to redeem. Paul speaks about "sin in our bodies" (Rom. 6:6), but he doesn't mean that our bodies are left out of God's plan for us:

> Therefore, never let sin rule your physical body so that you obey its desires. Never offer any part of your body to sin's power. No part of your body should ever be used to do any ungodly thing. Instead, offer yourselves to God as people who have come back from death and are now alive. Offer all the parts of your body to God. Use them to do everything that God approves of. Certainly, sin shouldn't have

power over you because you're not controlled by laws, but by God's favor. (Rom. 6:12–14)

Once we become followers of Jesus, our bodies remind us daily that as Christ died and rose again, so will we. Because he lives, we will live. He was raised with a body, and we are destined for the same experience (1 Cor. 15:42–44, 53–54).

The Body of Christ

Scripture gives the term two meanings: the first from the words of Jesus, and the second from the words of Paul. Jesus took bread to symbolize his body that would be given as a sacrifice and payment for the sins of humankind. The communion elements symbolize Jesus' willing acceptance of the pain, shame, and extreme suffering required to substitute for us on the cross. The combination of Jesus' bodily capacity to feel and his capacity to physically die became the unique offering that provided forgiveness and eternal life to those who would otherwise have no hope.

The body of Christ is also the rich New Testament symbol of all those who have been saved by him. Believers are parts of a body (Rom. 12:4–5; 1 Cor. 12:12–31). Our attachment to Christ, who is the head of the body, also means that we are attached to all others who have Jesus as Lord. This is true of believers presently alive but extends back to all believers. The body of

Christ represents those who will be together for all eternity, experiencing the presence of Christ in the new heaven and new earth in a way we can only experience with limits now.

As "members" of the body of Christ we have functions and roles within that body. Just as each part of the body is necessary, so each person has a valuable role within the body of Christ while at the same time depending on the rest of the body to do their parts (1 Cor. 12). The loss of any member limits the function of the body.

Key Verse

Instead, as we lovingly speak the truth, we will grow up completely in our relationship to Christ, who is the head. He makes the whole body fit together and unites it through the support of every joint. As each and every part does its job, he makes the body grow so that it builds itself up in love. (Eph. 4:15–16)

Each believer's body is portrayed as a temple for the indwelling Holy Spirit (Rom. 12:1–2; 1 Cor. 6:19–20). That means that the believer has a responsibility to use his or her body in ways that honor God. At the same time, this gives dignity to the body. It is not merely a physical element that is destined to decay, it is a tool that can be used to do Christ's work in the world.

Top, communion is a remembrance of Christ's bodily death on the cross for our salvation.

37

Book/Scroll

The word *Bible* is actually a borrowed term from Latin (*biblia*) meaning "book." For Christians, the Bible is the Book above and beyond all books. Jews and then Christians have long been called "the people of the Book," highlighting the point that Judaism and Christianity both see the Book God has given as the most reliable guide to God's direction for our lives. For Jews, this is restricted to the Old Testament; for Christians, both the Old and New Testaments form the complete Book that God authored.

The Scrolls

Almost everywhere in the Old Testament where we encounter the word *book* we should be thinking *scroll*: a long, sewn-together series of written sheets of leather or parchment-thick, primitive paper made from reeds. More specifically, *book* usually refers to the scrolls of Scripture. When Joshua is told by God, "Never stop reciting these teachings. You must think about them night and day so that you will faithfully do everything written in them. Only then will you prosper and succeed" (Josh. 1:8), the term *teachings* is literally *book* and refers to Moses' inspired collection—the Pentateuch or first five books of the Bible. In this sense, *book* is a symbol for all of the teachings of God by which Christians live.

The Book of Life

In Psalm 139 we read, "Every day of my life was recorded in your book before one of them had taken place" (v. 16). This idea of a book symbolizes God's record of events and lives. We find this concept in passages like Exodus 32:32, where being blotted out of the book is an image for death: "But will you forgive their sin? If not, please wipe me out of the book you have written."

Building on this imagery, the Book of Life mentioned in Daniel 12:1 and then in Revelation symbolizes God's judgment of individual people. Their eternal fate depends on whether their names have been recorded in the book:

> I saw a large, white throne and the one who was sitting on it. The earth and the sky fled from his presence, but no place was found for them. I saw the dead, both important and unimportant people, standing in front of the throne. Books were opened, including the Book of Life. The dead were judged on the basis of what they had done, as recorded in the books. The sea gave up its dead. Death and hell gave up their dead. People were judged based on what they had done. Death and hell were thrown into the fiery lake. (The fiery lake is the second death.) Those whose names were not found in the Book of Life were thrown into the fiery lake. (Rev. 20:11–15)

A Scroll

This idea of the book as a symbol of judgment comes up in the prophet Zechariah's vision (Zech. 5:1–2) of a flying scroll. In this sealed scroll is written God's judgment. This symbol of God's judgments sealed in a scroll is also a central picture in Revelation, and here we learn that only one Person is worthy to open it and reveal its contents. The scroll is introduced in chapter 5: "I saw a scroll in the right hand of the one who sits on the throne. It had writing both on the inside and on the outside. It was sealed with seven seals. I saw a powerful angel calling out in a loud voice, 'Who deserves to open the scroll and break the seals on it?'" (Rev. 5:1–2).

Access to the scroll that unfolds history depends on the Lamb, Jesus, who alone is qualified:

> When the lamb had taken the scroll, the four living creatures and the 24 leaders bowed in front of him. Each held a harp and a gold bowl full of incense, the prayers of God's holy people. Then they sang a new song,
>
> "You deserve to take the scroll and open the seals on it,
> because you were slaughtered.
> You bought people with your blood to be God's own.
> They are from every tribe, language, people, and nation.
> You made them a kingdom and priests for our God.
> They will rule as kings on the earth." (Rev. 5:8–10)

The Truth

God's book is a symbol of truth as well. The psalmist tells us that God desires truth in our inmost being (Ps. 51:6), and elsewhere we are told to meditate or chew on God's Word (Josh. 1:8). Sometimes this was done by literally eating the book. Ezekiel received a scroll from God and was required to eat it as a symbol of his acceptance of God's call: "He said to me, 'Son of man, eat this scroll I'm giving you, and fill your stomach with it.' So I ate it, and it tasted as sweet as honey in my mouth" (3:3). In Revelation 10, John also encountered a small scroll that revealed information he was forbidden from telling others. He was commanded to eat the scroll: "Take it and eat it. It will be bitter in your stomach, but it will be as sweet as honey in your mouth" (Rev. 10:9). Knowing the truth can be "sweetness," but sometimes the truth and what it reveals to us turns our stomachs.

Key Verse

I saw the dead, both important and unimportant people, standing in front of the throne. Books were opened, including the Book of Life. The dead were judged on the basis of what they had done, as recorded in the books. (Rev. 20:12)

The image of the Book of Life in Revelation came from the Jewish custom of keeping a citizenship book of the people who lived in each town (Neh. 7:5, 64). If your name was blotted out of that official register, your citizenship had been revoked. Similarly, only those whose names are written in the Lamb's Book of Life can enter heaven (Rev. 21:27).

Top, Jesus read from scrolls in the synagogue and as he taught.

39

Branch

Branches in the world of the Bible were either on trees or vines and were relatively rare given the arid climate, so the picture of a healthy and fruitful tree was a symbol of vigor and prosperity. "Branch" or "branches" could refer to families (Gen. 49:22) or rulers (Ezek. 31:3, 6). Broken or unfruitful branches symbolized judgment or the downfall of a person or nation (Job 15:32; 18:16; Dan. 4:14; Isa. 9:14; 17:6; Jer. 11:16). But God always gives the hope of restoration, and branches figure in the symbolism of redemption as well: "When that day comes, the branch of the LORD will be beautiful and wonderful. The fruit of the land will be the pride and joy of Israel's survivors" (Isa. 4:2). The image of judged or redeemed branches reaches its climax in the prophecies of the messianic Branch and the salvation he brings.

The Messianic Branch

The Old Testament includes six central passages in which the title *Branch* is used to refer to the coming Messiah (Isa. 4:2–6; 11:1; Jer. 23:5; 33:15; Zech. 3:8; 6:12). Jeremiah declares that the Branch will represent God like no other:

> "The days are coming," declares the LORD,
> "when I will grow a righteous branch for David.
> He will be a king who will rule wisely.
> He will do what is fair and right in the land.
> In his lifetime, Judah will be saved,
> and Israel will live in safety.
> This is the name that he will be given:
> The LORD is our righteousness."
> (Jer. 23:5–6)

This branch not only comes from David's royal line, but he also will be one grown by God, hinting at the divine nature of the Branch.

The term *branch* is not used in the New Testament in the form of a name as it is in the Old, but the prophetic voices that announced the coming Messiah didn't hesitate to include *branch* in their descriptions: "Listen, Chief Priest Joshua and your friends sitting with you. These men are a sign of things to come: I'm going to bring my servant, the Branch" (Zech. 3:8). When Matthew opened his Gospel with the genealogy of Jesus, he provided a description of the generational tree from which the Branch was delivered to his people in order to do his work of salvation. "Then say to him, 'This is what the LORD of Armies says: Here is the man whose name is Branch. He will branch out from where he is, and he will rebuild the LORD's temple'" (Zech. 6:12).

Believers as Branches

In a broader sense, the term *branch* can be used of people in general, with Israel described as a tree and its citizens as branches (Ps. 80:8–11; Ezek. 17:6, 23; Hosea 14:6). Jesus used this imagery in describing his relationship to followers. He is now the Branch who becomes the main trunk from which all branches grow:

> I am the true vine, and my Father takes care of the vineyard. He removes every one of my branches that doesn't produce fruit. He also prunes every branch that does produce fruit to make it produce more fruit.
> You are already clean because of what I have told you. Live in me, and I will live in you. A branch cannot produce any fruit by itself. It has to stay attached to the vine. In the same way, you cannot produce fruit unless you live in me. (John 15:1–4)

The branch is a fitting symbol for the essential union believers have with Christ, because without him their faith has no nourishment or support and it cannot grow or bear fruit.

The apostle Paul, describing the relationship between God and Jews and Gentiles, turns to the idea of grafting branches to explain what God is doing:

> If the root is holy, the branches are holy. But some of the olive branches have been broken off, and you, a wild olive branch, have been grafted in their place. You get your nourishment from the roots of the olive tree. So don't brag about being better than the other branches. If you brag, remember that you don't support the root, the root supports you. . . .
>
> If Jewish people do not continue in their unbelief, they will be grafted onto the tree again, because God is able to do that. In spite of the fact that you have been cut from a wild olive tree, you have been grafted onto a cultivated one. So wouldn't it be easier for these natural branches to be grafted onto the olive tree they belong to? (Rom. 11:16–18, 23–24)

The image of the branch comes to us with an invitation to share connection with a common trunk from which we all gain life and nourishment. As Jesus described the kingdom of heaven, "The kingdom of heaven is like a mustard seed that someone planted in a field. It's one of the smallest seeds. However, when it has grown, it is taller than the garden plants. It becomes a tree that is large enough for birds to nest in its branches" (Matt. 13:31–32).

Key Verse

I am the vine. You are the branches. Those who live in me while I live in them will produce a lot of fruit. But you can't produce anything without me. Whoever doesn't live in me is thrown away like a branch and dries up. Branches like this are gathered, thrown into a fire, and burned. If you live in me and what I say lives in you, then ask for anything you want, and it will be yours. You give glory to my Father when you produce a lot of fruit and therefore show that you are my disciples. (John 15:5–8)

> Let us yield ourselves to be pruned by the Word, that we may not need the pruning of awful sorrows. It is said that three out of five of the vine-berries are cut off that the remainder may attain their full size. How many of our own promptings have to be excised in order that our best fruit may be yielded!
>
> F. B. Meyer, *Devotional Commentary* (Wheaton: Tyndale House, 1989), 473

Top, Israel is portrayed as a vine—tended by God himself—that is sometimes healthy and sometimes fruitless.

41

Bread

In one form or another, bread is found all over the world. Its existence goes back to the roots of humanity, for when God described the results of the fall, he told Adam, "By the sweat of your brow, you will produce food [the Hebrew word for *bread*] to eat" (Gen. 3:19). Bread is basic to life and comfort. Bread has long been a symbol of hospitality and friendship, and "breaking bread" conveys a welcome to someone's table (see Gen. 14:18).

Bread as Provision

Bread often represents food in general, even survival. At the end of his forty-day fast in the wilderness, Jesus was presented with a powerful temptation that connected with his hunger: "If you are the Son of God, tell these stones to become loaves of bread" (Matt. 4:3). Jesus' answer highlights the importance of bread in comparison to the eternal significance of God's instructions: "Scripture says, 'A person cannot live on bread alone but on every word that God speaks'" (Matt. 4:4). Jesus quoted only the second half of a verse from Deuteronomy that points to God's purposes, including allowing hunger: "So he made you suffer from hunger and then fed you with manna, which neither you nor your ancestors had seen before. He did this to teach you that a person cannot live on bread alone but on every word that the LORD speaks" (Deut. 8:3).

Bread filled an important role in the events of the exodus not only in God's demonstration of care in providing food in the desert, but also in the departure meal. Passover bread was part of the Passover meal and was made without leaven/yeast. When the time came to travel, the people needed to be ready and would have no time to wait for dough to rise. "So the people picked up their bread dough before it had risen and carried it on their shoulders in bowls, wrapped up in their clothes" (Exod. 12:34). At their first stop on the journey they were able to prepare bread: "With the dough they had brought from Egypt, they baked round, flat bread. The dough hadn't risen because they'd been thrown out of Egypt and had no time to prepare food for the trip" (Exod. 12:39).

For forty years, God himself was in the bread business, providing manna for his people seven days a week as they traveled through the wilderness between Egypt and the Promised Land. In this sense bread is a symbol of God's daily provision. The familiar phrase "Give us our daily bread today" (Matt. 6:11) from the Lord's Prayer (vv. 9–13) has an often overlooked connection with God's provision of manna in the wilderness. In Exodus 16, when the people complained against Moses for leading them away from Egypt, which they now pictured as a place of "pots of meat" and "all the food we wanted" (v. 3), God answered with "food [bread] from heaven" (v. 4). God not only meant it was coming from him, but that it was also literally going to fall out of the sky every day—as manna. Except for the day before the Sabbath, the manna God provided would be good for that day only.

Jesus is the Bread of Life.

They should not be hoarding or worrying about tomorrow's provision. God would provide their daily bread. Those who doubted ended up with a wormy and smelly mess on their hands. Trusting God for our immediate needs is still the best way to express our overall dependence on God. Claiming to trust God with the long-term things while doubting him right now is not trust.

Jesus the Bread of Life

In John 6, Jesus repeatedly identifies himself as the Bread of Life. "Jesus told them, 'I am the bread of life. Whoever comes to me will never become hungry, and whoever believes in me will never become thirsty'" (v. 35). Coming to Jesus and believing in him are comparable to eating bread—the latter leads to maintaining physical life, the former leads to spiritual life. This truth was underscored by the miraculous provision of bread for five thousand people (John 6:5–13).

On the night he was betrayed, Jesus took the familiar elements of the Passover meal and transformed two of them forever. The bread of the old meal became the symbol of Jesus' body, which would suffer on the cross. Our physical sharing in a portion of the symbol of Jesus' body through communion doesn't represent "a piece of Jesus." We get all of him; all his work on our behalf, and all the promises he secured for us by delivering his body to death.

In the original languages, bread is also mentioned as part of the coming kingdom (Luke 14:15–24; Isa. 25:6–8; Rev. 19:9). Those who enter heaven participate in a wedding feast that includes bread from heaven (Neh. 9:15; Rev. 2:17)—God's provision for all spiritual needs in the person of Christ. Thus bread is a symbol that portrays salvation history: the daily provision of God, sustenance through desert times, partaking of Christ's death, and participation in the coming kingdom through faith in Christ.

Key Verse

Jesus said to them, "I can guarantee this truth: Moses didn't give you bread from heaven, but my Father gives you the true bread from heaven." (John 6:32)

> Jesus answered, "I am the bread." He was saying something like this: "You have to understand, there is more to life than daily bread. What you really need is life itself, not just now, but forever, and I am the only one who can give it to you." However real daily bread seems to us, it is still not the reality; it is only the picture. Jesus Christ is the reality.
>
> Philip Ryken, *When You Pray* (Phillipsburg, NJ: P&R, 2006), 115

Bride

Two brides take up most of the symbolic attention in the Bible. The bride of the Old Testament is Israel; the bride of the New Testament is the church, the bride of Christ. With the possible exception of the bride who takes the spotlight in Song of Solomon 4, the idea of a bride in the Old Testament was a daughter "paid for" by a bride-price and then wooed by her husband. Even in the case of Ruth, a widow, the proposal of marriage involved a cost: in this case, Boaz taking on responsibility not only for Ruth but also for Elimelech's widow, Naomi, and a potential child (Obed) who would inherit Chilion's estate as well as Boaz's inheritance.

Bride as a Spiritual Metaphor

The typical actions of a bride anticipating her wedding are understood to be natural parallels to spiritual behavior. Old Testament believers prepared themselves for the coming Messiah through their worship and service. Isaiah wrote on Israel's behalf, "I will find joy in the LORD. I will delight in my God. He has dressed me in the clothes of salvation. He has wrapped me in the robe of righteousness like a bridegroom with a priest's turban,

like a bride with her jewels" (61:10). The same hope of joyful faithfulness is echoed in Jeremiah: "This is what the LORD says: I remember the unfailing loyalty of your youth, the love you had for me as a bride" (2:2). He returns to this picture later in the same chapter: "A young woman can't forget her jewelry or a bride her veils" (v. 32).

Yet these lovely pictures are colored with disappointment, and the bride becomes a symbol for unfaithfulness. God is the heartbroken bridegroom, for the young woman he paid for and wooed has been repeatedly unfaithful:

> When Josiah was king, the LORD asked me, "Did you see what unfaithful Israel did? She went up every high mountain and under every large tree, and she acted like a prostitute there. I thought that after she had done all this that she would come back to me. But she didn't come back, and her treacherous sister Judah saw her. Judah saw that I sent unfaithful Israel away because of her adultery and that I gave Israel her divorce papers. But treacherous Judah, her sister, wasn't afraid. She also acted like a prostitute. Because she wasn't concerned about acting like a prostitute, she polluted the land and committed adultery with standing stones and wood pillars." (Jer. 3:6–9)

Both Ezekiel 16 and most of Hosea are extended metaphors regarding the wifely unfaithfulness of Israel and Judah, though they don't use the term *bride*. But God told Hosea a future relationship between God and his people would mirror the highest hopes for bridal beauty and marriage faithfulness: "Israel, I will make you my wife forever. I will be honest and faithful to you. I will show you my love and compassion. I will be true to you, my wife. Then you will know the LORD" (Hosea 2:19–20).

Israel was an unfaithful bride, but God is ever faithful to his people.

The Church as the Bride of Christ

The lovely picture of a faithful bride and wife is picked up by both Paul and John in the New Testament to symbolize the relationship God wants to have through Christ with all those who make up the church. Believers have been bought with the bride-price of Christ's blood and are now wooed by his love. Paul develops some key insights into a godly marriage, featuring the role of the wife's relationship to her husband as being parallel to the role of the church in her relationship with Jesus (Eph. 5:22–33). He drives home the point: "This is a great mystery. (I'm talking about Christ's relationship to the church)" (v. 32). Paul can even visualize his role as that of a father who is preparing to entrust his daughter (the church) to the only proper suitor. "I'm as protective of you as God is. After all, you're a virgin whom I promised in marriage to one man—Christ" (2 Cor. 11:2).

In the closing chapters of Revelation, the symbol of the bride, who ultimately represents all believers, comes into clear focus. First we read the formal announcement of the wedding: " 'Let us rejoice, be happy, and give him glory because it's time for the marriage of the lamb. His bride has made herself ready. She has been given the privilege of wearing dazzling, pure linen.' This fine linen represents the things that God's holy people do that have his approval" (19:7–9). Like the words of Isaiah and Jeremiah, the bride's meticulous preparations are a symbol and metaphor of the Christian's preparations for their heavenly home.

Then the bride of Christ is fully prepared, with an appearance far beyond anything imaginable when a bride stands at the back of a church waiting to step down the aisle: "Then I saw the holy city, New Jerusalem, coming down from God out of heaven, dressed like a bride ready for her husband. I heard a loud voice from the throne say, 'God lives with humans! God will make his home with them, and they will be his people. God himself will be with them and be their God. He will wipe every tear from their eyes. There won't be any more death. There won't be any grief, crying, or pain, because the first things have disappeared' " (21:2–4). In the end, the bride is a people—us. All who have been bought with the ultimate bride-price that Jesus paid on the cross with his life will be adorned in his righteousness for all eternity.

Key Verse

I will find joy in the LORD.
   I will delight in my God.
   He has dressed me in the clothes of salvation.
   He has wrapped me in the robe of righteousness
      like a bridegroom with a priest's turban,
      like a bride with her jewels. (Isa. 61:10)

Christ Jesus has no quarrel with His spouse. She often wanders from Him, and grieves Him—but *He does not allow her faults to affect His love.* He sometimes chides—but it is always in the tenderest manner, with the kindest intentions—it is "My love" even then. There is no remembrance of our follies. He does not cherish ill thoughts of us—but He pardons and loves as well after the offence—as before it!

Charles Spurgeon, *Morning and Evening*
(Nashville: Thomas Nelson, 1994), December 3, "Morning"

Top, the white bridal garment is a metaphor for the pure white garments Christ gives to those who trust him.

Bridegroom

Weddings are joy-filled and expectant events. We look forward to the couple's new life and the starting of a new family. In biblical times, the bridegroom was ending his adolescence and taking on the responsibility of starting a family line. Continuing the family name was of utmost importance. Because of this, the bridegroom was portrayed as a victor (Ps. 19:5). He had won the bride through the payment of a bride-price and had earned a position of importance in the community.

The Ultimate Bridegroom

Song of Solomon (often called Song of Songs) offers a beautiful picture of wedded bliss. The bride and bridegroom share a mutual love for one another. Their love is fresh and untainted by unfaithfulness or the trials of life. Song of Solomon is a portrait of a real marriage, but it is also an image for the relationship between God and his people. God is the bridegroom, and Israel is the beautiful bride.

Of course, sin and rebellion ruin that ideal marriage. The book of Hosea describes a marriage that is a metaphor for the relationship between God and Israel as it turned out to be. God is represented by Hosea, the faithful husband. Israel is represented by Gomer, the harlot and priestess in a pagan cult. The bride has been unfaithful to the bridegroom in the most heinous ways, yet the bridegroom pursues her and woos her back, time and again. God is the pursuing bridegroom of his wayward people.

The image of God's people as a bride for Christ is fleshed out in the New Testament with Paul's instructions on marriage in Ephesians 5:22–33. After commanding the wife to submit to her husband's leadership and the husband to love sacrificially, Paul says, "This is a great mystery. (I'm talking about Christ's relationship to the church)" (v. 32). Marriage should reflect the relationship between Christ and the church today, just as it was intended to reflect the relationship between God and his people in the Old Testament. The loving, sacrificial bridegroom who takes the appropriate leadership in the marriage relationship reflects God's care for the church.

The Wedding

One of the most memorable uses of the imagery of a wedding is in Jesus' parable about the ten foolish virgins (Matt. 25). These virgins were to be part of the wedding night festivities, proceeding with lamps to the bride and groom's bedchamber. But they failed to prepare properly and so were excluded from the wedding feast. Jesus is reminding us that he is the diligent bridegroom making preparations for

Weddings are joy-filled celebrations of love and commitment, but the ultimate marriage is of Christ to the church.

us (Matt. 9:15; John 3:29); and while we wait, we must remain alert and ready for his return (John 14:1–3).

The imagery of Christ as our bridegroom reaches a climax in Revelation. The whoring wife of Hosea has been redeemed and is now the resplendent, pure bride of Christ. "Let us rejoice, be happy, and give him glory because it's time for the marriage of the lamb. His bride has made herself ready" (19:7). The final four chapters of Revelation flesh this out as invitations are sent out for the marriage supper, the triumphant wedding host prepares the path and conquers his enemies, the new home is prepared and lit, the guests arrive and those whose names are written in the Lamb's Book of Life are admitted, and the guests are refreshed with the water of life and twelve kinds of fruit. The final invitation is offered in 22:17: "The Spirit and the bride say, 'Come!' Let those who hear this say, 'Come!' Let those who are thirsty come! Let those who want the water of life take it as a gift." The Bible's final picture of Christ is as a bridegroom. What image could be more fitting and appealing for his final invitation to us than that of a bridegroom? He is the loving victor holding out the glorious invitation to cherish and care for us eternally.

Key Verse

As a young man marries a woman,
*   so your sons will marry you.*
As a bridegroom rejoices over his bride,
*   so your God will rejoice over you.*
*   (Isa. 62:5)*

What is the secret of marriage? . . . The message that what husbands should do for their wives is what Jesus did to bring us into union with himself. And what was that? Jesus gave himself up for us. Jesus the Son, though equal with the Father, gave up his glory and took on our human nature (Philippians 2:5ff). But further, he willingly went to the cross and paid the penalty for our sins, removing our guilt and condemnation, so that we could be united with him (Romans 6:5) and take on his nature (2 Peter 1:4). . . . Jesus' sacrificial service to us has brought us into a deep union with him and he with us. And that, Paul says, is the key not only to understanding marriage but to living it.

Tim Keller, *The Meaning of Marriage*
(New York: Dutton, 2011), 45–46

Brimstone

*B*rimstone, literally "the stone that burns," is another name for the mineral sulfur. It is found at the surface around the Dead Sea, where it was deposited during the breakdown of sedimentary rocks. Sulfur, when burned, produces an acrid and poisonous smoke. It was sometimes used as a disinfectant, as a fumigant, or as an antiparasitic. It was also associated with volcanic activity. Sulfur's distinctive odor is present in odorized natural gas, skunk spray, grapefruit, and garlic. It was also used to make the most effective black gunpowder. Today it is used in fertilizer and pesticides, and is also an essential mineral for the human body.

Sodom and Gomorrah

Burning sulfur accompanied the destruction of Sodom and Gomorrah (Gen. 19:24). The city had become so evil that the angels told Lot, "We're going to destroy this place. The complaints to the LORD against its people are so loud that the LORD has sent us to destroy it" (v. 13). Not even ten righteous people could be found in the entire city (18:32). This historical event caused brimstone to become symbolic of divine judgment. This is where we get the phrase "fire-and-brimstone preacher" to signify a preacher who speaks exclusively on the judgment of God.

Jesus used Sodom and Gomorrah as the example of harsh judgment: "I can guarantee that judgment day will be easier for Sodom than for that city" (Luke 10:12). Later he used it as a symbol for sudden judgment, coming when least expected. "The situation will also be like the time of Lot. People were eating, drinking, buying and selling, planting and building. But on the day that Lot left Sodom, fire and sulfur rained from the sky and destroyed all of them. The day when the Son of Man is revealed will be like that" (Luke 17:28–30). The psalmist also uses brimstone as a symbol of ultimate judgment: "He rains down fire and burning sulfur upon wicked people. He makes them drink from a cup filled with scorching wind" (Ps. 11:6; see also Deut. 29:23; Ezek. 38:22; Luke 17:29). Ignited sulfur was not only a tool of punishment but also a purging of evil. The disinfectant properties of burning sulfur make it a purifying tool for the earth.

Prophecies of judgment contain warnings of coming brimstone and fire to judge sin in the world.

Final Judgment

At the final judgment, brimstone figures prominently. One of the plagues described in Revelation is burning sulfur (9:17–18). It also will be used in Satan's final punishment: "The devil, who deceived them, was thrown into the fiery lake of sulfur, where the beast and the false prophet were also thrown. They will be tortured day and night forever and ever" (Rev. 20:10). This Old Testament image for the punishment most appropriate for the greatest evils of man is a fitting symbol for the end-times judgment that awaits Satan, the most evil being that exists. The acrid smell of sulfur makes it a vivid and almost tactile image for judgment.

Key Verse

He rains down fire and burning sulfur upon wicked people.
He makes them drink from a cup filled with scorching wind. (Ps. 11:6)

Jonathan Edwards was well known for his vivid descriptions of the fires of hell, which were designed to invoke fear that would lead people to repent of their sins.

The world will probably be converted into a great lake or liquid globe of fire, in which the wicked shall be overwhelmed, which will always be in tempest, in which they shall be tossed to and fro, having no rest day and night, vast waves and billows of fire continually rolling over their heads, of which they shall forever be full of a quick sense within and without; their heads, their eyes, their tongues, their hands, their feet, their loins and their vitals, shall forever be full of a flowing, melting fire, fierce enough to melt the very rocks and elements; and also, they shall eternally be full of the most quick and lively sense to feel the torments; not for one minute, not for one day, not for one age, not for two ages, not for a hundred ages, nor for ten thousand millions of ages, one after another, but forever and ever, without any end at all, and never to be delivered.

Jonathan Edwards,
That Unknown Country, or, What Living Men Believe concerning Punishment after Death (Springfield, MA: C. A. Nichols, 1793), 226–27

Top, the cities of Sodom and Gomorrah were burned with sulfur and brimstone as a judgment for their sin, and pillars of salt were left when the destruction was over.

49

Building

uilding is both an effort and a result. If we build well, the product will be a structure we call a *building*. The Bible is full of people building altars, cities, houses, roads, towers, walls, and more. Quite a few significant buildings are mentioned: the Tower of Babel, the walled city of Jerusalem, the temple of Solomon. We read of cities being built and destroyed. The greatest builder of all time is God, the builder of creation from the foundation up (Pss. 102:25; 104:3; Isa. 48:13). He described in great detail the construction plans for the traveling worship center (tabernacle) that moved with the people of Israel as they wandered in the wilderness for forty years and also the plans for its permanent replacement, the temple. One of the regular cycles of life mentioned in Ecclesiastes 3 is "a time to kill and a time to heal, a time to tear down and a time to build up" (v. 3).

Building a Foundation for Life

The drive to construct is a symbol for the way we shape our lives and the impact we can have on other people. We can tear them down or build them up (Eph. 4:29 NIV). And while we are living, we are also constructing a life that has a certain structure, just like a building. God's role in that project is crucial: "If the LORD does not

build the house, it is useless for the builders to work on it. If the LORD does not protect a city, it is useless for the guard to stay alert" (Ps. 127:1).

Jesus concluded his famous Sermon on the Mount with the following application challenge to his listeners:

> Therefore, everyone who hears what I say and obeys it will be like a wise person who built a house on rock. Rain poured, and floods came. Winds blew and beat against that house. But it did not collapse, because its foundation was on rock.
> Everyone who hears what I say but doesn't obey it will be like a foolish person who built a house on sand. Rain poured, and floods came. Winds blew and struck that house. It collapsed, and the result was a total disaster. (Matt. 7:24–27)

The apostle Paul elaborated on this idea of our individual lives as buildings:

> You are God's building. As a skilled and experienced builder, I used the gift that God gave me to lay the foundation for that building. However, someone else is building on it. Each person must be careful how he builds on it. After all, no one can lay any other foundation than the one that is already laid, and that foundation is Jesus Christ. People may build on this foundation with gold, silver, precious stones, wood, hay, or straw. The day will make what each one does clearly visible because fire will reveal it. That fire will determine what kind of work each person has done. If what a person has built survives, he will receive a reward. If his work is burned up, he will suffer the loss. However, he will be saved, though it will be like going through a fire. (1 Cor. 3:9–15)

The church is illustrated by the metaphor of a building, each member a building block with Christ himself as the chief cornerstone and the apostles and prophets as the foundation.

This symbol of a building representing a person's spiritual life is carried over to the corporate relationship between believers. The church is a building of human lives. "You are built on the foundation of the apostles and prophets. Christ Jesus himself is the cornerstone. In him all the parts of the building fit together and grow into a holy temple in the Lord. Through him you, also, are being built in the Spirit together with others into a place where God lives" (Eph. 2:20–22). Colossians 2:7, 1 Timothy 3:15, and 2 Timothy 2:19 all echo this idea of believers bonded into a building.

An Eternal City

We see through prophecy that God has not only built and created builders, he is also building a great and eternal city. Abraham was anticipating that city: "Faith led Abraham to live as a foreigner in the country that God had promised him. He lived in tents, as did Isaac and Jacob, who received the same promise from God. Abraham was waiting for the city that God had designed and built, the city with permanent foundations" (Heb. 11:9–10). Revelation echoes this expectation in a picture of the new heaven and new earth: "He carried me by his power away to a large, high mountain. He showed me the holy city, Jerusalem, coming

down from God out of heaven. It had the glory of God. Its light was like a valuable gem, like gray quartz, as clear as crystal" (Rev. 21:10–11). But Jesus had already described, in a personal way, what we can anticipate in God's eternal construction project: "My Father's house has many rooms. If that were not true, would I have told you that I'm going to prepare a place for you? If I go to prepare a place for you, I will come again. Then I will bring you into my presence so that you will be where I am" (John 14:2–3). We are destined for an eternal city, a building where we will live forever with God.

Key Verse

We know that if the life we live here on earth is ever taken down like a tent, we still have a building from God. It is an eternal house in heaven that isn't made by human hands. (2 Cor. 5:1)

> The loftier the building, the deeper must the foundation be laid.
>
> Thomas à Kempis, *The Christian's Pattern, or, a Treatise of the Imitation of Jesus Christ*, trans. Dean Stanhope (London: William Tegg, 1865), 105

Bull/Calf

Cattle were primarily a measure or symbol of wealth in biblical times. They were both familiar and significant, good characteristics for symbolic use. Among his livestock, the wealthy Job had a thousand oxen (Job 1:3). Cattle not only provided meat, milk, leather, and other by-products, they were the main animal workforce in ancient agricultural societies. Oxen (castrated bulls) pulled plows as well as wagons.

Bulls

The size and strength of bulls made them ready symbols of power and virility (Deut. 33:17; Pss. 22:12; 68:30; 92:10; Isa. 66:3). They are naturally aggressive and difficult to domesticate. They were admired in ancient cultures to the point of being revered as gods. Sacrificing them would underscore their less-than-divine status and make them a valued offering to God as substitutes for humans.

Bulls were necessary for breeding purposes, but one bull was sufficient for several dozen cows. Significant numbers of bulls were also raised for sacrificial uses. Bulls are mentioned in connection with general sacrifices in which a "perfect animal" was not required (Lev. 22:23). Gideon was instructed to offer a seven-year-old bull as a protest sacrifice on the wrecked altar of Baal using the chopped-down wooden symbol of Asherah

as fuel (Judg. 6:25–32). When Hannah delivered young Samuel to Eli at the tabernacle in Shiloh, she included a three-year-old bull that was sacrificed on the occasion (1 Sam. 1:24–28).

Calves

Calves present a strong contrast of symbols in Scripture. The golden calf created by Aaron in the wilderness that was worshiped by the people was the poster image for idolatry. Aaron mistakenly thought this idol could represent the God who led his people out of Egypt; instead this episode stands as a lesson of how easily we can turn from the glory of the invisible Creator and worship created things that cannot begin to meet the need we have for God. The lasting memory of this event was captured in Psalm 106:19–23, though the lesson it should have taught the people remained unlearned.

The incident has a close parallel in 1 Kings 12:28 when Jeroboam (who, ironically, had recently returned from exile in Egypt) also created golden calves, telling the people, "Israel, here are your gods who brought you out of Egypt."

First Samuel 6 has an interesting mention of calves in a sign that was given after the Philistines had captured the ark of the covenant and discovered defeating Israel was one thing, but defeating the God of Israel was another matter entirely. The return of the ark was arranged by separating two cows from their recently born calves and hitching them to a cart bearing God's ark. If the cows behaved against their natural inclination to seek out their calves and instead pulled the cart back to Israel, that action would be a sign of God's intervention.

When Moses was up on Mount Sinai longer than the Hebrews expected, Aaron made a golden calf for them to worship.

But the calf can also be a positive metaphor. Jesus included the picture of the fatted calf in his parable of the prodigal son whose father is so overjoyed by his return that the calf is prepared for the welcome-home banquet. It becomes for the community a symbol of joy, forgiveness, and welcome (Luke 15:11–32). The fact that the calf was already fattened reminds us that the father was anticipating and hopeful of his son's return. This also speaks to the willingness to forgive, the expectation of a joyful reunion worth celebrating, and a prepared welcome long before the guest of honor shows up. The chapter begins with Jesus under attack for his compassionate treatment of society's undesirables: "This man welcomes sinners and eats with them" (Luke 15:2). By the end of the chapter, Jesus has made the case that his purpose in eating with sinners has to do with inviting them to join him in the great feast where the Father will prepare the fatted calf for *all* his prodigal children.

Isaiah promises a number of signs indicating that the "shoot" from Jesse's stump (Jesus) has established his eternal kingdom. Among them is a drastic new relationship between members of the animal kingdom, including calves: "Wolves will live with lambs. Leopards will lie down with goats. Calves, young lions, and year-old lambs will be together, and little children will lead them" (Isa. 11:6). Such a sight would definitely cause us to conclude that a whole new heaven and earth have come to be!

Key Verse

The blood of goats and bulls and the ashes of cows sprinkled on unclean people made their bodies holy and clean. The blood of Christ, who had no defect, does even more. Through the eternal Spirit he offered himself to God and cleansed our consciences from the useless things we had done. Now we can serve the living God. (Heb. 9:13–14)

Bulls were also specified in certain sacrifices. When God organized the priestly role of the tribe of Levi, priests were to be consecrated with the sacrifice of a bull (Exod. 29:1) as was the rest of the tribe that had been set aside for special service to God (Num. 8:5–14). When the altar was built for use in the tabernacle worship of God, it was dedicated with a bull sacrifice (Num. 7:87–88). This involved twelve young bulls (one for each tribe) that were "burnt offerings" and twenty-four bulls sacrificed as fellowship offerings. A number of other offerings (Num. 28–29) also included the sacrifice of bulls. The Feast of Tabernacles (Num. 29:12–38) involved the largest number of sacrificial bulls (seventy-one) spread out over the eight days of the festival commemorating the wilderness journey to the Promised Land.

Top, bulls were often worshiped in pagan religions, but in the Jewish faith they were sacrificed to make atonement for sin.

53

Camel

Camels were a common sight throughout Bible times, particularly in cities and villages along caravan routes, where these long-distance beasts of burden might pause for a night before trudging on to their destination. In addition to being a means of transportation, camels were also a source of milk and meat for Israel's neighbors (though they are listed among the unclean animals for Israel and therefore not used for food—Lev. 11:4). Camel hair was woven to create a rough but durable material from which Bedouins still create tents and people like John the Baptist occasionally sewed simple garments (see Matt. 3:4).

Wild and Unruly

Some camels, called *dromedaries*, were cultivated for riding and racing. Jeremiah used this type of camel as a symbol for wayward Israelites who followed other gods (Jer. 2:23). In this way camels parallel the symbolic use of donkeys—a supposedly cultivated and trained animal that has become wild and unruly.

Status Symbol

We can see in the life of Abram and Job that camels were considered a symbol of wealth. Someone who owned 3,000 camels, as Job did, would have been considered a millionaire in today's terms. Camels were also considered a powerful component of an army's battle resources. The Midianites who oppressed Israel in Judges 6 wielded a vast cavalry mounted on camels.

Hyperbole

Much later, Jesus created an unexpected symbolic picture with the camel by way of hyperbole: "It is easier for a camel to go through the eye of a needle than for a rich person to enter the kingdom of God" (Mark 10:25). The idea of a large animal like a camel being compressed to pass through a needle's eye is a ludicrous but effective way to emphasize that wealth has no standing when someone is seeking admission to God's kingdom.

Jesus said it is easier for a camel to go through the eye of a needle than for a rich man to enter the kingdom of heaven.

Jesus also found camels a handy symbol for important matters when he pointed out to the scribes and Pharisees, "You blind guides! You strain gnats out of your wine, but you swallow camels" (Matt. 23:24). He was highlighting the hypocrisy of giving great attention to an exacting idea of the tithe (making sure that you gave a tenth of every herb and spice in your possession) while neglecting the large matters of "justice, mercy, and faithfulness . . . the most important things in Moses' Teachings" (Matt. 23:23).

Key Verse

Indeed, it is easier for a camel to go through the eye of a needle than for a rich person to enter the kingdom of God. (Luke 18:25)

Not only those who heard the words when they were first spoken, but many others since have found the saying ["It is easier for a camel to go through the eye of a needle than for a rich man to enter heaven"] to be a hard one. Attempts have been made to soften it somewhat. The eye of a needle, we are sometimes assured, is a metaphor; the reference is to a small opening giving independent access or egress through a much larger city gate. . . . But this charming explanation is of relatively recent date; there is no evidence that such a subsidiary entrance was called the eye of a needle in biblical times. . . . No doubt Jesus was using the language of hyperbole . . . but the language of hyperbole was intended to drive the lesson home: it is impossible for a rich man to enter the kingdom of God—humanly impossible, Jesus concedes, for God, with whom nothing is impossible, can even save a rich man.

F. F. Bruce, *Hard Sayings of the Bible* (Downers Grove, IL: InterVarsity, 1996), 438

Canaan

The land of Canaan is the original name for what became the Promised Land of Israel in the Old Testament. It was named after Noah's grandson Canaan, who was the ancestor of various groups living in that region (Gen. 10:15–19). In general, the term *Canaanite* was applied to any and all peoples who lived along the eastern end of the Mediterranean and west of the Dead Sea.

Far from God's People

In biblical history, the original people who lived in the land of Canaan were to be displaced by God in favor of a people he had chosen to live there, the offspring of Abraham. God gave strict instructions that the values and religious practices of Canaan were *not* to be adopted by his people:

> The LORD your God will bring you to the land you're about to enter and take possession of. He will force many nations out of your way: the Hittites, Girgashites, Amorites, Canaanites, Perizzites, Hivites, and Jebusites—seven nations larger and more powerful than you. When the LORD your God gives them to you and you defeat them, destroy every one of them because they have been claimed by the LORD. Don't make any treaties with them or show them any mercy. Never marry any of them. Never let your daughters marry their sons or your sons marry their daughters. These people will turn your children away from me to worship other gods. Then the LORD will get very angry with you and will quickly destroy you.
>
> But this is what you must do to these people: Tear down their altars, smash their sacred stones, cut down their poles dedicated to the goddess Asherah, and burn their idols. (Deut. 7:1–5)

God's instructions for living were radically different from those practiced by the inhabitants of the land, but God's people gradually and then persistently chose to adopt religious traditions of the local people and neglect the God who had chosen them. Canaan thus became a symbol for the people who were farthest from him, for those who were either not chosen as his people or who had rejected him as their God.

The term *Canaan* rarely occurs in the New Testament, but a couple of occurrences are noteworthy. In Matthew 15 we read that Jesus had contact with a Canaanite woman. "Jesus left that place and went to the region of Tyre and Sidon. A Canaanite woman from that territory came to him and began to shout, 'Have mercy on me, Lord, Son of David! My daughter is tormented by a demon'" (Matt. 15:21–22). The exchange that follows reveals a woman of humility and faith who understood that, despite her background, she could appeal to Jesus for help. Being a Canaanite didn't cut her off from God's grace. What made this incident noteworthy to the disciples was that the woman was a Canaanite. She symbolized those who were farthest from the kingdom of heaven and least worthy of Jesus' mercy.

When the apostle Paul was preaching to Jews and Jewish converts in Antioch of Pisidia,

Canaan, part of the Promised Land, near the Sea of Galilee

he gave a quick overview of God's hand on the people of Israel through history:

> Then Paul stood up, motioned with his hand, and said, "Men of Israel and converts to Judaism, listen to me. The God of the people of Israel chose our ancestors and made them a strong nation while they lived as foreigners in Egypt. He used his powerful arm to bring them out of Egypt, and he put up with them for about forty years in the desert. Then he destroyed seven nations in Canaan and gave their land to his people as an inheritance. He did all this in about four hundred and fifty years.
>
> After that he gave his people judges until the time of the prophet Samuel. (Acts 13:16–20)

The Promised Land

The land of Canaan came to hold two symbolic meanings for believers. It can remind us of our life before Christ. Each of us was at one time his enemy, just like the Canaanites were (Rom. 5:10). But it also reminds us that once God has stepped into the picture, the land that was formerly saturated with sin becomes the Promised Land. God brings about radical change, redeeming those who are farthest from him. The land that was originally his creation, then used for evil for a time, remains his land and returns to usefulness for him as we live our new lives. That is why it was with such joy that the Israelites ate the fruit of the land of Canaan: "The day after that, the manna stopped. The people of Israel never had manna again. That year they began to eat the crops that grew in Canaan" (Josh. 5:12). In this sense Canaan is a symbol for heaven, the ultimate Promised Land for believers.

Key Verse

He confirmed it as a law for Jacob,
as an everlasting promise to Israel,
by saying, "I will give you the land of
Canaan.
It is your share of the inheritance."
(Ps. 105:10–11)

Israel's weary wanderings were all over, and the promised rest was attained. No more moving tents, fiery serpents, fierce Amalekites, and howling wildernesses: they came to the land which flowed with milk and honey, and they ate the old corn of the land. Perhaps this year, beloved Christian reader, this may be thy case or mine. Joyful is the prospect, and if faith be in active exercise, it will yield unalloyed delight. To be with Jesus in the rest which remaineth for the people of God, is a cheering hope indeed, and to expect this glory so soon is a double bliss.

Charles Spurgeon, *Morning and Evening*
(Nashville: Thomas Nelson, 1994), January 1, "Morning"

Top, Canaan was known for its fertile vineyards, which produced grapes so large it took two men to carry a cluster of them.

57

Candlestick/ Lamp Stand

The most notable candlesticks in the Bible are those created for use in God's house. The lamp stand or *menorah* that stood in the tabernacle was made of a single sheet of pure gold and had seven branches, each topped with a lamp in the shape of an almond blossom (Exod. 25:31–40). Solomon's temple had ten of these candles (1 Kings 7:49). Each lamp burned olive oil and was kept burning through the night as a symbol that God was with his chosen people at all times (Exod. 27:21; 1 Sam. 3:3). Extrabiblical sources suggest that in later times the middle lamp, which represented God himself, was kept burning around the clock.

God's Light

In temple worship, this object of beauty was symbolic of the light of God—the presence of the *shekinah* glory among the chosen people, housed in the tabernacle. As long as the lamps kept burning, the Jews were aware of God's presence and leadership among them. The act of trimming the lamps each day was a tactile reminder of God's promises. Additionally, the seven branches of the lamp stand represented the seven days of creation and the many other instances in Scripture of seven being the number of completeness. (See also SEVEN.)

The ever-burning light from the menorah was a sign that pointed to Jesus. He is Immanuel, "God with us," who brings the light of salvation to a dark world (Isa. 9:2; John 8:12). He is the light (John 1:4–10). Or as Jesus exclaimed, "I am the light of the world. Whoever follows me will have a life filled with light and will never live in the dark" (John 8:12). This symbolism is apparent in the prophecies of Christ: "My servant David will always have a lamp in my presence in Jerusalem, the city where I chose to place my name" (1 Kings 11:36; see also 2 Kings 8:19).

A Light to the Nations

The menorah also represented the nation of Israel, which was to be a "light to the nations" (Isa. 42:6). As such, they were to be led by the Lord's power and be the means through which he would bring salvation to the world—a point made in Zechariah's vision of the lamp stand (Zech. 4:2, 6). Even today the menorah is an important Jewish emblem, appearing on Israel's coat of arms to symbolize their role as a light to the world.

The New Testament sheds further light on this symbolism. Jesus said, "You are light for the world. A city cannot be hidden when it is located on a hill. No one lights a lamp and puts it under a basket. Instead, everyone who lights a lamp puts it on a lamp stand. Then its light shines on everyone in the house. In the same way let your light shine in front of people. Then they will see the good that you do and praise your Father in heaven" (Matt. 5:14–16). Since the coming of Christ, the church is now God's menorah to the world—the bringer of the light of Christ into a dark world.

In the book of Revelation, the lamp stand appears once again as a symbol of the churches. "The hidden meaning of the seven stars that you saw in my right hand and the seven gold lamp stands is this: The seven stars are the messengers of the seven churches, and the seven lamp

stands are the seven churches" (Rev. 1:20; cf. 1:12–13; 2:1; 11:4). The lamp stand is a symbol for the way the church is to represent God's presence in the world, just as in the Old Testament the menorah represented God's presence in Israel. The light that once was only for the chosen nation of Israel is now for all people. The literal lamp stand in the Old Testament is a symbolic one in the New, showing that God's light is for all nations, and his work is done through the church.

Key Verse

The city doesn't need any sun or moon to give it light because the glory of God gave it light. The lamb was its lamp. (Rev. 21:23)

This golden candlestick stood on the south side of the holy place, opposite the table of showbread with the altar of incense between. The light of the candlestick was indispensable in the service of the priests. There was no other light in the tabernacle. . . . Not a single ray of light was allowed to come from the outside by the light of nature. The oil in the light, representing the Holy Spirit, was the only source of light by which the priest was to serve in the tabernacle. The light of the candlestick points both to the Lord Jesus Christ, and also to the written Word of God, the two being inseparable. The believer is to walk only, therefore, by the light of the Word of God.

M. R. DeHaan, *The Tabernacle*
(Grand Rapids: Zondervan, 1955), 97–98

Top, Jesus reminded us that believers are to be light in a dark world, shining before men to bring glory to God.

59

Circumcision

The physical act of circumcision was a sign of the covenant between God and Israel in which he had chosen them and promised to be their God for all generations (Gen. 17:10–11; Acts 7:8). In this act, the foreskin of a male child's penis was removed (Lev. 12:3). More rarely, circumcision was performed on adults. When God made his covenant promises to Abraham, he insisted that they be sealed with the physical reminder that the Israelites were a people set apart. Those who failed to comply with this condition were excluded from the covenant community (Gen. 17:14; Exod. 12:48).

Circumcision in Old Testament Culture

Interestingly, circumcision existed in other cultures in Old Testament times. Most of the surrounding nations, including Egypt, participated in the practice. The significance of circumcision in these other cultures is unclear, although it did not seem to be practiced among infants, so perhaps it was a rite of passage during puberty. The Philistines were the only one of Israel's immediate neighbors who were uncircumcised, and that is why Saul was able to demand that David bring back one hundred foreskins as the bride-price for Michal (1 Sam. 18:25). The Old Testament refers to the Philistines and other peoples as "uncircumcised," meaning that they were wicked and godless (Gen. 34:14; 1 Sam. 14:6; 17:36).

Circumcision was a symbol of belonging to the people of God and adherence to covenant regulations, but it was not always practiced in Jewish history. During the wandering in the wilderness it was neglected, perhaps because the nation had broken their covenant with God. When the Israelites entered the Promised Land they circumcised all those who had been born in the wilderness (Josh. 5:2–9).

The Hebrew nation took great pride in circumcision and looked down on anyone who was uncircumcised. Instead of reaching out to other nations as God intended, they thought of themselves as spiritually superior. Because circumcision was a symbol of being right with God, those who were uncircumcised were assumed to be outside the circle of God's love. Such exclusivity was never God's intention. The symbol he gave as a reminder of his covenantal love became a cause of sin.

Circumcision of the Heart

Although circumcision is a physical sign, its true meaning is spiritual. Moses and the prophets used the term *circumcised* to refer to purity of heart. It was a symbol of being repentant and eager to obey. The physical act was intended to be an expression of inward obedience, and in those cases where the outward obedience was not matched by inward heart change, a circumcised person was no better off than an uncircumcised person. A good example of this symbolic use of the word is Leviticus 26:41–42: "If they

Baby boys were circumcised as a sign that they were part of God's covenant people, recipients of all of God's promises.

humble their uncircumcised hearts and accept their guilt, I will remember my promise to Jacob, Isaac, and Abraham. I will also remember the land." Similarly, Jeremiah said of rebellious Israel, "Even though these nations are circumcised, all Israel has uncircumcised hearts" (Jer. 9:26).

This symbolic meaning of circumcision caused controversy in the early church. Jewish believers tried to insist that Gentile converts submit to circumcision in order to be admitted to the church (Acts 15). The Jerusalem council settled the matter, stating, "Why are you testing God? You're putting a burden on the disciples, a burden neither our ancestors nor we can carry. We certainly believe that the Lord Jesus saves us the same way that he saves them—through his kindness" (vv. 10–11). Paul reaffirmed this decision in Romans 4: "Abraham's faith was the basis of his approval by God while he was still uncircumcised. . . . Therefore, he is the father of every believer who is not circumcised, and their faith, too, is regarded as the basis of their approval by God" (v. 11).

Circumcision was of no value apart from a repentant and obedient heart (Rom. 2:25–26). The symbol of circumcision points to the truth of salvation through faith alone. It is an old covenant symbol whose failure to ultimately save points to the need for a new covenant. And as is the case with many Old Testament symbols, this physical act of worship is replaced in the new covenant with a spiritual act—circumcision of the body is replaced with circumcision of the heart (Gal. 6:15).

But there is also a New Testament sacrament that is an outward symbol like circumcision, an external sign on the body of the internal change that takes place at salvation. That sacrament, of course, is baptism. Colossians 2:11–12 makes this explicit: "In him you were also circumcised. It was not a circumcision performed by human hands. But it was a removal of the corrupt nature in the circumcision performed by Christ. This happened when you were placed in the tomb with Christ through baptism. In baptism you were also brought back to life with Christ through faith in the power of God, who brought him back to life." Although the importance of circumcision centered on the internal state of the heart toward God, it was still a helpful sign and symbol, and so God provided a new covenant substitute in baptism.

Key Verse

Rather, a person is a Jew inwardly, and circumcision is something that happens in a person's heart. Circumcision is spiritual, not just a written rule. That person's praise will come from God, not from people. (Rom. 2:29)

This passage [Col. 2:11–12], therefore, teaches that baptism is the same to Christians, which circumcision was to the Jews. And that baptism has taken the place of circumcision, may also be proven from the fact that both sacraments have the same end. Both are signs of our adoption into the family of God.

Zacharias Ursinius, *Commentary on the Heidelberg Catechism*, trans. G. W. Williard (1852; repr. Phillipsburg, NJ: P&R, 1992), 375

Clear/Crystal/ Transparent

The concept of *transparency*, which is technically not a color, is relatively rare in the Bible. The idea is mostly connected with the marvels of crystal, a hard substance that can be seen through. It provided a measure of clarity, but was considered a gem. Glass was still practically unknown.

Job mentions crystal as he tries to express the value of wisdom (Job 28:17). Ezekiel sees a sight he struggles to explain (Ezek. 1:1–28) in which he is given a vision of the throne of God. First he sees creatures and wheels that float and hover in a fantastic display of unearthly power. "Something like a dome was spread over the heads of the living creatures. It looked like dazzling crystal" (v. 22).

Brilliant Transparency . . .

John's efforts in Revelation to describe what he sees in his vision of eternity make the most use of the brilliant transparency of certain items. When the scene opens in his vision of the great throne in heaven, John writes, "In front of the throne, there was something like a sea of glass as clear as crystal. In the center near the throne and around the throne were four living creatures covered with eyes in front and in back" (Rev. 4:6). And John's first glimpses of the

New Jerusalem highlight his awareness of clarity and transparency:

> One of the seven angels who had the seven bowls full of the last seven plagues came to me and said, "Come! I will show you the bride, the wife of the lamb." He carried me by his power away to a large, high mountain. He showed me the holy city, Jerusalem, coming down from God out of heaven. It had the glory of God. Its light was like a valuable gem, like gray quartz, as clear as crystal. (Rev. 21:9–11)

The amazing eternal dwelling place of God's rescued people has a wonderful river of life running through it. "The angel showed me a river filled with the water of life, as clear as crystal. It was flowing from the throne of God and the lamb" (Rev. 22:1). In the descriptive language of Scripture, God's chosen writers were telling us that everything about heaven will be high definition. We will know and see as we have not seen before. Suddenly, everything will be as clear as it can be—crystal clear.

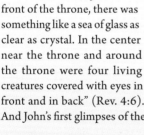

The descriptions Scripture offers of heaven are full of transparent and shiny surfaces that reflect the glory of God.

In his vision of heaven, John saw that "in front of the throne, there was something like a sea of glass as clear as crystal" (Rev. 4:6).

. . . Versus Veiled and Dim

By contrast, the way we see things now is veiled and dim. "Now we see a blurred image in a mirror. Then we will see very clearly. Now my knowledge is incomplete. Then I will have complete knowledge as God has complete knowledge of me" (1 Cor. 13:12). Spiritual truths can be known to us now through the power of the Holy Spirit, but only in part. When we reach heaven, the veil will be removed so we can see God face-to-face. Thus the images of crystal and transparence in heaven highlight the truth that the life we live here on earth is but a shadow of what is to come. It is a symbol that points to the greater spiritual truth that heaven is more real than earthly life.

Key Verse

In front of the throne, there was something like a sea of glass as clear as crystal. In the center near the throne and around the throne were four living creatures covered with eyes in front and in back. (Rev. 4:6)

C. S. Lewis offers a wonderful picture of the crystal of heaven as compared with the veiled shadows of earth:

When Aslan said you could never go back to Narnia, he meant the Narnia you were thinking of. But that was not the real Narnia. That had a beginning and an end. It was only a shadow or a copy of the real Narnia: just as our own world, England and all, is only a shadow or copy of something in Aslan's real world. You need not mourn over Narnia, Lucy. All of the old Narnia that mattered, all the dear creatures, have been drawn into the real Narnia through the Door. And of course it is different; as different as a real thing is from a shadow or as waking life is from a dream. . . . Your father and mother and all of you are—as you used to call it in the Shadow-Lands—dead. The term is over: the holidays have begun. The dream is ended: this is the morning.

—C. S. Lewis, *The Last Battle*
(New York: MacMillan, 1956), 160–61, 173

Top, while we are on earth we see spiritual truths dimly, distorted by our human limitations, but when we reach heaven we will see all things clearly.

63

Clothing

Garments are used as biblical symbols in almost as many ways as there are styles of clothing. Clothes are used as expressions of socioeconomic status, spiritual well-being, and emotional state. They can protect, conceal, or display an inner reality of the wearer. They can last for a long time or wear out quickly (Neh. 9:21; Matt. 6:19). They can consist of leaves (Gen. 3:7), animal skin (Gen. 3:21; Matt. 3:4), rags (Isa. 64:6), pure white linen (Dan. 7:9; Rev. 19:14), or anything in between. They can be literal or figurative. Yet despite all this variety, the use of clothing as a symbol falls into a few set patterns that yield a wealth of insight.

Clothing as Symbol in Scripture

Clothing is first of all a symbol for provisions important for daily life (Gen. 28:20; Isa. 23:18). We are perhaps the only creatures born without the necessary bodily covering to survive very long. Our remarkable skin can only adapt to a relatively narrow temperature fluctuation without needing additional protection. One of God's first acts after Adam and Eve sinned was to provide clothing for them as an act of care and mercy (Gen. 3:21). During the exodus he showed care by causing the Israelites' clothes not to wear out (Deut. 8:4; 29:5; Neh. 9:21). Hannah gave Samuel clothes to express her love (1 Sam. 2:19). The importance of clothing in a less affluent society was expressed in the fact that conquering kings would take clothes as part of their plunder (Exod. 3:22; 2 Kings 7:8; 2 Chron. 20:25), and being without clothes was viewed as a curse (Job 13:28; Isa. 50:9; 51:8). A person's social status was symbolized by how fancy their clothes were—whether they were provided with the barest necessities of life or with abundant riches. For instance, Isaac gave Joseph a fancy coat to show his importance

in the family (Gen. 37:3), and purple cloth was a sign of power (Ezek. 27:24).

Certain types of clothes in the Bible were worn as an expression of the inner emotional state of the wearer. Festive garments, such as for a wedding, connoted joy (Matt. 22:11–12). The Bible also mentions prison garments (Deut. 21:13; 2 Kings 25:29; Jer. 52:33) and lepers' garments (Lev. 13:45), which showed the wearers to be outcasts. Widows would wear clothes of mourning (Gen. 38:14, 19). And sackcloth was a well-known symbol of repentance or sorrow (Gen. 37:34; 1 Kings 20:31; Esther 4:1–2; Ps. 69:11; Isa. 37:1). Those in an extreme state of grief, fear, or anger would tear their clothes (Gen. 37:29; Isa. 37:1). God himself is said to be clothed with splendor and victory (Isa. 63:1) or with vengeance (Isa. 59:17).

Sometimes clothing was used as a disguise with the intent to deceive. False prophets come as wolves in sheeps' clothing (Matt. 7:15). Jacob tricked his father and stole Esau's blessing through the use of a disguise (Gen. 27:15, 27). Saul disguised himself when he visited the witch of Endor (1 Sam. 28:8). And the men of Gibeon dressed in worn-out clothes to trick the Israelites into making a treaty with them (Josh. 9:4–5). In these cases, clothes were used to conceal something about a person rather than to display his or her status.

Clothing and Spiritual State

The act of putting on and taking off clothes becomes a symbol of a person's spiritual state. Old Testament priests would don linen garments to perform their religious duties (Exod. 29:1–9; 40:12–15; Lev. 16:1–4). Their white garments symbolized the purity of God and the purification rites they had gone through to be worthy

to approach him. But evil people also would put on garments, in this case garments of violence (Ps. 73:6) or prostitution (Ezek. 16:16). Even the priests sometimes would wear defiled clothes (Lam. 4:13–14). In the New Testament, we read of putting off the deeds of darkness that belong to our old nature and putting on righteousness (Rom. 13:12; Eph. 4:22; Col. 3:9–10). Believers should be clothed in actions and attitudes that reflect the work of the Holy Spirit within them. Ultimately, believers will put on their eternal body like a garment (2 Cor. 5:2–4).

Taken together, the Bible's symbolic use of clothing provides a record of salvation history. Prior to the fall, Adam and Eve did not have any need for clothing—they were naked and unashamed (Gen. 2:25). After they sinned, they were ashamed and sought clothing as a way to hide their guilt (Gen. 3:7). God provided literal clothing for them (Gen. 3:21), which served their need temporarily, but they needed a permanent solution to their shame. Eventually God provided the promise of garments of salvation (Isa. 61:3, 10). He vowed to cover Israel's nakedness (Ezek. 16:8; Rev. 3:18). Salvation is portrayed symbolically as the changing of our filthy clothes for white robes—an action that only God can do (Isa. 64:6; Zech. 3:3–5; Rev. 7:14). The culmination of salvation is when the believer stands before God as a bride adorned for her husband (Isa. 61:10; Rev. 21:2).

Key Verse

I will find joy in the LORD.
I will delight in my God.
He has dressed me in the clothes of salvation.
He has wrapped me in the robe of righteousness
like a bridegroom with a priest's turban,
like a bride with her jewels. (Isa. 61:10)

In Christ, our rags are exchanged for robes of regal splendor, and we are seated at the same table with Abraham, Isaac, and Jacob. The clothing analogy is not original to Pauline theology. It occurs first with God's clothing of Adam and Eve after the fall, the vision of Joshua the high priest having his filthy clothes exchanged for a robe of righteousness in Zechariah 3, and a host of other passages. . . . So when Paul says that Christ is "our righteousness and sanctification and redemption" (1 Corinthians 1:30), and refers repeatedly to our being "clothed with Christ" and "having put on Jesus Christ," and calls us on that basis to "put on Christ" in our daily conduct, this same connection between justification and sanctification is being drawn.

Michael Horton, *Pilgrim Theology*
(Grand Rapids: Zondervan, 2013), 297

Cornerstone

The cornerstone of a building is the main foundation stone upon which the entire structure rests and therefore the most important stone in a building. In the construction techniques used in antiquity, the cornerstone was the first stone laid, and the integrity and stability of the building depended upon its being precisely squared. As a biblical image, Scripture has one reference to God laying the cornerstone of creation (Job 38:6); all other references are to Christ as the cornerstone of the church.

Christ the Cornerstone

The first use of *cornerstone* as a messianic symbol is in Psalm 118:22: "The stone that the builders rejected has become the cornerstone." This is first and foremost a defense of King David—the young man who had been rejected by his family was worthy of being made king. His royal line was built on the sure foundation of authority given by God himself and would endure forever. Jesus later interpreted this symbol as a reference to himself,

the true King in the lineage of David to whom all other kings pointed. He quoted this verse from Psalm 118 after telling the parable of the vineyard owner. The vineyard owner's son, who was rejected by the tenants, is a symbol for Jesus, the one who was rejected by the religious establishment (Matt. 21:33–46; Mark 12:1–12; Luke 20:9–19). Though rejected and killed, he would become the foundation of a new covenant of faith.

Jesus is the cornerstone of our faith because he is the foundation upon which all other matters of Christian belief rest. Without his perfect sacrifice, without him being the first stone laid in the church, we have no church at all. This point is made in Acts 4:10–11 and Ephesians 2:20, but it reaches its climax in 1 Peter 2:4–5, where the image is extended to include individual believers as part of the structure Jesus holds together: "You are coming to Christ, the living stone who was rejected by humans but was chosen as precious by God. You come to him as living stones, a spiritual house that is being built into a holy priesthood. So offer spiritual sacrifices that God accepts through Jesus Christ." Those who have received the true cornerstone become living stones, connected to one another and built into a temple made up of all believers through all time, resting on Jesus the cornerstone (1 Pet. 2:4–6).The temple of the Old Testament has been replaced by a living church made up of people, not stones. And all of it rests on the person and work of Jesus Christ.

A cornerstone must be perfectly square and perfectly straight in order for a building to have stability and strength.

Jesus is the chief cornerstone of the church, the foundation and the first stone laid.

The Stumbling Stone

The cornerstone is also seen in Scripture as a stone upon which some people stumble. It is a symbol for the truths of Christ that people either accept or reject but are rarely neutral about. People who cannot move beyond the Old Testament law to embrace the new covenant of grace in Christ stumble over the truths of the faith. Jesus and his claims are offensive to them, and they cannot get past their negative impressions to receive him by faith. Those who have faith see Jesus as the chosen foundation stone and build their life upon him. Those who do not have faith are blind to his truth and stumble upon it: " 'The stone that the builders rejected has become the cornerstone, a stone that people trip over, a large rock that people find offensive.' The people tripped over the word because they refused to believe it. Therefore, this is how they ended up" (1 Pet. 2:7–8; cf. Isa. 8:14).

Key Verse

You are built on the foundation of the apostles and prophets. Christ Jesus himself is the cornerstone. (Eph. 2:20)

God's presence makes us his people; the presence of Jesus constitutes the church as his temple, built of living stones, joined to him as God's elect Stone (1 Peter 2:4–6). The church itself is a temple, the house of God, sanctified by the presence of the Spirit (1 Corinthians 3:16).

Edmund P. Clowney,
The Church, Contours of Christian Theology
(Downers Grove, IL: InterVarsity, 1995), 46

Top, the cornerstone of a building is the first stone laid, and thus the most important stone.

67

Cross/ Crucifixion

Our familiarity with the cross has removed much of the obvious offensiveness that the symbol once represented. Crucifixion was the most humiliating form of execution known to the ancient world. Completely naked, victims would be hung on crosses or poles alongside heavily traveled highways. The victims served as object lessons of Roman rule. Indeed, Rome considered crucifixion so demeaning a form of death that it was outlawed for Roman citizens, and understandably so. The victim's hands would be nailed to a crosspiece and the feet fastened with spikes to an upright. The body's weight would be supported by a wooden peg driven into the upright, which the prisoner would straddle; otherwise, the nails would tear through the palms of the hands when the cross was dropped into its socket in the ground.

Naked, torn, and bleeding, under a blazing sun, the prisoner hung suspended between heaven and earth. Every rib became visible in the effort to breathe. Blood gathered in the abdominal cavity, causing swelling and pain. Fever and dehydration brought on a devouring thirst. To pain and thirst were added the further tortures of hunger, rigid fixation, swarming insects, and exposure to brutal spectators. Unless the executioners chose to hasten death by breaking the legs of the victims (done to both of the men crucified alongside Jesus), victims of crucifixion would slowly die on their crosses for as long as a week, suffering until they went completely mad. Eventually death would come through suffocation from bodily fluid collecting in the lungs. The victim would literally drown in his or her own bodily fluids.

The Cross of Christ

The death was horrible. The Christian church took some time to come to terms with the disgrace and horror of the cross. Church fathers forbade its depiction in art until the reign of the Roman emperor Constantine, who had seen a vision of the cross and who also banned it as a method of execution. Thus not until the fourth century did the cross become a symbol of the Christian religion. As C. S. Lewis pointed out, the crucifixion did not become common in art until all who had seen a real one died off.

Strange as this may seem, Christianity has become a religion of the cross. "The message about the cross is nonsense to those who are being destroyed, but it is God's power to us who are being saved" (1 Cor. 1:18) is the heart of the gospel. The preaching of the cross is the soul of the church's mission: "Our message is that Christ was crucified" (1 Cor. 1:23). More than the basis of salvation, Jesus' death on the cross was the central event in Christian history. Despite the shame and sadness of it all, what took place on that cross (and the subsequent resurrection) became the most important fact not only of Jesus' life but in all of human history. This indeed is foolishness to the world and ultimate divine wisdom.

Crucifixion was such a gruesome form of execution that it was outlawed for Roman citizens.

For this reason, the cross has become the symbol of the Christian faith. Its design couldn't be simpler. The horizontal beam reaches out—like God's love. The vertical beam reaches up—as does God's holiness. One represents the width of his love; the other reflects the height of his holiness. Jesus tasted what all people must taste—death—and conquered it. The cross is a symbol of his sacrifice on our behalf and his victory over death.

The Cross of Believers

The cross is a symbol of Christ's death, but it is also a symbol of the Christian life. Five times the Bible records Jesus using the cross as a symbol of radical discipleship and complete surrender to God (Matt. 10:38; 16:24; Mark 8:34; Luke 9:23; 14:27). Jesus challenged would-be followers, "Those who want to come with me must say no to the things they want, pick up their crosses every day, and follow me" (Luke 9:23). Jesus intended this symbolism, which was reflected in the Roman practice of convicted criminals bearing the crossbeam to the place of execution, to be lived out in two ways: dying to self—involving the sacrifice of one's desires for the purpose of following Jesus completely—and a willingness to imitate Jesus completely, even to martyrdom. Disciples cannot share the cross's salvation and triumph without sharing its responsibility. All who follow Jesus must be prepared to suffer and be crucified. Jesus' example becomes the disciples' path.

Paul builds on this symbolism of carrying the cross and embracing radical discipleship by speaking of the crucified life. "I no longer live, but Christ lives in me. The life I now live I live by believing in God's Son, who loved me and took the punishment for my sins" (Gal. 2:20). A believer's ego is sacrificed, replaced by Christ and faith in him. Self-centered desires are nailed to the cross (Gal. 5:24), and worldly interests are dead (Gal. 6:14). In both conversion and spiritual life, the disciple must relive the cross before experiencing the resurrection life. The cross (death) becomes the path to life.

Key Verse

Christ carried our sins in his body on the cross so that freed from our sins, we could live a life that has God's approval. His wounds have healed you. (1 Pet. 2:24)

> God's love to sinners was expressed by *the gift of His Son to be their Saviour*. The measure of love is how much it gives, and the measure of the love of God is the gift of His only Son to be made man, and to die for sins, and so to become the one mediator who can bring us to God. . . . The New Testament writers constantly point to the Cross of Christ as the crowning proof of the reality and boundlessness of God's love.
>
> J. I. Packer, *Knowing God*
> (Downers Grove, IL: InterVarsity, 1973), 114

Top, Christ's crucifixion and resurrection are the central events of Christianity, and indeed of all of human history.

69

Crown

Throughout history, crowns have been the primary image for authority and honor. In the Bible, it is clear that God is the one who crowns kings. All earthly authority comes from him (Rom. 13:1–2). In David's psalm describing the king, we read that God "welcomed him with the blessings of good things and set a crown of fine gold on his head" (Ps. 21:3). The king's crown was a symbol of his representative rule of the kingdom that was ultimately ruled by God. God is the only true authority, the everlasting King. One day we will see Christ with many crowns on his head, an image of his ultimate authority (Rev. 19:12). This carries through in the crown imagery when we read that "the LORD of Armies will be like a glorious crown for his few remaining people" (Isa. 28:5). Later on we learn that God removes the crown if a king fails to uphold the covenant (Ps. 89:39; Prov. 27:24).

The eternal reward of believers in heaven is portrayed in Scripture as a crown.

Crowns of Blessing

The Bible often uses the same figure in a number of contrasting ways, and the image of a crown is no exception. In a stunning reversal of the crown image, God bestows upon Jerusalem the honor of being *his* crown: "Then you will be a beautiful crown in the hand of the LORD, a royal crown in the hand of your God" (Isa. 62:3). Jerusalem has gone from being a desolate city, in rebellion against the true King's authority, to being Almighty God's adornment. God has raised his people up so that they are jewels in his crown (Zech. 9:16). What a beautiful picture of the redemption God works in the lives of those who love him.

The image of a crown also denotes God's blessing on his people. For example, Isaiah promised that after the Israelites returned from exile "everlasting happiness will be on their heads as a crown" (Isa. 35:10). God will crown his people with the blessings of children (Prov. 17:6), old age (Prov. 16:31), and wisdom (Prov. 4:9). These blessings of God will be external and visible to all, just like a crown.

Heavenly Crowns

In addition to being a symbol for literal kingship and for God's favor, crowns serve as an image of the eternal rewards for those who serve as God's ambassadors. Paul spoke of his congregations as his crowns (Phil. 4:1; 1 Thess. 2:19). Here the reference is to a victor's crown, like the one awarded to the winner of an athletic competition. Paul did not have much in the way of earthly treasure, but the souls of those he served were reward enough. In addition, his work on their behalf was storing up for him crowns in heaven, as he awaited

the "crown of righteousness" God would give him in return for his faithfulness to the gospel (2 Tim. 4:8 NIV).

Like Paul, all Christians anticipate the crowns that await us in heaven. As coheirs with Christ, we inherit the royal blessings of Christ. We are urged to "be faithful until death, and I will give you the crown of life" (Rev. 2:10). Not only has God allowed us to be jewels in his crown when we become part of his chosen people, he has given us our own imperishable crowns as we share in his glory: "Everyone who enters an athletic contest goes into strict training. They do it to win a temporary crown, but we do it to win one that will be permanent" (1 Cor. 9:25; see also James 1:12; 1 Pet. 5:4).

Key Verse

Then, when the chief shepherd appears, you will receive the crown of glory that will never fade away. (1 Pet. 5:4)

Hymn writers have long loved to borrow the biblical symbolism of crowns. Consider these examples:

Holy, Holy, Holy! All the saints adore thee, casting down their golden crowns around the glassy sea.

Reginald Heber

Crown him with many crowns, the Lamb upon his throne.

Matthew Bridges

When he cometh, when he cometh to make up his jewels, all his jewels, precious jewels, his loved and his own. Like the stars of the morning, his bright crown adorning, they shall shine in their beauty, bright gems for his crown. Little children, little children who love their redeemer, Are the jewels, precious jewels, his loved and his own.

William O. Cushing

Darkness

As a physical feature, darkness is nothing in and of itself. Darkness is instead defined as the absence of light. Synonymous with emptiness, darkness is used to describe the earth at the very beginning of creation when "darkness covered the deep water" (Gen. 1:2). Out of this absence, the first thing God created was light. In the beginning, Scripture pictures light and darkness as balanced parts of a single day and night: "So God separated the light from the darkness. God named the light *day*, and the darkness he named *night*" (Gen. 1:4–5).

From the Psalms we learn that the separation between darkness and light does not hinder God's continual presence in our lives:

> If I say, "Let the darkness hide me
>   and let the light around me turn into
>   night,"
> even the darkness is not too dark for you.
>   Night is as bright as day.
>   Darkness and light are the same to
>   you. (Ps. 139:11–12)

If God can see us even in the night, we can be sure he sees us all the time.

Hidden in Darkness

While the darkness doesn't pose a barrier to God, darkness is often used to symbolize God's hidden, inexplicable nature. God has "made the darkness his hiding place, the dark rain clouds his covering" (Ps. 18:11; see also 2 Sam. 22:12). Similarly, when presenting Moses with the Ten Commandments on Mount Sinai, God is pictured as a loud voice "coming from the darkness" (Deut. 5:23). Just as darkness literally obscures our vision, so the symbol of darkness represents a time when our spiritual vision is obscured.

Beyond these neutral descriptions, the majority of the references to darkness in the Bible have negative connotations. Darkness is most often pictured as God's judgment for the Israelites' sin throughout the books of the prophets: "The day of the LORD is one of darkness and not light" (Amos 5:18). In Ezekiel, God says, "I will darken all the lights shining in the sky above you. I will bring darkness over your land" (32:8). In Lamentations, the prophet Jeremiah mourns the destruction of Jerusalem, saying, "God has driven me away and made me walk in darkness instead of light" (3:2). The terror of being in absolute darkness, suddenly unable to see anything, is a fitting symbol for the dark day of judgment.

Darkness signifies the fearsome unknown or hidden truth.

The Light That Overcomes the Darkness

Evil deeds are portrayed throughout Scripture as a form of spiritual darkness. Ephesians 5:11 tells us, "Have nothing to do with the useless works that darkness produces. Instead, expose them for what they are." Not only are workers of evil destined for a punishment in darkness, but their very deeds are symbolized by darkness, and come from "misguided minds . . . plunged into darkness" (Rom. 1:21). This was Jesus' complaint about the Jews of his day: "This is why people are condemned: The light came into the world. Yet, people loved the dark rather than the light because their actions were evil" (John 3:19).

Pictured as the light of the world (John 8:12), Jesus was prophesied to be the ultimate conqueror of darkness: "The people who walk in darkness will see a bright light. The light will shine on those who live in the land of death's shadow" (Isa. 9:2). John affirms that the Word is also light and will conquer darkness: "The light shines in the dark, and the dark has never extinguished it" (John 1:5). Believers can have hope that Christ has the power to turn our "darkness into light" (2 Sam. 22:29).

Just as introducing a source of light into a pitch-black room overcomes the darkness and makes us able to see everything around us with clarity, so the work of Christ has overcome the darkness of sin and death. He is the light by which we can make sense of the world. As believers, we have no need to fear the darkness around us, but can dwell in the light of Christ and spread that light to those around us.

Key Verse

However, you are chosen people, a royal priesthood, a holy nation, people who belong to God. You were chosen to tell about the excellent qualities of God, who called you out of darkness into his marvelous light. (1 Pet. 2:9)

A man can no more diminish God's glory by refusing to worship Him than a lunatic can put out the sun by scribbling the word "darkness" on the walls of his cell.

C. S. Lewis, *The Problem of Pain*
(New York: Macmillan, 1962), 53

Top, Jesus is the light that overcomes darkness, the one who reveals truth to those who are walking in darkness.

73

Day

ay is one of the units of time we use to mark life. Typically, we think of day as the time between sunup and sundown, followed by night. But right from the beginning, God has exercised his divine authority over time by defining days in an unexpected manner. In the account of creation in Genesis 1, six times the record repeats, "There was evening, then morning—the first day" (v. 5), changing only the number of the day of the week. In Jewish thinking, days began at dusk and continued through the night and the following daylight hours. With the exception of day seven, the Sabbath, the Jewish people did not name the days of the week. But the Sabbath was also a day established in the order of creation for rest. God stopped creating on the seventh day, not because he was tired, but because he chose to cease and consider what he had accomplished. Enshrined among the Ten Commandments is the order Jesus said (in Mark 2:27) was for our benefit:

> Remember the day of worship [Sabbath] by observing it as a holy day. You have six days to do all your work. The seventh day is the day of worship dedicated to the LORD your God. You, your sons, your daughters, your male and female slaves, your cattle, and the foreigners living in your city must never do any work on that day. In six days the LORD made heaven, earth, and the sea, along with everything in them. He didn't work on the seventh day. That's why the LORD blessed the day he stopped his work and set this day apart as holy. (Exod. 20:8–11)

Symbolic Days

The words *day* and *days* are sometimes used to mean times or even years. As the writer of Chronicles puts it, "When David had grown old and had lived out his years, he made his son Solomon king of Israel" (1 Chron. 23:1). In Hebrew, the expression for David's aging is literally "full of days." Psalm 20:1 speaks of "times of trouble" (literally "day of trouble"), meaning not so much a certain day, but those periods of difficulty we often experience in life. The writer of Hebrews talks about the "last days," meaning the time we live in now, before the second coming of Christ (1:2).

The word *day* is also used as a symbol for what is right and good. First Thessalonians 5:5 states that believers' identities are tied to being people of the day: "You belong to the day and the light not to the night and the dark." As people who follow Jesus, the light of the world, our actions should bring light to others and be things we need not be ashamed of.

The Day of the Lord

The phrase "day of the LORD" is used with somber overtones, for it highlights God's control over events that will occur (or have occurred) on that day (Joel 1:18; Amos 5:18, 20). It is used as a symbol of God's intervention in human affairs. In Lamentations 2:22 Jeremiah looked back in deep sadness on the disaster that befell Jerusalem: "You have invited those who terrorize me on every side, as though they were invited to a festival. No one escaped or survived on the day of the LORD's anger. My enemy has murdered the children I nursed and raised."

Often, when the Old Testament prophets predicted the coming day of the Lord, their anticipation had a short-term as well as a long-term fulfillment. Isaiah predicted events that would come to pass in Babylon (Isa. 13:5–10), but Jesus extended and expanded the Old Testament's view of "that day" into a picture of the

The "day of the Lord" is the day when Christ will return and fulfill all he came to accomplish—a fearsome thing for unbelievers but a day of rejoicing and hope for believers.

final day of the Lord at the end of human history (Mark 13:24–37). Joel spoke of the coming "terrifying day of the LORD" (Joel 2:31), but Peter highlighted the hopeful side of that prophecy by pointing to what God promised to do among his people "in the last days" before the day of the Lord (Acts 2:16–21). In this case, "last days" represents years and centuries that come to a close when God reveals his day.

The term "day of the Lord" also makes specific reference to Jesus, pointing as a sign to the fulfillment of all that he came to accomplish (1 Cor. 1:8; 5:5; 2 Cor. 1:14; Phil. 1:10; 2:16). Although the day of the Lord will involve a terrifying last judgment on all sin and the difficult events leading to the renewal of the earth, the finality and justice of God's wrath are also reasons for great hope. The day of the Lord is the last day before eternity for those who are in Christ. Peter described both aspects of the day of the Lord in this way:

> The day of the Lord will come like a thief. On that day heaven will pass away with a roaring sound. Everything that makes up the universe will burn and be destroyed. The earth and everything that people have done on it will be exposed.

All these things will be destroyed in this way. So think of the kind of holy and godly lives you must live as you look forward to the day of God and eagerly wait for it to come. When that day comes, heaven will be on fire and will be destroyed. Everything that makes up the universe will burn and melt. But we look forward to what God has promised—a new heaven and a new earth—a place where everything that has God's approval lives. (2 Pet. 3:10–13)

What a day that will be!

Key Verse

Teach us to number each of our days so that we may grow in wisdom.
(Ps. 90:12)

Numbering your days means thinking about how few there are and that they will end. How will you get a heart of wisdom if you refuse to think about this? What a waste, if we do not think about death.

John Piper, *Don't Waste Your Cancer*
(Wheaton: Crossway, 2011), 9

Deer

Even in Bible times deer were game animals, and they were permitted in the Israelite diet because they chew the cud and "divide the hoof." They are admired for their agility and grace, even in difficult terrain, and when they sense danger they are able to run swiftly. As the sole caretakers for fawns, does are gentle. In an arid environment like that of Israel, deer would have had to travel long distances to find water. Beautiful, graceful, swift, and sure-footed, deer were often used by the writers of Scripture to portray personal and spiritual qualities.

Thirst

When David took his quill and wrote, "As a deer longs for flowing streams, so my soul longs for you, O God" (Ps. 42:1), he presented a compelling picture of the natural desire humans have for God. That longing may be distracted or even badly derailed by our experiences in life, but it lies at the heart of what being created in God's image truly means. The deer's simple, single-minded desire to have its thirst quenched points to what ought to always be true in our relationship with God—that we long to be satisfied in him.

Dexterity

Second Samuel 22 and Psalm 18 both record a powerful song of deliverance by David in which he writes, "He makes my feet like those of a deer and gives me sure footing on high places" (2 Sam. 22:34; Ps. 18:33). Freedom, nimbleness, and sure-footedness combine in David's simile of a deer in its natural mountain environment and remind us of the abundance of life that God has for us as we trust him. The Creator has fitted and designed his creatures for the places where they live. They thrive where other creatures cannot survive. The parallel between the deer's dexterity on high and hazardous terrain and our need for wise functioning in the equally dangerous "high places" of human society makes David's picture an apt one. The prophet Habakkuk can find no better symbol in his own psalm: "The LORD Almighty is my strength. He makes my feet like those of a deer. He makes me walk on the mountains" (Hab. 3:19). The agility

Deer are gentle and sure-footed animals.

of deer also makes them a fitting symbol for those who are healed by God: "those who are lame will leap like deer" (Isa. 35:6). When God restores the land, such will be people's joy that the best image the prophet could find to express it is lame people becoming as agile as deer.

Graceful Beauty

In the poetic language of Song of Solomon, deer or gazelles represent grace, beauty, and youthful energy (2:7, 9, 17). When alarmed they hurry off, but with a beautiful and long stride that epitomizes graceful motion. The groom sees admirable characteristics in his bride that remind him of those animals in motion, and he is so eager to be reunited with her that he urges her to come with similar haste. For her part, the bride sees her groom's approach as the tireless bounding of a stag. He comes to her quickly and purposefully.

Key Verse

The LORD Almighty is my strength. He makes my feet like those of a deer. He makes me walk on the mountains. (Hab. 3:19)

When Habakkuk started his book, he was "down in the valley," wrestling with the will of God. Then he climbed higher and stood in the watchtower, waiting for God to reply. After hearing God's Word and seeing God's glory, he became like a deer bounding confidently on mountain heights (Hab. 3:19)! His circumstances hadn't changed, but he had changed, and now he was walking by faith instead of sight. He was living by promises, not explanations.

Warren Wiersbe, *The Wiersbe Bible Commentary: The Complete Old Testament in One Volume* (Colorado Springs: David C. Cook, 2007), 1476

Top, David uses a deer longing for water as a metaphor for his longing for God.

Donkey

Donkeys were a familiar sight in Bible times. In Old Testament times, before horses became used more regularly, riding a donkey or mule was a common form of transportation, even for royalty (2 Sam. 13:29; 1 Kings 1:38). When laws were spelled out by God concerning the treatment of animals, donkeys were specifically mentioned in those instructions. Donkeys are included in the last of the Ten Commandments among the examples of a neighbor's property that should not be coveted: "Never desire to take your neighbor's household away from him. Never desire to take your neighbor's wife, his male or female slave, his ox, his donkey, or anything else that belongs to him" (Exod. 20:17).

Donkeys were also itemized in wealth portfolios in the ancient world and were symbolic of material blessing. Among Job's original holdings were five hundred donkeys, a number that doubled following his restoration (see Job 1:3; 42:12).

When Abraham's wealth is described in Genesis 12:16 and 24:35, donkeys are a featured item.

One of Samson's notable victories over the Philistines involved him using the jawbone of a donkey as a lethal weapon (see Judg. 15:15–16).

The Bible has two famous donkeys: Balaam's faithful steed, and the colt Jesus rode into Jerusalem during his triumphal entry. Balaam's donkey provides a symbol of just how far God will go to ensure that his will is done. Jesus' donkey was a sign of the rider's identity, which those creating the carpet of coats and palm branches failed to see.

The Donkey and the Angel

Balaam and his unfortunate donkey appear in Numbers 22. They were traveling to pronounce a curse on the people of God. Three times the donkey had to endure a beating when she refused to approach the angel of the Lord who was standing in the road with a drawn sword and whom Balaam could not see. Suddenly, the donkey spoke to Balaam and registered an eloquent complaint:

> Then the LORD made the donkey speak, and it asked Balaam, "What have I done to make you hit me three times?"
>
> Balaam answered, "You've made a fool of me! If I had a sword in my hand, I'd kill you right now."
>
> The donkey said to Balaam, "I'm your own donkey. You've always ridden me. Have I ever done this to you before?"
>
> "No," he answered.
>
> Then the LORD let Balaam see the Messenger of the LORD who was standing in the road with his sword drawn. So Balaam knelt, bowing with his face touching the ground. (Num. 22:28–31)

The story of Balaam and his donkey makes us laugh, but it also reminds us of God's power.

Much later, when writing about the destructive effects of false teachers, Peter used the contrast between Balaam and his donkey as an example: "These false teachers have left the straight path and wandered off to follow the path of Balaam, son of Beor. Balaam loved what his wrongdoing earned him. But he was convicted for his evil. A donkey, which normally can't talk, spoke with a human voice and wouldn't allow the prophet to continue his insanity" (2 Pet. 2:15–16).

Jesus and the Donkey

The donkey has always symbolized a combination of basic transportation with a generous dose of humility. Jesus rode into Jerusalem on a donkey (Matt. 29:1–11; Mark 11:1–11; Luke 19:29–44; John 12:12–15). An adult rider looks oddly mismatched on a donkey. If Jesus had arrived in Jerusalem on a magnificent steed or in a fancy horse-drawn chariot, a very different message would have been conveyed than the picture of a king arriving on a donkey colt. Riding on an unbroken animal pointed to the use of "perfect" animals for sacrificial purposes. Additionally, in a small way it showed Jesus' power over nature—even this inexperienced animal was submissive to him. As both Matthew and John point out, Jesus' actions were actually a sign that fulfilled the prophecy of Zechariah:

"Rejoice with all your heart, people of Zion! Shout in triumph, people of Jerusalem! Look! Your King is coming to you: He is righteous and victorious. He is humble and rides on a donkey, on a colt, a young pack animal" (9:9).

Key Verse

Rejoice with all your heart, people of Zion!
Shout in triumph, people of Jerusalem!
Look! Your King is coming to you:
    He is righteous and victorious.
    He is humble and rides on a donkey,
      on a colt, a young pack animal.
        (Zech. 9:9)

We who have the benefit of hindsight are amazed that the people missed the obvious clue that Jesus rode into Jerusalem on a donkey, yet how often we insist on God living up to our expectations rather than settling into a life of faith that anticipates and submits to God's will. He gives us what is best despite circumstances we may not enjoy. Jesus was the King arriving—but not to establish a kingdom in earthly terms. No amount of worship and extending to God a "triumphal entry" will force his hand into a different outcome than he has already planned.

Top, donkeys were used as beasts of burden and as farm animals.

79

Door/Doorpost

Doorways are so common that at first they might not seem like good candidates for symbolic use. Then we begin to look for them in Scripture and note how they play a significant role at key times.

The first mention of a door in the Bible is immediately symbolic: "If you do well, won't you be accepted? But if you don't do well, sin is lying outside your door ready to attack. It wants to control you, but you must master it" (Gen. 4:7). In a freshly fallen world, God was warning Cain that sinful behavior is as real as the dangers that might lurk outside one's house. The door represents access. It allows sin to have an exit from our hearts or an entrance into them. Doors throughout Scripture become significant places to meet God.

Doorways in Egypt

After the exodus, the doorway became forever connected with the Passover. The final plague that God used to measure out justice on Egypt was the killing of the firstborns. But the people of Israel were told to take specific precautions to insure that the plague did not visit their homes. The Passover lamb supplied meat for the final meal, and its blood provided a mark of protection:

> Take the branch of a hyssop plant, dip it in the blood which is in a bowl, and put some of the blood on the top and sides of the doorframes of your houses. No one may leave the house until morning. The LORD will go throughout Egypt to kill the Egyptians. When he sees the blood on the top and sides of the doorframe, he will pass over that doorway, and he will not let the destroyer come into your home to kill you. (Exod. 12:22–23)

The last time the Israelites walked out of their houses of slavery to begin the journey to the Promised Land, they walked under the protection provided by the lamb's blood on the doorways.

Doorpost Writing

When God revealed his law to his people during the wilderness trip from slavery in Egypt to the Promised Land, the doorway again took center stage. It became a symbol of the people taking seriously the guide to living that God had provided for them. Deuteronomy 6:6–9 says this:

> Take to heart these words that I give you today. Repeat them to your children. Talk about them when you're at home or away, when you lie down or get up. Write them down, and tie them around your wrist, and wear them as headbands as a reminder. Write them on the doorframes of your houses and on your gates.

God placed upon parents the burden of impressing, talking, illustrating, and exemplifying his commands throughout their lives and in the presence of their children. One prescribed way was to "write them on the doorframes of your houses and on your gates" (v. 9). The results of how Israel applied this final phrase can still be seen in objects called *mezuzot* on the doorways of devout Jewish homes. Taken from the Hebrew word meaning "doorpost," a *mezuzah* is a plaque about 3 or 4 inches long by about 1 inch wide. It can be made of various materials and consists of two pieces that form a shallow cavity inside. The space holds a tiny handwritten scroll of the Shema (which means "hear" in Hebrew and refers to the first word in God's Great Commandment from Deut. 6:4–5). Each

time a devout Jew enters or leaves through the doorway, the *mezuzah* is touched and then the fingers are kissed as the individual speaks the words of the Shema. The concept of continually remembering God and his claim on our devotion has great merit as a lifestyle. As long as it does not become a mindless habit, the discipline of this doorway devotion points to ordered living before God.

"I Am the Door"

Jesus used the door as a symbol for his role when he said, "I am the gate" (John 10:9). The Greek word *thura*, usually meaning "door," can also be used for "gate." Jesus was declaring himself to be the only passageway to salvation. Those who pass through that door are saved, but those who do not are shut out of salvation. He made this point again in John 14:6: "I am the way, the truth, and the life. No one goes to the Father except through me."

"I Stand at the Door"

In the first chapters of Revelation, Jesus instructed the aged apostle John to write seven letters to the churches in Asia (present-day western Turkey). At the close of those letters, Jesus mentioned a door (3:20). This passage refers to the kind of intimate fellowship that Jesus wants to have with us daily. The picture reminds us that Jesus never forces himself on us, but he provides numerous reminders (knocks on our door) to encourage us to spend time with him.

Revelation 4 opens with another door at the beginning of the visions that will make up the rest of this last book of the Bible: "After these things I saw a door standing open in heaven" (v. 1a). The future lies behind a closed door, but God knows everything behind that door. His Word reveals what he has chosen to let us know, yet much exists that we don't or can't know. For that, trust is required. For believers, one expression of our hope is to stop seeing death as a doorway through which we pass, for because of Christ it is no longer that. *He* is the doorway. Once we go through him, death is simply the access moment to eternal life.

Key Verse

Ask, and you will receive. Search, and you will find. Knock, and the door will be opened for you. (Matt. 7:7)

Today people may rail against what they perceive as God's unfairness in not offering numerous ways to heaven or his audacity to make Jesus the only way, but such complaints simply overlook or deny the condition of humanity apart from God. No doorway devised by humans, even by their most lofty ethical efforts, can overcome the separation created by sin. The reality is that apart from God's intervention there is *no* way to heaven. But God has intervened and he has offered a way, through his Son. Insisting on alternatives indicates that we have failed to correctly see our sinful and hopeless condition.

Dove/ Wild Pigeon

The dove appears in Scripture as a symbol not only of peace but also of the one who brings peace: the Holy Spirit. One of the compelling pictures in the New Testament of the relationship between the persons of the Trinity is on display in Matthew 3:16–17: "After Jesus was baptized, he immediately came up from the water. Suddenly, the heavens were opened, and he saw the Spirit of God coming down as a dove to him. Then a voice from heaven said, 'This is my Son, whom I love—my Son with whom I am pleased'" (see also Mark 1:9–11; Luke 3:21–22; John 1:32). This vivid image, combined with the arrival of the Holy Spirit on the early Christians as "tongues that looked like fire" (Acts 2:3), has led to the Spirit often being pictured as flames in the form of a dove. This use of the symbol emphasizes the peacefulness and affectionate love of the dove.

Doves in the Old Testament

In Bible times, doves were very much a part of life, seen as a source of meat and also used frequently in the sacrificial system. The eagle may be the most regal bird in Scripture, but the dove is probably the most important. Leviticus mentions several offerings that involve the sacrifice of a dove (1:14; 5:7, 11). After a woman bore a child, the ritual of purification involved the sacrifice of a dove (Lev. 12:6, 8), and healing from leprosy and other diseases would be marked by a dove offering (Lev. 14:22, 30; 15:14, 29).

Noah was the first to use doves/pigeons as messenger birds. He sent out a dove once a week for three weeks to test whether the waters of the great flood had receded enough to allow the ark's floating menagerie to disembark on dry land (Gen. 8:8–12). The first flight was unsuccessful; the second produced a "freshly plucked olive leaf" (v. 11), indicating the presence of new life; the third led to Noah's conclusion that the time had come to leave the ark because the dove did not bother to return.

Doves in Flight

The behavior of doves lent itself to being used in various symbolic ways. David used the defenseless fearfulness of a dove to describe his own desire for flight: "My heart is in turmoil. The terrors of death have seized me. Fear and trembling have overcome me. Horror has overwhelmed me. I said, 'If only I had wings like a dove—I would fly away and find rest'" (Ps. 55:4–6). Hosea highlighted the dove's lack of awareness and even silliness to picture the capture of Israel's northern kingdom (Hosea 7:11), yet he also used their homing instinct as symbolic of the people's eventual return from captivity: "'They will come trembling like birds from Egypt and like doves from Assyria. I will settle them in their own homes,' declares the LORD" (11:11). Other prophets used doves as effective symbols for return and nesting in their messages (Isa. 60:8; Jer. 48:28). Ezekiel spoke of the mourning wails of doves as a metaphor for moaning over sin (7:16). And speaking of behavior, one prophet's name meant "dove"—Jonah—which fit his timid response to God's call and the fact that his calling led him away from his own people.

Also, in Song of Solomon, *dove* is used as a term of endearment (2:14; 5:2; 6:9).

Doves in the Life of Christ

Doves make an appearance early in Jesus' life. Luke 2:24 mentions that Mary and Joseph went to Jerusalem, presented the child to the Lord, and "offered a sacrifice as required by the Lord's Teachings: 'a pair of mourning doves or two pigeons.'" Based on Leviticus 12:8, their offering indicates that they could not afford the usual lamb to sacrifice. The earthly parents of the Lamb of God did not have the means to offer the expected sacrifice at his arrival. Later, in his cleansing of the temple, Jesus drove out those who were desecrating the house of prayer by taking advantage of the many poor who had to obtain doves or pigeons to sacrifice (Matt. 21:12; Mark 11:15; John 2:14, 16).

But Jesus also mentioned doves in describing for us the character of those who would be his genuine disciples: "I'm sending you out like sheep among wolves. So be as cunning as snakes but as innocent as doves" (Matt. 10:16). In this sense he was using doves as a symbol for purity and innocence.

Key Verse

As Jesus came out of the water, he saw heaven split open and the Spirit coming down to him as a dove. (Mark 1:10)

The second way God remembered Noah was by giving him a sign. We see this sign in the story of the sending out and return of the dove. Noah wanted to see if the ground had become dry enough for the animals and people to disembark, so he sent out birds to test the environment. A raven was dispatched, but it just kept flying around. Next Noah sent out a dove. The first time it flew out and returned, but the second time it returned with a freshly plucked olive leaf in its beak. When Noah saw this he knew that the waters had receded, that the earth was renewing itself and that the judgment was past. The sign of a dove carrying an olive branch was so moving that the symbol is used as a token of peace even today.

James Montgomery Boice, "Remembered by God," from The Bible Study Hour, http://www.oneplace.com /ministries/the-bible-study-hour/read/articles /remembered-by-god-11789.html

Top, the Holy Spirit in the form of a dove descended on Jesus after his baptism.

Eagle/Vulture

The word most often translated *eagle* occurs in both the Old and New Testaments. And while it may not appeal to our more obvious notions of the regal appearance of eagles, the word used for these soaring, majestic creatures can also refer to vultures. In truth, particularly when observed from a distance, the flight patterns and other behaviors of eagles and vultures are fairly similar. The traits of these birds, which are used for symbolic purposes, have little to do with appearance. God certainly gave to both eagles and vultures certain abilities that provoke us to envy as we watch these feathered marvels sense the thermal lifts and ride the air currents—often without moving their wings but simply allowing the winds to take them to dizzying heights while they observe the world far below.

The Hebrew term for *eagle* or *vulture* is used almost exclusively for figurative purposes except in Leviticus 11 and Deuteronomy 14 where various unclean birds are listed: "You may eat any clean bird. But here are the birds that you should never eat: eagles, bearded vultures, black vultures, buzzards, all types of kites, all types of crows, ostriches, nighthawks, seagulls, all types of falcons, little owls, great owls, barn owls, pelicans, ospreys, cormorants, storks, all types of herons, hoopoes, and bats" (Deut. 14:11–18). The Israelites didn't eat eagles, but they certainly saw their value as signs in the sky.

The Majestic Eagle

The book of Proverbs includes a glimpse of the awe eagles inspire as they soar: "Three things are too amazing to me, even four that I cannot understand: an eagle making its way through the sky . . ." (Prov. 30:18–19). Isaiah includes what is probably the best known use of eagles as a symbol for power and spiritual vitality:

"Yet, the strength of those who wait with hope in the LORD will be renewed. They will soar on wings like eagles. They will run and won't become weary. They will walk and won't grow tired" (Isa. 40:31). The soaring bird becomes a sign of the way God responds to those who persist in counting on or waiting on him. The eagle isn't "working" but waiting for the thermals and winds to lift him. Waiting in hope isn't work; it's depending on God to do his work in us. Only by his power can we soar like eagles.

The eagle is a symbol for God's speedy and powerful deliverance. Exodus describes God's deliverance of Israel from Egypt this way: "You have seen for yourselves what I did to Egypt and how I carried you on eagles' wings and brought you to my mountain" (19:4). Similar descriptions are found in Deuteronomy 32:11 and Revelation 12:14.

The strength and majesty of eagles can also be fearsome—particularly when they are hunting prey—which makes them a fitting symbol for judgment. Ezekiel included an amazing riddle about eagles among his prophecies (see Ezek. 17:1–21), in which the birds represent the kingdoms that will execute God's judgment on his people. In Daniel's vision of the four creatures that represent the kingdom of Babylon and those to follow (chap. 7), the first looks like a lion but has the wings of an eagle, which are plucked off when that kingdom begins to stand and act like a human.

Eagles at the End of Days

Eagles don't appear often in the New Testament. Jesus used this term, though possibly referring to vultures, in his prophecies about the end times recorded in Matthew 24 and Luke 17. "'I can guarantee that on that night if two people

are in one bed, one will be taken and the other one will be left. Two women will be grinding grain together. One will be taken, and the other one will be left.' They asked him, 'Where, Lord?' Jesus told them, 'Vultures will gather wherever there is a dead body'" (Luke 17:34–37). Jesus was giving an ominous glimpse into the terrors that await those who are left behind when the Messiah returns.

In Revelation 4, the apostle John is shown a view of God's throne in heaven. "In front of the throne, there was something like a sea of glass as clear as crystal. In the center near the throne and around the throne were four living creatures covered with eyes in front and in back. The first living creature was like a lion, the second was like a young bull, the third had a face like a human, and the fourth was like a flying eagle" (vv. 6–7). These remarkable creatures can speak, and they repeatedly sing, "Holy, holy, holy is the Lord God Almighty, who was, who is, and who is coming" (v. 8).

Later, a woman is mentioned who receives the wings of a large eagle, which allows her to escape Satan ("the snake") and survive in a wilderness hideout for three and a half years (Rev. 12:14). Here the eagle's wings symbolize the swift getaway from danger that God provides for his people. Since John was describing what he saw, we can speculate that he was watching the woman airlifted out of danger. The woman, who may represent believing Israel or all believers on earth during the time of Satan's final rebellion, will receive God's protection until the struggle is complete.

Key Verse

Yet, the strength of those who wait with hope in the LORD
will be renewed.
> *They will soar on wings like eagles.*
> *They will run and won't become weary.*
> *They will walk and won't grow tired. (Isa. 40:31)*

The most powerful birds, eagles are known for their keen eyesight, allowing them to spot prey from hundreds of feet in the air and swoop down instantly to capture it. They are also able to glide for hours, barely moving their wings as they ride the currents. Their hunting ability, speed, and endless energy make them a well-loved and easily recognized biblical symbol.

Top, eagles have always been a symbol of royalty due to their size, power, and beauty.

85

Eden

Thoughts about Eden make us look back and look forward. The beautiful garden where the first human beings were created is a symbol of a perfect beginning before sin shattered the creation. It was a protected place where God provided for every creature's needs and had a face-to-face relationship with the man and woman, walking with them in the cool of the day. That Eden is gone. While the general location of the garden is indicated as the Tigris and Euphrates valley (along with two other water channels no longer functioning), all evidence of the paradise that was there has long been erased. The place exists, but the paradise is lost. What a fitting metaphor for the spiritual price we paid for the fall and the curse of sin. But a new heaven and new earth have been promised, an Eden-like place that will once again be the home of those who have been rescued from sin and given an eternal destiny with God.

Old Testament References

Apart from the opening chapters of Genesis and a passing mention in Isaiah 51:3 and Joel 2:3, Eden appears most often in Ezekiel (28:13; 31:9, 16, 18; 36:35). In all of these instances Eden is a symbol for paradise. It is the place where all was right in the world and everything was just as God had intended it to be. Eden is synonymous with perfection, with everything being the best it can be. Things are beautiful and fruitful there, with no thorns and difficulties to hamper daily life and no sin or shame to mar human relationships.

New Testament References

The garden isn't mentioned by name in the New Testament, but three significant reminders of Eden can be seen as God unfolds a glimpse of the new heaven and new earth in the closing chapters of the Bible: the Tree of Life, the presence of God, and redeemed humanity (Rev. 22). Every aspect of Eden, including rivers and trees, has been redeemed and re-created. And best

Eden was a paradise unmarred by sin and death.

The fall affected all aspects of natural life, and as a result all creation is in bondage, eagerly awaiting the redemption of Christ's final return.

of all, the close relationship between human beings and God has been rekindled as they see him face-to-face.

> The angel showed me a river filled with the water of life, as clear as crystal. It was flowing from the throne of God and the lamb. Between the street of the city and the river there was a tree of life visible from both sides. It produced 12 kinds of fruit. Each month had its own fruit. The leaves of the tree will heal the nations. There will no longer be any curse. The throne of God and the lamb will be in the city. His servants will worship him and see his face. His name will be on their foreheads. There will be no more night, and they will not need any light from lamps or the sun because the Lord God will shine on them. They will rule as kings forever and ever. (vv. 1–5)

Jesus hinted at this picture when he said to the believing thief on the cross, "I can guarantee this truth: Today you will be with me in paradise" (Luke 23:43). Like the first man and woman, those who become citizens in the kingdom of heaven "may have the right to the tree of life and may go through the gates into the city" (Rev. 22:14). The paradise that was lost has now been reclaimed.

Key Verse

So the Lord will comfort Zion.
> *He will comfort all those who live among its ruins.*
> *He will make its desert like Eden.*
> *He will make its wilderness like the garden of the Lord.*
>> *Joy and gladness will be found in it, thanksgiving and the sound of singing. (Isa. 51:3)*

John Milton wrote the famous poem *Paradise Lost*, which details in beautiful language humanity's fall and expulsion from the garden. These lines from Book 4 (lines 214–18, 246–47) portray his vision of the perfect Garden of Eden.

> *In this pleasant soil*
> *His far more pleasant garden God ordained;*
> *Out of the fertile ground he caused to grow*
> *All trees of noblest kind for sight, smell, taste.*
> *And all amid them stood the Tree of Life. . . .*
> *Thus was this place*
> *A happy rural seat of various view.*

Egypt

The Bible most often portrays the land of Egypt as the crucible in which the nation of Israel was forged. But Egypt played an important role earlier, in the lives of Abraham as well as his great-grandson Joseph. Abraham found shelter there during a famine but left in disgrace after lying to the Pharaoh about Sarai (Gen. 12:10–20). Joseph was sold into slavery in Egypt and became not only a great blessing to the nation, but also the means by which the rest of his family was kept safe during another devastating famine (Gen. 37–46). Eventually Egypt enslaved the young nation and treated them mercilessly for four hundred years.

Egypt the Oppressor

Because of the harsh treatment the Israelites received there, Egypt became almost entirely a negative symbol of oppression and lack of hospitality. The hard lessons learned in Egypt are remembered yearly in the Passover, and God's command for Israel to show kindness toward aliens and strangers stands in stark contrast to how they were treated there. God expected to be understood when he said, "Never oppress foreigners. You know what it's like to be foreigners because you were foreigners living in Egypt" (Exod. 23:9; also see Lev. 19:34; Deut. 5:12–15; 15:12–18; 16:9–12; 24:17–22). Yet God exercised compassion on Egypt in ways that parallel how he treats his chosen people. Later Ezekiel is told to prophesy against Egypt:

> I will make Egypt the most desolate country in the world. For 40 years Egypt's cities will lie in ruins. They will be ruined more than any other city. I will scatter the Egyptians among the nations and force them into other countries.
>
> This is what the Almighty LORD says: After 40 years I will gather the Egyptians from the nations where they have been scattered. I will bring back the Egyptian captives and return them to Pathros, the land they came from. There they will be a weak kingdom. They will be the weakest kingdom, and they will never rule the nations again. I will make them so weak that they will never rule the nations again. The nation of Israel will never trust Egypt again. The people of Israel will remember how wrong they were whenever they turned to Egypt for help. Then they will know that I am the Almighty LORD. (Ezek. 29:12–16)

The harsh treatment the Israelites received in Egypt made it a symbol of God's powerful deliverance. The exodus of the Israelites from Egypt was the turning point in Hebrew history, the event that is looked back on in all generations as the symbol of God's love and care during difficult times. Exodus 19:4 tells us, "You have seen for yourselves what I did to Egypt and how I carried you on eagles' wings and brought you to my mountain."

One interesting sidelight to Egypt's role in God's master plan can be found in the birth narrative of Jesus. Faced with a threat from Herod,

The Egyptians used Hebrew slaves to build their impressive buildings and landmarks.

Joseph was instructed to take Mary and Jesus to Egypt where they remained until the king died. Matthew sees a fulfillment of prophecy in this journey: "Joseph got up, took the child and his mother, and left for Egypt that night. He stayed there until Herod died. What the Lord had spoken through the prophet came true: 'I have called my son out of Egypt'" (Matt. 2:14–15). The irony is that Egypt, the land that had enslaved Israel, was for a time the land that protected Israel's Messiah.

Egypt the Place of Temptation

Throughout the Bible Egypt is portrayed as a place that might be visited, but living there would be dangerous. Power and temptation can be found in Egypt alongside slavery and judgment. The writer of Hebrews highlights the attraction of worldly values that Egypt symbolizes: "When Moses grew up, faith led him to refuse to be known as a son of Pharaoh's daughter. He chose to suffer with God's people rather than to enjoy the pleasures of sin for a little while. He thought that being insulted for Christ would be better than having the treasures of Egypt. He was looking ahead to his reward" (11:24–26). And in John's terrible vision of the end times, two powerful witnesses for God are struck down in Jerusalem. Jerusalem isn't named outright, but instead is referred to as the "important city where their Lord was crucified"

(Rev. 11:8a). John goes on to say, "The spiritual names of that city are Sodom and Egypt" (v. 8b).

Egypt is the recurring symbol for those places we know we should avoid yet toward which we still find ourselves drawn. We may think we want to go back to Egypt, but we must listen to the voice reminding us that only captivity and death await us there.

Key Verse

The God of the people of Israel chose our ancestors and made them a strong nation while they lived as foreigners in Egypt. He used his powerful arm to bring them out of Egypt, and he put up with them for about forty years in the desert. (Acts 13:17–18)

> The Exodus tells our story. Each of us has a personal journey to make, from our own Egypt to the Promised Land. We have left something behind in order to make this journey. We have had to break free from our former lives in order to begin afresh. *We* were in Egypt. *We* were delivered from bondage. *We* are in the wilderness, on our way to the Promised Land. The story of the Exodus involves us. . . . It is all part of the history of our redemption, of which we are part.
>
> Alister McGrath, *The Journey: A Pilgrim in the Lands of the Spirit* (London: Hodder & Stoughton, 1999), 23

Top, the Great Pyramid of Giza is the only one of the seven wonders of the ancient world that is still standing.

Eye

Gazing into someone's eyes can make us feel as though we are seeing into the person's soul. In the Bible, as in life, we find many types of eyes, including beautiful eyes (Gen. 29:17; Song of Sol. 1:15; 4:1); prideful, arrogant eyes (Prov. 6:17); lustful eyes (2 Pet. 2:14); sad eyes (Ps. 6:6); and desiring eyes (Zech. 2:8). People who are seeking revenge take "an eye for an eye" (Exod. 21:23–25; Lev. 24:20; Deut. 19:21). How a person judges morality is described as "doing right in [one's] own eyes" (Judg. 17:6; 21:25; 2 Kings 10:5, all ESV). This contrasts with doing "what was right in the eyes of the LORD" (1 Kings 15:5, 11; 2 Kings 14:3, all ESV). The use of *eyesight* as an image is varied and far-reaching, but two main uses emerge in Scripture.

Satan and his evil agents are frequently portrayed in Scripture as animals looking for prey to devour (1 Pet. 5:8; see also Gen. 49:27; Ps. 14:4).

Spiritual Truth

Sight is a common metaphor in the Bible for the ability to understand spiritual truth (Deut. 29:4; Ps. 119:18). We all start out life spiritually blind, and it is God who opens our eyes and gives understanding (Isa. 44:18; John 9). Our spiritual eyesight may be darkened through habitual rebellion: "The god of this world has blinded the minds of those who don't believe. As a result, they don't see the light of the Good News about Christ's glory" (2 Cor. 4:4; see also Acts 28:27). Turning away from God makes people spiritually blind, unable to see truth even when it is right in front of them.

Once we have had our eyes opened to spiritual truth, our eyes remain an important metaphor for the focus of our lives. The psalmist prays, "Turn my eyes away from worthless things. Give me a new life in your ways" (Ps. 119:37). More specific than the general direction of our gaze is what we choose to look at moment by moment, either good or evil. Jesus said, "Your eye is the lamp of your body. When your eye is unclouded, your whole body is full of light. But when your eye is evil, your body is full of darkness. So be careful that the light in you isn't darkness" (Luke 11:34–35; see also Ps. 101:3). This image makes clear that we have some control over the health of our spiritual eyesight. What we look at with our physical eyes determines how sharp our spiritual eyesight will be and how full of light our lives will be.

The God Who Sees

God's omniscience is often referred to in eye-related imagery. "The LORD's eyes scan the whole world to find those whose hearts are committed to him and to strengthen them" (2 Chron. 16:9). "The LORD's eyes are on those who fear him, on those who wait with hope for his mercy" (Ps. 33:18). He sees all people, inside and out, from before we are even conceived and throughout our lives (Ps. 139:16; Heb. 4:13). Making this truth more concrete, in Ezekiel the creatures that

surround God are portrayed as being covered with eyes (Ezek. 1:18; 10:12). God sees everything that takes place on earth (Job 34:21).

God has the ability to refuse to see, and thus refuse to help. God tells rebellious Israel, "So when you stretch out your hands in prayer, I will turn my eyes away from you. Even though you offer many prayers, I will not listen because your hands are covered with blood" (Isa. 1:15). This leads human beings to plead with God to turn his eyes toward us, as in these words from the dedication of the temple: "Day and night may your eyes be on this temple, the place about which you said your name will be there" (2 Chron. 6:20). Knowing that God seems to reserve this refusal to see for rebellious nations, rather than individuals, is comforting. We know that Christians need never fear that God will turn a deaf ear to their prayers (Ps. 4:3).

As we think of the God who sees us, we recognize our opportunity to see God either through clear eyes that have been made pure through the work of Christ and remain clear through our choices, or through eyes that have been made muddy by our own sin. Our hearts should echo the prayer of Paul: "I pray that the eyes of your heart may be enlightened in order that you may know the hope to which he has called you, the riches of his glorious inheritance in his holy people, and his incomparably great power for us who believe" (Eph. 1:18–19 NIV).

Key Verse

You will open their eyes and turn them from darkness to light and from Satan's control to God's. Then they will receive forgiveness for their sins and a share among God's people who are made holy by believing in me. (Acts 26:18)

In the July 13 entry from *My Utmost for His Highest*, Oswald Chambers offers these insights based on Isaiah's vision of the throne of God in Isaiah 6:

My vision of God is dependent upon the condition of my character. My character determines whether or not truth can even be revealed to me. Before I can say, "I saw the Lord," there must be something in my character that conforms to the likeness of God. Until I am born again and really begin to see the kingdom of God, I only see from the perspective of my own biases. What I need is God's surgical procedure—His use of external circumstances to bring about internal purification.

Father

Among the human relationships God designed to point to him in a special way, he included the role of father. While the picture of God as Father isn't dominant in the Old Testament, it is significant. Psalm 68:5 says, "The God who is in his holy dwelling place is the father of the fatherless and the defender of widows." David also wrote, "He will call out to me, 'You are my Father, my God, and the rock of my salvation'" (Ps. 89:26), and his expression appears prophetic of the way Jesus will speak of the Father. Then, as a reminder of fatherhood at its best, Psalm 103:13 takes a tender role of a father and applies it to God: "As a father has compassion for his children, so the LORD has compassion for those who fear him." The intense personal nature of this passage manages to convey the distinction that the relationship as children of God can only be claimed by those who fear him.

The Ideal Father

God's role as father intersects with human fathering in two ways: he is the ideal or perfect father, and he is able to overcome the disappointment that invariably occurs as fallen fathers attempt to live out their responsibilities with their children. The Bible doesn't give many pictures of successful fathers or even offer extended teaching about being a father. But it does give commands that point to what an ideal father looks like. He is a leader and caretaker, he offers religious instruction, and he blesses his children. He disciplines his children in love for their own good. For a father to give his children stones or snakes would be unthinkable (Matt. 7:9–11). The earthly office of father is a sign of the true Father, God, who perfectly fulfills all the commands given to fathers.

Some people dismiss God's fatherly guidance because of problems with their earthly fathers. They can find a way through their feelings when they realize that failure is the norm. When imperfect human beings live out a role that is intended to point to God in some way, the result will be far from perfect. We love our earthly fathers because they steer us toward God. Even when they don't, their all-too-real faults and inadequacies can remind us that at best they were only supposed to give us some sense of God's importance and were never intended to replace God in our lives. All the fathers in Scripture, from Adam to Zechariah, point to God the ultimate Father. They also exhibit some good or evil behaviors (often both) that drew their children to God or drove them from God.

God Our Father

Jesus persistently called God his Father, underscoring their unique relationship. But when asked by the disciples for some guidance in prayer, Jesus immediately said, "When you pray, say this: 'Father, let your name be kept holy. Let your kingdom come'" (Luke 11:2). We have Christ's permission and direction to address God as "Father." He repeats this instruction in the longer form prayer we call the Lord's Prayer (Matt. 6:9–13). In a glimpse of the inner workings of the Trinity, Jesus told his disciples, "My sheep respond to my voice, and I know who they are. They follow me, and I give them eternal life. They will never be lost, and no one will tear them away from me. My Father, who gave them to me, is greater than everyone else, and no one can tear them away from my Father. The Father and I are one" (John 10:27–30). Jesus spoke of his own relationship with the sheep as the divine Shepherd, the Son of God. Then, getting away from

the shepherding metaphors, Jesus said, "Don't be troubled. Believe in God, and believe in me. My Father's house has many rooms. If that were not true, would I have told you that I'm going to prepare a place for you?" (John 14:1–2). Again, God the Father's house was in mind, but Jesus was promising to "prepare a place."

The apostle Paul takes what is already an intimate invitation to address God as Father and deepens it to the endearing term *Abba*, a child's simple cry. "Certainly, all who are guided by God's Spirit are God's children. You haven't received the spirit of slaves that leads you into fear again. Instead, you have received the spirit of God's adopted children by which we call out, 'Abba! Father!' " (Rom. 8:14–15; see also Gal. 4:6). The Bible uses the figurative language of birth to describe our relationship with God as a miraculous transformation that brings new life (John 3:1–21; Eph. 2:1–10). But the language of adoption is also used, emphasizing God's choosing us. Salvation and God's forgiveness are neither earned nor deserved but are poured into our lives through the graciousness of God. Whether we are thinking of our new birth or our adoption, the words of John come to mind: "Consider this: The Father has given us his love.

He loves us so much that we are actually called God's dear children. And that's what we are. For this reason the world doesn't recognize us, and it didn't recognize him either" (1 John 3:1).

Key Verse

As a father has compassion for his children,
so the LORD has compassion for those who
fear him. (Ps. 103:13)

The Bible's most fleshed-out picture of the fatherhood of God is in the story of the prodigal son, also called the story of the Loving Father, in Luke 15. Henri Nouwen wrote about that story and Rembrandt's painting of it in *The Return of the Prodigal Son* ([New York: Doubleday, 1994], 95). He writes:

God, creator of heaven and earth, has chosen to be, first and foremost, a Father. As Father, he wants his children to be free, free to love. That freedom includes the possibility of their leaving home, going to a "distant country," and losing everything. The Father's heart knows all the pain that will come from that choice, but his love makes him powerless to prevent it.

Feast/Banquet

(*See also* Meal)

The word *feast* comes from the same Latin word that gives us *festival*. Today we think of a feast as primarily a very special meal. In the Bible feasts were more like festivals, and they commemorated great acts of God. Many of these festivals included a feast or banquet as a central part of the celebration. For a long time we have stopped using the term *festival* or *feast* in the old way, substituting the word *holiday*. Too bad we don't notice more often that the origin of that word is *holy day*. Symbols are often sneaky: we lose sight of them when they become such a part of our lives that we take them for granted. The delight in identifying symbols in Scripture and throughout Christianity is not the power of mystery but the power of the mundane. Special days can remind us of God's priceless gifts. The feasts that feed our bodies with delicious food can feed our souls with even deeper and more lasting satisfaction. Each one of these religious feasts is a symbol pointing to the greater reality of God's faithful love throughout Israel's history.

Feasts of Israel

Listed according to the Jewish calendar, the feasts of Israel were as follows:

Passover/Feast of Unleavened Bread (March/ April). Passover is the first and perhaps greatest of the Jewish holidays, celebrating the Jews' astounding release from slavery after four centuries of bondage in Egypt. It also serves as the birth anniversary of the nation of Israel. For more on the Passover, look for the entry by that name.

Feast of Pentecost (May/June). As the name suggests, this feast occurred fifty (*pente*) days after the Feast of Unleavened Bread. In the Jewish calendar Pentecost was a day to celebrate the harvest (Exod. 23:16; 34:22; Lev. 23:15–21; Num. 28:16–31). For Christians, this feast was made forever holy in that on this day the early church experienced the outpouring of the Holy Spirit.

Feast of Trumpets (Rosh Hashanah) (September/October). This feast is listed in Leviticus 23:24–25 and Numbers 29:1–40, but its particular purpose is somewhat unclear. It marked the beginning of the civil year of the Jews. Its status

Food is an image of God's provision and care for his people.

may have become greater during the exile, when the displaced Jews celebrated their heritage and tried to keep it alive for each generation, though they were far from Jerusalem.

Day of Atonement (Yom Kippur) (September). Technically not a feast but a fast, the Day of Atonement was the yearly time of accountability for sin by the nation. Leviticus 23:26–32 describes this day as "a special day for the payment of sins" (vv. 27–28). Leviticus 16 explains the fascinating symbol of a dual sacrifice that atonement requires, for on this day the sins of the people are dealt with by the death of one goat and the "living sacrifice" of another, the scapegoat. One goat's life represents payment for sin. The

other goat, bearing the sins of the people, is taken out and released in the wilderness. Those who read these instructions with New Testament history in mind can see how Jesus fulfilled all God's requirements for the atonement of sin. And the book of Hebrews explains this built-in sign as a centerpiece of how Jesus fulfilled the codes and commands of the Old Testament.

Feast of Tabernacles/Booths (Sukkoth) (September/October). This feast, celebrated with the construction of makeshift dwellings, invited the people of Israel to remember how God protected and provided for them in the wilderness after the exodus.

Feast of Lights (Hanukkah) (November/December). Not long before the life of Jesus, a group in Israel temporarily took power back from foreign invaders and held a great ceremony to cleanse the temple in Jerusalem. This feast celebrates their victory and the restoration of the temple.

Feast of Purim (February/March). This feast was a later addition to the calendar, attributed to Mordecai in Esther 9:18–28, and was a day to remember how God moved through Esther to preserve the lives of his people in Persia.

Feasts of the Church

Christians celebrate and anticipate two feasts: the Lord's Supper (see the entry on this event) and the Wedding Banquet of the Lamb.

The Wedding Banquet of the Lamb is the much-anticipated eternal celebration in Christ's presence when the Kingdom of God is fully revealed in the new heaven and new earth. Jesus repeatedly referred to this event in teaching and parables (Matt. 8:11; 22:1–14; Luke 14:15–24). It is foretold in Revelation 19:9. The symbol of a grand meal brings together all the themes of joy, satisfaction, and pleasure that the Bible highlights as God's intention for us. We may be prone to focus on what we assume is God's lack of provision, but his Word reveals that God never withholds anything from us that he doesn't intend to replace with something far better. We might settle for a meal as God's symbol of provision for our physical hunger; he intends us to remember at every meal that he is the giver of every good gift and that his plans for us are eternal and beyond our wildest imagination.

Key Verse

On this mountain the LORD of Armies will
    prepare for all people
a feast with the best foods,
a banquet with aged wines,
    with the best foods and the finest
      wines. (Isa. 25:6)

Feasts in the Bible are images of joyful voices, festive music and dancing, and abundant food. They are not simply parties, but celebrations of God's goodness toward his people. Feasts provide occasions of fellowship with one another and with the Lord to remember and to celebrate what wonderful things God has done.

Leland Ryken, James C. Wilhoit,
and Tremper Longman III, eds.,
Dictionary of Biblical Imagery
(Downers Grove, IL: InterVarsity, 1998), 278

Top, heaven's bounty is portrayed as a feast, the marriage supper of the Lamb to his bride, the church.

95

Feet

When asked where feet appear in the Bible, most people are likely to point to Psalm 119:105, "Your word is a lamp for my feet and a light for my path." Following the principle that we usually go where our feet go, the most common symbolic use for feet in the Bible is to represent our lives. The psalmist repeatedly praised God because "he makes my feet like those of a deer and gives me sure footing on high places" (Ps. 18:33) and because he makes "a wide path for me to walk on so that my feet do not slip" (18:36). When the apostle Paul wants the Ephesian Christians to understand what God expects of them, he writes, "I, a prisoner in the Lord, encourage you to live [literally, *walk*] the kind of life which proves that God has called you" (Eph. 4:1).

A Fresh Take on Tradition

In Bible times, most people walked barefoot or with simple sandals that left most of the foot exposed to whatever was on the road. Even today in most Middle Eastern cultures, entry into a home or worship space involves removing footwear. One of the most basic acts of hospitality in these cultures was to wash the feet of guests when they arrived. Such a task was assigned to the lowest member of the household servants. This makes Jesus' actions at the Last Supper all the more startling. During a special Passover celebration in the upper room, he got up from the table, put on a servant's apron, and washed his disciples' feet (John 13:4–17). The disciples, particularly Peter, were shocked at Jesus' action and ashamed at their oversight. And we see this interaction between Peter and Jesus: "Peter told Jesus, 'You will never wash my feet.' Jesus replied to Peter, 'If I don't wash you, you don't belong to me'" (13:8). In true Peter fashion, what he misunderstood one way he quickly misunderstood another way: "Lord, don't wash only my feet. Wash my hands and my head too!" (v. 9). After lovingly correcting Peter, Jesus made clear that he wanted the disciples to understand the importance of serving one another in the most mundane and truly servant-oriented aspects of living: "You call me teacher and Lord, and you're right because that's what I am. So if I, your Lord and teacher, have washed your feet, you must wash each other's feet" (vv. 13–14). Here Jesus used a daily task and turned it into a symbol for the way we should serve one another.

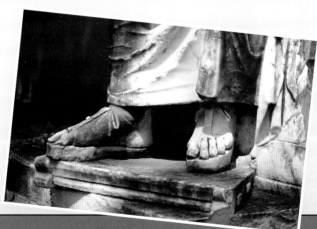

Jesus washed his disciples' dusty feet—taking the position of a slave—as an expression of his love for them.

Feet as Symbol

When the apostle Paul wants to describe the significance of a person sharing the gospel with someone else, he recalls the words of Isaiah and writes, "How can people tell the Good News if no one sends them? As Scripture says, 'How beautiful are the feet of the messengers who announce the Good News'" (Rom. 10:15, quoting Isa. 52:7). Again, the *feet* of the messenger become beautiful because of the value of the message being delivered. They are a symbol for the traveling and effort required in bringing the Good News to others.

In Daniel 2, feet are one of the parts of a statue that symbolize a succession of kingdoms. The feet made of clay and iron were crushed by a stone that was cut out but not by human hands. In this case, feet represent the weakest in a succession of kingdoms that will be overwhelmed by the rolling stone, which we now know was a picture of Christ's arrival in history. This symbolism is also related to the idea of a person being put under the feet of a conquering army—it shows authority (Josh. 10:24; 1 Kings 5:3; Ps. 8:6, all NIV). That is why Scripture tells us that one day all things will be put under Christ's feet (Matt. 22:44 NLT; 1 Cor. 15:25 NLT; Eph. 1:22 NKJV; Heb. 2:8 NKJV). And this is why we fall at his feet in worship (Rev. 1:17).

Feet that slip or stumble are a symbol for falling into sin (Job 12:5; Pss. 37:31; 56:13; 66:9; 73:2; 116:8; 121:3). People may even have their feet caught in a trap or be put in shackles (Pss. 25:15; 57:6; 105:18). By contrast, God makes our feet secure, keeping us on firm ground so we will not sin (1 Sam. 2:9; Pss. 17:5; 26:12; 31:8). He is the One who makes our steps sure as we walk through life.

Key Verse

My steps have remained firmly in your paths. My feet have not slipped. (Ps. 17:5)

The highest form of worship is the worship of unselfish Christian service. The greatest form of praise is the sound of consecrated feet seeking out the lost and helpless.

Billy Graham, "Faith Produces Works," http://billygraham.org/devotion /faith-produces-works/, May 17, 2014

Top, Paul told the Ephesians to fit their feet with a readiness to preach the gospel.

Fire

Both mesmerizing and mysterious, fire represents combustion, a chemical reaction that releases both heat and light. Today, fire seems to be at our fingertips—we just need to turn on the stove or light a match. Because we no longer have to work to get it, most of us take fire for granted. Yet we rely on fire for light, warmth, cooking, manufacturing, and refining. Fire figures into the Bible in numerous ways—in daily life, religious ceremony, and as an instrument of warfare. The ritual of animal sacrifice instituted by God in the Old Testament required the use of fire to consume burnt offerings. The burning of sacrificial meat with fire is described as "a soothing aroma to the Lord" (Lev. 23:18; Num. 28:13, 24; 29:6, 13).

Holy Fire

Other symbolic uses of fire in the Bible correspond to fire's practical uses. For example, in Zechariah 13:9, God is a refiner who brings the Israelites "through the fire" in order to "refine them as silver is refined" (see also Mal. 3:2). Fire is pictured as a purifying agent in people's lives. Proverbs 17:3 clarifies the relationship of fire with spiritual refinement: "The crucible is for refining silver and the smelter for gold, but the one who purifies hearts by fire is the Lord."

Throughout the Bible, we see the presence of God physically manifested as fire. In Genesis 15:17, God sealed his covenant with Abram by passing through the animal sacrifice

as "a smoking oven and a flaming torch." During the Israelites' exit from Egypt, the Lord appeared as a protective wall of fire at night: "So the Lord's column stayed over the tent during the day, and there was fire in the smoke at night. In this way all the Israelites could see the column throughout their travels" (Exod. 40:38; see also Exod. 13:21; Ps. 105:39; Zech. 2:5). The fire symbolized the guiding presence of God among the people. God also appeared to Moses in the form of a burning bush on Mount Sinai (Exod. 3:2). For biblical authors, the theophany of fire portrayed God's power, holiness, and protection over his people.

The Fires of Judgment

Fire also demonstrates God's anger and righteous judgment over humanity. In Deuteronomy, God's supremacy over false idols is demonstrated as fire: "The Lord your God is a raging fire, a God who does not tolerate rivals"

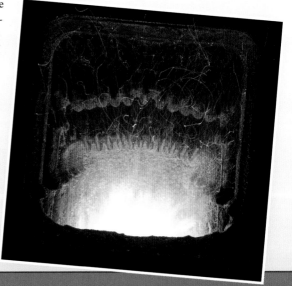

Fire is a metaphor for trials that enter a believer's life; such things purify character in the same way fire purifies precious metals.

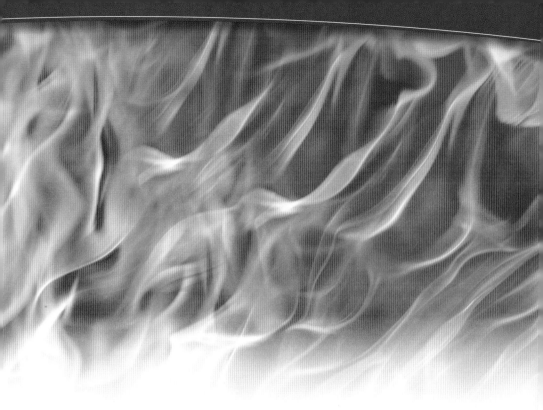

(4:24). In stories such as the condemnation of Sodom and Gomorrah, we see fire used in God's punishment for sin (Gen. 19:24). In the last days, fire is pictured as a tool of judgment that both burns up the dross and purifies the holy: "The day will make what each one does clearly visible because fire will reveal it. That fire will determine what kind of work each person has done. If what a person has built survives, he will receive a reward. If his work is burned up, he will suffer the loss. However, he will be saved, though it will be like going through a fire" (1 Cor. 3:13–15). Foreshadowing the fires of hell, John the Baptist explained Jesus' work in the final days: "He will gather his wheat into a barn, but he will burn the husks in a fire that can never be put out" (Matt. 3:12).

Metaphorical Fires

The Bible uses fire as a metaphor for the destructive capabilities of human action. The tongue can be a fire, with words leaving a path of destruction through human hearts (James 3:5–6).

Sometimes these destructive words are God's tool of judgment (Jer. 5:14). Jealousy can also be a fire that devours (Deut. 4:24). So can lust (Prov. 6:27), love (Song of Sol. 8:6), or anger (Num. 11:1; Ps. 89:46).

Key Verse

The crucible is for refining silver and the smelter for gold,
but the one who purifies hearts by fire is the LORD. (Prov. 17:3)

This stanza from the well-known hymn "How Firm a Foundation" illustrates the biblical image of purification by fire:

When through fiery trials thy pathways shall lie,
My grace, all sufficient, shall be thy supply;
The flame shall not hurt thee; I only design
Thy dross to consume, and thy gold to refine.

Top, fire is a refining agent, separating the dross from precious metals.

99

Fish

In the ancient world fish were a staple food and fishing was a common occupation. Of Jesus' twelve disciples, seven of them worked as fishermen. Jesus commissioned these men using familiar symbolism, saying, "Come, follow me! I will teach you how to catch people instead of fish" (Matt. 4:19). The fishing profession that was their livelihood became a symbol for their new calling of spreading the good news of salvation. Both at the beginning (Luke 5:1–11) and at the end of his ministry (John 21:1–8) Jesus provided a miraculous catch of fish that demonstrated his power and character.

Provision and Judgment

Given the cultural background of his audiences, it is no surprise that Jesus' miracles and teachings frequently employed the theme of fish and fishing. Jesus used fish in the miraculous feeding of four thousand people (Matt. 15:32–39; Mark 8:1–10) and five thousand people (Matt. 14:13–21; Mark 6:30–44; Luke 9:10–17; John 6:1–14). The provision of fish and bread on these occasions was a sign of God's ultimate provision through the death and resurrection of Jesus Christ. This symbolism of fish as provision is further carried out with the fish that provides the temple tax for Jesus and his disciples (Matt. 17:24–27).

In the Old Testament, the image of fish is at times connected with the uncertainty of life: "No one knows when his time will come. Like fish that are caught in a cruel net or birds caught in a snare, humans are trapped by a disaster when it suddenly strikes them" (Eccles. 9:12). Fish caught in nets are also frequently used by prophets to symbolize God's judgment over enemies of Israel (Ezek. 26:5, 14; 29:3–7) or concerning the Israelites' rebellion, specifically resulting in their foreign captivity (Amos 4:2; Hab. 1:15–17). In this case God is the fisherman gathering the people like fish for judgment or blessing.

Signs of Salvation

The book of Jonah describes the rebellious prophet's rescue from drowning in the storm-swept sea when God sent a fish to swallow him. Beyond the historical account, the great fish also stands as a picture of God's deliverance and mercy. The account clearly shows that the fish was Jonah's

Jesus multiplied five loaves and two fish into enough to feed five thousand men—a miracle that showed him to be the Bread of Life.

means of salvation. It was also a sign of the greater salvation offered through Christ. Jesus recalled the story of Jonah in his confrontation with the Pharisees and symbolically connected the three days and nights Jonah spent in the fish with the time that would lapse between his crucifixion and resurrection (Matt. 12:38–41).

Jesus signaled the diversity of the church by picturing the kingdom of heaven as a net that gathers all kinds of fish from the sea (Matt. 13:47). Fish were often employed in art and literature of the early church as it grew and spread in the first centuries. For these early Christians the Greek word for *fish*, ΙΧΘΥΣ (*ichthus*), took on added significance because the letters formed an acronym meaning, "Jesus Christ, God's Son, Savior." The fish symbol eventually became an identifying marker for believers in the early church, and today it continues to be one of the most easily identifiable symbols of Christianity as demonstrated by the popularity of fish decals placed on car bumpers.

Key Verse

Jesus said to them, "Come, follow me! I will teach you how to catch people instead of fish." (Mark 1:17)

You may feel that, from a human perspective, what you have to offer doesn't count for much, that it will never be very visible or dramatic. Jesus has made it clear: There is no truth in such a perspective. We serve the Lord of the Gift. The Lord of the Gift can take five fish and two loaves and feed the multitudes. . . . The Lord of the Gift can take twelve bumbling followers and create a community that has spread throughout the world with a dream that refuses to die.

John Ortberg, *If You Want to Walk on Water, You've Got to Get Out of the Boat* (Grand Rapids: Zondervan, 2001), 51

Top, a staple of daily life, fish figured prominently in the miracles of Jesus.

Five

The number *five*, with its immediate connection to the fingers of one hand, often represents a small amount in the Bible. The idea expressed in modern terms is "just a handful." When faced with the hunger of five thousand, all Jesus' disciples could come up with was a child's lunch of five loaves and two fish (John 6:9). Yet Jesus had no problem multiplying that small gift into abundance for the meal. Isaiah mentions five Egyptian cities that will be unusual as a foreign remnant from that land and that will "swear allegiance to the LORD of Armies" (Isa. 19:18). Numerous other passages indicate an alliance of five kings, a theme that arises so many times it seems like it must be symbolic of a handful of enemies as well as being a literal and historical number. Isaiah again uses the number *five* to point out the fear that will infect people so that "you will flee when five threaten you" (Isa. 30:17). So *five* carries the effect of a small number with potentially significant weight. The five books of Moses are certainly a handful in several ways.

Fairness

Five also appears in several places as a multiplier that indicates fairness or favor. When Joseph wanted to single out his maternal brother Benjamin from the rest of his brothers, he gave him five times more food than he gave each of the others (Gen. 43:34) and five changes of clothing (Gen. 45:22). Old Testament law stated that a livestock thief must "make up for the loss with five head of cattle to replace the bull" (Exod. 22:1b). When God set apart the Levites as a tribe of priests and his special servants, he designated them as "substitutes for all the firstborn Israelites" (Num. 3:45). But when the census was taken, the firstborn Israelites outnumbered the Levites by 273 males. So God settled on five shekels of silver for each of the extra Israelite males (Num. 3:47, "two ounces of silver").

The number *five* was often used to make restitution or repayment.

In art, five is the number of symmetry and beauty. For this reason it figured prominently in the construction of both the tabernacle and the temple.

Symmetry

The number *five* figures prominently in the structure of the tabernacle in the wilderness. In this case it is prized for its symmetry.

- The pillars were five cubits apart and five cubits high.
- The bronze altar was five cubits by five cubits.
- Five pillars stood at the entrance to the holy place.
- The sides of the tabernacle were reinforced by five crossbars on each side (Exod. 26:26–27).
- The inner covering of the tabernacle was composed of five curtains that were attached to five other curtains for a total of ten curtains (Exod. 26:3). These were attached with fifty loops and fasteners.
- The original priests numbered five: Aaron and his four sons (Exod. 28:1).

Standard

Five also naturally appears as a standard measurement and half of ten. The construction details for the outer covering of the tabernacle specified ten curtains in two sets of five (Exod. 26:3). In Jesus' parable of the virgins (Matt. 25:1–13), there are ten in the group, but only five prove to be wise.

Key Verse

Then he ordered the people to sit down on the grass. After he took the five loaves and the two fish, he looked up to heaven and blessed the food. He broke the loaves apart, gave them to the disciples, and they gave them to the people. All of them ate as much as they wanted. When they picked up the leftover pieces, they filled twelve baskets. (Matt. 14:19–20)

Five is a number of preparation in the following passages:

- The first five books of the Bible (the Pentateuch) prepare us for Israel's story throughout the rest of the Bible.
- The five wise virgins were prepared (Matt. 25:1–13).
- David, in preparing for Goliath, took up five smooth stones (1 Sam. 17:40).
- Paul lists five offices for spreading the gospel and building the church: apostles, prophets, missionaries, pastors, and teachers (Eph. 4:11–12).

Flowers

The beauty of flowers and the way they bloom and flourish makes them a good image for many spiritual themes, including love, transience, and the glory of God. Two Hebrew words are translated as "flower": *perach* means to break forth, bud, sprout, or burst; *tsuwts* evokes images of shining, sparkling, or gleaming. The first connotes spontaneous growth, while the second focuses on beauty.

The Beauty of Creation

In Song of Solomon, the image of a flower is used to describe the beloved. The beauty and delicate nature of flowers makes them a metaphor for love. The lover says, "I am a rose of Sharon, a lily growing in the valleys" (2:1). Both the woman and the man are described with flower imagery (e.g., 4:5; 5:13), and their love is consummated in a garden (7:12). Beautiful, sensuous, and carefully tended flowers are a metaphor for erotic love.

Flowers also point us to the glory of God. Jesus urges us to "notice how the flowers grow in the field. They never work or spin yarn for clothes. But I say that not even Solomon in all his majesty was dressed like one of these flowers" (Matt. 6:28–29). Flowers are an image of God's tender care of nature and his concern for beauty in addition to utility. Perhaps that is why the tabernacle (Exod. 28:31–36) and temple were so filled with depictions of flowers (1 Kings 6:18, 29, 32, 35; 7:49). When we see the beauty God has given us in nature, particularly the creativity, color, and delicate scent of flowers, we can't help but praise the Creator.

Here Today, Gone Tomorrow

One of the most common uses of flower imagery in the Bible is in connection with the transience of life. Flowers last but a few days, in much the same way that a person is here one day and gone the next. This image first applies to divine judgment, wherein evil people and their wicked deeds do not last. The psalmist explains that "wicked people sprout like grass and all troublemakers blossom like flowers, only to be destroyed forever" (Ps. 92:7). They will be trampled underfoot (Isa. 28:1–4) and cut down in their prime (Dan. 4:4–14). Their deeds will not outlast them.

This brevity is particularly true of earthly wealth, which lasts but

Flowers are a picture of rejuvenation and restoration, expressing the way God makes all things new.

a moment. James tells us, "Rich people will wither like flowers. The sun rises with its scorching heat and dries up plants. The flowers drop off, and the beauty is gone. The same thing will happen to rich people. While they are busy, they will die" (James 1:10–11). When one thinks of riches, the image of a flower fits well—it is flashy and bright but soon wilts and falls off. Earthly treasure does not last.

Restoration

God's Word stands in contrast to the brief life of a flower. "Grass dries up, and flowers wither, but the word of our God will last forever" (Isa. 40:8). Using the image of flowers to represent the short span of a person's life makes it an appropriate foil to the eternal Word of God.

As with most biblical images, flowers also have a redemptive use. After the judgment comes restoration. "The desert and the dry land will be glad, and the wilderness will rejoice and blossom. Like a lily the land will blossom. It will rejoice and sing with joy. . . . Everyone will see the glory of the LORD, the majesty of our God" (Isa. 35:1–2). The tree that has been cut down will once again sprout and blossom. God does not leave us in death, but brings the blossom of life from the dry stump.

Key Verse

And why worry about clothes? Notice how the flowers grow in the field. They never work or spin yarn for clothes. But I say that not even Solomon in all his majesty was dressed like one of these flowers. That's the way God clothes the grass in the field. Today it's alive, and tomorrow it's thrown into an incinerator. So how much more will he clothe you people who have so little faith? (Matt. 6:28–30)

In light of Solomon's great glory, some might think this illustration is overstated. Far from it! "Lilies of the field" are wildflowers, and a microscope applied to any of them reveals a magnificence that makes Solomon's robes look like rags! These wildflowers collectively decorate the green grass with exquisite beauty for a short time, but then they are mown down like mere weeds and are tossed into the furnace. . . . Since God takes care of inanimate flowers that cannot reason or toil, how much more will he care for us, his gifted creation, to whom he repeatedly gives his immediate and living presence.

R. Kent Hughes, *The Sermon on the Mount: The Message of the Kingdom*, Preach the Word, vol. 40 (Wheaton: Crossway, 2001), 223

Top, the beloved in Song of Solomon is compared to a white lily, perfect and beautiful.

105

Forty

We should note at the outset that in the era before clocks and precise record keeping, numbers were often an estimation. Three and five signified a little, and forty a lot more. That is not to say that forty was never an accurate number, only that precision was not the intent of biblical authors.

The number *forty* appears for the first time in Scripture in Genesis 7 describing the details of the great flood, which began with forty days and nights of rain and led to the death of "every living creature" (v. 4) God had made except the people and animals preserved in the ship constructed by Noah and his sons under God's direction. The last time *forty* appears in the Bible is Hebrews 3:10 and 17. There God's anger with Israel during the four decades in the wilderness after the exodus from Egypt is used to demonstrate the superiority of Jesus over Moses. The author also warns those who have the chance to know Christ not to display hard hearts like those of the people of Israel long ago.

Divine Judgment or Testing

Between these two examples, the number *forty* appears in such consistent settings that Christians have long equated it with a trial period or divine judgment, a time of hardship and difficulties.

The Bible notes that Moses stayed up on the mountain of God for forty days while the people waited below on the plain (Exod. 24:18). We don't know how difficult the time was for Moses, but we know that the people got tired of waiting for him and came up with an alternative god, a golden calf, who wouldn't demand as much as the real God and wouldn't say anything about whatever behavior they decided to display. Needless to say, their impatience under a forty-day delay was one factor that led to them having to endure a forty-*year* delay before entering the Promised Land.

The punishment for various transgressions was limited to forty lashes for Israelites (Deut. 25:3; 2 Cor. 11:24). During the time of the judges, one particularly difficult episode was a forty-year period when Israel was under the domination of the Philistines (Judg. 13:1). God raised up Samson to free the people from that bondage. Here again, the forty years was a symbol of God's punishment and testing.

On a later occasion, the prophet Elijah followed up a brilliant victory over the prophets of Baal by fleeing in terror when Queen Jezebel threatened his life. He ended up in the wilderness with no means of sustenance, so God fed him. He was so energized by the bread and water God provided that he traveled

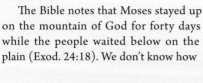
Both Elijah and Jesus faced a time of testing in the wilderness that lasted forty days; Jesus faced his with no food.

forty days and nights to Mount Horeb, the same place where Moses had spent his time alone with God (1 Kings 19:1–18). His fear of Jezebel had to be thoroughly crushed by an even greater fear of the God who met him on Mount Horeb. The forty-day journey was symbolic of the testing God was causing him to undergo in order to prepare him for greater service.

Lasting Image

During the days of the prophets, Ezekiel created a lasting image by lying on his right side for forty days (Ezek. 4:6) to symbolize the years of punishment Judah would experience. And Jonah's reluctant message finally delivered in Nineveh gave that great city forty days to repent (Jon. 3:4). Much to Jonah's chagrin, the people heard him and repented.

Alongside the people's forty-year wandering in the desert, Jesus' forty-day fast in the wilderness at the outset of his ministry is another recognizable use of the number (Matt. 4:2). But the comparisons between the two events go beyond numbers. Jesus' threefold temptation parallels the trials and failures of God's people. They, like he, were tempted with food (Exod. 16:1–8; Matt. 4:3).

Satan incited both the people and Jesus to put God to the test (Exod. 17:1–3; Matt. 4:5–7), and he tempted each of his targets to idolatry (Exod. 32; Matt. 4:8–10). The people failed; Jesus resisted using passages from Deuteronomy written as Moses led the people in the wilderness.

Key Verse

Moses was there with the LORD 40 days and 40 nights without food or water. He wrote on the tablets the words of the promise, the ten commandments. (Exod. 34:28)

The Bible is filled with examples of how God uses a long process to develop character, especially in leaders. He took eighty years to prepare Moses, including forty in the wilderness. . . . Contrary to popular book titles, there are no *Easy Steps to Maturity* or *Secrets of Instant Sainthood*. When God wants to make a mushroom, he does it overnight, but when he wants to make a giant oak, he takes a hundred years.

Rick Warren, *The Purpose-Driven Life*
(Grand Rapids: Zondervan, 2002), 222

Top, scriptural accounts of times of testing or trial often lasted for forty days.

107

Four

The number *four* and groups of four connect with our sense of place in the horizontal world. Everything around us is in one of four directions: east, west, north, or south. In the worldview of the Old Testament, complete descriptions were often developed in sets of four. When the tax collector Zacchaeus expressed his practical faith in Jesus, he included a promise to "pay four times as much as I owe to those I have cheated in any way" (Luke 19:8). Jesus accepted that commitment as a sign of genuine repentance, symbolic of completeness. And there are four Gospels, a complete picture of the life of Christ.

Four as a Literary Technique

Notice the various groups of four included by the prophet Isaiah (numbers added for clarity):

This is the kind of fasting I have chosen:
¹Loosen the chains of wickedness,
²untie the straps of the yoke,
³let the oppressed go free,
and ⁴break every yoke.
¹Share your food with the hungry,
²take the poor and homeless into
your house,
and ³cover them with clothes when
you see them naked.
⁴Don't refuse to help your
relatives.

Then ¹your light will break through like the
dawn,
and ²you will heal quickly.
³Your righteousness will go ahead of you,
and ⁴the glory of the LORD will guard you
from behind.

Then ¹you will call, and ²the LORD will
answer.
³You will cry for help, and ⁴he will say,
"Here I am!"

Get rid of that yoke.
Don't point your finger and say wicked
things.

¹If you give some of your own food to feed
those who are hungry
and ²to satisfy the needs of those who are
humble,
then ³your light will rise in the dark,
and ⁴your darkness will become as bright
as the noonday sun.
(Isa. 58:6–10)

These groupings provide a strong sense of direction covering every facet of life. The examples, listed in groups of four, are intended to symbolize or imply these specifics plus everything in between. This is similar to Amos's parallelism of "three . . . even . . . four" of a variety of sins (chap. 1–2 NIV). God is interested and will engage with us as we seek to follow his leading in every relationship.

Four in Apocalyptic Prophecies

In the prophetic writings of Scripture—primarily Ezekiel, Daniel, and Revelation—collections of four make frequent appearances to convey a sense of completeness, whether it has to do with God's judgment—as in the four horsemen of John's vision in Revelation 6:1–7 and the four winds of heaven in Daniel 7:2—or God's saving plan extended to "every tribe, language, people, and nation" (Rev. 5:9; see also 7:9; 10:11; 11:9; 13:7; 14:6). The eventual inclusion of representatives from all of humanity is a ringing endorsement of God's heart for the whole world.

In John's glimpse of heaven's throne room, he is mesmerized by the sight of four living creatures, one like a lion, one like a bull, one like a human, and one like an eagle. These creatures see everything and can't stop giving glory to God. They provide a prophetic echo to Ezekiel's first vision, which also involved a number of foursomes:

> In the center of the cloud I saw what looked like four living creatures. They were shaped like humans, but each of them had four faces and four wings. Their legs were straight, their feet were like those of calves, and they glittered like polished bronze. They had human hands under their wings on each of their four sides. All four of them had faces and wings. (Ezek. 1:5–8)

Four as a Term of Geographical Completeness

When John finally sees "New Jerusalem, coming down from God out of heaven" (Rev. 21:2), one of the features about the city that becomes apparent is its shape as a massive cube. "The city was square. It was as wide as it was long. He measured the city with the stick. It was 12,000 stadia long. Its length, width, and height were the same. He measured its wall. According to human measurement, which the angel was using, it was 144 cubits" (Rev. 21:16–17).

When God gave the precise instructions to Moses in the wilderness about the structure and components of the tabernacle (worship tent) that would stand in the middle of the Israelite camp,

those directions were filled with fours (Exod. 25–39). From the four golden rings attached to the ark of the covenant that would hold the carrying poles (25:12) to the four bronze carrying rings on the square altar for burnt offerings (38:5) and the "four posts set in four bronze bases" (38:19) that supported the screen of the outside entrance of the tabernacle, the number *four* figures prominently. And when God built the New Jerusalem, the jewel of the new heaven and new earth, it's not surprising that the repetition of *four* provides a sort of signature of the Designer.

Key Verse

All the angels stood around the throne with the leaders and the four living creatures. They bowed in front of the throne with their faces touching the ground, worshiped God, and said,

"Amen! Praise, glory, wisdom, thanks, honor, power, and strength
be to our God forever and ever! Amen!"
(Rev. 7:11–12)

In some early Christian traditions these animals represent the four gospel writers, so that Matthew (the human face), Mark (the lion), Luke (the ox), and John (the eagle) are thought of as the living creatures who surround, and worship, the Jesus of whom they speak.

N. T. Wright, *Revelation for Everyone*, New Testament for Everyone (Louisville: Westminster John Knox, 2011), 47–48

Top, groups of four show wholeness, indicating those specific things plus everything in between.

109

Gate

Doors allow access to or prevent us from entering a room or home. Gates are usually more imposing and important. They guard the access to large spaces: cities, estates, and the way to eternal life. In Bible times, most cities of any size were surrounded by walls, so gates were a constant feature in people's lives. No wonder, then, that the role of gates became symbolic of other values and ideas.

The Importance of Gates in Biblical Culture

Gates were primarily for protection. They were open during the day but closed at night (Josh. 2:5). Gatekeepers were posted to keep intruders out (Neh. 7:1–3). Sometimes gates even became personified as living guardians and representatives of a city: "Lift your heads, you gates. Be lifted, you ancient doors, so that the king of glory may come in" (Ps. 24:7). The opening of a gate symbolized a royal welcome. Conversely, a city without a gate was the ultimate target: "Attack the nation living peacefully and securely, declares the LORD. It is a nation with no gates or bars" (Jer. 49:31).

Because of their importance to a city, gates were often the place where leaders would meet to discuss affairs of state and settle legal matters. One such event is the climax of the book of Ruth, when Boaz negotiated with another relative over the fate of Naomi, Ruth, and the legacy of a man named Elimelech. When they reached an agreement, the witnesses spoke up: "All the people who were at the gate, including the leaders, said, 'We are witnesses. May the LORD make this wife, who is coming into your home, like Rachel and Leah, both of whom built our family of Israel. So show your strength of character in Ephrathah and make a name for yourself in Bethlehem'" (Ruth 4:11). A crucial moment in the ancestry of King David and Jesus the Messiah was decided by the exchange of a sandal at the city gate of Bethlehem (Ruth 4:1–22). In addition, the virtuous wife was praised in the city gates (Prov. 31:31), her husband was known there (Prov. 31:23), and wisdom cries out there (Prov. 1:21).

Metaphorical Gates

Jesus described the two basic approaches to life as a choice between two gates: "Enter through the narrow gate because the gate and road that lead to destruction are wide. Many enter through the wide gate. But the narrow gate and the road that lead to life are full of trouble. Only a few people find the narrow gate" (Matt. 7:13–14). He also described himself as the only gate through which we can find salvation: "I am the gate. Those

The Eastern Gate in Jerusalem was an important location in the biblical landscape.

who enter the sheep pen through me will be saved. They will go in and out of the sheep pen and find food" (John 10:9). The gate is a symbol for Christ himself, the only means of salvation. Just as one could only gain entrance to an earthly city through the gate, so one can only enter the heavenly city through the gate of Christ.

Jesus also mentioned a more ominous set of gates, the gates of hell, but he promised that the church to be born after his death and resurrection would confront hell victoriously: "You are Peter, and I can guarantee that on this rock I will build my church. And the gates of hell will not overpower it" (Matt. 16:18).

While the Old Testament prophecies of future well-being for the people of God feature secure gates (Isa. 60:11, 18; Ezek. 40–48), the New Testament book of Revelation displays the gates of the New Jerusalem in all their glory (Rev. 21:12–25). Although for most people a gate symbolized the security that was created when it was closed, one of the features of the New Jerusalem is that "its gates will be open all day. They will never close because there won't be any night there" (Rev. 21:25). In the new heaven and new earth, gates will be decorative memorials, no longer needed for protection since God's presence makes the grand city the ultimate safe place.

Key Verse

Enter through the narrow gate because the gate and road that lead to destruction are wide. Many enter through the wide gate. But the narrow gate and the road that lead to life are full of trouble. Only a few people find the narrow gate. (Matt. 7:13–14)

The first reason he gives us for entering in at this straight gate is the character of the two types of life that are open to us and possible for us. There is the broad way which you enter through the wide gate, and there is the other way which is entered through the straight gate, a way which is narrow the whole time. If we only realized the truth concerning the character of these two ways there would be no hesitation. Of course, it is so difficult for us to detach ourselves from life in this world, and yet the essence of this matter is that we should do so.

D. Martyn Lloyd-Jones, *Studies in the Sermon on the Mount* (Leicester, England: Inter-Varsity, 1971), 232

Top, gates were an important form of protection in the ancient world.

111

Goat

Flocks of goats were part of everyday life throughout Bible times. Hardier than sheep, goats provided milk, cheese, water skins, meat, and hair from which rough fabric was made for tents and other durable items. When God gave Moses the detailed instructions for creating the tabernacle that would be God's tent in the wilderness, he specified an outer layer of goat hair that protected the fine linen covering of the inner space called the Holy of Holies, where God's presence would be evident (Exod. 26).

The goat was considered a clean animal for the Israelites to consume. Goat meat is an acquired taste, since the animal's diet makes the flavor similar to wild game. Families often had a young goat on hand for special occasions or to extend hospitality. This is why, for instance, when Jacob and his mother, Rebekah, conspired to trick old, blind Isaac by having Jacob act as Esau and bring a special meal of wild game, they substituted a goat kid as the counterfeit main course (Gen. 27). Pretending to be Esau, Jacob claimed he was serving his father the wild game he had requested. Rebekah also used the goat's skin to cover Jacob's arms so he could pass for a hairy man like his brother.

Sacrificial Goat

All these practical uses for goats made them ideal symbols in the sacrificial system God instituted while the people of Israel traveled through the wilderness. The central act on the Day of Atonement involved the use of two goats. One goat was sacrificed and the other was exiled as the *scapegoat*. The live goat was led out into the wilderness bearing the sins of the people, representing those sins being taken away, even as the sacrificial death of the other goat was said to *atone* (make right, make amends, settle an offense) for the sins of the people. The instructions for this special day are found in Leviticus 16:7–22 and are later a central theme of the New Testament book of Hebrews, where the dual roles of the goats in the Day of Atonement are shown to be fulfilled by Jesus' sacrifice on the cross (see Heb. 10:1–18). Jesus not only atoned for our sins on the cross, he permanently carried their weight away from us. What the ancient Israelites had to do every year, Jesus accomplished in his single trip to the cross.

Visionary Goat

Throughout the Old Testament, leaders were often symbolized by goats (Jer. 50:8; 51:40; Ezek. 34:17, 23; Zech. 10:3). Among Daniel's visions, a goat is prominent in chapter 8. The vision features a powerful ram and an even more powerful goat. At first the ram seems invincible no matter what direction it moves, but a goat comes from the west and defeats the ram. At the height of its power, the goat's single massive horn breaks off and is replaced by four

On the Day of Atonement, one goat was sacrificed and a second goat was sent into the wilderness as a scapegoat, symbolically carrying the sins of the people.

horns. One of these develops an added small horn. The angel Gabriel explains to Daniel, "The hairy male goat is the kingdom of Greece, and the large horn between its eyes is its first king. The horn broke off, and four horns replaced it. Four kingdoms will come out of that nation, but they won't be as strong as the first king was" (Dan. 8:21–22). From the backward look of history, Daniel's visions were correct to an uncanny degree. Greece did replace the Medo-Persian juggernaut under Alexander and then split into four smaller kingdoms. Those determined to find naturalistic explanations for every event simply suggest that Daniel's book was written much later, after these events occurred, and is more record than vision. But if God who has perfect foreknowledge of all things chose to reveal in this way what would unfold in history, why would we not use it as a reason to remain in awe of him?

Jesus' description of the final judgment of humankind (Matt. 25:31–46) features goats used to represent those who are destined for eternal judgment. Although sheep and goats often grazed over the same territory, when evening came and the shepherds gathered their flocks, the sheep and goats were kept in different folds. Jesus used this simile to explain that the final separation between the saved and the lost doesn't rest on sheep being of greater value than goats; rather, like a shepherd's knowledge of his flock, God will not hesitate to determine those who are part of his eternal flock and those who will spend eternity apart from him.

Key Verse

He used his own blood, not the blood of goats and bulls, for the sacrifice. He went into the most holy place and offered this sacrifice once and for all to free us forever. (Heb. 9:12)

This was the ritual of the Day of Atonement, the day designed to cleanse all things and all people from sin. . . . Every year, this ceremony had to be gone through again. Everyone but the high priest was barred from the presence, and even he entered in terror. The cleansing was a purely external one by baths of water. The sacrifice was that of bulls and goats and animal blood. The whole thing failed because such things cannot atone for sin. In it all, the writer to the Hebrews sees a pale copy of the reality, a ghostly pattern of the one true sacrifice—the sacrifice of Christ.

William Barclay, *The Letter to the Hebrews*, New Daily Study Bible (Louisville: Westminster John Knox, 2002), 120

Top, a flock of goats and herdsmen were a common site in the Holy Land.

113

Gold

old has always been prized for its rarity and permanence. It is useful in its pure state even before it is refined, and it never tarnishes like other metals do. Gold's value and beauty caused it to become associated with wealth and royalty (Gen. 13:2; 41:42). The accoutrements of royalty were made of gold, including scepters and crowns (2 Sam. 12:30; Esther 4:11; 8:15). Thus the wise men's gift of gold to Jesus was a symbolic act—he was being declared to be a king (Matt. 2:11).

Symbol of Worship

Gold played an important part in the construction of the tabernacle and temple. The ark was overlaid with gold and many of the utensils were made of gold, as well as parts of the structure itself (Exod. 25:11–39; 1 Kings 6:20–35). Gold's symbolic association with royalty made it a natural choice for the house of the King of kings and the instruments used in worshiping him. Paul draws out the significance of gold being used to make items for noble purposes in his letter to Timothy: "In a large house there are not only objects made of gold and silver, but also those made of wood and clay. Some objects are honored when they are used; others aren't" (2 Tim. 2:20). The use of gold in the tabernacle and temple symbolized the value the worshiper placed on the God they were worshiping.

Image of Value

The poets of the Bible often use gold to represent superiority. The beloved in Song of Solomon refers to her lover's head, arms, and feet being made of gold (5:11, 14–15). The psalmist declares that the teachings of God's Word are "more desirable than gold, even the finest gold" (19:10). Wisdom is better than gold (Prov. 3:14), as evidenced by the fact that it cannot be bought with gold (Job 28:12–15). Gold is portrayed as the symbolic standard of ultimate value in the Bible.

The value of gold caused it to become misused and idolized. People began to worship gold idols rather than the One who created gold to begin with (Exod. 20:23; Acts 17:29). In addition, preoccupation with gathering wealth such as gold is condemned throughout Scripture (e.g., Job 31:24–28). This overvaluation of gold led God to declare, "The silver is mine, and the gold is mine, declares the LORD of Armies" (Hag. 2:8). Gold may be a standard of superiority and value, but God is of infinitely higher worth than any earthly standard.

The Purifying of Gold

The process by which gold is purified and formed makes it a fitting image for the sanctifying work that occurs in the life of a believer. Refiners carefully melt gold to bring out any

Gold has always been prized as a precious metal, a thing of great value.

impurities, a process that requires high heat and constant tending. The image of God refining believers is first used in the book of Job as Job declared, "When he tests me, I'll come out as pure as gold" (23:10; cf. Jer. 9:7). Following this imagery through to the New Testament, Peter reminded believers that suffering is a testing process: "The purpose of these troubles is to test your faith as fire tests how genuine gold is. Your faith is more precious than gold, and by passing the test, it gives praise, glory, and honor to God. This will happen when Jesus Christ appears again" (1 Pet. 1:7). The use of gold refining as an image for sanctification helps us understand the purpose of suffering in our lives and the role of God as he tends the fire and cares for us at each stage of the refining process.

Heaven

The final use of gold in Scripture is, of course, in the depictions of heaven. It is a city of pure gold with streets made of pure gold (Rev. 21:18, 21) and an eternal home for those who spent their lives living for the things that last—symbolized by the gold, silver, and precious stones, representing a life lived for Christ and his kingdom (1 Cor. 3:12). In the descriptions of heaven, gold as an image for value and permanence has come full circle, with gold covering God's house as it did the tabernacle and temple and God being honored as the true and worthy King by those who

have been brought through the fire. Those who have persevered to the end, whose faith has been proven to be as genuine as gold, enjoy eternal life in the city of gold with the King above all kings.

Key Verse

The purpose of these troubles is to test your faith as fire tests how genuine gold is. Your faith is more precious than gold, and by passing the test, it gives praise, glory, and honor to God. This will happen when Jesus Christ appears again. (1 Pet. 1:7)

The goldsmith lifts the gold out with a pair of tongs, lets it cool, rubs it between his fingers, and if not satisfied puts it back again in fresh medicine. This time he blows the fire hotter than it was before, and each time he puts the gold into the crucible the heat of the fire is increased: "It could not bear it so hot at first, but it can bear it now; what would have destroyed it then helps it now." "How do you know when the gold is purified?" we asked him, and he answered, "When I can see my face in it [the liquid gold in the crucible] then it is pure."

Amy Carmichael, *Learning of God: Readings from Amy Carmichael*, ed. Stuart and Brenda Blanch (Fort Washington, PA: Christian Literature Crusade, 1985), 50

Graft

The agricultural practice of grafting—joining a shoot or bud to a growing plant so they grow together into a new plant—was well known in the ancient world. It was usually done to promote new growth and increased fruit production among similar plant species. Grafting was a faster way to get a mature plant than starting from seeds. Often a branch from a cultivated tree would be grafted onto an already established wild tree, and the wild tree would then produce better fruit in greater quantity. As an image, grafting appears only once in Scripture, although it also reminds the reader of similar imagery related to vines, branches, and roots.

Chosen People

In Romans 11, the image of grafting is used to illustrate the relationship between Israel and Gentile believers. Gentile believers had been "grafted" into the "olive tree" and were now part of God's chosen people. They were not a separate nation but all one chosen people saved by God's grace. The whole church benefited from their presence, just as the whole tree benefits from a grafted branch. The nation of Israel could grow bigger and stronger and be more productive with the inclusion of Gentile believers. In addition, the grafted-in branches could enjoy the benefits of Israel's long history and the established roots of God's previous interactions with his people. They were not a vulnerable young plant, but part of a vibrant, thriving tree. As a result, more fruit would come from the grafted plant than from either of the two original plants.

Branches

But Paul reminded Gentiles not to think they were better than the original branches: "Some of the olive branches have been broken off, and you, a wild olive branch, have been grafted in their place. You get your nourishment from the roots of the olive tree. So don't brag about being better than the other branches. If you brag, remember that you don't support the root, the root supports you" (Rom. 11:17–18). Some Gentile believers had a sense of superiority over their Jewish brothers and sisters. Paul reminded them that they had been granted their position in God's kingdom by God's grace, not by their own effort, just as a branch cannot graft itself onto a tree. Paul goes on to remind Gentile believers that if God did not spare the original branches that failed to produce fruit, he would also not spare them. The penalty for not bearing fruit was the same for both Jews and Gentiles: being burned in the fire (Matt. 13:40; John 15:6).

Both the grafted-on branch and the original branches must bear fruit or they will be thrown into the fire.

Paul tells us that Gentiles have been grafted into Israel, and the resulting nation will be more fruitful than the original would have been.

Concerning Paul's metaphor in Romans 11 of Gentile Christians being grafted into the kingdom of God, Dr. Douglas Moo writes:

> Two aspects of Paul's metaphor in verse 17 require further comment. First is the significance of Paul's choice of the olive tree to fill out the imagery of root and branches. This probably reflects both its use as a symbol of Israel in the OT and Judaism and the fact that the olive tree was the most widely cultivated fruit tree in the Mediterranean area. The wild olive tree, by contrast, was notoriously unfruitful, and Paul's comparison of Gentiles to it may be intended to prick the Gentiles' pride and sense of superiority. The second point calling for attention is Paul's reference to the practice of grafting branches from a wild, or uncultivated, tree into a cultivated one—the reverse of the usual process. . . . Paul has allowed the theological process he is illustrating to affect the terms of his metaphor.

Douglas J. Moo, *The Epistle to the Romans*, New International Commentary on the New Testament (Grand Rapids: Eerdmans, 1996), 702–3

Key Verse

If the root is holy, the branches are holy. But some of the olive branches have been broken off, and you, a wild olive branch, have been grafted in their place. You get your nourishment from the roots of the olive tree. So don't brag about being better than the other branches. If you brag, remember that you don't support the root, the root supports you. (Rom. 11:16–18)

Top, *grafting* was an ancient process of joining two plants to make a more fruitful plant.

Grapes

Grapevines are a plant well suited to the climate of Palestine. Grapes were cultivated as far back as Noah's day (Gen. 9:20) and were eaten fresh, dried, or crushed to make juice, vinegar, or wine. In an area where water was often in short supply, the juice from grapes became crucial for life. Clusters of grapes as large as five kilograms (twelve pounds) have been reported in Palestine, giving validity to the spies' account of the grapes in Canaan in Numbers 13.

The importance of grapes in the Middle Eastern climate and culture made vineyards a symbol of abundance and prosperity. Grapes and the wine they produced were a crucial part of celebrations (Deut. 11:14; Judg. 9:27; Esther 1:7–8). This role of grapes is underscored by the fact that Nazirites refused grapes as part of their lifestyle of self-denial (Num. 6:3). Grapes were symbolic of all the best this world has to offer.

ultimate futility and frustration, but that was the fate promised to sinful Israel (Deut. 28:39; Mic. 6:15; Zeph. 1:13). The sinful life results in poverty and futility, while the righteous life produces abundant harvest and celebration.

Sour grapes are an image of sin in an ancient proverb quoted in Ezekiel 18:2: "Fathers have eaten sour grapes, and their children's teeth are set on edge." One of the most notable aspects of sin is that something that promises pleasure turns out to be distasteful and unpleasant, like the experience of biting into a sour grape when we expect something sweet. Sin appears good but leaves a bad taste in the mouth. Of course, children can't literally taste the grapes their parents eat, but metaphorically they suffer for the sins of their parents. One way this happens is when the sins of the fathers are repeated in subsequent generations as children imitate their parents' behavior.

Sin and Judgment

The failure of a grape crop was evidence of God's judgment (Isa. 18:5). Planting a vineyard and then not being able to enjoy it was a portrait of

The True Vine

Faithful Israel is portrayed as a vine that is lovingly tended by God, the vinedresser, and produces a bountiful crop (Isa. 5). The vine is a symbol for God's providential care and steadfast love toward his people. Yet despite all his loving care, Israel fails to produce a crop (vv. 2, 4). They refuse to act in justice and righteousness (v. 7), and so the vineyard is left unprotected to make way for a more productive crop (vv. 5–6). This is a fitting metaphor for the destruction Israel would suffer at the hands of her enemies as a result of her sin.

The Middle Eastern climate is well suited to growing grapes. They were used for wine and food.

In the New Testament this image is fleshed out in John 15, where Jesus himself is the vine, and Christians who abide in him are fruitful branches. In both uses of the image, grapes not being produced is considered unnatural and the branch is pruned until it bears fruit. Just as a grapevine should produce grapes, Christians should produce sweet spiritual fruit. The presence of spiritual fruit is evidence of God's blessing and work in the life of a believer, and the absence of fruit brings judgment and suffering with the end goal of bringing forth a harvest.

In the final judgment, God's wrath against sin is portrayed as a winepress, squeezing those who have been thrown into hell. This judgment was first fulfilled in the Old Testament by invading armies (Lam. 1:15) and will be fulfilled once for all in the end times (Isa. 63:3; Rev. 14). True believers need not fear falling into the winepress of God's wrath, but the severity of this image should drive us to warn others so they do not suffer that fate.

Key Verse

The LORD trampled the people of Judah in a winepress. (Lam.1:15)

The biblical image of God threshing out the grapes in judgment was made popular during the American Civil War era in "The Battle Hymn of the Republic" by Julia Ward Howe. The words of this hymn were the inspiration for the title of John Steinbeck's novel *The Grapes of Wrath*. The hymn is still used in patriotic settings today, an interesting mingling of biblical imagery with nationalistic fervor.

> *Mine eyes have seen the glory of the coming of the Lord;*
> *He is trampling out the vintage where the grapes of wrath are stored;*
> *He hath loosed the fateful lightning of His terrible swift sword:*
> *His truth is marching on.*

Top, the final judgment is symbolized by a winepress squeezing all the juice out of grapes.

119

Hand

Beyond their obvious use in holding objects, hands have long had two other significant roles for people: we count on our fingers, and we measure with the length or breadth of our hands. Finger width and palm width were standard units of measure in Bible times. In passages like Exodus 25:25 and 37:12, 1 Kings 7:26, and Ezekiel 40:43 the span is translated "three inches," but the original says "handbreadth."

Expressions of Power

In the figurative language of the Bible and beyond, hands have long represented power. When Moses says, "In fact, it was the LORD himself who got rid of all of them until none were left in the camp" (Deut. 2:15), his expressive phrase is literally, "the hand of the LORD was against them." When David prays, "Into your hands I entrust my spirit" (Ps. 31:5), he is claiming the protection of God's power and creating an expression Christ used in his closing moments of life on the cross (Luke 23:46). Symbolically, the right hand was the side of favor, so to sit there would be a place of honor: "You make the path of life known to me. Complete joy is in your presence. Pleasures are by your side forever" (Ps. 16:11; see also 110:1). In Mark 14:62, when Jesus said to the chief priest, "You will see the Son of Man in the highest position in heaven," his words were actually, "You will see the Son of Man sitting at the right hand of power," a claim to divinity that his enemies immediately seized to justify their rejection of him.

Reference to *hand* or *hands* could also indicate a person's will or attitude. When Jeroboam rebelled against Solomon and eventually split the kingdom, the expression used for his attitude in 1 Kings 11:26 is translated literally, "he lifted his hand against the king." Even more, when Paul is describing the way God has always offered correction and grace to people, he quotes Isaiah's words, "All day long I have stretched out my hands to disobedient and rebellious people" (Rom. 10:21; see also Isa. 65:2).

Clean Hands

Clean hands were much more than the product of washing; they were symbols of personal moral purity. Psalm 26:6 says, "I will wash my hands in innocence. I will walk around your altar, O LORD," claiming that the ritual of washing hands expressed a person's integrity. David made this a standard for approaching God: "Who may go up the LORD's mountain? Who may stand in his holy place? The one who has clean hands and a pure heart and does not long for what is false or lie when he is under oath" (Ps. 24:3–4).

The expression "washing one's hands of a situation" refers to Pilate's efforts to exempt himself from guilt in turning Jesus over to the people for crucifixion: "Pilate saw that he was not getting anywhere. Instead, a riot was breaking out. So Pilate took some water and washed his hands in front of the crowd. He said, 'I won't be guilty of killing this man. Do what you want!'" (Matt. 27:24).

The Laying On of Hands

One of the most profound symbolic acts in the Bible is the "laying on of hands." When someone offered a sacrifice to God as a way of seeking forgiveness for sin, the Old Testament instructions required the worshiper to place his hands on the head of the animal, symbolically transferring the sin from his own life to the animal about to die (Lev. 1:4).

Laying hands on someone was also a symbolic act conferring a blessing or responsibility on that person's life. When Moses passed over leadership responsibility to Joshua, God commanded him to do so in a public ceremony (Num. 27:18–20).

In the New Testament, the first leaders appointed by the apostles to serve the church as deacons were set apart by the laying on of hands (Acts 6:5–6). And the elders in the church of Antioch commissioned Paul and Barnabas for missionary duty by laying on hands and praying for them (Acts 13:3). Paul reminded Timothy of the importance of his ministry on behalf of those who had laid hands on him (1 Tim. 4:14; 2 Tim. 1:6). The act of touching someone this way functions like a prayer.

Raised Hands

Open hands and raised hands have often symbolized surrender or even worship and honor. Paul instructed Timothy to lead the church in fervent prayer that is more than audible: "I want men to offer prayers everywhere. They should raise their hands in prayer after putting aside their anger and any quarrels they have with anyone" (1 Tim. 2:8). He was preserving the physical aspects of prayer that are found throughout the Psalms: "Hear my prayer for mercy when I call to you for help, when I lift my hands toward your most holy place" (Ps. 28:2; see also 63:4; 88:9; 134:2; 141:2; 143:6).

Key Verse

I will wash my hands in innocence.
I will walk around your altar, O Lord,
*   so that I may loudly sing a hymn of*
*   thanksgiving*
*   and tell about all your miracles.*
*   (Ps. 26:6–7)*

> Dr. Robert E. Webber discusses the symbolic use of hands in the early church's celebration of the Eucharist:
>
> Two other actions were adopted by the ancient church to communicate the meaning of the offering. First, the washing of the hands (in keeping with Psalm 26:6: "I wash my hands in innocence, and go about your altar, O Lord") signified the innocence of those who serve at the altar. This action was first recorded by Cyril of Jerusalem in the fourth century and ought not be regarded as an early custom. Second, the imposition of hands on the elements may have been derived from the Old Testament practice of laying hands on the sacrificial animal (e.g., Leviticus 4:14–15).
>
> Robert E. Webber, *Worship Old and New* (Grand Rapids: Zondervan, 1994), 175

Top, in Scripture, clean hands are a metaphor for a pure heart, but mere external ritual cleansing is of no value without an internal focus on obedience.

Head

The head is in many ways the most important part of the body. It is the center of thought and emotion, and unlike other visible body parts (such as the hand or arm) it is essential for life. Biblical writers thought of it as the life of the individual, the body part that symbolized a person's entire being. In addition, it is the uppermost and most visible feature of a person. For these reasons the head serves as a fitting image for the center of life and leadership.

The Importance of the Head

The first biblical reference to the head comes in Genesis 3:15, where the curse on the serpent is that the woman's offspring will crush his head. The contrast between the serpent's bruising the heel of the woman's child and that child crushing the serpent's head pictures the difference between a wound and utter defeat. The Messiah will not conquer Satan as a slightly more powerful enemy; as a totally superior being he will completely destroy Satan.

Elsewhere, cutting off a person's head in warfare is a symbol of victory (1 Sam. 17:46; 31:8–10; 2 Sam. 20:22). The head is particularly vulnerable in warfare, so images of God as a shield often mention his protection over the head: "O LORD Almighty, the strong one who saves me, you have covered my head in the day of battle" (Ps. 140:7; see also Isa. 59:17; Eph. 6:17). God's protection in all of life's battles is symbolized by a head covering.

The head is the focal point of the body, so that is where kings were anointed (Exod. 29:7; 1 Sam. 10:1). When God anoints his sheep with oil in Psalm 23:5, images of the king's anointing come to mind. God is crowning his people with honor and blessing through the symbol of oil on the head. In addition, "Blessings cover the head of a righteous person" (Prov. 10:6), just as blessings throughout the Old Testament were delivered with a hand over a person's head (Gen. 48:14).

Blessing can symbolically center on a person's head, but so can sin and guilt. The priests put their hands on the head of the scapegoat to symbolize the transfer of the people's sin onto the animal (Exod. 29:10, 15; Lev. 3:2). People's sins return upon their own head (Obad. 1:15 NIV). Similarly, shame and guilt are symbolized by covering one's head with one's hand or with ashes (Jer. 14:3; Ezek. 27:30–31). Uncovering of the head by shaving one's hair was a symbol of mourning (Amos 8:10; Mic. 1:16).

The head is the command center of the body, the symbolic representation of the person's being as well as the leader of all the functions of the body.

Christ Our Head

Given the importance of the head to the entire body, it is fitting that Christ is pictured throughout the New Testament as the head of his church. God "has made Christ the head of everything for the good of the church" (Eph. 1:22) and "as we lovingly speak the truth, we will grow up completely in our relationship to Christ, who is the head" (Eph. 4:15). This relationship is to be portrayed in the earthly marriage relationship: "The husband is the head of his wife as Christ is the head of the church. It is his body, and he is its Savior. As the church is under Christ's authority, so wives are under their husbands' authority in everything" (Eph. 5:23–24). In the same way the tribes of Israel were led by "heads" or chief leaders throughout the Old Testament and husbands were heads over their families, so now Christ is the head over the entire church. And the universal church is connected to him as vitally as a body is connected to its physical head. Without his leadership and continuous feeding of all we need, the church could not exist. He is our life source as well as our leader. Just as a body cannot choose to disconnect itself from a head, so we cannot disconnect ourselves from Christ, our head, without suffering spiritual death in the process.

Key Verse

He existed before everything
*   and holds everything together.*
He is also the head of the church, which is his
*   body. (Col. 1:17–18)*

> The Bible emphatically tells us that Christ is the Head. One day God will head up everything in the universe under Christ. Today the universe has not come under the leadership of Christ yet, and everything is in a state of confusion. . . . The church is God's means of enlarging Christ, and this enlargement will go on until he fills the entire universe. The church is "the fullness of him who fills all in all" (Eph. 1:23). If the headship of Christ is not established in the church, it cannot be established in the universe.
>
> Watchman Nee, *The Mystery of Christ:*
> *Knowing Christ in the Church and As the Church*
> (Anaheim: Living Stream Ministry, 1997), 31

Heaven

In a literal sense, heaven is the eternal dwelling place of God (Gen. 24:7), the angels (Gen. 28:12), and the saints—Christians who have died (Eph. 2:6; Rev. 20:4). The imagery surrounding heaven in Scripture is filled with pictures of an otherworldly paradise, the world as it was meant to be in all of its original perfection. Heaven itself is not an image in Scripture—it is a real place, in the same way earth is a real place. But it is surrounded by images that express truths about heaven—a place so different from our daily experience on earth that we cannot comprehend it—and images for what heaven represents in our human experience. Heaven symbolizes the hoped-for destination of people, a place beyond death and better than anything we can imagine, where God himself prepares a place for us to live with him forever.

A Place Fit for a King

Heaven is so different from this fallen world that the only way biblical writers can explain it is through the use of cryptic images. It is a remote place that we can only see dimly, as if through a cloud, due to the limitations of our earthly

existence (Acts 1:9; 1 Cor. 13:12). Nevertheless, the Bible writers try to translate the realities of heaven into familiar pictures. One common theme in descriptions of heaven is that of a royal throne room where God sits in glory and judgment, with his robe filling the space in resplendence (Pss. 11:4; 47:8; 103:19; Isa. 6:1).

Heaven is also portrayed as a temple (Isa. 6:1; Rev. 3:12; 21:22). It is the eternal place of worship and the fulfillment of all that the earthly temple represents—a place where God dwells among his people (Rev. 21:3). Most frequently heaven is portrayed as a city: "Then I saw the holy city, New Jerusalem, coming down from God out of heaven, dressed like a bride ready for her husband" (Rev. 21:2). In all of these instances heaven is a place of splendor, majesty, and beauty. It is an enameled and regal city of jewels and gold (Ezek. 1; Rev. 21). Yet it is also a place designed with us in mind (John 14:1–6).

A Place of Perfection

Heaven is so otherworldly to us because it is a place of ultimate perfection and the satisfaction of every good desire. Those who live there have washed robes (Rev. 7:14) and white garments (Rev. 3:5). They are spotless (Rev. 14:4–5). In heaven, sin no longer separates us from God, because sin does not exist there. Every tear is dried, and every wound is healed (Rev. 21:4). Every thirst is satisfied (Rev. 21:6). Every person dwells in light, for no darkness is there (Rev. 21:23–27). All of these are aspects and images of the perfection that is integral to heaven. And heaven becomes a sign of all the good that God has waiting for us.

Jacob's vision of a ladder going up to heaven reminds us that Jesus has made a way through his work for us to enter heaven's rest as well.

A Place of Rest

Scripture also offers images of the fulfilled longings that heaven represents to human experience. Symbols of rest are common throughout Scripture (Isa. 66:1; Heb. 3:11; 4:9–11; Rev. 14:13). Hebrews 3–4 makes clear that the Sabbath is a symbol of the eternal rest we will find in heaven. Another common image for heaven is of a reward. As people are judged when they die, those who are found in Christ receive a reward for their righteous deeds (Matt. 6:2–4; 10:42; 2 Tim. 4:8; Heb. 11:26; 1 Pet. 5:4; Rev. 22:12). The imagery of rewards and crowns in heaven is in keeping with the royal throne room symbolism mentioned above. Despite all the glory and splendor, heaven is also pictured in Scripture as our home. Jesus prepares a room for each believer there (John 14:2–3). That is why Christians speak of death as a home-going—heaven is the place where we will truly be at home, unlike this world, where we are in some sense strangers on a journey through a hostile land (Eph. 2:19; Phil. 3:20; Heb. 11:13–16; 1 Pet. 2:11).

All of these images for heaven—both those that portray a reality about the place of heaven and those that portray a reality about what heaven will mean for us individually—make us long for the day we will be in the Lord's presence. In a prophetic sense, heaven holds out the hope God offers to each person because of what Jesus accomplished on the cross. Without God's gracious and singular alternative (faith in Christ), heaven would be an empty hope. With Christ as our way, truth, and life, we don't have to be troubled (John 14:1–3). Heaven symbolizes wholly positive images, and together they make up a picture that shows us the grand day when we enter our heavenly reward. Every longing we experience on earth will be perfectly fulfilled as we worship God for eternity in a place of ultimate beauty and comfort. We were made for heaven, and only there will we be truly at home.

One of the thieves crucified with Jesus realized that his only hope of heaven was in the unusual man who was dying next to him. Their brief exchange points to the moment of faith open to every person: "Then he said, 'Jesus, remember me when you enter your kingdom.' Jesus said to him, 'I can guarantee this truth: Today you will be with me in paradise'" (Luke 23:42–43).

Key Verse

My Father's house has many rooms. If that were not true, would I have told you that I'm going to prepare a place for you? (John 14:2)

Satan need not convince us that Heaven doesn't exist. He need only convince us that Heaven is a place of boring, unearthly existence. If we believe that lie, we'll be robbed of our joy and anticipation, we'll set our minds on this life and not on the next, and we won't be motivated to share our faith. Why should we share the "good news" that people can spend eternity in a boring, ghostly place that even *we're* not looking forward to?

Randy Alcorn, *Heaven* (Wheaton: Tyndale, 2004), 11

Top, heaven is the dwelling place of God, where Jesus sits in glory on his rightful throne.

125

Honey

In the Bible, honey was the sweet syrup produced by bees, either wild (1 Sam. 14:25–26) or domesticated (2 Chron. 31:5). It was a delicacy rather than a necessity of life, a sign of luxury and abundance. Occasionally it is referred to as a medicine: "Pleasant words are like honey from a honeycomb—sweet to the spirit and healthy for the body" (Prov. 16:24), although overindulgence is warned against (Prov. 25:16, 27). Honey's desirability and preciousness is underscored by the fact that it was occasionally used as a gift (Gen. 43:11; 2 Chron. 31:5).

Abundance and Delight

Honey most often symbolizes abundance and prosperity. Psalm 81:16 promises God's tender care for his people: "But I would feed Israel with the finest wheat and satisfy them with honey from a rock." The Promised Land is described as "a land flowing with milk and honey" twenty times (e.g., Exod. 3:8, 17). These words are a description of land that is good for both pasture and agriculture. Animals would have plenteous grazing land so they could produce milk, a necessity of life in Bible times, and people would be able to cultivate plants and bees to produce honey. The pairing of milk and honey symbolizes fullness of life. God was promising abundant satisfaction of both needs (milk) and desires (honey). When the twelve men came back from spying out the Promised Land, they verified that it was indeed flowing with milk and honey (Num. 13:27).

The sweetness of honey is used in the Bible as a metaphor for delight. In Psalm 19:10 the desirability of God's Word and the pleasure found therein is portrayed as the product of a honeycomb: "They are sweeter than honey, even the drippings from a honeycomb." The sweet taste of Scripture should linger in our mouths and make us long for more. The prophets echoed this sentiment about divine revelation. Ezekiel wrote, "He said to me, 'Son of man, eat this scroll I'm giving you, and fill your stomach with it.' So I ate it, and it tasted as sweet as honey in my mouth" (3:3). Meditating on God's Word enables it to enter our inmost being and have an effect on our lives, and its honey-like sweetness makes it a pleasure to do so.

God's Word is compared to honey from a honeycomb to show its sweetness.

Honey is a luxury and a delicacy, a product of the Promised Land that showed God's abundant provision for his people.

Judgment

Isaiah turns the usual symbolism of honey on its head when he speaks of Immanuel eating curds and honey in Isaiah 7:15: "He will eat cheese and honey until he knows how to reject evil and choose good." Foreign nations will invade Israel, and the few survivors of the invasion will be forced to eat off the land (Isa. 7:22). In these end-times prophecies, honey has changed from a symbol of abundance and delight into a symbol of scarcity and judgment. As further illustration of this negative symbolism of honey, John the Baptist consumed honey as part of his limited diet (Mark 1:6), living on what God provided at hand. John the Baptist's lifestyle of self-denial highlighted the nation's need for repentance and spiritual renewal.

Key Verse

*But I would feed Israel with the finest wheat
and satisfy them with honey from a rock.*
(Ps. 81:16)

For us too the everyday world seems strewn with rocks. We fear that we have been led out into this wilderness to perish. That our yearning for holiness will be forever unfulfilled. And then at that moment, from something as mundane as a rock, there glistens a drop of that eternal baby food, honey. Even here there is spiritual nourishment.

Lawrence Kushner, *Honey from the Rock*
(Woodstock, VT: Jewish Lights Publishing, 2000), 14

Top, bees are a picture of industry and hard work.

Horn

The horns of certain animals appear frequently in Scripture as symbols. These are often used in prophetic visions to represent the power of individuals or kingdoms (1 Kings 22:11). While horns were also fashioned into musical instruments (see TRUMPET/SHOFAR), their symbolic use is usually indicated when they are mentioned. Hornlike projections were included at the four corners of the altar of incense in the original tabernacle and in the Jerusalem temple. These horns were carved from wood and covered with bronze or gold. They were visual reminders of an encounter with the God of ultimate power as they surrounded the fragrant offerings before God. When David listed the dependable aspects of his relationship with God in Psalm 18, he began, "I love you, O LORD, my strength. The LORD is my rock and my fortress and my Savior, my God, my rock in whom I take refuge, my shield, and the strength of my salvation, my stronghold" (Ps. 18:1–2). The word *strength* is literally *horn*, playing off the idea of vigor and power that horns represent.

Animal Horns

The horns that appear in visions are usually attached to recognizable animals, though the number and shape of the horns indicate these are clearly figurative creatures. For example, Daniel saw an animal he couldn't really identify, the fourth image in a terrifying series that included a huge

flying lion, a bear, and a flying leopard. This last animal featured ten horns. When another horn sprouted, three of the previous horns were displaced (Dan. 7). Then he saw a ram in one of his visions that had a huge single horn that broke off and was replaced by four horns, one of which sprouted an additional horn (Dan. 8). The included interpretation of these visions indicated each of these horns represented a king/kingdom that would arise for a time. Daniel had seen a stunning display of the flow of history that would follow his life.

Horns of Power

This use of horns to visualize power also appears in John's visions in Revelation 13 and 17. The beasts pictured there have similarities to Daniel's beasts but also have unique features. The beast representing the Antichrist who rises from the sea combines parts of Daniel's vision (leopard-like general appearance with a bear's

A loud trumpet call will signal Christ's return.

feet and a lion's mouth), but it also has seven heads and ten horns bearing crowns. As the vision unfolds, the beast appears to be a human who wields the power represented by the ten horns, or controls the power associated with the ten kings. Then the first beast is joined by another one, who has "two horns like a lamb" (Rev. 13:11). This one functions as a religious spokesperson for the first beast, using powers given him by the serpent (Satan) to direct worship to the first beast. In Revelation 17:12–14, the horns in John's vision are given prophetic significance: "The ten horns that you saw are ten kings who have not yet started to rule. They will receive authority to rule as kings with the beast for one hour. They have one purpose—to give their power and authority to the beast. They will go to war against the lamb. The lamb will conquer them because he is Lord of Lords and King of Kings. Those who are called, chosen, and faithful are with him." John, recording these sights at the close of the first century, received a God-given glimpse of the closing days of this age. The lamb he mentions is helpfully identified as Lord of lords and King of kings, none other than Jesus Christ himself. In the end, he will be the victor. His is the ultimate horn of power.

Key Verse

Another sign appeared in the sky: a huge fiery red serpent with seven heads, ten horns, and seven crowns on its heads. (Rev. 12:3)

The Antichrist will be a man (2 Thess. 2:4), but at some point in his life, he will be indwelt by a powerful demon from the abyss. This demon-possessed man will be a gifted orator, an intellectual genius, possess great charm and charisma, and have immense leadership power. . . . His "family likeness" to Satan becomes strikingly apparent from John's description of him as having ten horns and seven heads, with ten diadems on his horns. That same grotesque description was applied to Satan in [Revelation] 12:3. . . . "Horns" in Scripture symbolize strength and power, for attack and defense. Here they represent the power of the kings who will rule under Antichrist's authority.

John MacArthur, *Because the Time Is Near: John MacArthur Explains the Book of Revelation* (Chicago: Moody, 2007), 215

Horse

Horses make their appearance in Scripture as early as Genesis 47:17, where they are mentioned among the possessions the Egyptians handed over to Joseph in exchange for food to survive the seven-year famine. An earlier reference to horses may be found in God's words to Job about the wonders of creation that humans cannot duplicate:

> Can you give strength to a horse
>   or dress its neck with a flowing mane?
> Can you make it leap like a locust,
>   when its snorting causes terror?
> It paws in strength and finds joy in its power.
>   It charges into battle.
> It laughs at fear,
>   is afraid of nothing,
>   and doesn't back away from swords.
> A quiver of arrows rattles on it
>   along with the flashing spear and javelin.
> Anxious and excited, the horse eats up the
>   ground
>   and doesn't trust the sound of the ram's
>   horn.
> As often as the horn sounds, the horse says,
>   "Aha!"
>   and it smells the battle far away—
>   the thundering orders of the cap-
>   tains and the battle cries. (Job
>   39:19–25)

Horses are thus a symbol of God's creative power, an example of the beauty and strength of his creatures.

Strength and Human Ingenuity

Mounted warriors occasionally had a role to play, but in biblical warfare, horses were primarily used to draw chariots into battle. Because of that military connection, horses are symbols of might that God says are not to be trusted above him: "Some rely on chariots and others on horses, but we will boast in the name of the LORD our God" (Ps. 20:7). That is why Israelite kings were forbidden to amass an army of horses (Deut. 17:16; 20:1).

The Lord's superiority over all human strength is symbolized by the fact that he will destroy the horses of his enemies (Jer. 50:37; Mic. 5:10; Hag. 2:22; Zech. 10:5; 12:4; 14:15). In his final rule over the earth, warhorses will disappear because there will be no need for them during his eternal reign of peace (Zech. 9:10).

Much like today, horsepower was considered both a luxury of the wealthy and a military necessity. King David gained many horses as a result of his victories in war. King Solomon collected horses and built lavish housing for them (2 Chron. 1:16; 9:24–28), though he was merely projecting military power, since his father had left him a peaceful kingdom. Solomon's stables, no less than his harem, were indications that wisdom alone, without continual fear of the Lord, will not prevent a person from drifting into a life that loses its central purpose.

Apart from Revelation, the only other clear mention of horses in the New Testament is James 3:3 (though Acts 23 records that Paul may well have ridden on horseback to travel from Jerusalem to Caesarea, the first leg of his journey to Rome). James uses the ability to direct a horse by means of a bit and bridle to symbolize the way controlling the tongue of a human being has a way of controlling the rest of the person. The picture is both humorous and truthful.

Role in the Final Judgment

The most famous horses in the Bible are the horses of Revelation. These are all warhorses,

and they signal the final war, the ending of history as we know it on this side of eternity. Four of them appear in John's vision in Revelation 6. Each horse is a different color (white, red, black, and pale), and each one symbolizes a form of judgment and disaster that falls on the earth at the close of history. These horses and their riders are known as the four horsemen of the Apocalypse who "kill people using wars, famines, plagues, and the wild animals on the earth" (Rev. 6:8). But a fifth horse, also white—and followed by a huge herd of white horses—appears in Revelation 19:11–16. This is one of the truly majestic descriptions of Jesus Christ in his glory:

> I saw heaven standing open. There was a white horse, and its rider is named Faithful and True. With integrity he judges and wages war. His eyes are flames of fire. On his head are many crowns. He has a name written on him, but only he knows what it is. He wears clothes dipped in blood, and his name is the Word of God.
>
> The armies of heaven, wearing pure, white linen, follow him on white horses. A sharp sword comes out of his mouth to defeat the nations. He will rule them with an iron scepter and tread the winepress of the fierce anger of God Almighty. On his clothes and his thigh he has a name written: King of kings and Lord of lords.

This horse is a continuation of imagery introduced in the Old Testament where God is a warrior with supernatural horsepower: "You march with your horses into the sea, into the mighty raging waters" (Hab. 3:15).

Key Verse

*Some rely on chariots and others on horses, but we will boast in the name of the L*ORD *our God. (Ps. 20:7)*

In Israel's world, horse and chariot were the supreme weapons of royal military might. . . . From the time David and Solomon introduced professional troops and chariotry, the kings of Israel and Judah were tempted to take the destiny of the nation into their own hands by building up military strength. But Israel's primary tradition of faith remembered that Israel had gained their land without chariots and horses. . . . The psalms reiterate that trust in weapons is a contradiction to faith in the LORD.

James Luther Mays, *Psalms: Interpretation: A Bible Commentary for Preaching and Teaching* (Louisville: Westminster John Knox, 1994), 102

Incense

Incense is a combination of aromatic spices, herbs, and oils that yields its strongest fragrance when warmed or burned. The incense used in the temple was made of stacte, onycha, galbanum, and frankincense; any combination other than this was not to be used for worship, and this combination was not to be used for any other purpose. When the high priest entered the Holy of Holies, he put a handful of incense on the hot coals from the altar. The incense immediately filled the room with a fragrant aroma and shrouded the throne of God on the ark of the covenant with smoke to prevent the priest from looking at the mercy seat. His senses of smell and sight had become part of the worship experience through the lighting of incense. Throughout the Old Testament, incense was a crucial part of the worship of Yahweh, and its importance is underscored by the fact that those who burned it in an unworthy manner were severely punished (2 Chron. 26:16–21).

The Aroma of Prayer

As with most aspects of Old Testament worship, incense was a symbol that pointed to a greater reality. The aroma of incense was a physical picture of the prayers of God's people wafting up to heaven: "Let my prayer be accepted as sweet-smelling incense in your presence. Let the lifting up of my hands in prayer be accepted as an evening sacrifice" (Ps. 141:2). The scent of incense mingled with the smell of burning sacrifices symbolizes the mingling of prayers of repentance and devotion. The book of Revelation portrays the blending of the physical reality of incense with the prayers of God's people as well: "The smoke from the incense went up from the angel's hand to God along with the prayers of God's people" (8:4). The perpetual worship of God in heaven includes incense as a sensory image for the internal reality of lives offered in devotion to God.

Frankincense is the resin from this tree and was one of the royal gifts given to Jesus by the Magi.

The aroma of incense made temple worship a multisensory experience, an image that carried over in the New Testament to Paul's command that believers should live in such a way that they are like a fragrant aroma to the people around them.

The importance of incense in worship and its link to prayer explains why the Israelites' burning incense to idols was so abhorrent: "It is because their people did evil, and they made me angry. They went to burn incense and serve other gods that neither you nor your ancestors heard of" (Jer. 44:3). Those who burned incense to idols were twisting a symbol of true worship and using it to worship false gods.

The Aroma of a Devoted Heart

The apostle Paul uses the image of incense to illustrate a life offered to God. "Wherever we go, God uses us to make clear what it means to know Christ. It's like a fragrance that fills the air. To God we are the aroma of Christ among those who are saved and among those who are dying" (2 Cor. 2:14–15). In the same way incense was used in sacrifices, so Christians are to offer the sweet fragrance of a life given to point others to the victory found in Christ. Some may dislike the aroma of Christ that lingers on us, but others will be drawn to it. Either way, our lives are offered up to God, and those around us cannot mistake that reality.

Key Verse

But I thank God, who always leads us in victory because of Christ. Wherever we go, God uses us to make clear what it means to know Christ. It's like a fragrance that fills the air. To God we are the aroma of Christ among those who are saved and among those who are dying. (2 Cor. 2:14–15)

Paul employs both metaphors (the triumphal procession and the fragrant aroma of sacrificial offering) to clarify the paradoxical nature of his ministry. Although he appears as a defeated and humiliated prisoner to the world, he is in fact exuding the sweet-smelling fragrance of Christ's sacrificial death by the gospel (the knowledge of God) he preaches and the ministry he exercises.

Frank J. Matera, *2 Corinthians: A Commentary*, The New Testament Library (Louisville: Westminster John Knox, 2003), 73–74

Top, the incense used in temple worship was a special blend that was not to be used for any other purpose.

Jar/Pottery/ Vessel

Working in clay is one of the ancient professions. Long before paper, damp clay served as a surface to receive the marks that represented early writing called cuneiform. And people discovered that baked clay contained water and could be used for cooking more efficiently than the tightest woven baskets. When one of our brilliant ancestors discovered the potter's wheel, the age of clay had arrived. Eventually, clay pots became widely used not only in daily life but for such unexpected applications as storage containers for the earliest forms of flexible writing surfaces: papyrus and parchment scrolls were often preserved in clay jars. The now-famous Dead Sea Scrolls were protected and preserved for a couple of millennia in large clay pots in a cave near Qumran on the shore of the Dead Sea.

Paul tells believers that they are like clay pots, common vessels containing the priceless treasure of the gospel.

God the Potter

The possibilities of clay are recorded in the early chapters of Genesis as we see God modeling the original man out of dust (Gen. 2:7). Job tells God, "Please remember that you made me out of clay and that you will return me to dust again" (Job 10:9). Clay is a symbol for the frailty and created nature of humans. Yet as Paul taught, even our fragile lives can be effective for eternity: "Our bodies are made of clay, yet we have the treasure of the Good News in them. This shows that the superior power of this treasure belongs to God and doesn't come from us" (2 Cor. 4:7).

Prophets like Jeremiah found clay pottery to be an effective metaphor in their preaching. "The LORD spoke his word to Jeremiah. He said, 'Go to the potter's house. There I will give you my message'" (Jer. 18:1–2). The lesson the prophet learned in the potter's house hasn't lost its power even today: "I went to the potter's house, and he was working there at his wheel. Whenever a clay pot he was working on was ruined, he would rework it into a new clay pot the way he wanted to make it. The LORD spoke his word to me. The LORD asked, 'Nation of Israel, can't I do with you as this potter does with clay? Nation of Israel, you are like the clay in the potter's hands'" (Jer. 18:3–6).

God the potter presents a powerful picture of his sovereign control over creation. The apostle Paul turned immediately to the rights of the potter when explaining God's ways with the world: "You may ask me, 'Why does

God still find fault with anyone? Who can resist whatever God wants to do?' Who do you think you are to talk back to God like that? Can an object that was made say to its maker, 'Why did you make me like this?' A potter has the right to do whatever he wants with his clay. He can make something for a special occasion or something for everyday use from the same lump of clay" (Rom. 9:19–21). As the Creator, God retains the right to fashion and use us as he sees fit.

Perhaps the greatest instance of understanding an effective use of clay can be found in John 9 and the story of a blind man healed by Jesus. We can't appreciate the symbolic use of mud in the story unless we close our eyes and imagine the heightened sense of hearing someone spit and the soft sounds of kneading as Jesus formed a clay paste in his palm and then smeared it on the man's eyes, saying, "Wash it off in the pool of Siloam" (v. 7). As he washed, the man's sight was restored. We should pause to consider why Jesus chose this particular means of healing. He didn't always use objects in his healing; sometimes he simply touched or spoke and the miracle happened. But why use clay? Because the Creator would be the first to simply use original parts to replace defective ones. Who better than Jesus to know how to use clay to fix a clay pot?

Key Verse

Our bodies are made of clay, yet we have the treasure of the Good News in them. This shows that the superior power of this treasure belongs to God and doesn't come from us. (2 Cor. 4:7)

Paul says that as believers we're clay pots, common earthenware jars meant to hold priceless treasure through the course of our lives. . . . Each of these earthenware jars has been handmade by God himself, our Creator and the master artisan—not stamped out in some mass-production factory in China. So as with all handmade items, we are unique. No two exactly alike. And if our life purpose is to display the treasure we contain within, that display often works best when there are faults and cracks and chips in the pot! It is through these that the radiant, resplendent glory of Jesus shines through to the wondering eyes of the world.

Joni Eareckson Tada,
A Place of Healing: Wrestling with the Mysteries of Suffering, Pain, and God's Sovereignty
(Colorado Springs: David C. Cook, 2010), 70–71

Jonah in the Great Fish

Jonah's story is summed up in one verse: "The LORD sent a big fish to swallow Jonah. Jonah was inside the fish for three days and three nights" (Jon. 1:17). Jonah was an ordinary man, called by God to preach to Nineveh. But he is also a satirical and ridiculous figure, an example of what a prophet should not be. Fearing that the hated Ninevites might repent, Jonah refused God's call and tried to run from God by boarding a ship bound for the opposite direction. So God sent a storm to get him back on course and then sent or commissioned a fish, as a king would appoint an ambassador, to swallow (not chew) Jonah. The fish is not described other than being called "big."

Into the Depths

Jonah had hit bottom. The sea was thought of as the abyss (see SEA OF GALILEE), a place of great fear, great terror, and death. Jonah was in the depths of the sea "inside the fish" (2:1). The belly of the fish pictures Jonah's spiritual condition. Spiritually he was as distant from God as the fish was from dry land. He was as spiritually dirty from rebellion and disobedience to God as he was physically dirty from the vile contents of the fish's stomach.

God brought Jonah down to a desperate place, and Jonah's desperation moved him to prayer. In the belly of the fish, Jonah turned to God because he had nowhere else to turn. "From inside the fish Jonah prayed to the LORD his God. Jonah prayed: 'I called to the LORD in my distress, and he answered

me. From the depths of my watery grave I cried for help, and you heard my cry'" (2:1–2). God is the only one who can help people out of their predicaments.

Jonah in the belly of the fish reminds us that the times when we are down and in the pits, while not pleasant, can be profitable. The belly of the fish is not a happy place to live, but it can be a good place to learn. Jonah had to experience the feeling of death before he could know the freedom of life. In a spiritual sense, people need to give up before they can be raised up, getting to that point where they can do nothing to help themselves. When Jonah gave up hope of surviving and could sink no lower, God intervened and saved him. Jonah had to die before he could live.

Up and Out

After running away from God, being cast into the depths of the sea, then being swallowed by a fish, death was imminent. But God was up to something great. From God's perspective, death and the depths are not a problem. Jonah ended up getting vomited onto the shore. "'Victory belongs to the LORD!' Then the LORD spoke to

The Bible does not tell us what kind of fish swallowed Jonah, only that it was big.

the fish, and it spit Jonah out onto the shore" (2:9–10). The Hebrew word for *spit* is graphic. Jonah was not a tragic figure covered with suffering, nor a heroic figure covered with glory, but a ridiculous figure covered with vomit. In the regurgitation, God reveals that stiff-necked rebellion will be dealt with. God laughs at pride and arrogance. In the end, God always has the final word. He always triumphs.

Parallels with Christ

The parallels between Jonah's story and the life of Christ are striking. Jonah was from a town called Gath-hepher (2 Kings 14:25), a few miles away from Nazareth. Jesus came from Nazareth. Jonah was asleep on a boat in a storm when everybody else on the boat panicked and woke him up, and because of his subsequent actions, the storm was stilled. Jesus fell asleep in a boat and then stilled a storm. Jonah's name translates to "the dove," which expands to mean "was given to a beloved one." Jesus once went down into the water and came up out of the water. Then a dove descended and a voice said, "This is my Son, whom I love" (see Matt. 3:16–17). Toward the end of his life, Jesus spelled out the connection between himself and Jonah in what he called the sign of Jonah: "The people of an evil and unfaithful era look for a miraculous sign. But the only sign they will get is the sign of the prophet Jonah. Just as Jonah was in the belly of a huge fish for

three days and three nights, so the Son of Man will be in the heart of the earth for three days and three nights" (Matt. 12:39–40). Jonah in the belly of the fish and his resulting deliverance are a foretaste of a believer's victory when Jesus meets them at the lowest place, defeating death.

Key Verse

Jonah prayed:

*"I called to the L*ORD *in my distress,*
and he answered me.
From the depths of my watery grave
I cried for help,
and you heard my cry."
(Jon. 2:2)

> For the Hebrews, Sheol was the place of death. The fact that Jonah was in a kind of Sheol for three days and three nights is symbolic of the mercy God has shown to sinners through the resurrection of Jesus Christ. . . . Jonah was the illustration; Jesus is the resurrected reality. . . . Now the same power by which God raised Jesus from the dead—the power of his ever-present grace—is available to everyone who trusts in him for salvation from sin and death.
>
> Philip Graham Ryken, *Discovering God*
> *in Stories from the Bible*
> (Phillipsburg, NJ: P&R, 1999), 50

Jordan River

The Jordan River played an important role in a number of memorable events from both the Old Testament and the New Testament. It is known for being a fertile valley and an important landmark. The first mention of the Jordan occurs in the story of Abram and Lot, where Lot chose for himself "all the plain of Jordan" (Gen. 13:11 KJV). The next time we come upon it, Jacob is wrestling with his adversary at the ford of the Jabbok, one of the major tributaries of the Jordan. Elsewhere the Jordan is crossed and is used as a place of baptism and provision.

A River Boundary

In the Bible, most references to the Jordan treat it as a boundary, with such phrases as "beyond the Jordan," "on this side of the Jordan," "on the other side of the Jordan," and "over Jordan." Because it is most often seen as the eastern boundary of Israel, the Jordan typically symbolizes crossing into or out of the Promised Land. Joshua led the nation of Israel into the Promised Land by crossing the Jordan "on dry ground" (Josh. 3:17). The water miraculously "rose up like a dam," as had the Red Sea at the exodus from Egypt. Both events were signs of God's miraculous power. The Jordan thus became associated in the Hebrew imagination with a glorious entry into the Promised Land.

Because the Israelites made a difficult and hazardous journey from slavery in Egypt to freedom in the Promised Land, the Jordan also refers to freedom. The actual crossing was the final step of the journey from bondage to freedom. It becomes a symbol of victory and deliverance: saying good-bye to slavery and hardship, and entering a new life of promise and hope.

In traditional Christian thought, the final transition from life on earth to life in heaven is symbolized by crossing the Jordan River. Because the Jordan River was the border of the earthly Promised Land, those who through faith in Christ are part of God's chosen people think of a symbolic Jordan River being the boundary of their eternal Promised Land—heaven. The symbolism of crossing the Jordan River does not end with salvation from sin and being born again (John 3:3). In daily life, as Christians face difficulties, experience doubt, and struggle against sin, they cross many "Jordans." The Bible teaches we may walk with confidence through them because God is with us to deliver us just as he was with Joshua.

The Jordan River is the boundary of the Promised Land and a location that features prominently in many Bible stories.

A Place of Provision and Preparation

The Jordan also is symbolic of God's provision. Elijah was miraculously

fed by ravens at the brook Cherith, east of the Jordan (1 Kings 17:2–7). Elijah was transported into heaven shortly after he and Elisha crossed the Jordan River (2 Kings 2:7–12). Naaman, the Syrian king, was healed of leprosy by dipping seven times in the Jordan (2 Kings 5:8–14). John the Baptist began his ministry of preaching at the Jordan, proclaiming the coming of the kingdom of heaven. Later, John baptized Jesus there, marking the beginning of Jesus' earthly ministry (Mark 1:9).

The Jordan River descends to the lowest of all river levels by the time it enters the Dead Sea, so we might expect it to be a symbol of death in the Bible, but it is not. Rather, it is the symbol of life, health, and fulfillment. In many respects it becomes a perfect analogy for the Christian life. For someone to become a Christian he or she must be brought down (to understand the depth of his or her sin), like the Jordan descends. Then the person must pass through (repenting and believing) as the Israelites passed through on dry land when Joshua led them to cross the Jordan (Josh. 3:16). Then they are baptized as John the Baptist was baptizing repentant sinners before he baptized Jesus in the Jordan River (Matt. 3:13; Mark 1:9). Paul wrote, "When we were baptized into his death, we were placed into the tomb with him. As Christ was brought back from death to life by the glorious power of the Father, so we, too, should live a new kind of life" (Rom. 6:4).

Key Verse

Elijah left and did what the word of the Lord had told him. He went to live by the Cherith River, which is east of the Jordan River. (1 Kings 17:5)

Numerous folk songs associate the Jordan River with crossing over from death to life, much like the rivers Styx and Lethe in classical literature. Two notable ones are "Michael, Row Your Boat Ashore" and "Swing Low, Sweet Chariot."

> *Jordan's river is deep and wide*
> *Hallelujah.*
> *Meet my mother on the other side*
> *Hallelujah.*
>
> *Jordan's river is chilly and cold*
> *Hallelujah.*
> *Kills a body but not the soul*
> *Hallelujah.*
>
> *I looked over Jordan, and what did I see*
> *Coming for to carry me home?*
> *A band of angels coming after me,*
> *Coming for to carry me home.*

Top, crossing over the Jordan River is a metaphor for entering heaven, the true Promised Land.

139

Key

Having the key to something denotes power and authority. You have the right to enter in and the right to refuse entry to others. In the ancient world, keys were given to the steward, a servant whom the master of the house trusted to care for the household. The long, large keys of that day were often carried on a person's shoulder.

Keys of the Kingdom

Isaiah capitalized on the symbolism of keys of authority and trustworthiness when he prophesied of a day when the false steward of Jerusalem (Shebna) would be unseated and a true steward (Eliakim) entrusted with the care of the city. He said that Eliakim would replace the corrupt leaders and "I will give him your authority. . . . I will place the key of the house of David around his neck. What he opens no one will shut. What he shuts no one will open" (Isa. 22:21–22). This new leader would be trusted with the responsibility to care for Jerusalem.

In Jesus' day, the experts in the law had also proved themselves unworthy to hold the keys. He said to them, "How horrible it will be for you experts in Moses' Teachings! You have taken away the key that unlocks knowledge. You haven't gained entrance into knowledge yourselves, and you've kept out those who wanted to enter" (Luke 11:52). These men had access to gain knowledge and share it with others—they knew how to read and interpret the law—but they did not fulfill their responsibility, so Jesus took the key away. This is similar to when Jesus said he had blinded those who refused to see. At some point disobedience leads to a hardened heart that is unable to be turned back to God, and in this case Jesus removed their authority, as symbolized by the key.

Jesus not only took the keys away from those who were unworthy; he also gave them to worthy men. After Peter's confession of Christ's identity, Jesus said, "I will give you the keys of the kingdom of heaven. Whatever you imprison, God will imprison. And whatever you set free, God will set free" (Matt. 16:19). Peter had unlocked the knowledge of who Christ was, so he could be trusted with the authority to bind and loose in a spiritual sense. He was given the authority to explain gospel truth to others, thereby opening the kingdom to them. This same authority rests with the church today. We bear a responsibility to unlock the knowledge of the kingdom of heaven for others.

Ultimate Authority

Of course, the true steward of the kingdom of heaven is Christ himself, as we see in Revelation. Jesus is the one who

The keys to unlocking truth are given to true ministers of the gospel, an important charge that they must not take lightly.

holds "the keys of death and hell" (1:18). He is the one entrusted with the authority to give access to heaven or to cast into hell: "The one who is holy, who is true, who has the key of David, who opens a door that no one can shut, and who shuts a door that no one can open, says: I know what you have done. See, I have opened a door in front of you that no one can shut" (3:7–8).

The symbol of the key reminds us of the interworking of human agency with divine authority. We have been given the keys to help others, but the ultimate locking or unlocking of hearts rests with God alone. Any authority we have is given by him, and the final authority is his.

Key Verse

I will give you the keys of the kingdom of heaven. Whatever you imprison, God will imprison. And whatever you set free, God will set free. (Matt. 16:19)

Keys are the ensigns of treasurers, and of stewards, and such the ministers of the Gospel are; they have the rich treasure of the word under their care, put into their earthen vessels to open and lay before others; and they are stewards of the mysteries and manifold grace of God, and of these things they have the keys. So that these words have nothing to do with church power and government in Peter, nor in the pope, nor in any other man, or set of men whatever; nor to be understood of church censures, excommunications, admissions, or exclusions of members: nor indeed are keys of any such similar use; they serve for locking and unlocking doors, and so for keeping out those that are without, and retaining those that are within, but not for the expulsion of any: but here they are used in a figurative sense, for the opening and explaining the truths of the Gospel, for which Peter had excellent gifts and abilities.

John Gill, *Gill's Exposition of the Bible,*
http://www.biblestudytools.com/commentaries
/gills-exposition-of-the-bible/matthew-16-19.html

Top, having a key signifies the authority and the right to enter into a place.

Kingdom

The themes of God's kingship and the establishment of his eternal kingdom run throughout Scripture. God's kingdom is a favorite motif of the psalmists and prophets, and was an especially comforting symbol to the Israelites who struggled under unjust and oppressive kings throughout history. In a general sense God is King over all creation because he made all things: "LORD of Armies, God of Israel, you are enthroned over the angels. You alone are God of all the kingdoms of the world. You made heaven and earth" (2 Kings 19:15). Elsewhere we read, "Greatness, power, splendor, glory, and majesty are yours, LORD, because everything in heaven and on earth is yours. The kingdom is yours, LORD, and you are honored as head of all things" (1 Chron. 29:11). More specifically, God is King over Israel. In fact, that is the reason it was a problem when Israel sought an earthly king: "You told

Jesus came to establish the kingdom of heaven on earth, but the kingdom he established was spiritual—not earthly, as the Jews expected.

me, 'No, a king should rule over us,' though the LORD your God was your king" (1 Sam. 12:12). Earthly kings ruled over Israel as symbols of the true King who would bring his eternal kingdom to earth. After the coming of Christ, God's rule extends to all nations (Rev. 15:3–4) rather than being restricted to Israel alone.

A Kingdom That Defies Expectations

When Jesus came on the scene, it was clear that the Israelites were expecting an earthly, political Messiah to rule over them (Luke 2:25, 38). Jesus made clear that his kingdom is not political. "The Pharisees asked Jesus when the kingdom of God would come. He answered them, 'People can't observe the coming of the kingdom of God. They can't say, "Here it is!" or "There it is!" You see, the kingdom of God is within you'" (Luke 17:20–21). By this he meant that the kingdom was within their grasp, present in the ministry of Christ. Paul echoed this idea when he told the Romans that "God's kingdom does not consist of what a person eats or drinks. Rather, God's kingdom consists of God's approval and peace, as well as the joy that the Holy Spirit gives" (Rom. 14:17). It does not consist of external rules or political power, but of true power that comes from God working within each person.

A Kingdom That Is Near

Jesus' arrival on earth ushered in the beginning of the fulfillment of his kingdom. He declared repeatedly that he fulfilled the law and that the kingdom was near (Matt. 3:2; 4:17; 10:7; Mark 1:15; Luke 10:9). But in one sense it is not completely fulfilled, and the kingdom of heaven is still in some ways symbolic until the second coming of Christ when it reaches its full effect. The imagery Jesus used to describe his coming kingdom is full of violent terms, indicating that conflict between good and evil is ongoing: "the kingdom of heaven has been forcefully advancing, and forceful people have been seizing it" (Matt. 11:12).

The kingdom of God, though near and accessible to all, must be entered into intentionally,

through a conscious and sincere decision. The Beatitudes in Matthew 5 illustrate this beautifully. Those who wish to enter into the kingdom must do so through repentance (Matt. 21:28–32), and those who are part of the kingdom yield the fruit of changed hearts (Matt. 21:43). At the same time, the kingdom of God is said to be inherited (1 Cor. 6:9–10; 15:50; Gal. 5:21). In this way it is a symbol that illustrates the mysterious cooperation between human agency and divine predestination.

Images for the Kingdom

The kingdom of God is represented by various images that illustrate further truths about it. It is a place of festive abundance, a time of feasting rather than fasting (Matt. 22, 25; Mark 2; Luke 14). It is also an exclusive place, one that welcomes some and rejects others (Matt. 18:23–35; 25). Most of all it is a thing of extreme value, compared to a treasure in a field (Matt. 13:44) and a pearl of great worth (Matt. 13:45–46).

The kingdom of God is an image that reminds us of salvation history. It started with the nation of Israel alone and then expanded to include people from every nation. This ongoing revelation of salvation began with the inferior earthly kings who pointed out our need for a Messiah and continued with the unfolding promise of a Messiah. The story entered a new phase with Christ's first coming and sacrificial death and will culminate in the full flowering of the new heaven and new earth at his second coming. Through all of these acts of God, we eagerly await the final day when "the kingdom of the world has become the kingdom of our Lord and of his Messiah, and he will rule as king forever and ever" (Rev. 11:15). What a glorious day that will be, when we can rest in a time of eternal peace under the rule of a holy and loving king.

Key Verse

Turn to God and change the way you think and act, because the kingdom of heaven is near. (Matt. 3:2)

Most biblical scholars agree that the "kingdom of God" means the dynamic rule or reign of God. The reign involves God's intentions, authority, and ruling power. It doesn't refer to a territory or a particular place. Nor is it static. It's dynamic—always becoming, spreading, and growing. . . . The kingdom appears whenever women and men submit their lives to God's will.

Donald Kraybill, *The Upside-Down Kingdom* (Harrisonburg, VA: Herald Press, 2011), 18

Lamb/Sheep

Sheep appear more often than any other animal in the pages of the Bible, mentioned over seven hundred times. They often represent people, and in a special case, one particular person (discussed below). Sheep are gentle and social creatures that function best in a flock, but their individual tendencies lead them to wander. That combination requires an attentive shepherd to guide and tend a large flock.

Because of their usefulness in providing milk, meat, and wool, vast numbers of sheep were part of daily living in Bible times. More importantly, lambs played an important role in sacrifices. Lambs were sacrificed every morning and evening (Exod. 29:38–42), along with lambs presented as personal sacrifices. When Jesus cleared the temple court (John 2:13–17), he was reacting to the way his Father's house had been taken over as a marketplace for sheep and other items used in worship.

The Good Shepherd

Humankind is represented as one large flock when Isaiah writes, "We have all strayed like sheep. Each one of us has turned to go his own way, and the LORD has laid all our sins on him" (53:6). Jesus highlighted just how seriously God takes this description of our condition as sinners when he told the parable of the shepherd with ninety-nine sheep in the fold and one out wandering and lost (Matt. 18:12–14; Luke 15:3–7). God cares for lost sheep, and he is willing to humble himself and identify with the lowest occupation in the ancient world to rescue them. Jesus didn't shy away from the title of Good Shepherd as he indicated what he would do: "I am the good shepherd. The good shepherd gives his life for the sheep" (John 10:11). He is a guide, protector, and leader for his people; yet he is so close to them that he sleeps among them, and they know his voice (John 10:1–18).

One of the best known and most loved passages in the Bible features the confession made by the author speaking as a sheep and declaring, "The LORD is my shepherd" (Ps. 23:1). David applied all the lessons he had learned as a young man about caring for sheep in expressing how he understood God's care for him as a sheep-like creature.

Shepherds of the Church

Our identification as sheep is not limited to our sinfulness but remains a picture of our need for a spiritual shepherd throughout life. False religious leaders are described as bad shepherds. They care more for themselves than their flock (Ezek. 34) and lead them astray (Jer. 10:21; 50:6). By contrast, when Jesus pulled Peter aside for reconciliation and commissioning, he told his disciple three times, "Feed my sheep" (John 21:15–19). Godly leaders who follow the Good Shepherd help their flock stay on the straight and narrow path.

Lamb of God

God surprises us by not only picturing himself as our Shepherd but also by identifying with us in a unique way as the sacrificial Lamb of God. John the Baptist, sent to be the forerunner for Christ, pointed out Jesus to the crowd and announced, "Look! This is the Lamb of God who takes away the sin of the world" (John 1:29). The following day he repeated this description (John 1:36). This was apparently John's personal insight, for the title *Lamb*

of God is used nowhere else in Scripture. The idea of bringing a sacrificial lamb to create atonement for their sins was familiar to John's audience, but God stepping in and offering his *own* Lamb to cover the sin of the world was startling news.

In Revelation, the Lamb *of* God is seen as the Lamb *with* God. The apostle John's vision presents Christ in the form of a lamb, taking certain roles in salvation that no one else can. When John sees a sealed scroll that no one can open, he weeps bitterly (5:1–4). But then he sees

> a lamb standing in the center near the throne. . . . The lamb looked like he had been slaughtered. . . . He took the scroll from the right hand of the one who sits on the throne.
>
> When the lamb had taken the scroll, the four living creatures and the 24 leaders bowed in front of him. Each held a harp and a gold bowl full of incense, the prayers of God's holy people. Then they sang a new song,

> "You deserve to take the scroll and open the seals on it,
>   because you were slaughtered.
>   You bought people with your blood to be God's own.
>   They are from every tribe, language, people, and nation.
> You made them a kingdom and priests for our God. They will rule as kings on the earth." (5:6–10)

The imagery of Christ as the once-for-all sacrificial Lamb continues throughout Revelation. Those who are victorious against Satan even in death are honored in Revelation because of their connection to the Lamb (12:11). The final marriage, banquet, and city that represent life in the new heaven and the new earth will be overseen by "the throne of God and the Lamb" (22:1, 3). From the first sacrificial lamb in Genesis (chap. 21) to the final pages of Revelation, salvation comes through the blood of the lamb.

Key Verse

Like a shepherd he takes care of his flock.
He gathers the lambs in his arms.
He carries them in his arms.
He gently helps the sheep and their lambs.
(Isa. 40:11)

> It is no accident that God has chosen to call us sheep. The behavior of sheep and human beings is similar in many ways. . . . Our mass mind (or mob instincts), our fears and timidity, our stubbornness and stupidity, our perverse habits are all parallels of profound importance. Yet despite these adverse characteristics Christ chooses us, buys us, calls us by name, makes us his own, and delights in caring for us.
>
> Phillip Keller, *The Shepherd Trilogy*
> (Grand Rapids: Zondervan, 1996), 14

Top, the lambs offered as sacrifices were to be without blemish or spot of any kind.

Lamp

In the ancient world lamps were usually made of pottery shaped like a shell with a rim across the top and a spout at one end to hold the wick. The lamps of Christians were decorated with Christian symbols. Olive oil was the most common fuel, and although lamps could hold enough oil to last through the night, housewives had to get up during the night and trim the wick. In Jesus' day, the most common lamp was a wheel shape, and these stayed lit for five hours. The foolish virgins in Jesus' parable didn't plan ahead and bring enough fuel to refill their lamps after the five hours were up (Matt. 25:1–12).

Lamps in Worship

The most frequent images of lamps in the Bible relate to worship. The lamps on the seven-branched lamp stand in the tabernacle were to be constantly lit (Exod. 30:7–8) as a symbol of God's perfection and constant guidance. The enduring light is a metaphor for God's covenant blessing on the Davidic dynasty, his promise to be with them and lead them: "But the LORD, recalling the promise he had made to David, didn't want to destroy David's family. The LORD had told David that he would always give him and his descendants a shining lamp" (2 Chron. 21:7). Of course, the Davidic line eventually culminated in the birth of Christ, and the lamp symbolism continues in him as well. We are told that the coming kingdom needs no lamps because "the glory of God [gives] it light. The lamb [is] its lamp" (Rev. 21:23). The lamp in the temple has been replaced by the true light, Jesus.

Lamps to Guide the Way

Lamps are also symbols of guidance. The guidance of a parent is likened to a lamp (Prov. 6:23), and "a person's soul is the LORD's lamp. It searches his entire innermost being" (Prov. 20:27). God's Word is also compared to a lamp that gives light for the steps ahead (Ps. 119:105). In the ancient world, so few light sources were available that the darkness could be terrifying and dangerous, so people would have resonated with and been comforted by the image of a light to guide their path.

The light we receive from Jesus is meant to be shared with others. John the Baptist was compared to a lamp for the Good News he brought: "John was a lamp that gave off brilliant light. For a time you enjoyed the pleasure of his light" (John 5:35). Jesus called his disciples to be lights in the world. He

Lamps were made out of pottery and burned olive oil.

said, "You are light for the world. A city cannot be hidden when it is located on a hill. No one lights a lamp and puts it under a basket. Instead, everyone who lights a lamp puts it on a lamp stand. Then its light shines on everyone in the house. In the same way let your light shine in front of people. Then they will see the good that you do and praise your Father in heaven" (Matt. 5:14–16). The light of Jesus shining through our lives will show others the way to true life. Just as those who have a lamp have a desire and responsibility to share the light it gives with others, so we have a desire and responsibility to share the light of Christ with those who have not seen it.

The fact that Jesus calls each believer a lamp not only shows how we reflect his light but also symbolizes the movement of the location for worship from the temple into the heart of each believer through the indwelling of the Holy Spirit. The literal lamp of God's presence used to be in the temple; then it was preserved figuratively through David's line. After that, Jesus, the true Light, came to dwell among us. Now that light is present in each believer through the Holy Spirit, and one day we will no longer need lamps because we will be in the presence of the true Light for all eternity. The lamp symbolism has come full circle, mirroring the story of redemption spreading from one people, the Jews, to all nations through Christ.

Key Verse

No one lights a lamp and puts it under a basket. Instead, everyone who lights a lamp puts it on a lamp stand. Then its light shines on everyone in the house. In the same way let your light shine in front of people. Then they will see the good that you do and praise your Father in heaven. (Matt. 5:15–16)

The truth of the gospel is the light, contained indeed in fragile earthenware lamps, yet shining through our very earthenness with the more conspicuous brightness. We are called both to spread the gospel and to frame our manner of life in a way that is worthy of the gospel.

John R. W. Stott, *The Message of the Sermon on the Mount* (Leicester, England: Inter-Varsity, 1978), 67

Top, Christians are to be lights in a dark world, beacons of hope as we share the gospel.

147

Leprosy

The biblical word translated "leprosy" does not refer to what we know today as leprosy—Hansen's disease—but rather to a variety of skin diseases, including psoriasis, leukodermia, and urticaria. Hansen's disease did not even exist in the days when Leviticus, with all its regulations regarding leprosy, was written.

Leprosy at that time was a chronic, infectious skin disease characterized by sores, scabs, and shining white patches, and was incurable apart from supernatural means. These diseases were associated with ritual uncleanness (Lev. 3:3, 8–17; Num. 5:2) and required separation from others. Lepers were forced to live by themselves and had to call out, "Unclean, unclean!" to warn others of their condition (Lev. 13:45–46). Anyone who came in contact with a leper was defiled and ritually unclean. The isolation and uncleanness of leprosy make it a symbol of sin and human vulnerability. At the same time, provision was made right from the beginning not only for diagnosis of leprosy, but also for what to do when a person was healed from leprosy (Lev. 13–14).

Leprosy as Punishment

Some people in the Bible became ill with leprosy as a divine punishment. King Uzziah became proud and burned incense in the temple; as punishment, he suffered with leprosy for the rest of his life (2 Chron. 26:16–21). Miriam spoke out against Moses' authority and then became leprous (Num. 12:1–12). Gehazi was also punished with leprosy when he greedily attempted to secure from Naaman the presents that had already been declined by Elisha (2 Kings 5:27). The punishment in these cases was a tragic outward manifestation of the internal decay of humanity lost in sin.

The Cure for Leprosy

Lepers were thought of as the living dead (Num. 12:12; Job 18:13). When the king of Israel was asked to heal a leper, he responded, "Am I God? Can I kill someone and then bring him back to life?" (2 Kings 5:7). Leprosy, then, was a symbol of being dead in sin. But like the curse of sin, leprosy was curable through the mercy and healing of God. Miriam was healed in Numbers 12. Naaman was healed (2 Kings 5:1–14), and Jesus healed lepers (Mark 1:40–45;

Leprosy was a dreaded skin disease. It is an image of the isolating effects of sin.

Luke 17:11–19). In these instances of healing from leprosy, the cure was a sign that the healer was a prophet. Elisha declared that Naaman would "find out that there is a prophet in Israel" when he healed him (2 Kings 5:8). The only other instance of healing from leprosy is at the hands of the disciples (Matt. 10:8).

Jesus declared that his ability to make clean "those with skin diseases" was a sign that he was the coming one (Luke 7:22). He then shocked his witnesses and later Jewish readers of the Gospels by touching lepers—which would normally bring spiritual and possibly physical defilement—as he healed them. Jesus' healing of the lepers was a sign and symbol of his compassion to touch sinful humanity and his ability to heal us from the curse of sin. He is willing to reach down and identify with us in our worst possible moments of spiritual death and decay and touch us to heal us. The punishment and isolation caused by sin is reversed by the healing touch of Jesus as the unclean leper, the living dead person, is made clean and restored to the community of believers. The physical disease of leprosy, then, is the occasion for a beautiful picture of redemption.

Key Verse

A man with a serious skin disease came and bowed down in front of him. The man said to Jesus, "Sir, if you're willing, you can make me clean."

Jesus reached out, touched him, and said, "I'm willing. So be clean!" Immediately, his skin disease went away, and he was clean. (Matt. 8:2–3)

Concerning the story of Jesus healing the leper recorded in Matthew 8, Dr. Warren Wiersbe writes,

That the leper ran up to Jesus and violated the code is evidence of his great faith that Jesus would heal him. . . . When Jesus touched the leper, he contracted the leper's defilement, *but he also conveyed his health!* Is this not what he did for us on the cross when he was made sin for us (2 Corinthians 5:21)? The leper did not question his *ability* to heal; he only wondered if [Jesus] were willing. Certainly God is willing to save!

Warren W. Wiersbe, *The Wiersbe Bible Commentary* (Colorado Springs: David C. Cook, 2007), 28

Top, although Jesus healed ten lepers, only one returned to thank him.

149

Light

ight was the first thing created and among the first words spoken by God that were written in Scripture: "Let there be light!" (Gen. 1:3). As the first created thing and something necessary for life, light holds primary significance in the Bible. Throughout Scripture, light imagery is consistently used to symbolize life itself, particularly life lived in a way that pleases God. The psalm writer praises God, saying, "You have rescued me from death. You have kept my feet from stumbling so that I could walk in your presence, in the light of life" (Ps. 56:13). When Job curses the day he was born, he depicts the living as those who have light (Job 3).

The Light of Truth

Beyond the physical element, *light* in the Bible stands for spiritual illumination and truth. It encompasses all that is pure, good, and holy, as opposed to the darkness of evil. God's Word is "a lamp for my feet and a light for my path" (Ps. 119:105). It guides us in following his commands throughout our lives. In the New Testament, the theme of God's ways being light is continued: "The Lord has filled you with light. Live as children who have light. Light produces everything that is good, that has God's approval, and that is true" (Eph. 5:8–9). The symbolic light of truth and goodness is contrasted with deeds of darkness, which we are told to get rid of (Rom. 13:12).

Light also characterizes God himself, the source of all truth. In 1 John 1:5, we see that "God is light, and there isn't any darkness in him." In Revelation, God's glory is the light that illuminates heaven (21:23). The nature of God's transcendence is also pictured through light imagery: "He lives in light that no one can come near. No one has seen him, nor can they see him" (1 Tim. 6:16). In this sense light is a symbol for God's holiness and mystery as well as the purity of God himself.

Light also reveals what is hidden. That's why we say things "come to light" when they are discovered. For the psalm writer, light describes God's knowledge of our sins: "You have set our sins in front of you. You have put our secret sins in the light of your presence" (Ps. 90:8). John makes it clear that to draw close to God means that we must "live in the light," a relationship that is shown by demonstrating sincere love to those around us (1 John 2:10). Paul tells us that God shines light on men's hearts: "bring to light what is hidden in the dark and reveal people's motives" (1 Cor. 4:5).

The Light of Blessing

In 2 Samuel, David sings a song connecting light with God's deliverance: "O LORD, you are my lamp. The LORD turns my darkness into light" (22:29). In a world where the dark night was fraught with danger, light was a fitting image for safety. Light

Truth is portrayed in Scripture as light; it brings clarity to a situation just like light shining from above.

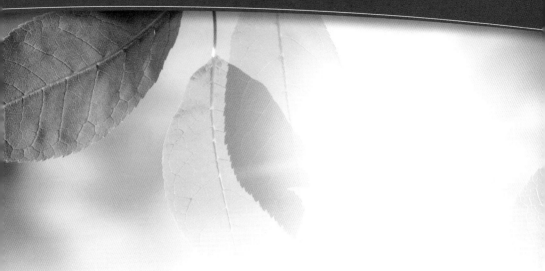

from God is similarly featured in the deliverance of the Israelites from Egypt: "But because of your endless compassion, you didn't abandon them in the desert. The column of smoke didn't leave them during the day, but it led them on their way. The column of fire didn't leave them during the night, but it gave them light to see the way they should go" (Neh. 9:19). Here the physical light of the column of fire is a symbol of God's presence, much as the light of the lamp in the temple later signified God's presence there.

The Light of the World

Speaking to the Pharisees, Jesus alluded to his divinity by declaring, "I am the light of the world. Whoever follows me will have a life filled with light and will never live in the dark" (John 8:12). Isaiah had prophesied centuries before that the Messiah's coming was like light dawning (Isa. 9:2). This symbolism harks back to the light of God's presence in the pillar of fire and the lamp of the temple. Then it was a sign of something to come; with Jesus' arrival on earth the reality was present.

By extension, the light of Christ present in the people's hearts is a symbol for salvation. Those who follow him do not walk in darkness, but in light (John 12:46). Peter describes believers as those who were called "out of darkness into his marvelous light" (1 Pet. 2:9). The powers of Satan are the dominion of darkness, but those who have received salvation are transferred to the kingdom of light (Col. 1:13). Just as bringing light into a dark room changes the atmosphere and enables one to see, so the presence of Christ changes one's heart and illuminates all aspects of life. And Christians are called to be bearers of that light. Jesus said, "You are light for the world" (Matt. 5:14), signifying that we carry his light within us and are responsible to illumine the truth of Christ to others.

Key Verse

You are light for the world. A city cannot be hidden when it is located on a hill. No one lights a lamp and puts it under a basket. . . . In the same way let your light shine in front of people. Then they will see the good that you do and praise your Father in heaven. (Matt. 5:14–16)

> We are to live in such a way that, as men and women look at us, we shall become a problem to them. They will ask, "What is it? Why are these people so different in every way, different in their conduct and behavior, different in their reactions?" . . . And they will be driven to the only real explanation, which is that we are the people of God, . . . we have become reflectors of Christ, reproducers of Christ. He is "the light of the world" so we have become "the light of the world."
>
> D. Martyn Lloyd-Jones, *Studies in the Sermon on the Mount* (Grand Rapids: Eerdmans, 1959), 156

Top, Scripture sometimes uses light as a metaphor for the blessing of God.

151

Lion

During Bible times, the Holy Land was still occupied by lions. These majestic animals, then as now, do not typically prey on humans, though older or disabled lions sometimes see people as easy food to capture. Observable lion behavior lies behind the comparisons that we find in the Scriptures. Their roaring tends to provoke fear (Amos 3:8), so Peter can write, "Keep your mind clear, and be alert. Your opponent the devil is prowling around like a roaring lion as he looks for someone to devour" (1 Pet. 5:8). Lions tend to be fearless, so Proverbs 28:1 uses them as a comparison to righteous living: "A wicked person flees when no one is chasing him, but righteous people are as bold as lions." Courageous behavior is seen as lionlike: "Even the bravest man with a heart like a lion would lose his courage, because all Israel knows that your father is a warrior and the men with him are brave" (2 Sam. 17:10).

Lion Sightings

In the writings of the prophets (Hosea 5:14; Mic. 5:8), lions symbolize the destructive results when God and his people act to dispense judgment. In Daniel's vision of four strange creatures, the first is part lion: "The first animal was like a lion, but it had wings like an eagle. I watched until its wings were plucked off and it was lifted off the ground. It was made to stand on two feet like a human and was given a human mind" (Dan. 7:4). This animal represented one of the kingdoms that would rule the world after Daniel's time.

Lions appear directly in two Bible stories. The first involves Samson (Judg. 14:5–20) and a lion who dared to roar in the strong man's path. Samson killed it and later used the animal as part of a riddle to entertain his wedding guests. Much later, in the best known lion encounter in Scripture, Daniel is lowered into a den of hungry lions in an effort to eliminate his godly influence in Persia (Dan. 6:1–28). Not only did Daniel survive, but those who had conspired to kill him ended up being the substitute meal for the lions and God was given even greater glory in the Medo-Persian Empire.

Lion of Judah

The phrase "Lion of Judah," referring to Jesus Christ, appears once in Scripture. Revelation 5:5 says, "Then one of the leaders said to me, 'Stop crying! The Lion from the tribe of Judah, the Root of

Lions are majestic and powerful animals, so it is fitting that Jesus was called "the Lion of Judah."

David, has won the victory. He can open the scroll and the seven seals on it.'"

This is the ultimate fulfillment of Jacob's blessing/description in Genesis 49:9–10: "Judah, you are a lion cub. You have come back from the kill, my son. He lies down and rests like a lion. He is like a lioness. Who dares to disturb him? A scepter will never depart from Judah nor a ruler's staff from between his feet until Shiloh comes and the people obey him." As noted above, the lion was often a symbol of royal power in the Old Testament (Job 10:16; Ps. 10:9; Prov. 20:2; Ezek. 32:2; Dan. 7:1–4). David was from the lineage of Judah, and his eminence as king gave rise to the messianic hope that God would send a political ruler to finally set Israel as chief among the nations. Jesus' fulfillment of Jacob's prophecy was far greater than settling the immediate turmoil that Israel was experiencing under the Romans, but for the most part those around him could not see it.

The source of this Lion of Judah title is almost an aside in Revelation 5, which focuses on describing the place and ministry of the Lamb who is God and who alone can open the scroll that determines the final chapters of history. Jesus was the Lion who did his work as the Lamb. The reign of Christ at the end of time will fulfill the prophecy about lions and lambs that says, "Calves, young lions, and year-old lambs will be together, and little children will lead them" (Isa. 11:6).

Key Verse

Then one of the leaders said to me, "Stop crying! The Lion from the tribe of Judah, the Root of David, has won the victory. He can open the scroll and the seven seals on it." (Rev. 5:5)

The Lion of Judah inspired C. S. Lewis's famous lion, Aslan, in the Chronicles of Narnia. This interchange from *The Lion, the Witch and the Wardrobe* captures something of what the image of Christ as the Lion of Judah represents.

"Who is Aslan?" asked Susan.

"Aslan?" said Mr. Beaver. "Why, don't you know? He's the King. He's the Lord of the whole wood. . . ."

"Is—is he a man?" asked Lucy.

"Aslan a man!" said Mr. Beaver sternly. "Certainly not. I tell you he is the King of the wood and the son of the great Emperor-Beyond-the-Sea. Don't you know who is the King of Beasts? Aslan is a lion—*the* Lion, the great Lion."

"Ooh!" said Susan, "I'd thought he was a man. Is he—quite safe? I shall feel rather nervous about meeting a lion." . . .

"Safe?" said Mr. Beaver; ". . . Who said anything about safe? 'Course he isn't safe. But he's good. He's the King, I tell you."

C. S. Lewis, *The Lion, the Witch and the Wardrobe* (New York: MacMillan, 1950), 63–64

Top, Satan is portrayed as a prowling lion, seeking someone to devour.

153

Locust

Locust insects (today's grasshopper) were plentiful in Bible times and are an image with which the original hearers would have been familiar. They were ceremonially clean insects (Lev. 11:20–23) and a crucial part of John the Baptist's ascetic wilderness diet (Mark 1:6). Locusts are voracious eaters at all stages of their development (larva, pupa, and adult); thus, a swarm can strip an area bare of all crops. This is what the locusts did the first time we see them swarm in the Bible, sent as a plague from God to judge the Egyptians. Throughout the Bible, locusts are usually used as an image of terror and destruction.

Locusts in Battle

Joel's description of a plague of locusts is indeed terrifying:

> In front of this army a fire burns.
>> Behind it flames are blazing.
>> In front of it the land is like the garden of Eden.
>> Behind it the land is like a barren desert.
>> Nothing escapes it!
> The soldiers look like horses.
> They run like war horses.
> As they leap on mountaintops,
>> they sound like rattling chariots,
>>> like crackling fire burning up straw,
>>>> and like a mighty army prepared for battle.
>>>> (Joel 2:3–5)

Of greater concern to Joel is how the locusts are a sign of God's judgment against Israel. The invasion may be a natural phenomenon, but the locusts are sent as God's army to bring justice to a nation that has turned its back on God.

The physical resemblance of a locust to a horse and the unbroken, thunderous manner in which they strip the land (Job 39:20; Prov. 30:27; Nah. 3:15–17; Rev. 9:9) make them a good metaphor for an advancing army. The apocalyptic vision in Revelation is rife with locust imagery:

> The locusts looked like horses prepared for battle. They seemed to have crowns that looked like gold on their heads. Their faces were like human faces. They had hair like women's hair and teeth like lions' teeth. They had breastplates like iron. The noise from their wings was like the roar of chariots with many horses rushing into battle. They had tails and stingers like scorpions. They had the power to hurt people with their tails for five months. The king who ruled them was the angel from the bottomless pit. In Hebrew he is called Abaddon, and in Greek he is called Apollyon. (Rev. 9:7–11)

Locusts in Judgment

These are not literal, physical descriptions but rather images to show how powerful, swift, fierce, and complete the final judgment will be. The image of human faces describes malicious intent, the lions' teeth portray their destructiveness, and the roar of chariots connotes a loud approaching army. These fearsome enemies will have armor-like

Locust swarms devastate the land, leaving a barren wilderness in their wake.

insect exoskeletons and lethal weapons like scorpion stingers. These depictions of locusts are used to give a concrete picture of a terrifying time of destruction. In an age when human air travel was inconceivable and armies like those of today were unimaginable, locusts offered an image of unspeakable devastation. Today we can read these words as an almost literal description of what the armies and weapons at the final battle of Armageddon might be like.

Key Verse

Then I will repay you for the years
that the mature locusts, the adult locusts,
the grasshoppers, and the young
locusts ate your crops.
(They are the large army that I sent
against you.) (Joel 2:25)

Who can make the all-devouring locust restore his prey? No man, by wisdom or power, can recover what has been utterly destroyed. God alone can do for you what seems impossible. And here is the promise of His Grace—"I will restore to you the years that the locust has eaten." By giving to his repentant people larger harvests than the land could naturally yield, God could give back to them, as it were, all they would have had if the locusts had never come. And God can restore your life which has up to now been blighted and eaten up with the locust and sin, by giving you Divine Grace in the present and in the future. He can yet make it complete and blessed and useful to his praise and glory. It is a great wonder—but Jehovah is a God of wonders and in the kingdom of his Grace miracles are common things.

C. H. Spurgeon, "Truth Stranger than Fiction,"
No. 2081, delivered on Lord's Day Evening, May 30, 1886,
by C. H. Spurgeon at the Metropolitan Tabernacle, Newington,
http://www.spurgeongems.org/vols34-36/chs2081.pdf

Lord's Supper/
Last Supper/Lord's Table
(*See also* PASSOVER; BREAD; WINE; MEAL)

Some events are so rich in significance that they receive multiple names. On the night Jesus was betrayed, he held his last meal, a Passover celebration with his twelve disciples. This was such a key event that all four Gospels include descriptions of the arrangements and the meal itself. During the meal, Jesus presided as the host, and he reinterpreted the elements of the meal as symbols of his impending death as the sacrificial Lamb.

The Last Supper was a Jewish Passover meal. The table held numerous elements that Jesus could have used symbolically for his special role, but he chose two: bread and cup. The bread represents his body and the cup his blood. These two elements highlighted Jesus' upcoming suffering (the bread as his body capable of experiencing pain) and the giving up of his life (the cup as his blood, echoing the Old Testament teaching that "life is in the blood," see Lev. 17:11–14). Jesus could have suffered greatly and not died, or died without suffering greatly, but he did both in his role as bearer of our punishment and substitute for our death.

The Interpretation of New Testament Writers

John's account, written years after the events described, has less to do with the meal and Jesus' inauguration of the ordinance or sacrament of communion, and more to do with all that Jesus said and did during the meal (see John 13–17). John also includes an incident during Jesus' ministry (John 6:48–58) when he looked ahead to his sacrifice and made some statements his hearers found highly offensive: "Those who eat my flesh and drink my blood live in me, and I live in them" (v. 56). They could not imagine what he meant, even though he pointed out that the bread he was offering was more like "the bread that came from heaven" (v. 58), which their ancestors ate in the wilderness. Their ancestors had died in the wilderness after living on God's manna, but "those who eat [my] bread will live forever" (v. 58). The general response on that occasion was to turn away from Jesus because his words were "hard to accept" (v. 60).

A fifth account of the Lord's Table is found in 1 Corinthians 11:23–34, in a section where Paul is dealing with the Corinthians about the way they gathered for meals and some negative behavior that was developing into the opposite of communion. Paul makes clear that the communion meal, often called the *Eucharist* from the Greek word for "thanks," is about our fellowship with Christ. When we partake of the Lord's Supper, we are participating in the benefits of

The Lord's Supper, also called *communion* or the *Eucharist*, is a remembrance of our deliverance from sin.

Christ's death, symbolized by the cup that represents his blood and the bread that represents his broken body. Thus, the symbols of Passover that Christ reinterpreted as referring to himself now unite us with him. We remember his death for us, in our place (Luke 22:19). This idea is communicated in 1 Corinthians 10:16: "When we bless the cup of blessing aren't we sharing in the blood of Christ? When we break the bread aren't we sharing in the body of Christ?"

The two direct commands of Jesus (to celebrate the Supper and to practice baptism) have been considered normative for most Christians throughout history. These are the symbols that God chose to give us as the most important marks and celebrations that help us understand and participate in all he has done for us. Some groups have added other sacraments, but these two remain the central responses of obedience agreed upon by believers in Jesus.

A Sacrament of Remembrance

The Lord's Supper was instituted as a remembrance. Jesus said, "Do this to remember me" (Luke 22:19). Just as those who celebrated the Passover did so as a remembrance of their deliverance from the bondage of Egypt, so believers remember in the Lord's Supper our deliverance from sin. We partake of the meal with hearts thankful for all Christ has done for us.

We also take time to look ahead, to test ourselves (1 Cor. 11:28–29), and to renew our commitment to follow Christ "until he comes" (1 Cor. 11:26). An interesting note is that communion has always been celebrated with the living Christ. The only time since that first Lord's Supper that we are fairly certain had no celebrations of the meal was during the three days that Jesus was actually dead. The disciples were in hiding, and they did not seem to have understood the significance of Jesus' actions until he had risen from the grave. Every time we share communion we remember Christ's death until he comes back to gather his own for an eternal banquet with him.

Key Verse

On the night he was betrayed, the Lord Jesus took bread and spoke a prayer of thanksgiving. He broke the bread and said, "This is my body, which is given for you. Do this to remember me." When supper was over, he did the same with the cup. He said, "This cup is the new promise made with my blood. Every time you drink from it, do it to remember me." (1 Cor. 11:23–25)

> The Lord's Supper is an act of worship whereby the community of faith gathered in the name of Jesus participates in a symbolic meal in which we encounter Christ afresh. It is an experience in which we find spiritual nourishment. Thus, it is with good reason that the evangelical Protestant tradition calls it a "supper." It is a liturgical and spiritual meal.
>
> Gordon T. Smith, *A Holy Meal: The Lord's Supper in the Life of the Church* (Grand Rapids: Baker Academic, 2005), 83

Top, Jesus instituted a new covenant in his blood at the Last Supper, a symbolic meal to replace the Passover with a celebration of his death and resurrection.

Mark/Seal

In Bible times, a *seal* was a personal symbol that could be transferred to soft clay or wax, which was connected to an object or scroll that couldn't be opened by anyone not authorized to break the seal. A seal left a mark similar to what is left by a rubber stamp on paper or an indentation in soft clay or wax. Long before people were signing their names to documents, they were authenticating them with personal seals.

A Sign of Authority

Seals are significant details in many Bible stories because they symbolize the authority of the person using them. When Joseph moved from the prison to the palace in Egypt, he was given the king's signet ring, which allowed him to seal orders and wield the authority of the king (Gen. 41:41–45). Jezebel used the signet ring of her husband, King Ahab, to seal the fate of poor Naboth in an evil exercise of power (1 Kings 21:8–13). Daniel's trip to the lions' den was sealed by the king's orders—as was the den itself with Daniel inside (Dan. 6). Presumably the amazing declaration of praise to Daniel's God issued by Darius after Daniel survived the lions was also sealed with the king's ring. Esther and Mordecai faced a difficult dilemma after they unmasked Haman's scheme because the plot to murder all the Jews had already been set in motion under the king's seal (Esther 8:8).

In a vain effort to prevent the resurrection of Jesus, the Jewish leaders asked Pilate to place his seal on the tomb and guard it with soldiers (Matt. 27:62–66). The seal of Rome didn't keep Jesus in the tomb or prevent the angels from rolling aside the stone to show the space was no longer occupied (Matt. 28:1–10; Mark 16:1–8; Luke 24:1–7; John 20:1–10).

Sealed by God

As a symbol of power, authority, and ownership, seals are used symbolically in several places in the Old Testament. God asks Job to consider the exalted nature of his own power: "Have you ever given orders to the morning or assigned a place for the dawn so that it could grab the earth by its edges and shake wicked people out of it? The earth changes like clay stamped by a seal, and parts of it stand out like folds in clothing" (Job 38:12–14). What a vivid picture of God shaping the world as easily as a signet ring impresses its image in soft clay! This intimate connection between seal and owner is applied to the relationship between Jesus and his Father: "After all, the Father has placed his seal of approval on him" (John 6:27). This is extended to us by Paul in explaining the role of the Holy Spirit: "You heard and believed the message of truth, the Good News that he has saved you. In him you were sealed with the Holy Spirit whom he promised" (Eph. 1:13; see also 2 Cor. 1:22). When God looks at us he sees the mark or seal of the Holy Spirit on our lives once we have placed our faith in Christ.

Seals at the End of Time

In John's vision in Revelation 5, he sees a scroll that has been sealed with seven seals. Only the Lamb of God is able to break those seals because he has established his right by shedding his blood for people from "every tribe, language, people, and nation" (v. 9). The seven seals symbolize God's ultimate authority over history, controlling the timing and details of the final events. In Revelation 7, individual people are "sealed" by God and set apart. Presumably

this also applies to the "large crowd from every nation, tribe, people, and language" (v. 9) who gather before the throne of the Lamb. Verses 13–17 remind us that being sealed by God does not mean protection from suffering in this life, but the anticipation of an eternity with God where the Lamb "will wipe every tear from their eyes" (v. 17).

John also reports that the forces of evil in the closing days of history have their own form of seal to apply to people: "The second beast forces all people—important and unimportant people, rich and poor people, free people and slaves—to be branded on their right hands or on their foreheads. It does this so that no one may buy or sell unless he has the brand, which is the beast's name or the number of its name" (Rev. 13:16–17). This "seal" may seem to give temporary preferential treatment to people here on earth, but their future is unfortunately tied to the fate of the beast with whom they will spend eternity in hell.

Key Verse

You heard and believed the message of truth, the Good News that he has saved you. In him you were sealed with the Holy Spirit whom he promised. (Eph. 1:13)

What did Paul mean in Ephesians 1:13 when he said that believers are sealed with the Holy Spirit? . . .

1. If the Spirit seals shut, the point must be that he seals in faith and seals out unbelief and apostasy.
2. If the Spirit seals us as a sign of authenticity, then he is that sign and it is the Spirit's work in our life which is God's trademark. Our eternal sonship is real and authentic if we have the Spirit. He is the sign of divine reality in our lives.
3. Or if the Spirit marks us with God's seal, he protects us from evil forces which won't dare to enter a person bearing the mark of God's own possession.

However you come at this message contained in this word "sealed," it is a message of safety and security in God's love and power. God sends the Holy Spirit as a preserving seal to lock in our faith, as an authenticating seal to validate our sonship, and as a protecting seal to keep out destructive forces. The point is that God wants us to feel secure and safe in his love and power.

John Piper, "Sealed by the Spirit to the Day of Redemption," sermon preached May 6, 1984, http://www.desiringgod.org/resource-library/sermons /sealed-by-the-spirit-to-the-day-of-redemption

Top, seals were used to close the tomb where Jesus was buried.

Marriage

Marriage and the related symbols of *bride* and *bridegroom* play as large a role in Scripture as they did in real life in the ancient world. Whether we consider the Old Testament picture of Israel as the bride and God as her bridegroom (Isa. 62:4–5; Jer. 2:2) or the New Testament picture of the church as the bride and Jesus as the bridegroom (2 Cor. 11:2; Eph. 5:21–32; Rev. 21:2, 9), the message points to a special relationship God longs to have with his people. (See also BRIDE, BRIDEGROOM.)

The Image of God

Genesis 1:27 explains that God not only "created humans in his image" but also created them "male and female." The human image of God involves male and female in unique relationship. Then God summarized the practical purpose of that relationship: "God blessed them and said, 'Be fertile, increase in number, fill the earth, and be its master. Rule the fish in the sea, the birds in the sky, and all the animals that crawl on the earth'" (Gen. 1:28). But more significantly for the symbol of marriage, God conducted the first wedding ceremony and described the significance of what he had created:

> Then the LORD God said, "It is not good for the man to be alone. I will make a helper who is right for him."
> So the LORD God caused him to fall into a deep sleep. While the man was sleeping, the LORD God took out one of the man's ribs and closed up the flesh at that place. Then the LORD God formed a woman from the rib that he had taken from the man. He brought her to the man.
> The man said,

> "This is now bone of my bones and flesh of my flesh.
> She will be named woman
> because she was taken from man."

> That is why a man will leave his father and mother and will be united with his wife, and they will become one flesh. The man and his wife were both naked, but they weren't ashamed of it. (Gen. 2:18, 21–25)

The relationship between a man and a woman was blessed by God and is intended not only to multiply and preserve the race but also to create a living symbol of the relationship that is possible and desirable between God and people.

Interestingly, God's description of marriage in Genesis 2:24 is not repeated again in Scripture until Jesus uses it several times in his teaching about marriage. Then Paul quotes it when he presents the beautiful working relationship between husband and wife (Eph. 5:21–32) as the ultimate example of the way God has intended us to see our corporate relationship with him: "We are parts of his [Christ's] body. That's why a man will leave his father and mother and be united with his wife, and the two will be one. This is a great mystery. (I'm talking about Christ's relationship to the church)" (Eph. 5:30–32).

A Picture of God's Faithfulness

In both the Old and New Testaments, unfaithfulness in marriage is used as a picture of people rejecting God and all he offers. The heartbreaking account of Hosea and his efforts to preserve his marriage with Gomer reflect the grief God expresses over the people for whom he had done so much for so long and who persistently rejected his love: "When the LORD first spoke

to Hosea, the LORD told him, 'Marry a prostitute and have children with that prostitute. The people in this land have acted like prostitutes and abandoned the LORD'" (Hosea 1:2). Although Gomer had prostituted herself into slavery, Hosea redeemed her and continued to treat her as his wife. When Jesus on at least three different occasions said, "The people of an evil and unfaithful era look for a miraculous sign" (Matt. 12:39; see also 16:4; Mark 8:38), the word he used for *unfaithful* means "adulterous." This is an indelible lesson about the lengths to which God will go to keep his promises.

Jesus also made clear that the marriage he had in mind was a future event. What God desires to have with his people he will eventually get. In Jesus' parable of the wedding feast (Matt. 22:1–14), he says, "The kingdom of heaven is like a king who planned a wedding for his son" (v. 2). Here the theme of rejection focuses on those who have been invited to the wedding but ignore the invitation. The bride isn't mentioned in this parable, setting up the possibility that those who treat the invitation with disdain do not realize that they are not simply expected to attend as observers but have actually been offered a place as part of the bride. This picture of the ceremony of marriage finally comes to full completion in Revelation 21:2 when John sees a city and a people ready to marry and live with a husband: "Then I saw the holy city, New Jerusalem, coming down from God out of heaven, dressed like a bride ready for her husband."

In marriage, the first human relationship, we find the ultimate sign of God's purpose in creating us; that we might live with him forever in the holy bonds of matrimony! "I heard a loud voice from the throne say, 'God lives with humans! God will make his home with them, and they will be his people. God himself will be with them and be their God'" (Rev. 21:3).

Key Verse

As a bridegroom rejoices over his bride,
so your God will rejoice over you. (Isa. 62:5)

> The reason God became flesh was so that we might know him; correspondingly, God did not create marriage just to give us a pleasant means of repopulating the world and providing a steady societal institution for the benefit of humanity. He planted marriage among humans as yet another signpost pointing to his eternal, spiritual existence.
>
> Gary Thomas, *Sacred Marriage*
> (Grand Rapids: Zondervan, 2000), 29–30

Top, the faithfulness of God is reflected in the book of Hosea as a husband who continually seeks after his wayward and unfaithful wife.

Meal

Convenience, fast food, and the loss of the family table have put us in a poor place to understand the importance of meals throughout the Bible. Meals were never eat-on-the-run, with the rare exception of the original Passover, during which the people ate with their bags packed, ready for God's power to release them from slavery in Egypt (Exod. 12:6–11). Meals among Bible cultures were significant social events. In addition to the feasts and other special meals, eating together was a part of the fabric of daily living. The importance of hospitality was also highlighted by guests at the table. When Abraham welcomed three strangers into his home, he was only behaving as a responsible man of honor (Gen. 18:1–8). God himself indicated the spiritual significance of meals by designating them as one of the times in family life when conversations about the law of the Lord should take place (Deut. 6:4–9). The writer of Hebrews extended this idea in his letter to the early Christian church: "Continue to love each other. Don't forget to show hospitality to believers you don't know. By doing this some believers have shown hospitality to angels without being aware of it" (Heb. 13:1–2).

Fellowship

One of the interesting constants in the life of Jesus and his disciples was their meals together. As is still the custom in many places in the world, daily sustenance consisted primarily of a midday and evening meal. We can estimate that in their three years together, the disciples shared over two thousand meals with Jesus. Some of them, like the Last Supper, were historic, but many of them seem to have been significant sharing times. Certain patterns are apparent: Jesus often began the meal by thanking his Father, symbolically inviting his presence at the meal. Then he broke the bread, an expression that has come to mean sharing a meal. The two disciples who walked with Jesus from Jerusalem to Emmaus on Resurrection Sunday (Luke 24:13–35) may not have recognized him visually, but once they sat down to a meal, Jesus revealed himself to them with his familiar actions. The long established habit of praying over a meal has its roots in Jesus' consistent pattern.

Although a physical table was not always present, the ministry of Jesus, beginning with the wedding in Cana and ending with the breakfast on the beach in Galilee, was often advanced during meals. In the early years of the church, meals alongside the celebration of the Lord's Supper were a significant part of practical fellowship, providing food for the less fortunate among those who were equal in Christ. Paul included warnings about the danger of losing the benefits of meals together by forgetting that they were part of the shared life of the body of Christ (1 Cor. 11:17–22).

A rediscovery of hospitality and renewal of the table as a central part of family life would certainly make an impact on today's society, where many families seldom have a meal together. God has designed the family as the most effective context for learning. What happens during meals matters when the topics include all that God has to say to us. "Repeat them to your children. Talk about them when you're at home or away, when you lie down or get up" (Deut. 6:7).

The Eschatological Meal

Meals were symbols of God's abundant provision, and none more so than the prophesied

marriage supper of the Lamb. This meal was first prophesied by Isaiah: "On this mountain the LORD of Armies will prepare for all people a feast with the best foods, a banquet with aged wines, with the best foods and the finest wines" (25:6). John also saw it in his revelation of heaven: "Let us rejoice, be happy, and give him glory because it's time for the marriage of the lamb" (Rev. 19:7).

When someone mentioned to Jesus the banquet in the kingdom of God, Jesus used it as an opportunity to tell a parable (Luke 14). Those who were first invited to a wedding banquet were too busy to attend, so the poor and lame were invited in their place. The banquet, with its abundance and joy that is only available to those who have received an invitation, is a fitting symbol for the kingdom of God. The meals we enjoy on earth, especially the covenant meals enjoyed by the Jews in the Old Testament and the breaking of bread with other believers that we see in the New Testament, are a foretaste of

the joyous fellowship we will enjoy with God in heaven.

Key Verse

Then the angel said to me, "Write this: 'Blessed are those who are invited to the lamb's wedding banquet.'" (Rev. 19:9)

Joyful eating recognizes God as Creator of heaven and earth and of you and me. God has made food for our bodies, and our bodies for food, including all the sensations and associations that make eating pleasurable and satisfying. We should revel in—not be ashamed of!—our enjoyment of the simple pleasures of smelling, tasting and chewing. When we are fed, it is God who feeds us.

Rachel Marie Stone, *Eat with Joy: Redeeming God's Gift of Food* (Downers Grove, IL: InterVarsity, 2013), 37

Top, Jesus shared many meals with his disciples, even after his resurrection.

163

Mirror

Mirrors in the ancient world consisted of flat metal discs (made of bronze, copper, or silver) that were polished to be as reflective as possible (Exod. 38:8; Job 37:18). Mirrors are used symbolically in three New Testament passages.

Blurred Mirrors

First Corinthians 13:12 uses the image of a mirror to contrast earthly and heavenly knowledge: "Now we see a blurred image in a mirror. Then we will see very clearly. Now my knowledge is incomplete. Then I will have complete knowledge as God has complete knowledge of me." Mirrors in the ancient world yielded only cloudy, blurred images, so Paul used a mirror as a metaphor for the fact that we do not understand spiritual things as well now as we will in heaven. In addition, a mirror only reflects an object indirectly, in much the same way that spiritual truths need interpretation to become clear to us. We know God in part now, but one day we will see him face-to-face and know him fully.

James compares a person who hears the Word of God but does not obey it to a person who looks at himself or herself in a mirror and then forgets what he or she looks like, or ignores the implications of the image in the mirror and does nothing to improve his or her appearance (James 1:23–25). The law reflects back to us who we are—sinners in need of salvation. But if we ignore the mirror-like purpose of the law, it does us no good. We have wasted our time, just as if we had looked in a mirror and then not remembered what we saw there. If our Bible reading makes no change in our attitudes and behavior, the problem lies not with the Word of God, but with the inattentive reader.

Reflecting God's Glory

Just as mirrors are made to reflect back the most accurate image possible, so we as God's creatures should strive to reflect back the glory of the Creator in whose image we are made. Second Corinthians 3:18 says, "As all of us reflect the Lord's glory with faces that are not covered with veils, we are being changed into his image with ever-increasing glory. This comes from the Lord, who is the Spirit." (The Greek term translated *reflect* means "to look at in a mirror.") Paul contrasts Moses' donning a veil to shade the glory of God after receiving the

Blurry reflections are an image for our incomplete or skewed view of spiritual truth.

law (Exod. 34:33) with the unveiled heart and mind of a Christian after salvation. Jesus liberates believers so that they can reflect the glory of God as in a mirror. We shine his glory back so others can see more of him, in effect multiplying his greatness. Those who look at us should see Jesus reflected back.

Key Verse

As all of us reflect the Lord's glory with faces that are not covered with veils, we are being changed into his image with ever-increasing glory. This comes from the Lord, who is the Spirit. (2 Cor. 3:18)

In *The Weight of Glory*, C. S. Lewis discusses the privilege and responsibility believers have to reflect God's glory.

The load, or weight, or burden of my neighbour's glory should be laid on my back. . . . It is a serious thing to live in a society of possible gods and goddesses, to remember that the dullest and most uninteresting person you can talk to may one day be a creature which, if you saw it now, you would be strongly tempted to worship, or else a horror and a corruption such as you now meet, if at all, only in a nightmare. All day long we are, in some degree, helping each other to one or the other of these destinations. It is in the light of these overwhelming possibilities, it is with the awe and the circumspection proper to them, that we should conduct all our dealings with one another, all friendships, all loves, all play, all politics. There are no *ordinary* people. You have never talked to a mere mortal. Nations, cultures, arts, civilisations—these are mortal, and their life is to ours as the life of a gnat. But it is immortals whom we joke with, work with, marry, snub, and exploit—immortal horrors or everlasting splendors.

C. S. Lewis, *The Weight of Glory* (repr.; New York: HarperCollins, 2001), 45–46

Mountain/Hill

Although most Westerners would think of mountains and hills as very different from one another, in the biblical landscape the two terms were used almost interchangeably. We often see mountains and hills used in parallel to illustrate the same idea. For instance, in Psalm 114 we read, "The mountains jumped like rams. The hills jumped like lambs" (v. 4). The two terms are not contrasted, but rather represent the same idea.

Mountains are often used as images of wilderness and extreme conditions. They are usually barren and unpopulated areas and are used in the Bible for refuge or hiding. Lot fled to the hills with his daughters after the destruction of Sodom and Gomorrah (Gen. 19:30). David ran to the hills to escape from Saul (1 Sam. 26:1). Armies ran to the hills when they were defeated (1 Sam. 14:22). During the exile, the Israelites were described as lost people who "wander around on the mountains. They go from mountains to hills. They have forgotten their resting place" (Jer. 50:6).

Mountaintop Experiences

More positively, mountains are used for covenant making and renewal. The visible presence of a mountain served as a reminder of commitments made (Exod. 19–20; Deut. 27–28). Many notable events of the Old Testament occurred on or near mountains, including the Garden of Eden (Ezek. 28:13–15), Abraham's sacrifice of Isaac (Gen. 22:1–14), Moses and the burning bush (Exod. 3:1–2), and Moses meeting with God (Exod. 19). In these cases the mountain was symbolic of a transcendent encounter with God ("the mountain of God"). Individuals ascended physically to meet with God spiritually.

Unfortunately, the mountains often became places of pagan worship as well. The Israelites were told to "completely destroy all the worship sites on the high mountains, on the hills, and under every large tree. The people you're forcing out worship their gods in these places" (Deut. 12:2). This is a common Old Testament theme.

Jesus looked to the mountains as places of transcendent spiritual experience when he went up on a mountain to be with God. The rugged beauty and solitude of these high places enabled him to commune with his Father (Matt. 14:23; John 6:15). The transfiguration, one of the most striking spiritual encounters the disciples had, occurred on a mountain (Matt. 17:1–8; Luke 9:28–36).

Mountains also serve as an image of mystery and divine power. Quaking mountains instill fear and point back to the God who controls nature (Ps. 46:2; Isa. 64:3). The psalm writers praise God for being "more majestic than the ancient mountains" (76:4) and having "righteousness . . . like the mountains of God" (36:6). God's eternal power is measured against the seemingly eternal nature of mountains: "Before the mountains were born, before you gave birth to the earth and the world, you were God" (Ps. 90:2). The wild, ancient beauty of mountains evokes expressions of awe and wonder at their Creator.

The Mountain of God

The most important scriptural mountain is the *mountain of God*: first near Eden (Ezek. 28:14); then Mount Horeb (Exod. 3:1), which was later called Mount Sinai (Exod. 19); and finally Mount Zion (Isa. 24:23), where the temple stood in Jerusalem. These places carried with them a sense of transcendence, but added to that are images of holiness (Exod. 19:23; Isa. 11:9) and authority (Ps. 43:3; Isa. 24:23). As people

looked up to the mountains, visible for miles around, they were reminded of God's presence among them and above them.

The mountain of God that is to come will, like Mount Sinai, be the birthplace of God's law (Isa. 2:1–5; see also Exod. 19–20) and will be covered by cloud and fire (Isa. 4:5; see also Exod. 19). But unlike Sinai, which was primarily a place of fearsome judgment, Zion will be a place where people are welcomed and nurtured (Isa. 2; see also Exod. 19). It will be a place of holy celebration rather than condemnation. The people of God will be planted on God's mountain (Exod. 15:17), transforming it from a place of wild barrenness to a place of cultivated fruitfulness. The mountain of judgment and mystery is transformed into the prominent symbol of redemption and communion with God.

Key Verse

When Jesus saw the crowds, he went up a mountain and sat down. His disciples came to him. (Matt. 5:1)

> Before he went to the masses, he went to the mountains. Before the disciples encountered the crowds, they encountered the Christ. And before they faced the people, they were reminded of the sacred. . . . Take a trip with the King to the mountain peak. It's pristine, uncrowded, and on top of the world. Stubborn joy begins by breathing deep up there before you go crazy down here.
>
> Max Lucado, *The Applause of Heaven* (Nashville: Word, 1999), 20–21, 24

Top, in Scripture, mountains are places of covenant making and renewal.

167

Mount Moriah

ount Moriah was the location of two events in the Old Testament. First, it was the mountain on which God commanded Abraham to sacrifice his son Isaac as a burnt offering (Gen. 22). From Abraham's home in Beersheba to Mount Moriah was a three-day journey, and Abraham took the journey with Isaac and two servants in obedience to God's shocking command to kill his own son. Isaac was the child God had promised to Abraham as part of his covenant promise, the child for whom Abraham had waited so many years. This sacrifice was no small thing for Abraham, but he was trusting that God would fulfill his promises even when all human hope was lost. He even expressed the belief that perhaps God would raise Isaac from the dead, even though no similar event had ever taken place. Hebrews 11:19 explains, "Abraham believed that God could bring Isaac back from the dead. Abraham did receive Isaac back from the dead in a figurative sense."

A Place of Faith

Abraham got as far as tying up Isaac, placing him on the altar, and raising his arm to kill his only son before an angel stopped him and God said, "Do not lay a hand on the boy. . . . Do not do anything to him. Now I know that you fear God, because you did not refuse to give me your son, your only son" (Gen. 22:12). God then provided a ram to be the sacrifice, and "Abraham named that place The LORD Will Provide. It is still said today, 'On the mountain of the LORD it will be provided'" (Gen. 22:14). The Hebrew word *ra'ah* means "to see, provide,

or appear," and the ending *-iah* is a shortened form of the name of the Lord (also *yah*). God had seen Abraham's obedience and his need, and he provided the sacrifice himself. He also renewed and expanded his covenant promise to Abraham on the mountain.

A Place of Worship

Mount Moriah later became the location of Solomon's temple. The site had been the threshing floor of Ornan the Jebusite (1 Chron. 21; named Araunah the Jebusite in 2 Sam. 24:18). God appeared to David on the mountain, and then David purchased the threshing floor from Ornan and built an altar there. His son Solomon later built the temple on the site. Most scholars place this at the same location as Abraham's sacrifice, while others think they are two different places. The link between the temple and Abraham's sacrifice makes the location of the temple all the more significant because it was the place where God provided the sacrifice,

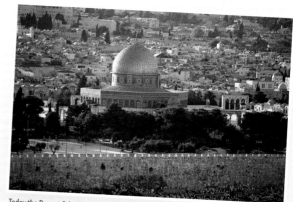

Today the Dome of the Rock marks the place where the second temple stood.

just as he would later do through Christ. The temple's location foreshadowed the ultimate, once-for-all sacrifice that God would provide.

Mount Moriah was the place where God met his people. First he met Abraham there, and later he met David there—both fathers of the Jewish faith. For this reason, the mountain became a symbol for the relationship between God and his people. God asked his people for complete obedience, and in return he provided for their salvation and made a way for them to be in relationship with him. On the mountain, God saw his people and met their needs abundantly through his sacrifice and covenant promises.

Key Verse

Abraham named that place The Lord Will Provide. It is still said today, "On the mountain of the Lord it will be provided." (Gen. 22:14)

How fitting it is, then, that the first time we see God as our Jehovah-jireh [the Lord our Provider] we see a father offering his only son on Mount Moriah. Love, worship, and obedience become three in one! Besides being the place where Abraham offered Isaac, Mount Moriah was significant too because "Solomon began to build the house of the Lord in Jerusalem on Mount Moriah, where the Lord had appeared to his father David, at the place that David had prepared, on the threshing floor of Ornan the Jebusite" (2 Chronicles 3:1). So on Mount Moriah every temple sacrifice for sin would echo Abraham's words, "The Lord Will Provide [Jehovah-jireh], as it is said to this day, 'In the mount of the Lord it will be provided'" (Genesis 22:14). Every lamb, every goat, every sacrifice would point to the one ultimate sacrifice.

Kay Arthur, *Lord, I Want to Know You*
(Colorado Springs: Waterbrook Press, 2000), 66

Top, Abraham was willing to offer his son Isaac as a sacrifice on Mount Moriah, proving his faith in God.

169

Mount Sinai

We sometimes think of the Old Testament as a book in which God makes repeated appearances of many kinds. But when we put a time line next to the account, we quickly realize that God's manifest presence was far more rare and purposeful than we realized. The last time God made a direct appearance in Genesis he visited Jacob in a dream (46:1–7) and assured him his family would become "a great nation" while in Egypt (v. 3). Over four hundred years would pass before God would make another recorded appearance.

Burning Bush

Moses was an energetic eighty-year-old tending sheep in the desert when God showed up at "Horeb, the mountain of God" (Exod. 3:1). Most scholars believe that Horeb and Sinai are two names for the same place. God made this his mountain. There God spoke from a burning bush and instructed Moses to retrieve his people from Egypt and bring them back to that very location. Moses wasn't sure he was up to the task. He had already botched his chance at

leading and helping his people by becoming a wanted killer. So he told God, "Who am I that I should go to Pharaoh and bring the people of Israel out of Egypt?" (v. 11), to which God answered, "I will be with you. And this will be the proof that I sent you: When you bring the people out of Egypt, all of you will worship God on this mountain" (v. 12).

Ten Commandments

Moses did return to Mount Sinai followed by the nation of Israel. He climbed up the mountain twice to hear from God (Exod. 19–20; 24). Regarding the second ascent, Exodus 24:16–18 states: "The glory of the LORD settled on Mount Sinai. For six days the cloud covered it, and on the seventh day the LORD called to Moses from inside the cloud. To the Israelites, the glory of the LORD looked like a raging fire on top of the mountain. Moses entered the cloud as he went up the mountain. He stayed on the mountain 40 days and 40 nights" (Exod. 24:16–18). During this time on the mountain, Moses received two tablets on which God inscribed the words of the Ten Commandments.

Mount Sinai symbolizes our link to God. Like a personal moment of deep meaning and life-changing intensity, Sinai may be described as the cosmic event in which we feel an internal avalanche that shakes the foundations of our being and our view of the world. It also may be a moment of stunning calm and composure in which we feel that we see the world with new clarity. Perhaps this is why Jewish tradition describes the moment of Sinai in such contradictory

Moses received the Ten Commandments during the forty days he spent with God in the cloud of God's glory on Mt. Sinai.

terms—it is both the storm and the stillness at its center. The Ten Commandments are the Jewish people's collective afterglow from their Sinai moment. They felt God among them when he revealed himself and his laws at Sinai. They carried with them a reminder of that experience, the Ten Commandments, in the ark of the covenant. They vowed to live differently than the peoples around them, and Mount Sinai symbolizes that vow. They promised to change their manner of living, abiding by a new code of morality.

Key Verse

I'm going to use these historical events as an illustration. The women illustrate two arrangements. The one woman, Hagar, is the arrangement made on Mount Sinai. Her children are born into slavery. Hagar is Mount Sinai in Arabia. She is like Jerusalem today because she and her children are slaves. But the Jerusalem that is above is free, and she is our mother. (Gal. 4:24–26)

As the mother who bore children into slavery, [Hagar] stands for the covenant from Mount Sinai, the Mosaic law. This is clear, Paul adds in a parenthesis, because "Sinai is a mountain in Arabia," and the Arabians were known as "the sons of Hagar." It is even more clear from the fact that the children of the law, just like Hagar's children, are slaves. So Hagar stands for the covenant of the law. . . . But Sarah was different. . . . If Hagar, Ishmael's mother, the slave woman, stands for the earthly Jerusalem or Judaism, then Sarah, Isaac's mother, being a free woman, stands for the heavenly Jerusalem or the Christian church. . . . We are bound to the living God by a new covenant, and this citizenship is not bondage, but freedom.

John R. W. Stott,
The Message of Galatians, The Bible Speaks Today
(Downers Grove, IL: InterVarsity, 1984), 125

Nineveh

As a city symbolic of man's power in rebellion against God, Nineveh ranks second only to Babylon. Yet it also stands out as an example of cultural repentance—the population of a large city recognizing the holiness of God and humbling themselves before him. Three of Israel's prophets—Jonah, Nahum, and Zephaniah—had dealings with the city. Nineveh flourished from about 800 to 612 BC on the eastern bank of the Tigris River. Its ruins are across the river from the modern-day city of Mosul, in northern Iraq.

A Wicked City

Nineveh was the greatest of the capitals of Assyria, the mortal enemy of Israel. It is first mentioned in the Old Testament as one of the cities established by Nimrod (Gen. 10:9–12). It is better known as the city to which God called the reluctant prophet Jonah in the eighth century BC. The book of Jonah calls it "the important city" (1:2; see also 4:11) and "a very large city" (3:3), adding "it took three days to walk through it" (3:3) to describe its size. This phrase may indicate the city's actual size, or it may be an idiom referring to the first day for travel to, the second for visiting, and the

third day for the return. The phrase "120,000 people . . . [who] couldn't tell their right hand from their left" (4:11) is most likely a reference to the entire population, offering a picture of God's amazing compassion for those who are unaware of spiritual truth.

Nineveh was a wicked city, the epitome of everything Jewish people hated in the Gentile world. Its name became a synonym for godless tyranny. When God said Nineveh was evil (Jon. 1:2) or wicked, that was an understatement. The inhabitants had a reputation for cruelty that is hard to fathom in our day. Their specialty was brutality of a gross and disgusting kind. When their armies captured a city or a country, unspeakable atrocities would occur, such as skinning people alive, decapitation, mutilation, ripping out tongues, making a pyramid of human heads, piercing the chin with a rope, and forcing prisoners to live in kennels like dogs. Ancient records from Assyria boast of this kind of cruelty as a badge of courage and power. To call them the terrorists of their day would be accurate. We could also fairly say that everyone feared and hated the Assyrians.

Everyone, including Jonah, hated Nineveh. He didn't want the slightest thing to do with those people even though God sent him there. He was a prophet of Israel, not a preacher to the degenerate Assyrians. Nineveh was not in Jonah's comfort zone. Nineveh represents the places God calls us where we do not want to go, anywhere that looks like trouble or danger. Nineveh represents the places we fear.

Nineveh was a powerful enemy of Israel, but after Jonah's preaching they repented.

A City on Its Knees

As perverse and immoral as Nineveh was, it is remembered for the people's desire for God's compassion (Jon. 4:11). They responded with repentance and conversion "from the most important to the least important" (3:5). This reputation for repentance is what endures in the New Testament. Jesus said, "The men of Nineveh will stand up with you at the time of judgment and will condemn you, because they turned to God and changed the way they thought and acted when Jonah spoke his message. But look, someone greater than Jonah is here!" (Matt. 12:41). As famous as the Ninevites were in their depravity, they repented when Jonah preached to them of a coming judgment, whereas Jesus' own generation ignored his warnings.

In a dual lesson that repentance is neither permanent nor transferable to the next generation, the story of Nineveh has a sad conclusion. A hundred years after Jonah, the city had returned to its state of horrendous moral perversion. Both Nahum and Zephaniah declared God's judgment on the city. This time, no repentance was expressed. The famed Assyrian city was destroyed in 612 BC by the Babylonian army, which wiped out the remainder of the empire in the following years.

Key Verse

Leave at once for the important city, Nineveh. Announce to the people that I can no longer overlook the wicked things they have done. (Jon. 1:2)

In [God's] mind, Nineveh is not a quantity but a quality, not a mere metropolis but an immorality. He takes the symbol of the ancient world's most impressive evil, magnifies and intensifies it by mass, and sends his timorous prophet into the middle of it.

Edwin M. Good, *Irony in the Old Testament*, 2nd ed. (Sheffield, UK: Almond Press, 1981), 48

Top, Nineveh was a center for the worship of the false god Ishtar.

Oil

Most uses of the word *oil* in the Bible have ceremonial rather than food connections. Oils were harvested from animal fats, minerals, and vegetables. Oil also had medicinal purposes (Ps. 23:5; Luke 10:34) and was used to fuel lamps (Matt. 25:1–13). In a bartering economy, oil was a commodity of value. In 2 Kings 4:1–7 Elijah helps a widow and her two sons by telling them to gather as many containers as possible and pour her meager supply of oil into the jars. The oil didn't run out until every available jar had been filled. Elisha then told her to sell the oil and live on the proceeds.

In Jesus' day olive oil was made using an olive press. A large trough was created in a massive stone, and a stone wheel was hewn to match the trough. Olives were dumped into the trough and the wheel was pushed or pulled around the groove to crush the olives. The Garden of Gethsemane where Jesus spent hours in prayer was not only on the Mount of Olives, but the name *Gethsemane* means "oil press," a description that fits the pressure and anguish Jesus experienced in the garden as he prepared for the final journey to the cross.

Olive oil was used for food and medicinal purposes as well as for anointing.

Anointing with Oil

Anointing with oil symbolizes the idea of being set apart and blessed for a task. Oil was often used in the dedication of priests and special leaders. When Samuel was commanded to go to Bethlehem to anoint a replacement for King Saul, God said, "Fill a flask with olive oil and go. I'm sending you to Jesse in Bethlehem because I've selected one of his sons to be king" (1 Sam. 16:1). Then, when David finally showed up, "Samuel took the flask of olive oil and anointed David in the presence of his brothers. The LORD's Spirit came over David and stayed with him from that day on" (1 Sam. 16:13). Much earlier, God had given Moses specific instructions about the recipe for anointing oil:

> The LORD said to Moses, "Take the finest spices: 12 ½ pounds of powdered myrrh; half as much, that is, 6 ¼ pounds of fragrant cinnamon; 6 ¼ pounds of fragrant cane; 12 ½ pounds of cassia—all weighed using the standard weight of the holy place—and 4 quarts of olive oil. Have a perfumer make these into a holy oil, a fragrant mixture, used only for anointing. This will be the holy oil used for anointing." (Exod. 30:22–25)

This oil was to be used for anointing holy places and holy people and was to be preserved for those purposes alone (Exod. 30:26–33). When Jesus was anointed with oil, it was in the sense of being set apart and prepared for death and burial (John 12:3–8).

Oil was also used to anoint people for healing. James urges us, "If you are sick, call for the church leaders. Have them pray for you and anoint you with olive oil in the name of the Lord" (5:14). This is also the type of anointing mentioned in Psalm 23:5, Isaiah 1:6, Mark 6:13, and Luke

10:34. If being anointed with oil symbolizes God's mark of blessing on someone, it makes sense that it would also symbolize his healing.

Symbolic Oil

Because it was so widely useful, oil became symbolic of several significant ideals. An abundance of oil was mentioned in descriptions of wealth as a mark of God's blessing (Job 29:6; Joel 2:24). When the exiles returned to Israel, they were promised oil along with grain and new wine (e.g., Joel 2:19). The joy of the Lord was frequently compared to being anointed with oil: "You have loved what is right and hated what is wrong. That is why God, your God, has anointed you, rather than your companions, with the oil of joy" (Ps. 45:7; see also Pss. 23:5; 92:10; Heb. 1:9).

When David wrote a psalm of worship and meditated on the delight of gathering with others before God, he said, "See how good and pleasant it is when brothers and sisters live together in harmony! It is like fine, scented oil on the head, running down the beard—down Aaron's beard—running over the collar of his robes" (Ps. 133:1–2). Unity and fellowship are like anointing oil in someone's life. And the similarity between the Hebrew words for *oil* and *name* yields a nice wordplay in Ecclesiastes 7:1a, where personal integrity is highly prized: "A good name is better than expensive perfume." *Perfume* here refers to aromatic oil.

Occasionally *oil* is used as a negative symbol. The words of an enemy are "more soothing than oil, but they are like swords ready to attack" (Ps. 55:21). The kiss of an adulteress is "smoother than oil" (Prov. 5:3). These images are common in our vocabulary today when we speak of a "slick-talking salesman." The underlying significance in these uses of *oil* is that they point to the way evil corrupts good.

Key Verse

If you are sick, call for the church leaders. Have them pray for you and anoint you with olive oil in the name of the Lord. (James 5:14)

In New Testament times, oil was used medicinally. The Good Samaritan poured on oil (Luke 10:34) as a soothing ointment and Isaiah 1:6 takes that practice even further back. Both . . . aspects of the use of oil, the medicinal and the spiritual, would be in the minds of the elders and of their sick brother [in James 5:14]. . . . In itself [the oil] would speak of soothing and healing, and by linking it with *the name of the Lord* it would become a visible expression and token of the descent of the healing authority and the efficacy of the Name.

J. A. Motyer, *The Message of James*, The Bible Speaks Today (Downers Grove, IL: InterVarsity, 1985), 195–96

One

The word *one* is used more than two thousand times in Scripture. For the most part, these are simply natural uses of the number to indicate a solitary individual or item. But in several distinct instances the singular number carries special and symbolic weight. These refer, in order of importance, (1) to God's revelation of himself as one; (2) to a characteristic of unity related to a group or nation; or (3) to a significant individual.

One Lord

The people of Israel worshiped the God who is one, symbolic of his supremacy over all things. When God introduces himself in Scripture, as in Deuteronomy 6:4, the emphasis is on the divine singularity of his being: "Listen, Israel: The LORD is our God. The LORD is the only God." That last phrase also means "the LORD is one." God is a unique category in which he is the only occupant. Others may be compared to God, but he is not to be compared to anyone else. Others may be called "god," but they cannot measure up to God, nor are they divine—whatever might be claimed about them. Divine attributes like God being all-powerful imply that only one has that attribute.

Today the three large monotheistic religious groups (Christianity, Judaism, and Islam) all retain the same firm concept of the oneness of God derived from the same revelation of God—the Old Testament. Apart from these three religions, the world may be more or less pluralistic in its acceptance of many alternatives to the oneness of God.

Our understanding of the God who is one expands in the New Testament to accommodate the idea that one God can also be one divine, inseparable relationship of three—the Trinity: God the Father, God the Son, and God the Holy Spirit. Jesus declared, "The Father and I are one" (John 10:30). Later he introduced the third person in the Trinity as the Helper: "However, the helper, the Holy Spirit, whom the Father will send in my name, will teach you everything. He will remind you of everything that I have ever told you" (John 14:26). Here all three persons of the Trinity that is one God are seen in their functions as they impact Jesus' followers.

One Church

The one God is God for all nations and people groups. Throughout the Old Testament, God may have chosen Israel for a special purpose, but he also consistently declared that he is the God of all people. Psalm 22:28 says, "The kingdom belongs to the LORD and he rules the nations." When Paul preached to the philosophers in Athens in Acts 17, he didn't hesitate to tell his audience that the "unknown god" they were acknowledging was in fact the one true God, Maker of heaven and earth.

Jesus gave the number *one* a further significant application when he compared the unity that exists in the Trinity with the unity that ought to exist within the church: "I have given them the glory that you gave me. I did this so that they are united in the same way we are. I am in them, and you are in me. So they are completely united. In this way the world knows that you have sent me and that you have loved them in the same way you have loved me" (John 17:22–23). In other words, we are to be one in much the same way the Father, Son, and Holy Spirit are one.

The Significance of a Life

The number *one* also has important meaning when it comes to the value God places on individual lives. Several of Jesus' parables highlight the significance of God's care for individual people much as a shepherd singles out a sheep needing special care (Luke 15:1–10). Each person is a "one" God cares about. The great evangelistic verse John 3:16 includes the global perspective of one God who loves the world he created, but it also includes the individual response in the phrase "everyone who believes in him." God has great plans for us as a group, but he also sees us as individual people he loves and draws to himself.

Finally, when the one God created humans in his image (Gen. 1:27), he made them male and female. And when God instituted marriage, he devised a relationship that would parallel on the human level the relationship in the Trinity: "That is why a man will leave his father and mother and will be united with his wife, and they will become one flesh" (Gen. 2:24). The oneness of marriage points to the unity found in the Godhead.

Key Verse

Through the peace that ties you together, do your best to maintain the unity that the Spirit gives. There is one body and one Spirit. In the same way you were called to share one hope. There is one Lord, one faith, one baptism, one God and Father of all, who is over everything, through everything, and in everything. (Eph. 4:3–6)

Christ died to make his church one body out of a diversity of ethnic groups, and the Spirit lives within the church to keep this unity. . . . There is only one Lord, and all Paul's readers confess him as Lord. There is only one body of truth about this Lord and his significance, and all Paul's readers believe it. There is only one immersion in the Spirit at conversion (signified by water baptism), and all Paul's readers have experienced it. There is only one God who created all things and is summing all up in Christ, and he is the object of worship of all of Paul's readers. If Paul's readers are unified with one another in their willingness to confess these truths, then they should be willing to engage in the practical attitudes and actions that foster the unity of the church for which Christ died.

Frank Thielman, *Ephesians*, Baker Exegetical Commentary on the New Testament (Grand Rapids: Baker Academic, 2010), 261

One Hundred Forty-Four Thousand

The number 144,000 is used in only one book of the Bible: Revelation. The number relates to a group mentioned in Revelation 7:4–8 made up of twelve thousand people from each of the twelve tribes of Israel. The significance of *twelve* is heightened by using twelve times twelve as a number. This large, exact number is immediately followed by an even larger and more expansive number in verse 9 ("a large crowd from every nation, tribe, people, and language. No one was able to count how many people were there"). This may mean that 144,000 indicates God's specific inclusion of his original chosen people as part of heaven's throng, or it may symbolize a final harvest of believers. While some groups like Jehovah's Witnesses use the number 144,000 in a restrictive or selective sense, this doesn't seem to be the point of these passages.

Inclusive Body

By the end of the New Testament age, Paul's insight on the inclusiveness of the gospel was accepted by the church. Instead of insisting, like some of the early Jewish followers of Jesus, that all non-Jews must become Jews before being eligible to believe in the Jewish Messiah, Paul taught that God had actually created one new people out of both Jews and Gentiles and did not exclude anyone who believed. As he put it to the Galatians:

> You are all God's children by believing in Christ Jesus. Clearly, all of you who were baptized in Christ's name have clothed yourselves with Christ. There are neither Jews nor Greeks, slaves nor free people, males nor females. You are all the same in Christ Jesus. If you belong to Christ, then you are Abraham's descendants and heirs, as God promised. (Gal. 3:26–29)

As Paul explains at length in Romans 9–11, God gave a special task to the Jewish nation to be the people from which the Messiah would be born. But as human beings they stand in the same position as Gentiles: spiritually separate from God because of sin and needing the Savior as much as anyone. "In the past, you disobeyed God. But now God has been merciful to you because of the disobedience of the Jewish people. In the same way, the Jewish people have also disobeyed so that God may be merciful to them as he was to you. God has placed all people into the prison of their own disobedience so that he could be merciful to all people" (Rom. 11:30–32). So the

God's kingdom is made up of people from every tribe, tongue, and nation.

144,000 could conceivably be made up of Jewish believers in the final days, but not necessarily. This number reminds us that the blood descendants of Abraham as well as the rest of us who are adopted under the grace of God all become citizens of God's kingdom in the same way—by spiritual birth into that citizenship.

Heavenly Choir

The other three uses of 144,000 in Revelation (14:1, 3–4) number a group no longer identified by race but by a unique song. "They were singing a new song in front of the throne, the four living creatures, and the leaders. Only the 144,000 people who had been bought on earth could learn the song" (Rev. 14:3). Twice in these verses, the group is described as people who were "bought," a frequent expression in Scripture for Christ's work on the cross. They had been through the crucible of life and emerged blameless. Out of their experience comes a song that only they can sing, which they lift continuously as they follow the Lamb who bought them with his life. The picture of a heavenly choir of 144,000 raising their voices in a special song comes with an overwhelming sound John can only describe as "a sound from heaven like the noise of raging water and the noise of loud thunder" (Rev. 14:2). We are given in this number a hint of the power of worship in the presence of God.

Key Verse

These 144,000 virgins are pure. They follow the lamb wherever he goes. They were bought from among humanity as the first ones offered to God and to the lamb. They've never told a lie. They are blameless. (Rev. 14:4–5)

The description of the 144,000 in [Revelation] 14:1–5 should convict all of us who claim to be followers of Christ. Look again at the stunning description of those faithful saints:

- They are sexually chaste.
- They follow the Lamb without hesitation.
- They have no lies on their lips.
- They are blameless.

We might generalize that description in another way. In their relationship with others, they are pure. In their relationship with God, they are obedient. Surrounded by deception and lies, they exhibit remarkable integrity. They have an unimpeachable character that results in an impeccable record. They are a living reproof to their peers, displaying proof of the gospel by their very lives.

Charles R. Swindoll, *Insights on Revelation*,
Swindoll's New Testament Insights
(Grand Rapids: Zondervan, 2011), 196

Top, Revelation mentions a group of 144,000 people—12,000 from each of the twelve tribes of Israel.

179

Passover

We begin to understand the significance of Passover when we realize that the word is actually two words: *pass over*. Passover originated in one of the greatest events recorded in the Old Testament, when the people of Israel were released after four hundred years of slavery in Egypt. God ensured the nation's exit from bondage with a tenth plague on those who had mistreated his people for centuries: an angel of death visited the homes of Egypt and killed the firstborn males (Exod. 11:1–12:42).

God instructed his own people to begin keeping a new calendar because their release from bondage would be such a history-making event. Passover would be the first event in each year, commemorating the birth of a nation.

Salvation through Blood

The exodus was activated with blood and remembered with a feast. Each family unit was told to choose an unblemished lamb whose blood was to be painted on the doorposts of their house and whose meat would become the centerpiece of their journey meal. God let them know through Moses that the angel of death would "pass over" any home that had been marked with blood, and the firstborn in that family would be safe. The life of the lamb, represented in the blood, substituted for the firstborn's life. The tragedy that fell on the Egyptian people was the crisis that expelled the people of Israel from captivity.

The significance of the blood of the Passover lamb parallels and is ultimately replaced by the Lamb of God, who takes away the sins of the world. Just as the lamb's blood painted on doorjambs protected those within, so the blood of Jesus, painted on our lives, represents God's acceptance of his sacrifice on the cross on our behalf. Jesus' death was the ultimate Passover, making the exodus from sin a possibility for humankind. Peter makes this connection explicit, saying, "Rather, the payment that freed you was the precious blood of Christ, the lamb with no defects or imperfections" (1 Pet. 1:19).

The Feast

The original Passover meal (also called a *Seder*) featured two elements: the lamb and

The last plague before the Hebrews were released from captivity in Egypt was the night the angel of death killed all the firstborns in Egypt; the firstborns among the Israelites who smeared blood on their doorposts were spared.

the unleavened bread. The food symbolized God's supply for the journey and his promise of freedom. Eating had a hurried aspect. The bread was not allowed to rise, and the meat was meant to be entirely consumed. No leftovers were kept because no one would be left to eat them. Over time several other elements were added to the meal: cups of wine, bitter herbs, and a mixture of fruit and nuts called *cheroseth*. The wine cups (four or five of them, depending on particular traditions) are shared throughout the meal. Two of these were used by Jesus during the Last Supper to draw attention to his special role. The bitter herbs symbolize the hardship of bondage and are eaten to remember that dark chapter in the nation's history. The nut and fruit paste is reminiscent of the mortar used between the bricks that were produced daily by enslaved Jewish ancestors. Though these elements symbolize hardship, the tone of the Seder meal is one of joy and gladness, seeing God as the liberator.

God and his judgment passed over the faithful people of Israel, and he continues to "pass over" those who have been marked by the blood of his Lamb.

Key Verse

When your children ask you what this ceremony means to you, you must answer, "It's the Passover sacrifice in the LORD's honor. The LORD passed over the houses of the Israelites in Egypt and spared our homes when he killed the Egyptians." (Exod. 12:26–27)

The innocent Passover lamb foreshadowed the one who would come centuries later to be God's final means of atonement and redemption. The parallels are striking:

- The Passover lamb was marked out for death (Isaiah 53:7; 1 Peter 1:19–20).
- They watched the Passover lamb to see that it was perfect (Deuteronomy 15:20; Hebrews 4:15; 1 Peter 1:19).
- They roasted the Passover lamb with fire, a symbol of judgment (2 Corinthians 5:21).
- Not a bone of the Passover lamb was broken (Psalm 34:20; John 19:36).

Ceil and Moishe Rosen, *Christ in the Passover* (Chicago: Moody, 1978), 26–27

Pigs

Throughout the Bible, pigs are presented with a consistent tone of uncleanliness. The people of Israel were expressly forbidden from eating the meat of swine (Lev. 11:7; Deut. 14:8). All that was filthy, untouchable, and ugly was symbolized by pigs. Thus, when Jesus inserted in his parable of the wandering son (Luke 15) the decision to seek employment feeding pigs, he was giving his audience an almost unspeakable description of desperation and humiliation.

In the Sermon on the Mount, Jesus balanced his forceful words against judging others and his pithy picture of how our own faults obscure our view of others with an equally startling warning in the other direction: "Don't give what is holy to dogs or throw your pearls to pigs. Otherwise, they will trample them and then tear you to pieces" (Matt. 7:6). Given the context, Jesus was forbidding his followers to become judgmental of others while at the same time urging caution when dealing with those who demonstrate a pattern of carelessness or disdain for the gospel.

A Symbol of Foolishness

Peter echoes this picture to describe the sad condition of those who come to a passing knowledge of the gospel but reject it. "It would have been better for them never to have known the way of life that God approves of than to know it and turn their backs on the holy life God told them to live. These proverbs have come true for them: 'A dog goes back to its vomit,' and 'A sow that has been washed goes back to roll around in the mud'" (2 Pet. 2:21–22). Those who reject the gospel after having heard it are unreasonable and lack a sense of value, just like pigs.

In Proverbs an attractive but foolish woman is compared to a pig: "Like a gold ring in a pig's snout, so is a beautiful woman who lacks good taste" (11:22). A beautiful woman would often have a gold ring in her nose. Just as a gold ring was out of place on a pig, so lack of discretion was out of place in the life of a woman.

Because Jews avoided pigs, their presence in the Holy Land was usually evidence of an area with a large Gentile population. When Jesus was traveling through the lands of the Gadarenes (Matt. 8:28–34; Mark 5:1–20; Luke 8:26–29), he was confronted by demon-possessed men whom he liberated by sending their tormentors into a herd of pigs that was grazing nearby. While this has often been seen as a confirmation of the low esteem for swine that Jesus would have reflected as a Jew, it is probably better to see Jesus' action as a lesson in how highly he valued the lives of the men who were suffering harassment by demons.

A Symbol of Uncleanness

For people long accustomed to bacon, ham, and pork chops in our

Pigs were unclean animals for the Israelites. When the prodigal son was forced to feed them, he had hit rock bottom.

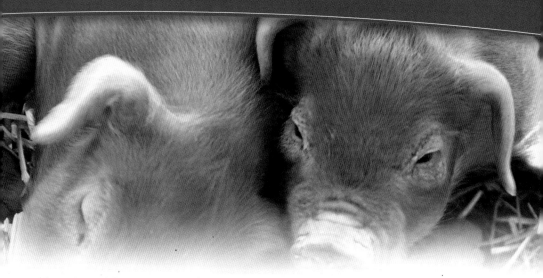

diets, the prohibition against pork seems surprising to us. Several explanations have been suggested. Because pork can carry a parasite that causes trichinosis, care must be taken in cooking the meat. God may have forbidden his people from eating pork as a health measure. The diet and an affinity to filth on the part of pigs also lead to suspicions about their use for human food. But the explanation that makes most sense is simply that God did not tell his people why pork was off the menu. He distinguished pigs from acceptable food and sacrifice animals because, although they have a divided hoof (like cattle and sheep), they do not chew the cud.

By the time of Jesus, pigs were the poster animal for the term *abomination*, which refers to obscene uncleanliness and unholiness. Jews avoided using the word *swine* and simply referred to them as *abomination*.

Daniel's prophecy (Dan. 9:27) points to a not-too-distant future when the temple in Jerusalem would be desecrated. This occurred during the reign of Antiochus IV Epiphanes when the temple was vandalized and the altar was defiled by sprinkling it with pig's blood. That act provoked the revolt of the Jewish people under the Maccabees that gave Israel a measure of autonomy before the Roman conquest. Daniel's prophecy also points to a time in the future when Israel will again deal with an evil ruler who insists on desecrating the temple and mocking their God (Matt. 24:14–18).

Key Verse

People can know our Lord and Savior Jesus Christ and escape the world's filth. But if they get involved in this filth again and give in to it, they are worse off than they were before. It would have been better for them never to have known the way of life that God approves of than to know it and turn their backs on the holy life God told them to live. These proverbs have come true for them: "A dog goes back to its vomit," and "A sow that has been washed goes back to roll around in the mud." (2 Pet. 2:20–22)

Concerning the proverb that Peter quotes in 2 Peter 2:22, Douglas Moo writes,

> Jews viewed both animals negatively. Dogs in the ancient Near East were not "man's best friend." They were not mild-mannered house pets but wild and savage beasts that often stole food and preyed on weak people. And, of course, pigs were anathema, declared "unclean" in the Old Testament and avoided by pious Jews. Dogs and pigs were thus often grouped together as despised animals. The meaning of the proverb is clear enough: Returning to the corruption of the world is like a dog returning to its vomit. . . . The false teachers, having gotten a taste for depravity, come to enjoy it; they are like pigs who, it is well known, love to wash in mud.

Douglas Moo, *The NIV Life Application Commentary: 2 Peter and Jude* (Grand Rapids: Zondervan, 1996), 147

Top, pigs are symbols of filth and foolishness.

Precious Stones

Jewels and precious stones are a scriptural image that is not very far removed from our present-day experience. As a whole in the Bible they symbolize beauty, value, and permanence, just as they do in our imagination today. The first mention in the Bible of precious stones is in the description of the high priest's breastplate in Exodus 28:17–21. The types of stones are not of any particular importance, but together they represent the enduring value and preciousness of the twelve tribes of Israel in God's eyes.

In the ancient world, jewels acted as a bank account. Jewelry, accessible only to royalty or very wealthy individuals, was a visual reminder of a person's status and authority. It was also a common spoil of war, so the owner of valuable gemstones was known to be powerful in battle (2 Sam. 1:10). For these reasons precious stones became symbols for wealth and power.

Jewels were primarily used for adornment. The beloved in Song of Solomon is resplendent with jewels (1:10–11). Brides wore jewels as part of their wedding attire (Isa. 49:18; 61:10; Jer. 2:32). And, of course, royal crowns were set with gems.

Character Jewels

Of more value, however, is adorning oneself with metaphorical jewels of wisdom and gentleness. Proverbs 1:9 asserts that "discipline and teachings are a graceful garland on your head and a golden chain around your neck." Furthermore, "wisdom is better than jewels. Nothing you desire can equal it" (Prov. 8:11). And Peter reminds us that "beauty doesn't come from hairstyles, gold jewelry, or clothes. Rather, beauty is something internal that can't be destroyed. Beauty expresses itself in a gentle and quiet attitude which God considers precious" (1 Pet. 3:3–4). A wife with these qualities is more precious than jewels (Prov. 31:10). The earthly value placed on jewels pales in comparison with the value believers should place on inner character.

Kingdom Jewels

Precious stones were used to metaphorically portray the value of God's kingdom. In the parable of the treasure hidden in a field, a man was willing to sell all he had to buy a field that contained a treasure—the jewels were a better investment than the rest of

Jewels and precious stones were associated with wealth in the ancient world, just as they are today.

his wealth combined (Matt. 13:44). In the adjoining parable, a merchant sold everything he had for one valuable pearl (Matt. 13:45–46). These parables use jewels and precious stones as symbols to show that the kingdom of heaven and those destined for it are more valuable than anything else found on earth.

God is portrayed in numerous places in Scripture as a king with jewels that display his incomparable power and wealth. Zechariah portrays the chosen people as "jewels in a crown" that "sparkle in his land" (9:16). In Revelation 21 we read that the heavenly city is constructed of gold and precious jewels, built on a foundation of precious stones representing the twelve tribes of Israel. The high priest's breastplate was a miniature representation of this ultimate reality. The gates to the city are huge single pearls, engraved with the names of the twelve tribes of Israel. The resplendence and beauty of the precious stones in heaven are symbols representing the infinite power and worthiness of God, the King above all kings.

Key Verse

The foundations of the city wall were beautifully decorated with all kinds of gems: The first foundation was gray quartz, the second sapphire, the third agate, the fourth emerald, the fifth onyx, the sixth red quartz, the seventh yellow quartz, the eighth beryl, the ninth topaz, the tenth green quartz, the eleventh jacinth, and the twelfth amethyst. The 12 gates were 12 pearls. Each gate was made of one pearl. The street of the city was made of pure gold, as clear as glass. (Rev. 21:19–21)

Scripture speaks of a New Jerusalem made of precious stones. Some of the jewels listed in Revelation 21:19–21 are among the hardest substances known. They indicate the material solidity of the New Earth.

Randy Alcorn, *Heaven*
(Carol Stream, IL: Tyndale, 2004), 79

Purim

On the fourteenth and fifteenth days of the Jewish month of Adar, about a month before Passover, devout Jews celebrate Purim. This holiday usually falls in March on our modern calendar. This joyous and sometimes even raucous holiday commemorates the deliverance of the Jews from Persian king Ahasuerus (Xerxes) and his evil royal vizier, Haman, through the daring work of Esther and her relative Mordecai. Purim celebrates the fact that time and again people have risen up to destroy the Jews, but each time God has delivered them and triumphed over their enemies.

Purim is celebrated with gifts of food and drink, acts of charity to the poor, a celebratory meal, and public recitation of the scroll of Esther. As the story of Esther is read, listeners boo, hiss, and rattle noisemakers whenever evil Haman's name is mentioned. This is a way to "blot out" his name. Celebrations include drinking wine and wearing masks and costumes. Purim was the one holiday that Jews predicted would be celebrated even in the Messianic age due to its joyful mood.

God's Will

Purim is the Hebrew word for "lots." The name comes from the point in the story of Esther when Haman selected the date for annihilation of the Jews by casting lots (Esther 3:7). That Haman used lots, which were used to determine God's will, as a way to choose when to kill God's people, is strikingly ironic. Solomon tells us, "The dice are thrown, but the LORD determines every outcome" (Prov. 16:33). The story of Haman illustrates God's control over human affairs, even when all hope seems to be lost. The Jewish people were on the verge of being wiped out, but God saved them. And in the process, Haman met his demise.

God's Faithfulness

Purim is not mentioned outside of the book of Esther, but it is a valuable symbol of God's faithfulness no matter how dire our circumstances

Throughout history God saved his people when all hope seemed lost.

may be. This holiday instituted by God and celebrated by Jews throughout history commemorates the sovereignty of God to save his people even when it seems as though all hope is lost. It was particularly poignant at times throughout history when the Jews had been discriminated against, such as in World War II.

Purim is the Hebrew word for *lots*; casting lots was a method of discerning God's will.

Key Verse

So the Jews called these days Purim, based on the word Pur. Therefore, because of everything that was said in this letter—both what they had seen and what had happened to them—the Jews established a tradition for themselves and their descendants and for anyone who would join them. The tradition was that a person should never fail to observe these two days every year, as they were described and at their appointed time. So these days must be remembered and observed in every age, family, province, and city. These days of Purim must not be ignored among the Jews, and the importance of these days must never be forgotten by the generations to come. (Esther 9:26–28)

Jewish commentators see [the story of Esther] not as a celebration of human power, but rather as an example of God's subtle ways in working through people. Jewish tradition sees God as creating the miracle of Purim through the intervention of Esther, even though God is never mentioned. Just as people wear masks on Purim to look like someone else, so too, perhaps, does God wear a mask. The strange frivolity of Purim may be a hint to us to look for God in places where God is not evident.

Rabbi Kerry M. Olitzky and Rabbi Daniel Judson,
Jewish Holidays: A Brief Introduction for Christians
(Woodstock, VT: Jewish Lights Publishing, 2007), 71

Purple

In the ancient world, color came through nature. The scope of colors was limited to naturally occurring hues, so things were categorized as the color of the sky, or plants, or blood. Hebrew has only three distinct color words and no concept or vocabulary for hue or color variation. Most of the words translated as *color* literally mean "eye," "appearance," or "aspect."

Over time, certain colors became associated with specific contexts, much as the colors red and green have become associated with Christmas in the modern world. Symbolic meanings for color evolved from their association with a context. This was particularly true of the color purple. Purple dye was derived from the murex shellfish found in the Mediterranean Sea, and 250,000 mollusks were needed to make one ounce of dye. Because purple dye was so expensive in the ancient world, it was used only by people of high status. Thus purple became a symbol for power, wealth, and royalty.

Purple as a Symbol of Wealth

Purple was the color of royalty in the Old Testament. One of the spoils of war that Gideon took from the kings of Midian was their purple robes (Judg. 8:26). Mordecai also wore a purple robe (Esther 8:15), and the color purple figured prominently in King Xerxes' royal splendor (Esther 1:6). King Belshazzar's riches included his purple accoutrements (Dan. 5:7, 16, 29). Even governors and lesser rulers in Assyria wore purple in Ezekiel's day (Ezek. 23:6), and it was an important commodity for Tyre (Ezek. 27:7, 16, 24).

Purple continued to be highly prized in the New Testament. It was an important and expensive item of trade for Lydia (Acts 16:14), and we know from that description of her that she was a successful tradeswoman and a prominent member of the church. The absence of purple trade in the book of Revelation is an indication of Babylon's fall (18:12). If people no longer trade in purple, the city has lost its wealth and power.

Dyes in the ancient world came from nature, and because purple is a more rare color in nature, purple dye was difficult to obtain.

Purple for the True King

The first time the color purple is seen in the Bible is in the fabric used for the curtains and hangings in the tabernacle. Its preciousness and rarity made it appropriate for God's dwelling place. The King above all kings should have all the honor due a king, including the copious use of purple in his throne room. Later, purple was also prominent in the temple that Solomon built, and he sought out "a man who has the skill to work with gold, silver, bronze, and iron as well as purple, dark red, and violet cloth" (2 Chron. 2:7).

In the New Testament, the most notable use of the color purple was when the soldiers placed a purple robe on Jesus to mock him: "The soldiers twisted some thorny branches into a crown, placed it on his head, and put a purple cape on him. They went up to him, said, 'Long live the king of the Jews!' and slapped his face" (John 19:2–3; see also Mark 15:17, 20). Because the color purple was connected with royalty, the use of purple in this instance completed their mockery. And of course the irony is that Jesus truly is the King of kings.

Key Verse

The Lord continued, "Make the inner tent with ten sheets made from fine linen yarn. Take violet, purple, and bright red yarn, and creatively work an angel design into the fabric." (Exod. 26:1)

The three colors woven into the veil [of the tabernacle] are symbolic of Christ's incarnation, ministry, and second advent. . . . The purple was produced from a secretion of the purple snail (murex). Purple is the color of royalty and speaks of Christ's kingship. Jesus was from the kingly line of David (Luke 1:32), born a King (Matthew 2:2), mocked as a King (Matthew 27:29), declared to be King at his crucifixion (Matthew 27:32), and is coming back as King of kings and Lord of lords (Revelation 19:16) to rule as King forever (Luke 1:33).

David M. Levy, *The Tabernacle: Shadows of the Messiah* (Bellmawr, NJ: The Friends of Israel Gospel Ministry, 1993), 72

Top, purple is the color of wealth and royalty.

Quail

Quail make a single but memorable appearance in the biblical story. Interestingly, quail are native migratory birds whose yearly travels in the spring take them across the Sinai Peninsula, traveling from northern Africa back to Europe—the very time of year depicted in Exodus and Numbers when the people of Israel were trudging toward the Promised Land. Their migration leaves them so exhausted that they collapse on the ground and can be caught by hand. Thus, their appearance in Exodus is partly a naturally occurring event, although the number appearing in that account is greater than would be typical. Most likely the Hebrews had eaten quail in Egypt, so they would have been accustomed to the taste.

Complaints

Numbers 11 tells a tragic account of complaints, ungratefulness, pride, greed, and God's response. Murmuring seemed to flow like the tides among the recently freed slave nation. No sooner had the fire of judgment provoked by complaints receded (Num. 11:1–3) than a new offense began to rise in the demand for meat. The attitude of entitlement on the part of the people angered God as well as Moses. In their complaints, people rewrote the history of their experience in Egypt. Their crushing subsistence as slaves was now described as a life of luxury and fine cuisine: "Remember all the free fish we ate in Egypt and the cucumbers, watermelons, leeks, onions, and garlic we had? But now we've lost our appetite! Everywhere we look there's nothing but manna!" (Num. 11:5–6).

The people were soon hip-deep in quail, which God said they would have as a steady diet for a month to teach them a lesson. Apparently, the migration pattern indicates that God had intended to provide them with meat all along, but their attitudes turned the gift into an unpleasant experience. As God himself explained, "This is because they rejected the Lord who is here among them and cried in front of him, asking, 'Why did we ever leave Egypt?'" (Num. 11:20).

Provision

Even Moses was amazed at God's provision. Verses 21–22 describe his awareness that even if they slaughtered all the livestock they had with them, they would not be able to feed the armed men of Israel, let alone the whole nation. "The Lord asked Moses, 'Is there a limit to the Lord's power? Now you will see whether or not my words come true'" (Num. 11:23).

Quail became the symbol not only of God's amazing, creative abundance, but also of the fine line between a generous gift and an unappreciated gesture that is wasted on the ungrateful.

Quail make an annual migration across the Holy Land.

Key Verse

The LORD sent a wind from the sea that brought quails and dropped them all around the camp. There were quails on the ground about three feet deep as far as you could walk in a day in any direction. All that day and night and all the next day the people went out and gathered the quails. No one gathered less than 60 bushels. Then they spread the quails out all around the camp. While the meat was still in their mouths—before they had even had a chance to chew it—the LORD became angry with the people and struck them with a severe plague. That place was called Kibroth Hattaavah [Graves of Those Who Craved Meat] because there they buried the people who had a strong craving for meat. (Num. 11:31–34)

En route [to Canaan] the Israelites complained and rebelled. Pressed and perplexed, Moses appealed to God in prayer. In response he was instructed to select seventy elders whom God endued to share his responsibilities. In addition God sent a great wind to bring an abundant supply of quails to the Israelites. The intemperate and indulgent people ate them uncooked, so that the gratification of their lust became a plague which caused the death of many. Appropriately this place was named Kibroth-hattaavah, meaning "graves of lust."

Samuel J. Schultz, *The Old Testament Speaks: A Complete Survey of Old Testament History and Literature*, 5th ed. (New York: HarperCollins, 2000), 80

Top, God provided meat for the Israelites in the wilderness by sending quail in such abundance that they became tired of it.

Rainbow

The rainbow is the primary biblical symbol most people can identify. Children in Sunday school learn early on about Noah's ark and the rainbow that accompanied God's promise to never again destroy the whole earth by flood:

> "I am making my promise to you. Never again will all life be killed by floodwaters. Never again will there be a flood that destroys the earth."
>
> God said, "This is the sign of the promise I am giving to you and every living being that is with you for generations to come. I will put my rainbow in the clouds to be a sign of my promise to the earth. Whenever I form clouds over the earth, a rainbow will appear in the clouds. Then I will remember my promise to you and every living animal. Never again will water become a flood to destroy all life. Whenever the rainbow appears in the clouds, I will see it and remember my everlasting promise to every living animal on earth."
>
> So God said to Noah, "This is the sign of the promise I am making to all life on earth." (Gen. 9:11–17)

The storm clouds retreat, making way for God's sign of mercy.

In theological terms the rainbow is the symbol that accompanies God's covenant with humanity, his promise to be in relationship with them as he grows them to be his people in his place under his rule. The rainbow is a visible sign and reminder that God will restore the relationship between God and humanity that was damaged at the fall. Unlike the Abrahamic covenant that followed later, this covenant had no stipulations attached to it. God made the covenant, and he promised to uphold it.

Mercy Triumphs over Judgment

In that sense, rainbows are a symbol for God's mercy in the midst of judgment. Humanity deserves judgment, but God in his grace reaches out to us. Rainbows are a fitting symbol for this reality because only God can place a rainbow in the sky, just as only he can provide salvation for his covenant-breaking people. The beautiful rainbow with its arc of blending colors after a rainstorm is a reminder of the fact that in God, justice and mercy are complementary rather than contradictory: "Mercy and truth have met. Righteousness and peace have kissed" (Ps. 85:10). Though God is angry with sin and enacts judgment, his rainbow of mercy peeks out after the storm. In addition, the rainbow stretches from heaven down to earth, a visual image of God reaching down to humanity.

Some scholars make much of the fact that a rainbow is shaped like a weapon. Indeed, the Hebrew word means "my bow" and is usually translated as a weapon. As the storm clouds of judgment retreat in the sky, the sun comes out and God lays his bow across the sky in a promise to be gracious to his creation. In wrath he will remember mercy.

Visions of Glory

Two other places in Scripture use rainbows in visions of God's glory. Ezekiel's vision of God includes a rainbow: "The brightness all around him looked like a rainbow in the clouds. It was like the LORD's glory" (Ezek. 1:28). A rainbow also surrounds God's throne in John's vision: "There was a rainbow around the throne which looked like an emerald" (Rev. 4:3). The presence of a rainbow in these settings is an allusion back to Genesis 9. Each one is a reminder of God's mercy that triumphs over judgment. The reigning King of kings places a rainbow in his throne room as a sign and symbol to his people that he is the covenant maker and covenant keeper.

Key Verse

God said, "This is the sign of the promise I am giving to you and every living being that is with you for generations to come. I will put my rainbow in the clouds to be a sign of my promise to the earth. Whenever I form clouds over the earth, a rainbow will appear in the clouds. Then I will remember my promise to you and every living animal. Never again will water become a flood to destroy all life. Whenever the rainbow appears in the clouds, I will see it and remember my everlasting promise to every living animal on earth." (Gen. 9:12–16)

God gave assurance that he would never send another flood to destroy life on the earth. The covenant included not only man but also birds, cattle, and the beasts of the field (Ezekiel 1:10; Revelation 4:7). The sign of the covenant was the rainbow, a bridge of beauty that joins heaven and earth. Whether we look at the rainbow or not, God looks upon it and remembers his promises. Noah saw the rainbow after the storm; Ezekiel saw it in the midst of the storm (Ezekiel 1:4ff); and John saw it before the storm of judgment (Revelation 4:1–3).

Warren Wiersbe, *Nelson's Quick Reference Chapter-by-Chapter Bible Commentary* (Nashville: Thomas Nelson, 1991), 21

Raven/Crow

The first bird specifically mentioned in the Bible is the raven. While most people remember that Noah sent out a dove from the ark to find out if dry land was available for the rescued humans and animals after the flood, fewer recall that he first sent out a raven (Gen. 8:6–7). The fact that the raven didn't return provided Noah with only part of the answer he was seeking: the bird had found some food to scavenge, but Noah still had no way to tell how much land was visible. The dove's thoughtful return with a branch gave the original ship captain confidence that the earth was returning to normal, but the dove hadn't found enough vegetation to survive on, and so it returned.

Comparison

The raven's distinct all-black plumage led to the bird being used in comparisons. The bride in Song of Solomon calls her lover's hair "black as a raven" (5:11). And a wise man named Agur, who contributed a chapter to the book of Proverbs in the Old Testament, included this warning to children: "The eye that makes fun of a father and hates to obey a mother will be plucked out by ravens in the valley and eaten by young vultures" (Prov. 30:17). This behavior was probably observed by Agur, as ravens have been known to pluck out the eyeballs of their prey, sometimes even before it is dead.

Provision

While ravens were considered an unclean bird (Lev. 11:15; Deut. 14:14), they make an appearance in the Bible not only as examples of God's provision but also as messengers *with*

God's provision. God told Job that part of the evidence for God's care of his creation was that he fed the ravens (Job 38:41), a theme that both a psalmist (Ps. 147:9) and Jesus echoed: "Consider the crows. They don't plant or harvest. They don't even have a storeroom or a barn. Yet, God feeds them. You are worth much more than birds" (Luke 12:24). Ravens are a particularly good symbol for God's providential care because they engage in a behavior called "caching." They eat some food right away, but some they save in a particular spot and come back for later. And they are smart enough to remember where their caches are, unlike some animals.

When Elijah was a fugitive in the wilderness, God supplied his basic needs by sending ravens with food (1 Kings 17:4–6). Here the raven that symbolized God's care for the animal world was the tool God used to care for Elijah in his hour of need. It is similar to the way God cares for us and then expects us to pass that comfort along to others (2 Cor. 1:3–6).

Biblical writers used the jet-black color of ravens to illustrate items that are dark.

Key Verse

*Then the L*ORD *spoke his word to Elijah: "Leave here, turn east, and hide beside the Cherith River, which is east of the Jordan River. You can drink from the stream, and I've commanded ravens to feed you there."*

*Elijah left and did what the word of the L*ORD *had told him. He went to live by the Cherith River, which is east of the Jordan River. Ravens brought him bread and meat in the morning and in the evening. And he drank from the stream. (1 Kings 17:2–6)*

Water would have been a precious commodity in that parched landscape described in the first book of Kings. So it's reasonable to think that the ravens would've spent time hanging out at Elijah's hideout at the brook—the only oasis around. It doesn't take long for clever ravens to realize someone is not a threat. Although they would probably still have been wary, they may have accepted Elijah as part of the family, or, at least, not an enemy. Food was super abundant, thanks to the major die-off in the drought, so there would've been plenty to share. . . . Did the ravens deliberately bring food to Elijah? It's possible. Or did they bring their finds to the brook to dip in the water or eat at leisure, and Elijah survived by sharing their leftovers? Another plausible explanation based on natural behavior.

Sally Roth, *An Eye on the Sparrow:*
The Bird Lover's Bible
(LaPort, CO: Happy Crab Corp., 2013), 85–86

Top, ravens were the unlikely delivery method for the meat that kept Elijah alive at the Cherith River.

195

Red/Scarlet

The Bible has two kinds of *red*. One is the natural color red, seen in such objects as blood, fire, and some human and animal skins and hair. The other *red* refers to the artificial color red, which was created using extracts from the bodies of insects. This man-made red is often called *scarlet*.

While the main word for *red* in Hebrew is derived from the word *blood*, the color of blood is rarely mentioned. One exception is 2 Kings 3:22: "When the Moabites got up early in the morning as the sun was rising over the water, they saw the water from a distance. It was as red as blood." Interestingly, in describing the first plague that God delivered on the people of Egypt in Exodus, the *color* of the water is never stated—the Nile river simply turned into blood (Exod. 7:14–25).

In Genesis 25:25, the newborn Esau is described as "red," probably because of the color of the hair that seemed to cover his body. Fast-forward a mere five verses to Genesis 25:30, and Esau's brother Jacob is preparing a red stew that tempts Esau to barter away his inheritance for a single meal. Numbers 19:2 specifies that a red cow must be sacrificed and its ashes mixed in the water that was used for purification. The explanation follows: "A man who is clean will collect the ashes from the cow and put them in a clean place outside the camp. They will be kept by the community of Israel and used in the water that takes away uncleanness. The cow is an offering for sin" (Num. 19:9).

Images of War

In the larger picture of symbolic uses of color, red usually indicates bloodshed, war, and destruction. Red appears in Revelation, first as part of prophetic horse colors. Among John's four apocalyptic horsemen, the second is riding a red horse: "A second horse went out. It was fiery red. Its rider was given the power to take peace away from the earth and to make people slaughter one another. So he was given a large sword" (6:4).

In the aftermath of the devastation caused by the horsemen, a powerful earthquake creates terrifying atmospheric conditions: "I watched as the lamb opened the sixth seal. A powerful earthquake struck. The sun turned as black as sackcloth made of hair. The full moon turned as red as blood" (6:12). When Satan the dragon appears in Revelation 12, John notes that his appearance is "fiery red" (v. 3).

Images of Sin and Cleansing

Throughout the Bible, the term *scarlet* is almost exclusively used to describe a dyed thread or fabric. Even the familiar passage in Isaiah 1:18 is making use of *scarlet* as a symbol of comparison, which GOD'S WORD highlights by translating it *red*: " 'Come on now, let's discuss this!' says the LORD. 'Though your sins are

Red is often associated with passion and love, and in the Bible it is inextricably linked with the shedding of Christ's blood on our behalf, the ultimate expression of love.

bright red, they will become as white as snow. Though they are dark red, they will become as white as wool.' " Revelation uses the reversed thought in picturing Babylon, the power of evil on earth, as a woman dressed in "bright red" (scarlet) who relishes the consumption of worldly goods. She will be judged: "How horrible, how horrible for that important city which was wearing fine linen, purple clothes, bright red clothes, gold jewelry, gems, and pearls. In a moment all this wealth has been destroyed!" (18:16–17).

We should not miss the significance of the scarlet (bright red), representing sin and the death and destruction that it brings about, and the way Christ's red blood transforms the scarlet into white, forgiveness, and righteousness. The author of Hebrews writes,

> As Scripture tells us, Moses told all the people every commandment. Then he took the blood of calves and goats together with some water, red yarn, and hyssop and sprinkled the scroll and all the people. He said, "Here is the blood that seals the promise God has made to you." In the same way, Moses sprinkled blood on the tent and on everything used in worship. As Moses' Teachings tell us, blood was used to cleanse almost everything, because if no blood is shed, no sins can be forgiven." (9:19–22)

God fights and conquers the fiery red of evil with his own cleansing blood.

Key Verse

"Come on now, let's discuss this!" says the LORD.
"Though your sins are bright red,
*   they will become as white as snow.*
Though they are dark red,
*   they will become as white as wool."*
*   (Isa. 1:18)*

Scarlet was the color of the cord that the prostitute Rahab hung outside her window as a signal to the Israelite spies to save her and her household (Josh. 2). This color may have had greater significance than just being easily seen:

> To Rahab, the scarlet cord was a simple, expedient emblem suited to mark her window discreetly so that her house would be easily distinguishable from all the rest of the houses in Jericho. To Bible commentators, the scarlet color is reminiscent of the crimson sign of the blood sprinkled on the doorposts at the first Passover. Others see this scarlet cord as a deliberate symbol related to the shed blood of the ultimate Sacrificial Lamb, Jesus Christ.

John MacArthur, *Twelve Extraordinary Women Workbook* (Nashville: Nelson Impact, 2006), 188

Top, the color red is usually associated with sin and the blood that cleanses from sin.

197

Ring

While we almost always think first of marriage when the subject of rings comes up, the Bible records no instances where a ring is used as a symbol of marriage or wedding vows. But surprisingly, the first time a ring is mentioned in Scripture involves an interesting account of surrogate courtship. When Abraham's servant Eliezer arrived in Haran on a mission to find a wife for young Isaac, he met a young woman at the city well whose name was Rebekah (Gen. 24:1–67). Discovering that Rebekah's parents were relations of Abraham, he knew he had found a match for his master's son. According to verses 22 and 47, Eliezer began his proposal to Rebekah on Isaac's behalf by putting a golden ring in her nose!

Gold was highly valued, and wearing one's worth in the form of rings was considered part of displaying wealth attractively. Before coins were widely used, precious metals were kept in this practical way, and lists of offerings, taxes, or gifts have rings among the items given (Num. 31:50).

Symbols of Authority

Rings, whether worn in the nose or on the fingers, were popular as jewelry throughout Scripture. When they were given as gifts, they symbolized honor. One of the most touching pictures of forgiveness is seen in Jesus' parable of the prodigal son (Luke 15), whom the father welcomes home and restores. "The father said to his servants, 'Hurry! Bring out the best robe, and put it on him. Put a ring on his finger and sandals on his feet'" (Luke 15:22).

Kings would often wear rings to symbolize their status and power. These were decorated with distinct carvings or shapes that became official signatures when the king pressed his ring into wax that sealed a document or letter. The term *signet ring* indicates a particular object that was used for making a royal sign. When Joseph graduated from prison to prince of Egypt, the Pharaoh publicly affirmed his new role: "Then Pharaoh said to Joseph, 'I now put you in charge of Egypt.' Then Pharaoh took off his signet ring and put it on Joseph's finger. He had Joseph dressed in robes of fine linen and put a gold chain around his neck" (Gen. 41:41–42). This designated Joseph's position and status in the kingdom. Someone wearing the king's ring could exercise the king's authority.

Rings were symbols of authority and honor.

A signet ring is used in several places in Scripture as a symbol for the way God knows and cherishes his people.

In the story of Esther, King Xerxes' ring became a central symbol for danger and delivery for the Jewish people. First, Haman received the ring and immediately set about to use its authority to pass a law dooming the Jews (Esther 3:8–14). Later, when Haman's scheme was exposed, the ring was taken from him on his way to the gallows and presented instead to wise Mordecai, who then devised a way for the Jewish people to lawfully resist the previous law that would have meant their death. He had to do this because the law passed by Haman could not be canceled. As the king himself noted:

> King Xerxes said to Queen Esther and Mordecai the Jew, "I have given Haman's property to Esther, and Haman's dead body was hung on the pole because he tried to kill the Jews. You write what you think is best for the Jews in the king's name. Seal it also with the king's signet ring, because whatever is written in the king's name and sealed with the king's signet ring cannot be canceled." (8:7–8)

Several times in Scripture God describes his chosen people as his signet ring, a visual reminder of his power and the value he placed on them (Jer. 22:24; Hag. 2:23). In this way, God was telling his people that he "wore" his promises to them and would not forget them.

Key Verse

The father said to his servants, "Hurry! Bring out the best robe, and put it on him. Put a ring on his finger and sandals on his feet. Bring the fattened calf, kill it, and let's celebrate with a feast. My son was dead and has come back to life. He was lost but has been found." Then they began to celebrate. (Luke 15:22–24)

[The ring in Luke 15:22 is] a token of the relationship between the Father and his child. It is a public acknowledgement from God that this one is his child and his son. It is a mark of identification in regard to relationship, as well as authority.

Walter L. Wilson, *A Dictionary of Bible Types*
(Peabody, MA: Hendrickson, 1999), 344

Top, the only time rings are mentioned in Scripture as being part of a wedding are in the story of Isaac and Rebekah's courtship.

199

Rome

In the book of Daniel, written years before Rome burst on the world scene, a Jewish exile in Persia interpreted a dream for King Nebuchadnezzar. The dream featured a huge statue made of different layers of material: gold, silver, bronze, iron, and iron mixed with clay. Daniel's interpretation revealed that each layer of the towering image represented a kingdom that would rise, with the golden section representing Babylon, the reigning superpower of that day. Comparing this sequence to history, we discover that the third world power after the Babylonians was Rome. Other than this prophetic vision, the Old Testament does not allude to or mention by name the Roman Empire. The Romans are mentioned in First and Second Maccabees, books written between the Old and New Testament during the time that Rome was overrunning the world.

New Testament Empire

By the time of the New Testament, the Roman Empire had conquered much of the world and had established order, which actually became a perfect environment in which the gospel of Jesus Christ could spread like wildfire. A glimpse of the pervasive power of Rome can be seen in the opening chapters of Luke's Gospel:

> At that time the Emperor Augustus ordered a census of the Roman Empire. This was the first census taken while Quirinius was governor of Syria. All the people went to register in the cities where their ancestors had lived. (Luke 2:1–3)

God used Rome to arrange for the movement of people that would ensure that his Son would be born in Bethlehem. The empire assumed the role of a powerful force behind the scenes that often participated in what God wanted to accomplish. So it came to be that a Roman ruler (Pilate) signed the death certificate that allowed the Jewish people to crucify Jesus. Later, Roman soldiers put Paul the apostle into protective custody and then transported him to Rome to appear before the emperor. Since Rome was the greatest city of the time, Paul could hardly wait to take the gospel to that place.

A New Babylon

The book of Revelation seems to offer an added symbolic role for Rome. The original writing was meant for first-century Christians to apply to their present circumstances as well as for the future, and we can see the similarities between the description of "Babylon" and some of the characteristics of Rome. Peter was the first to express the connection between the role of historical Babylon in the exile of Israel and the new Babylon (Rome) in the life of the growing church: "Your sister church in Babylon, chosen by God, and my son Mark send you greetings" (1 Pet. 5:13). The power and ruthlessness of Rome could be seen as both an obstacle to and a vehicle

The statue of St. Michael stands near the Vatican.

for the spread of the gospel, just the way Babylon had both opposed God and been used by him.

By the time John wrote Revelation, official persecutions were already being carried out under the authority of the Roman Empire. Christianity was becoming an outlawed religion, curiously called "atheist" because believers refused to accept the divinity of the emperor! The observation in Revelation 17:6, "I saw that the woman was drunk with the blood of God's holy people and of those who testify about Jesus," accurately describes the conditions when Christians were being tortured and torn apart by beasts for the entertainment of the masses in Rome. Further on, John says, "In this situation a wise mind is needed. The seven heads are seven mountains on which the woman is sitting" (Rev. 17:9), a topographical clue that points to the capital of the empire. Rome was known as a city on seven hills. Many scholars believe references to Babylon in Revelation 14:8; 16:19; 17:5; and 18:2, 10, and 21 also apply to first-century Rome. Revelation seems to reveal much more than simply a veiled picture of conditions and an encouraging prophecy regarding the eventual fall of Rome. The powerful symbol of that city and the empire it represented loomed over the early Christians in a way that has become a pattern for believers across the centuries who must courageously keep the faith in the face of strong opposition from ruthless, pagan governments.

Most ironic and perhaps even humorous is the fact that the seat of a major part of Christianity has for many centuries occupied the center of Rome. God has demonstrated through history that his use of symbols can take unexpected turns and is never mechanical. God remains the ultimate creative Author in the unfolding of his plan for those made in his image.

Key Verse

The Lord stood near Paul the next night and said to him, "Don't lose your courage! You've told the truth about me in Jerusalem. Now you must tell the truth about me in Rome." (Acts 23:11)

The Romans did not govern primarily for the welfare of the people in the provinces. Their system was not designed, even if it had worked ideally, to promote justice among the provincials. It was designed to support the interests of the leaders back in Rome, whether that meant collecting the maximum amount of taxes possible or protecting the Empire from threats to its stability from within or without. In this context, it is not hard to understand the resentment that developed toward Rome in Judea and elsewhere.

James S. Jeffers, *The Greco-Roman World of the New Testament Era* (Downers Grove, IL: InterVarsity, 1999), 110

Top, the Colosseum, once the site of gladiatorial contests, remains one of the most distinctive landmarks from ancient times.

201

Root

In the agrarian society of the ancient world, hearers of the Bible would have resonated with plant imagery. They knew even better than we do how a strong root system works to produce healthy crops. If a root withers, the plant dies. But if a root is attached to a water source, the plant grows healthy and strong. It is able to produce good fruit.

The same is true with people. The wicked may appear to be strong and successful, but their roots are shallow and they cannot survive a crisis (Job 5:3; 18:16; Ps. 1:4). On the other hand, those who trust in the Lord are like trees planted by a stream (Ps. 1:3; Jer. 17:7–8). They continue to produce fruit and thrive even during a drought when all the plants around them are dying: "the roots of righteous people produce fruit" (Prov. 12:12). Believers can rely on God's care for them, and so they do not fear calamity.

The Roots of a Nation

The nation of Israel is pictured as having strong roots that enable it to become a large vine.

> You brought a vine from Egypt.
>   You forced out the nations and planted it.
> You cleared the ground for it
>   so that it took root and filled the land.
> Its shade covered the mountains.
>   Its branches covered the mighty cedars.
> It reached out with its branches to the Mediterranean Sea.
>   Its shoots reached the Euphrates River. (Ps. 80:8–11; see also Ezek. 19:10–11)

God prospers the vine of Israel and helps it grow. The roots are a symbol of Israel's relationship with God, a connection that is at times healthy and at times anemic. Unfortunately, Israel's repeated rebellion causes its roots to wither and decay (Isa. 5:24; Hosea 9:16). Eventually God uproots them (1 Kings 14:15; Jer. 45:4), but even then he promises to preserve a remnant and one day restore Israel's greatness. Isaiah prophesies, "In times to come Jacob will take root. Israel will blossom, bud, and fill the whole world with fruit" (Isa. 27:6).

The nations that fall under God's judgment are also symbolized as uprooted plants. The Amorites will fall when God destroys their root system (Amos 2:9). Ekron would be "torn out by the roots" (Zeph. 2:4). Perhaps the most memorable use of this image is in relation to King Nebuchadnezzar. God allowed him to flourish like a great tree, but one day, similar to a tree that is chopped down, he descended into madness. After King Nebuchadnezzar learned his lesson, he was restored to some prominence, like a new shoot that comes up from a tree's roots (Dan. 4:26).

The Roots of a Believer

Jesus also used roots as a symbol for the health of a person's spiritual life. The Pharisees were not planted by God—he did not sanction their spiritual leadership—so they would be uprooted (Matt. 15:13). The entire generation of Jews in Jesus' days would be judged by their root system, just as the fruitless fig tree withered from the roots up (Matt. 3:10; Mark 11:12–14, 20–21; Luke 3:9). Jesus told the parable of the soils to illustrate the spiritual health of his hearers. When the Word of God fell on rocky soil, the believers' roots did not go deep enough, and their spiritual life withered and died. Jesus described it like this: "They don't develop any roots. They believe for a while, but when their faith is tested, they abandon it" (Luke 8:13). Just like in the Old Testament use of the image

of a root, those who have shallow roots cannot stand in times of trial.

The Root of Jesse

Elsewhere in Scripture we read that Jesus comes from the root of Jesse (Isa. 11:1, 10). He finds his source in the Davidic line, thereby confirming his identity as the Messiah. The symbolic root of Israel in the Old Testament is fulfilled in Christ. In addition, Israel itself will form the root of the people of God. People from other nations will be joined to the nation of Israel by finding their source in God (Rom. 11:16, 18). They, like the nation of Israel, will be judged by their roots—healthy roots will produce holy lives.

The Bitter Root

In a negative use of root imagery, idolatry and sin are likened to a bitter root that poisons the community of believers (Deut. 29:18 NIV; Heb. 12:15). Here the problem is bigger than a shallow root—the entire root system has gone bad, guaranteeing not just a poor harvest but a poisoned one. Such imagery should motivate us to pursue a life that is rooted in the living stream (John 7:37), just like the picture of a healthy tree offered in Psalm 1 and Jeremiah 17. The health of our root system will determine the spiritual fruit in our lives.

Key Verse

Since he doesn't have any root, he lasts only a little while. When suffering or persecution comes along because of the word, he immediately falls from faith. (Matt. 13:21)

The second type of soil stands for the *shallow heart*. . . . When the seed fell there it sank in, but only to a very shallow depth. It sprang up quickly, but it also faded quickly in the sun's heat because it had no root. . . . Many people fit that description. We see them in our thriving evangelical churches. Their shallow hearts are attracted to the joy and excitement of a church where much is happening. They hear the gospel and seem to fit in. Many even make a profession of faith. But then some difficulty comes—loss of a job, misunderstandings with other Christians, sickness, even a bad romance—and just as suddenly as they once seemed to embrace the faith, they fall away, because they were never really born again.

James Montgomery Boice,
The Parables of Jesus (Chicago: Moody, 1983), 17

Top, the health of a plant depends on the strength of its root system; so also the fruitfulness of a person's life depends on their being rooted in God's Word and character.

Sabbath

The term *Sabbath* comes from the Hebrew word for "cease." This day of stopping normal activity and work was to serve as a reminder of God's rest after the work of creation (Gen. 2:2–3). God set aside this day as holy and blessed it as a gift to humankind.

> Remember the day of worship by observing it as a holy day. You have six days to do all your work. The seventh day is the day of worship dedicated to the LORD your God. You, your sons, your daughters, your male and female slaves, your cattle, and the foreigners living in your city must never do any work on that day. In six days the LORD made heaven, earth, and the sea, along with everything in them. He didn't work on the seventh day. That's why the LORD blessed the day he stopped his work and set this day apart as holy. (Exod. 20:8–11)

During the exodus, the Sabbath became institutionalized in the Hebrew nation when people were forbidden to gather manna on that day (Exod. 16:23–30). The ceasing of work was a mandate rather than a suggestion. In time it became apparent that God's intention for the Sabbath was not only rest but also worship. In the Old Testament this consisted of sacrifices (e.g., Num. 28:9–10), and in the New Testament the day of worship was centered on the reading and teaching of God's Word (e.g., Mark 6:2; Luke 4:16).

A Covenant Promise

The Sabbath first of all symbolizes the covenant promise. God set this day apart as holy for his people. The surrounding nations did not participate in the Sabbath rest, only the chosen people Israel. It called to mind the promise God had made to preserve and save his people (Lev. 24:8) and was an expression of the Israelites' faith in God as they upheld their part of the covenant. The Lord said, "I also gave them certain days to worship me as a sign between us so that they would know that I, the LORD, made them holy" (Ezek. 20:12). Even today, keeping the Sabbath is an expression that we trust God to provide for our needs. We can rest from our work because we know that our well-being is not ultimately dependent on our own effort but on God's grace.

The importance of the Sabbath as part of the covenant is underscored by the fact that Jesus deliberately portrayed himself as Lord of the Sabbath. He repeatedly healed on the Sabbath and declared that "the day of worship was made for people, not people for the day of worship. For this reason the Son of Man has authority over the day of worship" (Mark 2:27–28). Over and over again Jesus affirmed that the Sabbath was a gift rather than a burden, one that is able to be enjoyed more freely because he came to fulfill the regulations of the law that we are unable to fulfill ourselves.

A Sign of Eternal Rest

The Sabbath, although a literal day of rest, also serves as a symbol for the eternal rest of heaven. Hebrews 4 fleshes this out fully, drawing a connection between the Sabbath rest of the Old Testament and the "place of rest" found by those who obey God (vv. 1–11). The author of Hebrews seems to go back and forth between the Sabbath day and salvation, using the two images almost interchangeably, and then concludes with these words: "Therefore, a time of rest and worship exists for God's people. Those who entered his place of rest also rested from their work as God did from his. So we must

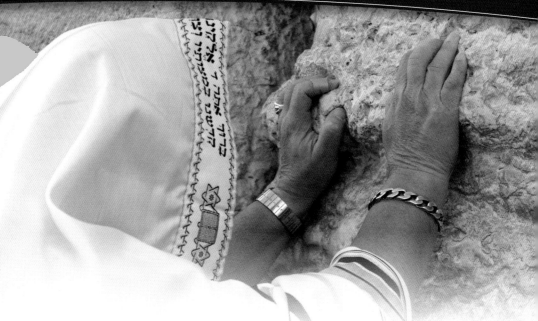

make every effort to enter that place of rest. Then no one will be lost by following the example of those who refused to obey" (vv. 9–11). Believers' participation in a weekly Sabbath is a symbol that reminds us of the Creator who rested from the work of creation and invites us into covenant relationship, as well as the eternal rest that awaits us as the final fulfillment of that covenant. We can rest and be at peace, trusting in God to meet our needs in the here and now, in part because we know that our true home and final rest is in heaven.

Key Verse

"The Spirit of the Lord is with me.
 He has anointed me
  to tell the Good News to the poor.
 He has sent me
  to announce forgiveness to the
   prisoners of sin
  and the restoring of sight to the
   blind,
 to forgive those who have been
  shattered by sin,
 to announce the year of the Lord's favor."

Jesus closed the book, gave it back to the attendant, and sat down. Everyone in the syna-gogue watched him closely. Then he said to them, "This passage came true today when you heard me read it." (Luke 4:18–21)

What Jesus says in his very first sermon is that *he* is the Sabbath—and not just any Sabbath. "The time of the LORD's favor" has also been translated as "the acceptable year of the Lord." What is an acceptable year of the Lord? Certainly it is much more than a single Sabbath, and even more than a month of Sundays. The Hebrew people stopped one day a week. In addition, every seventh year was to be a special sabbatical year, one in which the land was allowed to lie fallow. Every seven cycles of seven years was followed by a year of ceasing, christened a jubilee year. In a jubilee year, all debts are canceled, all slaves are set free, and all property reverts to its original owners. . . . The minute Jesus steps into his ministry, he stakes his claim on the Sabbath. Jesus declares himself both the Lord of the Sabbath (Matthew 12:8) and the meaning of the day (Luke 4:21). To walk with Jesus through the Gospels and watch him work is to see Sabbath restored to its original intent.

Matthew Sleeth, *24/6*
(Carol Stream, IL: Tyndale, 2012), 50–51

Sacrifice/Offering

In order to understand the idea of sacrifices and offerings, we must go back to the very beginning of the Bible. By Genesis 4, the first sons, Cain and Abel, were practicing an early form of sacrifice: "Later Cain brought some crops from the land as an offering to the LORD. Abel also brought some choice parts of the firstborn animals from his flock. The LORD approved of Abel and his offering, but he didn't approve of Cain and his offering. So Cain became very angry and was disappointed" (Gen. 4:3–5). From the beginning, offerings and sacrifices generally expressed two attitudes: gratitude and repentance. In the case of Cain and Abel, later history of sacrifice might lead us to think that God's rejection of Cain's offering was because it wasn't a blood sacrifice, but the text doesn't indicate such a conclusion. Cain's offering was casual and perhaps careless; Abel's was costly. Cain brought "some crops"; Abel presented "some choice parts." Cain's response to God's correction revealed his heart.

Heart Sacrifice

This emphasis on attitude over performance appears again and again throughout the Bible. God repeatedly confronted his people over their persistent tendency to get worship wrong even when they got the offerings and sacrifices technically right. The prophets had this problem as a central theme in their preaching. Hosea reported God's words: "I want your loyalty, not your sacrifices. I want you to know me, not to give me burnt offerings" (Hosea 6:6). Samuel had to rebuke King Saul's efforts to cover his disobedience with sacrifice: "Is the LORD as delighted with burnt offerings and sacrifices as he would be with your obedience? To follow instructions is better than to sacrifice. To obey is better than sacrificing the

fat of rams" (1 Sam. 15:22). We find the healthy expression of this attitude in David's psalm of repentance: "The sacrifice pleasing to God is a broken spirit. O God, you do not despise a broken and sorrowful heart" (Ps. 51:17).

Sacrifices and offerings were an important part of worship. When Israel was freed from slavery in Egypt, God spent significant time teaching the new nation not only their individual responsibilities but also how they could function before him as an obedient corporate people. The numerous sacrifices and offerings prescribed by God might at first appear to benefit God, who needs nothing; in reality, all these worship actions ultimately benefited those who worshiped. The framework for sacrifices as detailed in Leviticus 23 had as its foundation the sacrifice of a day each week—the Sabbath. God gave his people seven days from which he expected them to return one day of honor to him—the day of rest. As Jesus later explained, the Sabbath was modeled by God in creation even though he needed no rest, in order that humans might eventually understand the healthy benefits of working up to six days but resting on the seventh. In Jesus' brief words, "The day of worship [Sabbath] was made for people, not people for the day of worship" (Mark 2:27).

Substitutionary Atonement

The idea behind sacrifice, particularly blood sacrifice, required the substitution of one life (the animal) for another (the worshiper or the people). A sacrifice was necessary because of sin. Failure to obey God or deliberate efforts to disobey God created an offense or debt that could not be settled by mere apology. The damage was as real as a broken window; forgiveness for throwing the rock doesn't fix the shattered window. The

sacrifice became the payment for the window—a symbolic settling of accounts—and an assurance of the forgiveness God was willing to give. This elaborate system prepared God's people and the rest of the world for the grand sacrifice of God's own Son, once on the cross, as payment and settlement for sin. His death demonstrates and guarantees God's forgiveness, paying the debt for our offense. "God had Christ, who was sinless, take our sin so that we might receive God's approval through him" (2 Cor. 5:21).

The various sacrifices and offerings sometimes involved burning of the fat from animals as an incense to God, but the meat and other edibles that were brought were used to feed the priests and Levites as well as to serve in the communal meals during the festivals. So, for example, the opening chapter of 1 Samuel shows a Jewish man named Elkanah coming to Shiloh with a yearly sacrifice: "Whenever Elkanah offered a sacrifice, he would give portions of it to his wife Peninnah and all her sons and daughters. He would also give one portion to Hannah because he loved her, even though the LORD had kept her from having children" (1 Sam. 1:4–5). The animal was offered, but the meat was shared after the sacrifice.

This was also symbolic of Christ's sacrifice. We have the dual, priceless blessing of a Savior who willingly sacrificed himself on our behalf and yet whose fellowship we can enjoy now and forever since he, though dead, rose from the grave. The sacrifice of Jesus, painful though it was, made our eternity infinitely delightful because we get to spend it with him.

Key Verse

Every day each priest performed his religious duty. He offered the same type of sacrifice again and again. Yet, these sacrifices could never take away sins. However, this chief priest made one sacrifice for sins, and this sacrifice lasts forever. Then he received the highest position in heaven. Since that time, he has been waiting for his enemies to be made his footstool. With one sacrifice he accomplished the work of setting them apart for God forever. (Heb. 10:11–14)

When God brought Israel out of Egypt he set up as part of the covenant relationship a system of sacrifices that had at its heart the shedding and offering of the blood of unflawed animals "to make atonement for yourselves" (Lev. 17:11). These sacrifices were *typical* (that is, as *types*, they pointed forward to something else). Though sins were in fact "left . . . unpunished" (Rom. 3:25) when sacrifices were faithfully offered, what actually blotted them out was not the animals' blood (Heb. 10:11) but the blood of the *antitype*, the sinless Son of God, Jesus Christ whose death on the cross atoned for all sins that were remitted before the event as well as the sins committed after it.

J. I. Packer, *Concise Theology: A Guide to Historical Christian Beliefs* (Wheaton: Tyndale, 1993), 135

Salt

alt was one of the most common substances in the ancient world. Roman soldiers were paid in salt and would revolt if they didn't get their ration. The English word *salary* comes from the Latin *salarium*, which literally means "salt-money." And the expression "that man isn't worth his salt" is a reminder of salt's high value. The biblical writers made generous use of salt imagery. Salt has many positive qualities and also some negative qualities.

Salt in the Old Testament

Early in Jewish tradition, the salt covenant (Lev. 2:13; Num. 18:19; 2 Chron. 13:5), capitalizing on salt's preserving qualities, symbolized a permanent, indissoluble relationship between God and his people. Salt was also used for its preserving quality for all burnt offerings (Ezra 6:9).

Salt symbolized a curse and a desolate landscape. Abimelech laid waste to the captured city of Shechem as he "tore down the city and scattered salt all over the land" (Judg. 9:45). The Dead Sea (Salt Sea), the Valley of Salt, and the City of Salt all imply death, desolation, despair, and deserts. "They will see all the soil poisoned with sulfur and salt. Nothing will be planted. Nothing will be growing. There will be no plants

in sight. It will be as desolate as Sodom, Gomorrah, Admah, and Zeboiim, cities the LORD destroyed in fierce anger" (Deut. 29:23).

The Salt of the Earth

Perhaps the best known salt symbolism comes from Jesus' Sermon on the Mount. Jesus contrasted salt's positive and negative potential: "You are salt for the earth. But if salt loses its taste, how will it be made salty again? It is no longer good for anything except to be thrown out and trampled on by people" (Matt. 5:13). Jesus used salt to symbolize the impact believers can have on society. In the ancient world, salt primarily functioned as a preservative. It retarded spoilage. Likewise, believers act as a preservative in the world. Believers spread the kingdom's influence into culture, protecting society from the full sway of evil that would otherwise be present.

Jesus declared, "You are salt for the earth" (Matt. 5:13). Absent from Jesus' instruction are the words *like* or *as*. Believers are commanded to *be* salt, not just to be like salt. The essence of salt is its uniqueness, its distinctness. Nothing is quite like salt. Just as salt is different from pepper, Christians are distinct from the world. The Christian's distinctiveness is what makes a difference in the world, impacting culture. Salt was used as a flavoring or seasoning (Job 6:6). In a similar fashion, Christianity brings spice and zest to life. The Christian is the personification of how life is to be lived.

Salt is an antiseptic. In ancient times newborn babies were rubbed with salt so that the cuts and infections of primitive birth methods could be healed (cf. Ezek. 16:4). While this

Christians are to be salt in the world—to make people thirsty for God, to preserve the culture, and to heal wounds.

sounds painful, the cleaning out of a wound with salt was very effective in fighting infection. Christians have a responsibility of not only pointing out sin, but practically offering healing and help. By exerting our influence we can prevent the ravages of disease and death caused by sin.

Salt creates thirst. A familiar statement asserts that we can lead a horse to water but we can't make him drink. That may be true, but we can give him a salt tablet, making him thirsty. As Jesus made people thirsty for God the Father, so do Christians make people thirsty for the real life found only in Christianity.

Jesus warned his followers, "But if salt loses its taste, how will it be made salty again? It is no longer good for anything except to be thrown out and trampled on by people" (Matt. 5:13). Perhaps the most important fact about salt is that in its purest form it never loses its taste. Salt will always be salt. It is an extremely stable compound. We can put it in a dish, walk away, come back ten years later, and it will still be sodium chloride—salt. The only way salt can lose its saltiness is to be mixed with something else. Jesus is making the point that it is dangerously easy for Christians to become diluted and lose their salty, preserving influence in the world. If believers are not affecting the world, the world is affecting them. If they are not salting the world, the world is rotting them. In order to prevent the world from affecting us, we must stay in close contact with the ultimate influence—Christ himself.

Key Verse

You are salt for the earth. But if salt loses its taste, how will it be made salty again? It is no longer good for anything except to be thrown out and trampled on by people. (Matt. 5:13)

We are to be unlike the world. There is no need to stress that, it is perfectly obvious. Salt is essentially different from the medium in which it is placed and in a sense it exercises all its qualities by being different. . . . The very characteristic of saltness proclaims a difference, for a small amount of salt in a large medium is at once apparent. Unless we are clear about this we have not even begun to think correctly about the Christian life. The Christian is a man who is essentially different from everybody else. He is as different as the salt is from the meat into which it is rubbed. He is as different as the salt is from the wound into which it is put. This external difference is to be emphasized and stressed.

D. Martyn Lloyd-Jones,
Studies in the Sermon on the Mount
(Grand Rapids: Eerdmans, 1959), 132

Top, salt was often used as a preservative in the days before refrigeration.

Sea of Galilee

Those who visit the Sea of Galilee today are surprised to realize that it is not a sea at all but a lake. And the mountains that surround much of this body of water can always be seen in the distance, at least by day. We can imagine that back when lighting consisted of simple candles and fires, the darkness in the middle of the lake would have created a profound sense of isolation. That body of water is not so much a symbol as a location where some startling events occurred in Bible times.

The name translated as the Sea of Galilee means "circle." In some translations of the Old Testament this sea is called Chinnereth. In the New Testament it is sometimes translated Lake of Gennesaret, Sea of Tiberias, and "the lake." It is the largest freshwater lake in Israel, nestled in the hills of northern Palestine. It is

Several of the disciples were fishermen on the Sea of Galilee.

approximately thirty-three miles in circumference, about thirteen miles long and eight miles wide, with a total area of sixty-four square miles. The Sea of Galilee is nearly seven hundred feet below the level of the Mediterranean (sea level), some thirty miles to the west, making it the lowest freshwater lake on earth and the second lowest lake overall (after the Dead Sea,

a saltwater lake). Though fed partly by underground springs, its chief source is the Jordan River, which flows into it at its northern end and out of it at its southern end.

The Abyss

Although the Sea of Galilee often looks beautiful and calm, it is quite deep and is one of the large bodies of water that biblical writers describe as an abyss. The term *abyss* is a Greek word meaning "depths," but is translated *depth* or *deep* in the Old Testament (Gen. 1:2; 7:11; Job 7:12; Ps. 42:7). Symbolically, the abyss is the abode of the demonic beings who oppose God. Clearly, it is a fearsome place of darkness and chaos. In the New Testament, the depths of the sea are seen as the home of demons, a place called the Abyss, the home of evil spirits according to Jewish tradition. The demons begged Jesus not to send them into the "bottomless pit" (Luke 8:31), but he did.

Furthermore, the Jewish people were not seafarers; they were desert people—nomads and Bedouins. They were comfortable in the wilderness, wandering the land. They rarely ventured to the seacoast. They saw the sea as an alien and threatening power. Few could swim, and even fishermen avoided deep water. For them the sea was a place of terror and danger.

The Storms

Due to the hills surrounding the Sea of Galilee, it is subject to sudden and violent storms that are usually short in duration. We now know that these storms often developed when an east wind dropped cool air over the warm air rising from the lake. This sudden change produced surprisingly furious storms (see Matt. 8:24) that could endanger people in boats.

While the disciples feared the wind and the waves of the sea, Jesus always displayed confidence that his power was greater than any evil in the sea. Jesus acted to demonstrate his authority over the sea and its destructive power. He walked on the stormy water (Matt. 14:22–33; Mark 6:47–50; John 6:16–20). He calmed the storms on the sea (Matt. 8:23–27; Mark 4:35–41; Luke 8:22–25). He even empowered one of his disciples to walk on the water (Matt. 14:28–32). Peter's cry of "Lord, save me!" as his lack of faith caused him to sink into the deep takes on intense meaning in light of the symbolism of the sea (Matt. 14:30). The reaction of the disciples was profound. They were amazed (Matt. 14:33; Mark 6:51) and terrified (Mark 4:41) at Jesus' power. They recognized that his power was more than just authority over the elements of nature. God controls the Abyss. The stilling of the storm produced not only awe at the power of God within Jesus, but also the realization that he was God. The sea and what it represented gave Jesus opportunities to demonstrate that he was truly God.

Key Verse

They were overcome with fear and asked each other, "Who is this man? Even the wind and the sea obey him!" (Mark 4:41)

The Sea of Galilee is not really a sea at all. It is a lake, and not a very large one at that. In most of the ancient literature, the Sea of Galilee is called a lake. . . . By calling it a sea, Mark and other early Christians associated the lake with the primal abyss, the watery chaos that prevailed when God first created the heavens and the earth. The sea was the abode of the great monsters, such as Leviathan, and jaws of death that swallowed Jonah. The sea was the dwelling place of the dark and ever-threatening unknown. . . . In this context, it should be easy to understand why Jesus' walking on the sea and his calming of a storm at sea were extremely powerful Christological images. Jesus was lord of creation. Like God, his Father, he could command order into the unformed and chaotic universe. In his company, no one needed to fear the abyss.

Eugene LaVerdiere, *The Beginning of the Gospel: Introducing the Gospel according to Mark* (Collegeville, MN: Liturgical Press, 1999), 42

Seed

Deceptively small, seeds contain the pure potential for life. A tiny seed can transform into a beautiful flower, a towering tree, or life-giving food. Given the right environment, seeds are self-sustaining: the plants that grow from seeds produce more seeds to continue the reproductive cycle. Seeds have formed the foundation of agriculture since the very first seeds were sown in the Garden of Eden, when God said, "Let the earth produce vegetation: plants bearing seeds, each according to its own type, and fruit trees bearing fruit with seeds, each according to its own type" (Gen. 1:11). As a picture of generation, fertility, and potential, seed imagery abounds through both the Old and New Testaments.

Human Seeds

One of the central uses of the seed image throughout Scripture denotes human ancestry and heritage. The Hebrew word translated as "descendant" literally means "seed." Specifically, Christ is referred to as the "seed of David." This connection stresses Jesus' royal lineage and messianic claim (Rom. 1:3). Similarly, God promised Abraham that his offspring or seed would be blessed and inherit the Promised Land (Gen. 12:7). As direct descendants of Abraham, the Jewish people are called the "seed of Abraham." In Galatians, the promise of God's salvation is extended to Gentiles: "If you belong to Christ, then you are Abraham's descendants and heirs, as God promised" (3:29).

The image of the seed appears in several parables in Matthew 13. Jesus uses the seed as a picture of cultivating the spiritual life. Seeds planted in four different soils (hard, rocky, thorny, and fertile) describe four different responses to the gospel. The seed planted in fertile soil, Jesus tells the disciples, is someone who has a willingness to understand and apply the Word of God. Like a seed that needs care to grow, only an open response to God's truth creates the perfect conditions for the spiritual life to grow. In another parable, Jesus pictures Christians themselves as seeds and warns against phony believers who are sown among them. God will allow the false and true believers to "grow" together until the end of the age, when they will be separated (Matt. 13:24–30).

The Seed of Faith

The size of a seed is also used to illustrate the unique power of faith. Although a seed appears tiny, it contains a hidden potential to produce a large plant. So too, even though a believer's faith is as

In Jesus' parable of the soils, the seed of the gospel falls on five different kinds of soil, representing five different heart responses.

"small as a mustard seed," it is enough to powerfully change the world (Matt. 13:31–32; 17:20; Mark 4:30–32; Luke 17:6). We may feel like our faith is small or just beginning to grow, but even in those early stages God can do powerful things through us as he helps us to grow.

Paul continued this symbol of seeds of faith when he discussed the process of evangelism. "I planted, and Apollos watered, but God made it grow. So neither the one who plants nor the one who waters is important because only God makes it grow. The one who plants and the one who waters have the same goal, and each will receive a reward for his own work. We are God's coworkers. You are God's field" (1 Cor. 3:6–9). Sharing the gospel with others can be thought of as planting a seed of faith. Just as with plants, we never know when it will germinate and what it will become, but we can faithfully do our part, trusting God for the outcome. Indeed, the kingdom of heaven itself is compared to a seed that grows into a huge tree. It starts small, but as each person spreads the good news of the gospel to others, the kingdom grows exponentially into a living organism. Such a promise should give us hope that God can cultivate a good work in us no matter how confident we feel about ourselves.

Key Verse

Jesus used another illustration. He said, "The kingdom of heaven is like a mustard seed that someone planted in a field. It's one of the smallest seeds. However, when it has grown, it is taller than the garden plants. It becomes a tree that is large enough for birds to nest in its branches." (Matt. 13:31–32)

The mustard seed and the leaven represent the extensive and intensive, the outward and inward, the objective and subjective aspects of Christianity. Sometimes when the Church is reaching its branches to the farthest, its heart is being corrupted by the slow spread of evil. See 1 Corinthians 5:7–8. See what stress our Lord lays on unnoticed beginnings! What seed is smaller than the mustard! Yet it may be the gateway through which Nature may pour her inner energies, forcing the rootlet down and the green shoot up. . . . Bigness is not greatness. Watch the first speck of sin; cherish each grain of holy impulse.

F. B. Meyer, *Devotional Commentary* (Wheaton: Tyndale, 1989), 405

Serpent on a Pole

During the exodus, the people of Israel repeatedly rebelled against God and didn't trust his Word, so God sent "poisonous snakes" (Num. 21:6) into the camp as a punishment for their sin. Some translations call them "fiery serpents." When the Israelites repented and begged for deliverance, God told Moses to create a bronze serpent and put it on a pole. Anyone who had been bitten could look at the bronze snake and be healed (Num. 21:4–9). The saving power came not from the bronze serpent itself but from God, who saved the people when they trusted him by looking at the bronze serpent.

A Symbol of Salvation

Some scholars connect this event to the time when Moses' staff (or pole) became a snake, swallowed up the snake-staffs of Pharaoh's magicians, and then turned back into a staff (Exod. 7:8–12). In Bible times, serpents were deified by both Egyptian and Canaanite religions, so the triumph of God's serpent over the Egyptian serpents symbolized his superiority over all other gods. Likewise, the triumph of the bronze serpent in the wilderness over the certain death caused by a poisonous snakebite signified God's power over all the forces of nature and the false gods the Egyptians associated with them. But the main focus in this event was God's provision of salvation. The serpent was a symbol of salvation because everyone who looked at it on the pole, in faith, was saved from death.

The Israelites brought the serpent on a pole with them when they entered the Promised Land as a remembrance of God's salvation in the desert. When Hezekiah embarked on his religious reforms he destroyed it, because by that time it had become an idol (2 Kings 18:4). People had forgotten that the serpent on a pole was a symbol of God's deliverance from death through faith and had begun to worship the object itself. This is similar to the way people of later generations confused symbols and icons representing God with God himself, giving them undue attention and neglecting acts of true worship such as showing mercy.

A Messianic Sign

Jesus compared his crucifixion to this saving event in the wilderness: "As Moses lifted up the snake on a pole in the desert, so the Son of Man must be lifted up. Then everyone who believes in him will have eternal life" (John 3:14–15). His Jewish hearers would have immediately remembered the story from Numbers about the judgment of poisonous snakes in the desert and the salvation that came through the bronze serpent on a pole. The fact that the serpent is usually a symbol for Satan and sin underscores the fact

When the Israelites were dying from a plague, God told Moses to put a statue of a bronze serpent on a pole, and those who looked to it were healed.

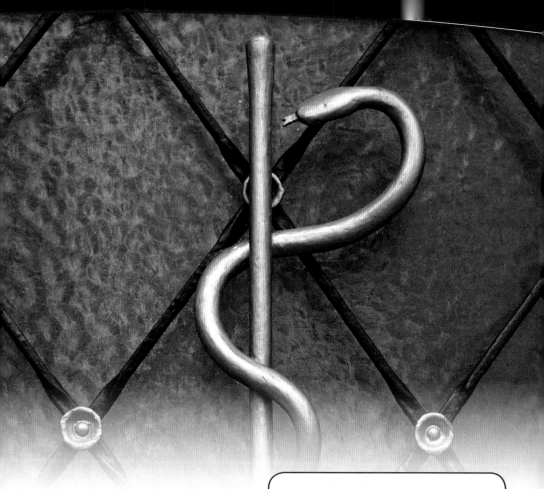

that "He made Him who knew no sin to be sin on our behalf, so that we might become the righteousness of God in Him" (2 Cor. 5:21 NASB). God redeemed a symbol of evil (the serpent) and turned it into a symbol of salvation.

The bronze serpent on a pole that saved people from poisonous snakebites was a sign of the true deliverance that came through Jesus when he was hung on the cross. Just as the Israelites had looked in faith to the serpent on a pole to be saved from death, we also look in faith to the crucified Savior to have eternal life.

Key Verse

As Moses lifted up the snake on a pole in the desert, so the Son of Man must be lifted up. Then everyone who believes in him will have eternal life. (John 3:14–15)

There was no healing virtue in the bronze serpent in the wilderness. In itself it was a mere *nehushtan*, a piece of bronze; when in later days people paid homage to it as though it had some inherent sanctity or power, good King Hezekiah broke it in pieces (2 Kings 18:4). It was the saving grace of God that healed the bitten Israelites when they believed his word and obeyed his command. But in the Son of Man who was lifted up there resides infinite healing virtue, far more potent than anything which was experienced by the Israelites in the wilderness. They were cured of a physical disease and received a prolongation of mortal life, but it is eternal life that the Son of Man ensures to those who look to him.

F. F. Bruce, *The Gospel of John: Introduction, Exposition, and Notes* (Grand Rapids: Eerdmans, 1983), 88–89

Serpent/Dragon

When the Bible introduces Satan in the story of humankind, it describes the tempter as a serpent or snake. "The snake was more clever than all the wild animals the LORD God had made" (Gen. 3:1). Was Satan a serpent? Much later, the apostle Paul makes a startling point when he writes, "And no wonder, even Satan disguises himself as an angel of light" (2 Cor. 11:14). We should not be surprised that the "father of lies" would use the strategy of changing appearances in order to fool those he is trying to tempt. Showing himself to Eve as a serpent who can talk should have been a warning to her, but she and Adam were both fooled by his argument.

animals as long as you live. I will make you and the woman hostile toward each other. I will make your descendants and her descendant hostile toward each other. He will crush your head, and you will bruise his heel.'" Both John the Baptist and Jesus called out the Pharisees as "poisonous snakes" (Matt. 3:7; 12:34) because their view of righteousness and Christ was entirely consumed by their desire for power and control rather than true faith. The deceptive way snakes can conceal themselves in plain sight is used as an illustration in Proverbs 23:31–32: "Do not look at wine because it is red, because it sparkles in the cup, because it goes down smoothly. Later it bites like a snake and strikes like a poisonous snake."

A Fearsome Animal

By the time Moses was recording the first volume (Genesis) of his five-book collection under the inspiration of God, humanity already had a lengthy experience with serpents. Their stealthy nature and poisonous bites made serpents an easy choice as a symbol of evil or life-threatening experiences in the world. The Bible uses at least fifteen different terms related to serpents or snakes. Although some traits of serpents are occasionally used as symbols of desirable characteristics in people, in general, serpents represent danger. Jesus could tell his followers to be "cunning as snakes" (Matt. 10:16), pointing to a certain wisdom and craftiness on the part of serpents that is consistent with their nature.

The symbolic uses of serpents in the Bible tend to rest on their dangerous aspects and reflect the truth of God's curse back in Genesis 3:14–15: "So the LORD God said to the snake, 'Because you have done this, you are cursed more than all the wild or domestic animals. You will crawl on your belly. You will be the lowest of

Serpents in the Exodus

Two instances of serpents during the exodus account deserve special attention. One of these you will find in a separate entry, SERPENT ON A POLE. The other instance occurs when God calls Moses to leave his lengthy exile in the desert and go back to Egypt to lead the children of Israel out of bondage. Moses is not eager to assume this role. God provides him with several authenticating signs that will demonstrate God's sanction of his mission. Among these is a demonstration of God's power through Moses' simple shepherd's staff:

Then the LORD asked him, "What's that in your hand?"

He answered, "A shepherd's staff."

The LORD said, "Throw it on the ground."

When Moses threw it on the ground, it became a snake, and he ran away from it.

Then the LORD said to Moses, "Reach out and grab the snake by its tail." He reached out and grabbed it, and it turned back into a staff as he held it. The LORD explained, "This is to

convince the people that the LORD God of their ancestors, the God of Abraham, Isaac, and Jacob, appeared to you." (Exod. 4:2–5)

Interestingly, when Moses and Aaron performed this sign before Pharaoh, the magicians of Egypt were able to duplicate it (Exod. 7:10–13). Their staffs turned into snakes also (possibly an indication that they were representing Satan's evil power to counterfeit God's actions). God's snake, however, consumed the snakes of the magicians, demonstrating the superiority of his power to theirs.

The Final Defeat of the Serpent

When Revelation 12 describes the appearance of Satan in the vision of the last days, he is called a *drakon* in Greek, the original language of the New Testament, from which we get the word *dragon*. This term is used twelve times in Revelation and nowhere else in Scripture (see 12:3, 4, 7, 9, 13, 17; 13:2, 4, 11; 16:13; 20:2). In 12:9, the identity of the serpent/dragon is made clear: "The huge serpent was thrown down. That ancient snake, named Devil and Satan, the deceiver of the whole world, was thrown down to earth. Its angels were thrown down with it." Satan, the original enemy of all God created, is the last enemy to be defeated along with his most powerful tool—death (see Rev. 20:10). The defeats he experienced at the fall, during the exodus, and at the crucifixion are nothing in comparison with his final judgment and defeat at the end of time.

Key Verse

Moses and Aaron went to Pharaoh and did as the LORD had commanded. Aaron threw his staff down in front of Pharaoh and his officials, and it became a large snake. Then Pharaoh sent for his wise men and sorcerers. These Egyptian magicians did the same thing using their magic spells. Each of them threw his staff down, and they all became large snakes. But Aaron's staff swallowed theirs. (Exod. 7:10–12)

Of all the signs that God could have given to Pharaoh, he chose to turn Aaron's staff into a serpent. The more we know about the Egyptians and their snakes, the clearer it becomes that by doing this, God was waging war against Satan. The Egyptians were fascinated with snakes, partly because they were so afraid of them. Many of them carried amulets to protect them from Apophis, the serpent-god who personified evil.... It was this fear of snakes that led Pharaoh to use the serpent as the symbol of his royal authority.... [Aaron] was taking the symbol of the king's majesty and making it crawl in the dust. This was a direct assault on Pharaoh's sovereignty; indeed, it was an attack on Egypt's entire belief system.

Philip Graham Ryken, *Exodus: Saved for God's Glory* (Wheaton: Crossway, 2005), 206–7

Seven

Almost from the very beginning of the Bible, the number *seven* takes on special if not symbolic importance. God not only created the world in seven days, he also reserved the seventh day of creation as a personal day of recreation, or rest. Later, when God delivered the Ten Commandments (Exod. 20:1–17), the seventh day, or *Sabbath*, was identified as "the day of worship dedicated to the LORD your God" (v. 10). The reason given for this rule is, "In six days the LORD made heaven, earth, and the sea, along with everything in them. He didn't work on the seventh day. That's why the LORD blessed the day he stopped his work and set this day apart as holy" (v. 11). This early use of *seven* in Scripture creates the foundation for understanding this particular number as a symbol of perfection and completeness.

The significance of *seven* is further carried into the spiritual practices of Israel. In carrying out sacrifices for his sins and the sins of the people (Lev. 16:14–19), Aaron and the priests who would follow him were directed to "sprinkle some of the blood with [their] finger seven times in front of the throne of mercy" (v. 14). The pattern of the Sabbath was applied not only to the weekly cycle, but to the yearly one. Every seventh year was to be a sabbatical; and every fiftieth year, the year following a cycle of seven times seven years, was to be a Jubilee year of special celebration in which debts were forgiven and commitments settled.

The Number of Completeness

Use of the number *seven* to symbolize completeness or representatives of a larger group is illustrated in many settings throughout the Bible. Sets of seven are not always obvious, but when identified they can be significant. Proverbs lists

seven deadly sins (6:16–19). The lamp stand had seven branches (Exod. 25:37). Seven priests with seven rams' horns preceded the march around Jericho, which was performed seven times (Josh. 6). Seven baskets of food were left over after the feeding of the four thousand (Mark 8).

Groupings of seven events also appear. Matthew's collection of Jesus' parables that makes up the bulk of chapter 13 in his Gospel includes seven of these stories, and all of them teach various aspects of the kingdom of heaven. The Gospel of John includes seven major miracles or signs that display the glory of God in Jesus (2:11, 18–19; 4:54; 6:2, 14, 26; 9:16; 12:18). In his Gospel, John also incorporated two sevenfold sets of "I am" statements of Jesus. One set echoes the "I AM" self-description of God in the Old Testament (Exod. 3:13–14), recognized as such by Jesus' hearers (John 4:26; 6:20; 8:24, 28, 58; 13:19; 18:5, 6, 8). The other group includes Jesus' special ministry claims beginning with "I am the bread of life" (John 6:35; 8:12; 10:7, 9, 11, 14; 11:25; 14:6; 15:1, 5). The writer of Hebrews, demonstrating from the Old Testament the superiority of Jesus over angels, uses seven passages to make the case (Heb. 1:5–14). When James describes wisdom, he gives it seven primary characteristics (James 3:17). When Jesus comes to John with a message for his churches, he specifies seven of them to represent all the churches (Rev. 2–3). The book of Revelation also has seven specific blessings, beginning with the promised blessing for those who read the book (1:3; 14:13; 16:15; 19:9; 20:6; 22:7, 14).

The Number *Seven* in Prophecy

In Scripture's prophetic books, seven serves as a symbolic pointer to completeness, sometimes even complete evil. In Zechariah 4:10, God's

intimate awareness of all things is described as the "seven eyes of the LORD." Daniel's interpretation of Nebuchadnezzar's dream included the sobering news that the king would be out of his mind for seven years (Dan. 4:19–37). On several occasions the book of Revelation refers to the "seven spirits of God" (1:4; 3:1; 4:5; 5:6), attributing them to Christ. Jesus is further described as the Lamb with seven eyes (complete knowledge) and seven horns (power) in Revelation 5:6.

Contrast that picture with the image of the seven-headed serpent of Revelation 12:3, representing the ancient serpent Satan, and the seven-headed beast who assists him in carrying out his plans on earth (Rev. 13:1; 17:3, 9–11). In Revelation, the unfolding of God's final judgment on earth is described in sets of seven seals, seven trumpets, and seven bowls. In each of these, the seventh item contains the next set of horrors. But when the final bowl of wrath is poured out, John writes, "One of the seven angels who had the seven bowls full of the last seven plagues came to me and said, 'Come! I will show you the bride, the wife of the lamb.' He carried me by his power away to a large, high mountain. He showed me the holy city, Jerusalem, coming down from God out of heaven.

It had the glory of God" (Rev. 21:9–11). After God's judgment has been fully completed, the true perfection of eternal life in his presence will become reality.

Key Verse

One of the seven angels who had the seven bowls full of the last seven plagues came to me and said, "Come! I will show you the bride, the wife of the lamb." (Rev. 21:9)

[Seven was] a sacred number to the ancient Hebrew people. The word is used often in the Bible to symbolize perfection, fullness, abundance, rest, and completion. This number was also considered holy or sacred by other cultures of the ancient world. It may have received its significance from the seven 'planets' visible in the heavens—the sun and moon and the five planets known to the ancients. Or perhaps it was chosen because the lunar month is composed of four periods of about seven days.

Ronald F. Youngblood, F. F. Bruce, R. K. Harrison, eds., *Nelson's New Illustrated Bible Dictionary* (Nashville: Thomas Nelson, 1995), 1149–50

Top, the seven candles in the menorah reflect the importance of this number in Jewish symbolism.

219

Ship/Boat

Today, we connect boating with recreation or even affluence. For people living in ancient times, boats were considered work vehicles (for fishermen) and a primary mode of transportation (Acts 15:39; 18:18–22; Rom. 15:24–28). Employed for fishing, pilgrimages, or trade, the boats and ships of biblical times were driven by sails or oars and carried people and cargo throughout the Mediterranean, Caspian, Red, and Black Seas. Although sea travel was common in ancient times, it was not without significant risk. Descriptions of sea journeys in the Bible are often replete with hazards, including violent storms, shipwrecks, and pirate attacks (1 Kings 22:48; 2 Chron. 20:37; Jon. 1; 2 Cor. 11:25–26; Rev. 8:9).

Security and the Protection of God

Biblical symbolism attached to boats and ships tends to illustrate the range of human experience, representing both security and human vulnerability. Boats as symbols of safety and security can be found throughout the Old Testament, from the very large ship that protected Noah and his family and an amazing menagerie during the flood (Gen. 6–8), to the small craft that conveyed the baby Moses to safety (Exod. 2). These two events are often thought of as symbolic of salvation. God provided the only means of escape for both Noah and Moses because of their faith (or in the case of Moses, the faith of his parents), just as our only escape from judgment is the salvation we find in Christ. Peter draws the connection by saying, "They are like those who disobeyed long ago in the days of Noah when God waited patiently while Noah built the ship. In this ship a few people—eight in all—were saved by water" (1 Pet. 3:20). This symbolism of boats of salvation is further illustrated when Jesus kept his disciples safe in a boat (Matt. 8:23–27; Mark 4:35–41; Luke 8:22–25).

Because ships were used to deliver goods over long distances, they are often used throughout Scripture to symbolize provision. The wise woman of Proverbs 31:13–14 is pictured as a ship: "She seeks out wool and linen with care and works with willing hands. She is like merchant ships. She brings her food from far away."

God's authority in our lives is also frequently portrayed in nautical terms. For those who place their confidence in the Lord, God is symbolized as a "sure and strong anchor for our lives" (Heb. 6:19). The psalm writer describes how those who "sail on the sea in ships, who do business on the high seas, have seen what the LORD can do, the miracles he performed in the depths of the sea" (Ps. 107:23–24). To sail a ship is to become intimately acquainted with God's power to control the storms of life and ultimately guide a boat "to the harbor they had longed for" (Ps. 107:30).

Beginning with Noah's ark and continuing through Jesus' interactions with his disciples, boats are symbols of God's protection.

Weakness and Vulnerability

We can assume that if God is portrayed throughout the Bible as the one who keeps sailors safe, then boats are also an image for human frailty and vulnerability. The destructive power of the tongue is compared to the rudder of a ship in James 3:4–5. Boat symbolism is especially prominent in the apostle Paul's writing. His mission work included extensive sea travel and a shipwreck in Acts 27:1–28:14. In Ephesians 4:14, Paul speaks of those whose lack of spiritual depth causes them to be "tossed and carried about by all kinds of teachings that change like the wind," and in 1 Timothy 1:19, he warns that those who refuse to let their faith guide their conscience will have their faith "destroyed like a wrecked ship."

In Revelation 18, ship imagery is used to symbolize the foolishness of seeking fleeting, worldly treasures as opposed to orienting one's life to the permanent blessings promised by God. This is portrayed in reactions to the destroyed city of Babylon: "Every ship's captain, everyone who traveled by ship, sailors, and everyone who made their living from the sea stood far away. . . . Everyone who had a ship at sea grew rich because of that city's high prices. In one moment it has been destroyed!" (vv. 17, 19).

Key Verse

The Lord said to Noah, "Go into the ship with your whole family because I have seen that you alone are righteous among the people of today." (Gen. 7:1)

Noah's faithfulness—in the form of a great ark—became one of the early church's symbols for refuge. The interiors of many great cathedrals were built to resemble the inside of a boat—a shelter in the time of storm, a reminder of an obedient man who went before us and was saved.

Ann Spangler and Robert Wolgemuth,
*Men of the Bible: A One-Year
Devotional Study of Men in Scripture*
(Grand Rapids: Zondervan, 2002), 36

Top, James uses the rudder of a ship to illustrate the power that the tongue can exert.

221

Silver

Silver is one of the precious metals mentioned frequently in the Bible. It symbolizes value. Proverbs uses silver along with gold as significant measures of the even greater value of wisdom: "The profit gained from wisdom is greater than the profit gained from silver. Its yield is better than fine gold" (3:14).

A Symbol of Purification

The process of heating silver to burn off the dross and other imperfections is a metaphor used throughout Scripture. God's Word itself is described in value beyond silver: "The promises of the LORD are pure, like silver refined in a furnace and purified seven times" (Ps. 12:6). The purification process was sometimes used as a symbol for the way God tests and refines people: "You have tested us, O God. You have refined us in the same way silver is refined" (Ps. 66:10; see also Isa. 48:10). A silversmith would have to attentively watch the silver, getting it to just the right heat, in order to purify the metal. God also watches us as he puts us through fiery trials, never leaving us for an instant and only allowing the situation to progress to the point where it is helpful for our sanctification.

Not as Valuable as It Seems

Frequently, however, the presence of silver indicates that something extremely valuable is being overlooked. A chief example of this is Judas's willingness to betray Jesus for thirty pieces of silver. Another example from the Old Testament involves the payment of ransom or tribute by Israel to gain or retain the favor of other nations in direct disobedience to God. King Menahem of the northern kingdom used silver to buy off the king of Assyria: "King Pul of Assyria came to attack the country. So Menahem gave Pul 75,000 pounds of silver to gain his support and help strengthen his hold on the kingdom. Menahem raised the money from all the wealthy men in Israel. Each gave 20 ounces of silver for the king of Assyria. Then the king of Assyria left the country" (2 Kings 15:19–20). Later, Hezekiah, the king of Judah, tried this approach with King Sennacherib of Assyria, offering silver and gold, but eventually he realized that the only way of escape for him and his people was to trust in God (2 Kings 18–19).

In the New Testament, silver is usually mentioned as the equivalent of money, used in exchange for goods. But Peter makes clear in his first letter that silver cannot purchase what is most valuable: "Realize that you weren't set free from the worthless life handed down to you from your ancestors by a payment of silver or gold which can be destroyed. Rather, the payment that freed you was the precious blood of Christ, the lamb with no defects or imperfections"

Jesus told his disciples to "give the emperor what belongs to the emperor, and give God what belongs to God" (Mark 12:17), indicating that a human life rightfully belongs to its Creator.

(1 Pet. 1:18–19). Shortly after the resurrection of Jesus, when Peter and John were asked by a lame beggar for help, they gave an unexpected answer: "But Peter said, 'I don't have any silver or gold for you. But I'll give you what I have. In the name of Jesus Christ the Nazarene, get up and walk!'" (Acts 3:6 NLT).

The picture of future Babylon in Revelation includes mention of great wealth in silver and gold that not only proves useless against evil but reinforces resistance to God. Valuable items from a worldly point of view become part of the symbolic false ideal that must be destroyed as the kingdom of God comes in fullness (see Rev. 18). Peter was right; silver is one of many things that we consider valuable but that has no potential in providing for us what we really need the most—a resolution of our sins and hope of eternal life.

Key Verse

The promises of the Lord are pure,
like silver refined in a furnace and purified
seven times. (Ps. 12:6)

Most people seem to prefer things golden. We even speak "words that are golden." But when God speaks, it's *silver*. Psalm 12:6 says, "The words of the Lord are flawless, like silver refined in a furnace . . . purified seven times." Purity and silver go together best when it comes to describing God's Word. Why does God choose this precious metal? Perhaps it's because gold requires impurities so it can bond. But not silver. God is less interested in attractiveness and more interested in purity. Dentists understand this—one unusual quality of silver that accentuates its purity is its ability to kill bacteria that comes in contact with it. So too the Word of God is not only pure, it has the ability, when applied by faith, to cleanse the reader of his or her sin. God is not as concerned about people finding his words "golden," all beautiful and attractive, as he is about people's lives being touched by the "silver" of his Word—becoming changed, holy, and pure.

Joni Eareckson Tada, "Before You Begin,"
in *More Precious than Silver*
(Grand Rapids: Zondervan, 1998)

Six Hundred Sixty-Six

When it comes to numbers in the Bible, it's quite possible that 666 is the most famous and infamous of the numbers. People who know little else about the Bible know that 666 is a number connected with some kind of evil character or movement.

The Number of the Beast

A practice called *gematria* gives a numerical value to the letters of a word, then uses their combined numerical value to express a name or a witty association of ideas. Gematria can be used as a simple code to hide an identity. Scripture gives only one clear number code, the number of the beast. This is given as the number of a man, 666: "In this situation wisdom is needed. Let the person who has insight figure out the number of the beast, because it is a human number. The beast's number is 666" (Rev. 13:18). If,

as many scholars believe, a name is hidden in the numbers (the value given to the letters that add up to the word form of 666), and if it is assumed that the writer was using the Hebrew or Aramaic alphabet (which only use consonants), one name seems to emerge. The consonants for Nero Caesar are as follows:

nun (n) = 50

resh (r) = 200

waw (w) = 6

nun (n) = 50

qoph (q) = 100

samekh (s) = 60

resh (r) = 200

These total 666 and seem to be the best solution.

The number 666 is associated with an evil leader in end-times prophecy.

The letters in the name Nero Caesar add up to 666, indicating that perhaps he is at least a partial fulfillment of end-times prophecy.

Six is a traditional symbol for humans, possibly because man was created on the sixth day. And because seven is the number of perfection and six is one less than that, the number *six* is a reminder of human incompleteness. People without God will always be incomplete, always falling short of the perfect number. In addition, the Bible often repeats things three times for emphasis—repeating a word three times, for example, as in "Holy, holy, holy" (Isa. 6:3). Thus, some have suggested that the threefold use of *six* could indicate an emphatic description of imperfection. This symbolism may also have been in John's mind.

Key Verse

In this situation wisdom is needed. Let the person who has insight figure out the number of the beast, because it is a human number. The beast's number is 666. (Rev. 13:18)

It is more or less certain that the number 666 represents, by one of many formulae well known at the time, the name *Nero Caesar* when written in Hebrew characters. (Many people, and many languages, used letters as numbers, as we would if we devised a system where A=1, B=2 and so on.) The monster who was, is not, and is to come looks pretty certain to be Nero. But the number 666 isn't just a cryptogram. It's also a parody. The number of perfection would be 777. For John there is little doubt that Nero, and the system he represented and embodied, was but a parody of the real thing, one short of the right number three times over. Jesus was the reality; Nero just a dangerous, blasphemous copy.

N. T. Wright, *Revelation: 8 Studies for Individuals and Groups*
(Downers Grove, IL: InterVarsity, 2012), 77

Top, the beast represented by the number 666 cannot be definitively identified, but it is nonetheless a fearsome symbol.

Sodom

Sodom was a city in ancient Canaan that became a symbol for God's justice applied. It ceased to exist as a place when God's messengers unleashed a storm of fire on the village and consumed it and all its inhabitants. It now serves only as a sad reminder that deliberate sin will be punished, sooner or later. The tragic Sodom episode is told in Genesis 18–19. Our awareness of the depravity of Sodom in the account of the Old Testament doesn't prepare us for Jesus' words: "And you, Capernaum, will you be lifted to heaven? No, you will go down to hell! If the miracles that had been worked in you had been worked in Sodom, it would still be there today. I can guarantee that judgment day will be better for Sodom than for you" (Matt. 11:23–24).

Sodom and the close-by city of Gomorrah are part of a significant chapter in Abraham's life. Lot chose to settle in the evil cities of Sodom and Gomorrah because it was "well-watered like the LORD's garden or like Egypt" (Gen. 13:10). This imagery echoes Eve's temptation to eat fruit that was "good to eat, nice to look at, and desirable" (Gen. 3:6) and foreshadows the temptations Lot would face in these sinful cities. While Lot was tolerating and trying to get along with his neighbors, God came to Abraham with his plans to destroy the cities. Abraham pled for their survival. In a classic and almost humorous example of bartering, Abraham argued for the sparing of the city if ten innocent men could be found there. God rescued Lot and his two daughters,

When Lot's wife disobeyed God's command and looked back as they fled Sodom, she was turned into a pillar of salt.

but Lot's wife decided to look back, perhaps with curiosity or with longing for what she was leaving, and she was lost. "Then the LORD made burning sulfur and fire rain out of heaven on Sodom and Gomorrah. He destroyed those cities, the whole plain, all who lived in the cities, and whatever grew on the ground" (Gen. 19:24–25).

A Symbol for Sin

The prophets mention Sodom frequently, using the name not so much to confront sexual perversity but as a symbol to represent blatant sin of all kinds. For example, Ezekiel rails against Jerusalem: " 'As I live,' declares the Almighty LORD, 'your sister Sodom and her daughters never did what you and your daughters have done. This is what your sister Sodom has done wrong. She and her daughters were proud that they had plenty of food and had peace and security. They didn't help the poor and the needy. They were arrogant and did disgusting things in front of me. So I did away with them when I saw this' " (16:48–50).

An Example of Judgment

Alongside Jesus' use of Sodom as a sobering example to his contemporaries, other New Testament writers mention Sodom in symbolic language. Paul quotes Isaiah's point that the ultimate difference between Israel and Sodom is the grace of God, not the moral

superiority of God's chosen people (Rom. 9:29). Peter points to Sodom as "an example to ungodly people of what is going to happen to them" (2 Pet. 2:6). Jude points out the specific sins of Sodom to demonstrate that they were not singled out for the punishment that will fall on all sin: "What happened to Sodom and Gomorrah and the cities near them is an example for us of the punishment of eternal fire. The people of these cities suffered the same fate that God's people and the angels did, because they committed sexual sins and engaged in homosexual activities" (1:7). And at one point in Revelation, John's description of Jerusalem equates the conditions in the city with that ancient example: "Their dead bodies will lie on the street of the important city where their Lord was crucified. The spiritual names of that city are Sodom and Egypt" (11:8).

The tragedy of Sodom lies buried in history, but the lessons of Sodom continue with us every day. The day of the Lord will bring the total and irrevocable judgment of God epitomized by Sodom and Gomorrah.

Key Verse

God condemned the cities of Sodom and Gomorrah and destroyed them by burning them to ashes. He made those cities an example to ungodly people of what is going to happen to them. Yet, God rescued Lot, a man who had his approval. Lot was distressed by the lifestyle

of people who had no principles and lived in sexual freedom. Although he was a man who had God's approval, he lived among the people of Sodom and Gomorrah. Each day was like torture to him as he saw and heard the immoral things that people did.

Since the Lord did all this, he knows how to rescue godly people when they are tested. He also knows how to hold immoral people for punishment on the day of judgment. (2 Pet. 2:6–9)

In his exposition of 2 Peter 2:6–9, John MacArthur writes,

Peter knew his readers, living in the midst of their corrupt culture, could identify with Lot's difficult position. Their own situations were equally soul-distressing as they witnessed the immoral excesses of the false teachers and their followers (cf. 2:18–20). Like Noah and his family, Lot stood against the sin of his day and refused to follow the demonic doctrines and immoral practices that permeated society. By recalling the account of God's judgment on Sodom and Gomorrah, Peter warns his readers of the doom that all of God's enemies (and, specifically, false teachers) will face. But, by highlighting the salvation of Lot, the apostle simultaneously comforts the righteous, reminding them that they have nothing to fear.

John MacArthur, *Second Peter and Jude*, The MacArthur New Testament Commentary (Chicago: Moody, 2005), 91

Top, the cities of Sodom and Gomorrah, the wicked cities where Lot lived, were burned with sulfur and brimstone as a judgment for their sin.

Son

Just as the most significant use of the term *father* has to do with God, likewise the word *son* gets its highest meaning when used to describe Jesus Christ, the Son of God. The greatest affirmation of Jesus to human listeners came on the occasions of his baptism and his transfiguration. During the former, God said, "This is my Son, whom I love—my Son with whom I am pleased" (Matt. 3:17). Later, when Jesus was glorified before three of his disciples, the Father again said, "This is my Son, whom I love and with whom I am pleased. Listen to him!" (Matt. 17:5). Jesus' final words from the cross tell us how deeply and fully he understood his role as God the Father's Son: "Jesus cried out in a loud voice, 'Father, into your hands I entrust my spirit.' After he said this, he died" (Luke 23:46). From the birth of Cain and Abel to the arrival of Jesus in Bethlehem, God prepared the world to understand his plan for solving the curse of sin by allowing the human race to develop a special interest in the idea of sons.

Customs Concerning Sons

In Bible cultures, a son carried on the name (and, in a sense, the life) of his father, and the first son received the primary inheritance in his family. The killing of the firstborn sons of Egypt as the final punishment by God on that nation struck at the heart of that culture (Exod. 11). One of the ways God described the importance of Israel was by calling the people his son: "Then tell Pharaoh, 'This is what the LORD says: Israel is my firstborn son. I told you to let my son go so that he may worship me. But you refused to let him go. So now I'm going to kill your firstborn son'" (Exod. 4:22–23). Later, Hosea will repeat this fact; then Matthew will refer to it in describing the significance of Jesus' escape to Egypt from the murderous intentions of Herod: "He stayed there until Herod died. What the Lord had spoken through the prophet came true: 'I have called my son out of Egypt'" (Matt. 2:15; quoted from Hosea 11:1).

The Son of God

The New Testament includes numerous references to Jesus using the term *Son* (around 150). These uses are considered foundational to our understanding of God as Trinity. But notice that sonship and even the phrase *only begotten* used in John 3:16 (often shortened to *only*) are not meant to imply that Jesus was created in Mary or was some temporary form/emanation that God adopted in order to visit earth. Jesus' place in the Trinity as God is eternal past, and he was present and active in creation. In the context of the Trinity, *Son* and *Father* serve primarily as relational descriptors and point to the intimacy that always has existed within God.

Jesus Christ, the Son of God who died on the cross to save us, is the person to whom all of Scripture points.

Becoming God's Child

Parallel to the Old Testament understanding of Israel as God's son, the New Testament teaches that those who follow Jesus and are transformed by him become "sons of God," a phrase intended to mean "children of God," since it includes both males and females: "However, he gave the right to become God's children to everyone who believed in him. These people didn't become God's children in a physical way—from a human impulse or from a husband's desire to have a child. They were born from God" (John 1:12–13). Because we are God's children, he provides for us as surely as an earthly father provides for his children—in our case, an eternal inheritance: "If we are his children, we are also God's heirs. If we share in Christ's suffering in order to share his glory, we are heirs together with him" (Rom. 8:17). The glory of the gospel is that through the sacrifice of the Son of God, we can be adopted into God's family as siblings of Christ with all the rights and privileges inherent in that relationship.

In the eternal kingdom of God, all symbols, including the idea of sonship, will reach their fulfillment and full understanding. So when all things are renewed at the arrival of the New Jerusalem and the re-creation of a new heaven and earth, God will make his declaration: "Everyone who wins the victory will inherit these things. I will be their God, and they will be my children" (Rev. 21:7). Because of God's Son, we will all be God's children.

Key Verse

God sent him to pay for the freedom of those who were controlled by these laws so that we would be adopted as his children. Because you are God's children, God has sent the Spirit of his Son into us to call out, "Abba! Father!" So you are no longer slaves but God's children. Since you are God's children, God has also made you heirs. (Gal. 4:5–7)

Concerning the image of adoption as a metaphor for salvation, Brenda B. Colijn writes,

> Adoption also involves new responsibilities. Like all of Paul's salvation metaphors, adoption has ethical implications. In the Greco-Roman world, an adopted son left his old family behind and took on the honor and obligations of his new family. He owed allegiance to his new father, not to his biological father, and he was obligated to live in a way that would bring honor to his new family. Similarly, believers in Jesus are adopted into the family of God. Their allegiance to their new Father supersedes all prior allegiances, whether to their biological parents or even to the "divine father," the emperor. They are obligated to follow the leading of God's Spirit (Rom. 8:9, 12–14). Likewise, they take on new responsibilities to other believers, their brothers and sisters in Christ.

Brenda B. Colijn, *Images of Salvation in the New Testament* (Downers Grove, IL: InterVarsity, 2010), 186

Top, the image of father and son is a portrait of the relationship God has with those who believe in him.

229

Stone/Rock

(See also CORNERSTONE)

In the ancient world, before the explosives and powerful tools we have today, rocks were impervious, seemingly eternal, and solid. In times of danger, a cliff formed a secure foundation or a safe hiding place, as David found when he was a fugitive being chased by Saul (2 Sam. 22:2–4, 32). The physical safety offered by rocks made them a fitting image for the security offered by God: "He alone is my rock and my savior—my stronghold. I cannot be severely shaken" (Ps. 62:2; see also 31:2–3; 62:6–7). God is the solid foundation upon which a believer builds his or her life.

Stone of Stumbling

A rock or a stone can also be an obstacle that causes one to stumble or gets in the way. God is a rock in this sense of the term as well, for "the LORD of Armies is holy. . . . He will be a place of safety for you. But he will be a rock that makes people trip and a stumbling block for both kingdoms of Israel" (Isa. 8:13–14; cf. Dan. 2:34; Rom. 9:32–33). Those who wish to earn their salvation through adherence to the law will stumble over the Messiah who offers salvation freely to those who come to him to be saved (Rom. 11:9, 11–12; 1 Cor. 1:23). On the other hand, those who take refuge in Christ and claim him as their Rock will not stumble (Ps. 91:12).

Images of Lifelessness

The lifelessness and hardness of stones makes them a fitting symbol for people who are spiritually dead. Ezekiel prophesied that God will remove the hearts of stone from his people and replace them with hearts of flesh—a picture of an unresponsive, hard, nonliving thing being replaced with something that is responsive and alive (36:26 NIV). Paul picked up this imagery in 2 Corinthians 3:3 as he contrasted the dead law, written on stone, with living letters written on people's hearts. The Christian life is one of spirit-filled warmth and action, not one of dead works.

Jesus used rocks as an image of lifelessness when he told the Pharisees that if the disciples were quiet, the rocks would cry out (Luke 19:40). Even the nonliving parts of creation will praise God if people are so spiritually blinded that they don't praise him, because he is worthy of all praise.

Living Stones

The solid timelessness of stone makes it an appropriate symbol for the eternal kingdom of God. Other kingdoms will come and go, but God's kingdom is eternal, just as a stone is more permanent than Nebuchadnezzar's statue made by human hands (Dan. 2:34–44).

The temporary manifestation of the kingdom of God, the universal church, is built on a rock as well. In the short term, the image of the apostle Peter (or perhaps his simple declaration of Christ's identity) represents the foundation God would use to build his church that would stand firm through the ages (Matt. 16:13–20). But in an eternal sense, Peter builds on this imagery further by saying that all believers are living stones built into a spiritual temple. We were once spiritually dead like a stone but have been given a heart of flesh through Christ and are now living stones. In this metaphor Christ himself is, of course, the cornerstone, the one who is

Jesus is a rock of safety for those who flee to him, but a stumbling block to those who reject him.

the most important stone, the first one laid, and who holds the building up (Isa. 28:16; Acts 4:11; Eph. 2:2–21; 1 Pet. 2:4–8). The rock of refuge and safety of the Old Testament has become the chief cornerstone in the New Testament.

Key Verse

As you come to him, the living Stone—rejected by humans but chosen by God and precious to him—you also, like living stones, are being built into a spiritual house to be a holy priesthood, offering spiritual sacrifices acceptable to God through Jesus Christ. (1 Pet. 2:4–5)

We think of stones as being inert, as having no vitality flowing through them. Yet when Peter speaks of coming to Jesus, he says it is like coming to a living stone. When the disciples were rebuked for praising Christ, He responded, "I tell you that if these should keep silent, the stones would immediately cry out" (Luke 19:40, NKJV). What could be more impossible than that? Stones do not speak, because they are not alive, but here Peter says that when we come to Christ, we come to a stone that is alive. . . . This is the stone that the people despised. We have come to a living stone that other people flee from. They have rejected him, but this stone, in the language of Peter, is the elect stone, the One whom the Father has elected, and the One that in God's eyes is considered precious. What is odious to us in our fallen condition is considered precious by God himself.

R. C. Sproul, *1–2 Peter*, St. Andrew's
Expositional Commentary
(Wheaton: Crossway, 2011), 62

Sword

One of the earliest uses of iron was in making swords. The sword was the primary weapon of warfare throughout the ancient world. As such, it became the primary symbol of warfare in general. The Israelites "put [cities] to the sword" (Deut. 13:15 NIV) and "smote [them] with the edge of the sword" (Num. 21:24 KJV). The defeated enemy was "cut . . . down with swords" (Jer. 19:7). Warfare was part of day-to-day life in the ancient world, so Isaiah's prophecy that in the end times people would beat their swords into plowshares and not lift up swords against other nations (2:4) was significant. When the new heaven and the new earth come, we will no longer need weapons and swords, since no evil or warfare will exist.

The sword is a symbol for anything that inflicts injury to others, including the tongue (Ps. 57:4; Prov. 12:18) and the actions of a promiscuous woman (Prov. 5:4). Those who exploit the poor are described as having teeth like swords as they metaphorically devour their victims (Prov. 30:14). A false witness is like a sword in the hands of an unjust prosecutor (Prov. 25:18).

The Divine Sword

More fearsome than the swords of earthly enemies is the sword that represents divine judgment (1 Chron. 21:12; Ps. 7:12). The Lord's enemies died not by the swords of other men, but by "swords not made by human hands" (Isa. 31:8). The judgment of God is again symbolized by a sword in verses such as Genesis 3:24 ("After he sent man out, God placed angels and a flaming sword that turned in all directions") and Isaiah 66:16 ("He will judge all people with his sword. Many people will be struck dead by the LORD"). This imagery carries through to Revelation, where in John's description of the Son of Man we are told, "Out of his mouth came a sharp, two-edged sword" (1:16). We later find out that this sword will "defeat the nations" (Rev. 19:15).

Sometimes earthly authorities bear the sword as instruments of God's judgment (Rom. 13:4 NIV). Believers are encouraged to submit to the discipline of earthly governments, viewing them as ambassadors who are ultimately subject to God's will. Earthly governments have a divine role in carrying out God's will because he is the one who gives all earthly authority. They wield the sword at the mercy of God's sovereign plan.

The Sword of the Spirit

In the New Testament, God's Word is symbolized by a sword: "It is sharper than any two-edged sword and cuts as deep as the place where soul and spirit meet, the place where joints and marrow meet. God's word judges

Swords are primarily a symbol of warfare, whether wielded by an earthly enemy or by God himself.

a person's thoughts and intentions" (Heb. 4:12). The Word of God is able to penetrate people's hearts in the same way as a sword—with precision and in a way that inflicts pain, in this case the pain of guilt. Such pain yields good results, just as a surgeon's scalpel cuts away diseased flesh.

Even better, once it has done its work of bringing us to repentance, we are able to take up the sword of God's Word as a weapon to use in our battle against Satan. The sword of the Word of God is part of the armor believers are to put on each day as they fight against the powers of evil (Eph. 6:17). In this we follow Christ's example as he fought Satan's temptations (Matt. 4:1–11). The sword is a symbol representing the power of God to fight the influences of evil and bring people to repentance, for it has "divine power to destroy strongholds" (2 Cor. 10:4 ESV).

Key Verse

Also take salvation as your helmet and the word of God as the sword that the Spirit supplies. (Eph. 6:17)

Machaira, the Greek word translated "sword," refers not to a big battle sword, but to a small dagger for use in hand-to-hand combat. *Rhema*, the Greek word translated "word," refers not to a Bible, but to an exact spoken word. Therefore, the idea here is that you'll have just the right word for the right person at the right time. As you study and meditate upon the full counsel of the written Word of God—the *rhema* word—the precise word—will come to you the moment you need to do exacting "surgery" regarding any specific situation.

Jon Courson, *Courson's Application Commentary, New Testament* (Nashville: Thomas Nelson, 2003), 266

Top, Christians are to use the Bible as their sword in the fight against Satan.

Tabernacle

The tabernacle was a religious structure built during the exodus when God's people lived in tents. The Hebrew word *mishkan*, translated "tabernacle," literally means "residence" or "dwelling place." It is related to the word for God's glorious presence, *shekinah*. Thus, the very word *tabernacle* connotes God's indwelling presence among his people.

Symbolic Structure

The tabernacle was a portable tent structure that could be moved when the Israelites moved. God was sending the message that he would dwell among his people. The tabernacle was beautiful, full of color and expert craftsmanship—a fitting place to worship the glorious Creator God. It consisted of three parts: the outer court, the

God gave his people detailed instructions for how to construct the tabernacle because it was a symbol that ultimately would point them to Jesus Christ.

holy place, and the Holy of Holies. Some other temples of the time, including Egyptian and Canaanite temples, were also three-part structures. But those temples had shrines to multiple deities, whereas the tabernacle was built for one God, and graven images of him were prohibited.

The structure of the tabernacle helped the Israelites understand that their God was different from all other gods, a God above all others.

Other differences between the tabernacle and shrines to false deities are notable as well. In the Israelite tabernacle the priests consumed the offerings, rather than a deity consuming them. Israelite offerings were not made for the purpose of persuading a reluctant god to send rain or other favors. Instead, Yahweh promised to bless his people if they simply kept the covenant. Unlike other deities, God did not require a footstool, lamp, table, and bed. The true God does not sleep (Ps. 121:4) and has no bodily needs (1 Kings 18:27). In the design of the tabernacle, God made it clear that he was unlike—and greater than—all other gods.

The tabernacle was to be located in the midst of the tribes of Israel. This symbolized God's presence among his people and his role as warrior king. When the tabernacle was taken down, the ark of the covenant led the march. God led his people and fought for them. When the ark rested, God's presence returned to the midst of his people (see Num. 10:35–36).

Christ, the True Tabernacle

Even after the tabernacle was destroyed at Shiloh (1 Sam. 4:11–22; Ps. 78:60; Jer. 7:12–15), the image of the tabernacle remained prominent in the minds of the Israelites. That imagery was high in John's mind when he wrote that "the Word became flesh and tabernacled among his people" (John 1:14, in its literal translation). Jesus Christ was Emmanuel, God with us. The true tabernacle—God's holy presence—had come to dwell among his people on earth.

The writer of Hebrews expounds on the imagery of Jesus as the true tabernacle by comparing the structure and religious practices of the Old Testament tabernacle to Christ's work as our High Priest.

> The first part of the tent is an example for the present time. The gifts and sacrifices that were brought there could not give the worshiper a clear conscience. . . . But Christ came as a chief priest of the good things that are now here. Christ went through a better, more perfect tent that was not made by human hands and that is not part of this created world. He used his own blood, not the blood of goats and bulls, for the sacrifice. He went into the most holy place and offered this sacrifice once and for all to free us forever. (Heb. 9:9, 11–12)

The tabernacle is a key image to show believers how Christ's once-for-all sacrifice breaks down the barrier between sinful humanity and a holy God. Because Christ came to tabernacle among us, we can now enter the Holy of Holies—the throne room of God—through his blood rather than through ritual animal sacrifices and the work of a human priest.

In Revelation we read that God's throne room builds on the images that were present in the tabernacle. We find an altar of incense (5:8), an altar of sacrifice (6:9), and the ark (11:19). Most importantly, the voice from the throne declares, "God lives with humans! God will make his home with them, and they will be his people. God himself will be with them and be their God" (21:3). The earthly image of a God who lives among his people in tents, traveling with them and leading them, portrays the ultimate reality that God will be with his people forever.

Key Verse

The main point we want to make is this: We do have this kind of chief priest. This chief priest has received the highest position, the throne of majesty in heaven. He serves as priest of the holy place and of the true tent set up by the Lord and not by any human. (Heb. 8:1–2)

> In the plan of the tabernacle or temple, we saw several things. First, the inner sanctuary represented the presence of God. No one could enter that sanctuary without the proper sacrifice. Second, the veil that separated God from the populace was no idle symbolism, but must have said something about the ontology, the being, of things. Thirdly, no one could enter the inner sanctuary without a sacrifice of blood, a symbol not only of the wealth of a nation and its food, but also of life which the blood carried.
>
> Louis H. Evans Jr., *The Preacher's Commentary: Hebrews* (Nashville: Thomas Nelson, 1985), 177

Temple

The five temples in the Bible deserving special mention are Solomon's great temple, Ezekiel's temple, Zerubbabel's reconstructed temple, Herod's renovated temple, and God's human temple. Each of these temples is important because God's presence was there in a special way that went beyond the general understanding that God is omnipresent (everywhere). Yet we should not assume that God ever limited his presence to a human structure. The temple buildings in the Bible were not places where God lived but places where God was willing to meet people who gathered to worship.

Solomon's Temple

Both King David and his son Solomon were involved in building the magnificent temple in Jerusalem. Second Samuel 7:2 records David's first mention of the idea for a temple: "So the king said to the prophet Nathan, 'Look, I'm living in a house made of cedar, while the ark of God remains in the tent.'" But God reserved the task of building the temple for David's son Solomon.

By all indications, Solomon's temple was one of the wonders of the world when it was finished around 950 BC. So strong was the identification between Jerusalem, the temple, and God, that generations of Jews could not imagine the city ever being conquered or the temple destroyed. But that is exactly what happened when Israel moved progressively away from true worship. That magnificent structure was destroyed by the Babylonians around 590 BC.

Ezekiel's Temple

The prophet Ezekiel described in great detail a temple revealed to him in a vision (Ezek. 41–44). To the Jewish exiles, it pictured a time of complete restoration, a time when God would return to his people.

Ezekiel's temple vision has been interpreted in four main ways: (1) It is the intended building plan for the temple Zerubbabel should have built in 520–515 BC. Because of disobedience (Ezek. 43:2–10), it was never followed. (2) It pictures a literal temple that will be built during the millennial reign of Christ. (3) It symbolizes the true worship of God by the Christian church now. (4) It symbolizes the future and eternal reign of God when his presence and blessing fill the earth.

Whatever interpretation is true, it clearly is a vision of God's final and perfect kingdom.

The Rebuilt Temple

Seventy years after the fall of Judah, Zerubbabel led a large group of displaced Jews back from Babylon with the purpose of rebuilding Jerusalem and the temple. Although this rebuilt temple was considered inferior to the previous one (Hag. 2:3), and even though it also suffered desecration at times, it remained a symbol to God's people that he had not abandoned them.

About twenty years before Jesus was born, King Herod began a massive renovation of the temple in Jerusalem. Work was going on throughout Jesus' life, though the building he and his disciples visited many times was certainly an impressive structure. In many ways it reawakened belief in many Jewish people that God was again present in his temple and would not let any harm come to it. Herod's temple was demolished in AD 70 by the Romans.

Jesus and the Temple

The idea of *temple* takes on special and personal significance in the New Testament. Jesus was

presented at the temple by his parents (Luke 2:22–24). Temple visits became an annual pilgrimage. By twelve years of age, Jesus was calling the temple "my Father's house" (Luke 2:49; see vv. 41–52). As an adult, Jesus cleansed the temple courts twice (Matt. 21:12–13; John 2:13–16) and grieved over his knowledge that it would be destroyed along with Jerusalem (Luke 19:41–44). But after the first cleansing, Jesus used the word *temple* to talk about himself: "Jesus replied, 'Tear down this temple, and I'll rebuild it in three days.' . . . The temple Jesus spoke about was his own body. After he came back to life, his disciples remembered that he had said this. So they believed the Scripture and this statement that Jesus had made" (John 2:19, 21–22). Jesus was God's presence among his people, the true temple of which the physical temple was a sign.

The shift in understanding worship as not being limited to a physical location was highlighted in Jesus' conversation with the woman at the well (John 4). She wanted to talk about legitimate locations for worship; he pointed to the crucial reality of a relationship with God: "true worshipers will worship the Father in spirit and truth" (John 4:23).

While the followers of Jesus spent a lot of time in the temple after Jesus' resurrection, the shift continued away from the temple as a place to the temple as a people. Paul made this very personal when he wrote, "Don't you know that you [this is a plural *you*] are God's temple and that God's Spirit lives in you? If anyone destroys God's temple, God will destroy him because God's temple is holy. You are that holy temple!" (1 Cor. 3:16–17; see also 2 Cor. 6:16; Eph. 2:21).

The symbol of the temple became complete in the prophetic picture in John's vision of the New Jerusalem in Revelation. Ultimately, John reported, a physical temple will not be necessary. As he looked at the New Jerusalem, he noticed a significant feature absent: "I did not see any temple in it, because the Lord God Almighty and the lamb are its temple" (Rev. 21:22). In its earliest form, the temple symbolized God's willingness to live among his people; in its later understanding, the temple became a forward-looking picture of a time when a visible building would no longer be required as a reminder of God's presence.

Key Verse

But the temple Jesus spoke about was his own body. After he came back to life, his disciples remembered that he had said this. So they believed the Scripture and this statement that Jesus had made. (John 2:21–22)

During his Galilean ministry, Jesus acted and spoke as if he was in some sense called to do and be what the Temple was and did. . . . He was undercutting the official system and claiming by implication to be establishing a new one in its place.

N. T. Wright, *The Challenge of Jesus: Rediscovering Who Jesus Was and Is* (Downers Grove, IL: InterVarsity, 1999), 65

Top, as important and beautiful as the temple was, the greater spiritual truth is that Jesus' death and resurrection made all those rituals obsolete. Now each individual believer is a temple of the Holy Spirit.

Thousand

The number *thousand* (or *thousands*) in the Bible is sometimes a literal number, but in many cases it is used to create a large round number. Hebrew and the other Semitic languages used approximations to express large numbers because they were rarely needed for small populations and tiny kingdoms. Examples of this can be found in Exodus 20:6; Deuteronomy 5:10 and 7:9; 1 Samuel 18:7; and Psalms 50:10, 90:4, and 105:8. Ten thousand (Hebrew *ribbō, ribbōth, rebhābhāh*; Greek *myrias, myrioi*) is also used as a round number in places like Leviticus 26:8, Deuteronomy 32:30, Song of Solomon 5:10, and Micah 6:7. The higher the figures in thousands of thousands, the more likely the numbers are distinctly hyperbolic, intended to convey large counts.

Extravagance or Multiplication

In the Old Testament, the use of the term *thousand* frequently has to do with an extravagant multiplication, such as when Moses prays over the people of Israel: "May the LORD God of your ancestors make you a thousand times more numerous, and may he bless you as he has promised" (Deut. 1:11). As an example of the generous and faithful character of God, Moses also says, "Keep in mind that the LORD your God is the only God. He is a faithful God, who keeps his promise and is merciful to thousands of generations of those who love him and obey his commands" (Deut. 7:9). By way of comparison, a note of seriousness is included in the Ten Commandments related to the importance of worshiping God alone and the real dangers of idolatry: "Never worship them or serve them, because I, the LORD your God, am a God who does not tolerate rivals. I punish children for their parents' sins to the third and fourth generation of those who hate me. But I show mercy to

thousands of generations of those who love me and obey my commandments" (Exod. 20:5–6).

God's legitimate relationship with his creation is also expressed in Psalm 50:10: "Every creature in the forest, even the cattle on a thousand hills, is mine." And our response to him must recognize that we were ultimately designed for intimacy with God: "One day in your courtyards is better than a thousand anywhere else" (Ps. 84:10). Days can be easily measured in thousands with God because time is relatively meaningless to him: "Indeed, in your sight a thousand years are like a single day, like yesterday—already past—like an hour in the night" (Ps. 90:4). Peter will later use this idea to address the apparent delay in Christ's return and the importance of God's willingness to bide his time (2 Pet. 3:8–9).

The New Testament accounts of Jesus' ministry usually describe the crowds that followed him as merely large, but in a couple of instances involving the miraculous feeding of significant gatherings, the numbers *five thousand* and *four thousand* are used to indicate the count of men in the crowd (Matt. 14:21; 15:38). Later, when the young church was launched following the resurrection of Jesus, the responses to the gospel were reported in thousands (Acts 2:41; 4:4). These numbers are all given not as exact counts, but as estimates of very large groups.

The Millennium

The most recognized use of the word *thousand* in the Bible is found in Revelation 20 and is referred to as the *millennium* (Latin for "one thousand years"). In that chapter, John records two simultaneous significant events in end times chronology: the binding of Satan in the "bottomless pit," and the reign of Christ on earth for a thousand years. The metaphorical use of

thousand is familiar to the Old Testament, and this may be the way John uses it in Revelation.

In the Old Testament, visions of an eventual golden age for Israel when the Messiah will rule are not generally measured in thousands of years but simply described as a future amazing time when the unusual will be the new normal. Isaiah 11:6–9 describes such a time:

> Wolves will live with lambs.
>> Leopards will lie down with goats.
>> Calves, young lions, and year-old lambs
>>> will be together,
>> and little children will lead them.
> Cows and bears will eat together.
>> Their young will lie down together.
>> Lions will eat straw like oxen.
> Infants will play near cobras' holes.
>> Toddlers will put their hands into vipers'
>>> nests.
> They will not hurt or destroy anyone any-
>>> where on my holy mountain.
> The world will be filled with the knowl-
>>> edge of the LORD
>> like water covering the sea.

Although biblical scholars disagree on what the millennium is, how long it is, and whether it is a current or future event, we can all agree that it is another use of *thousand* that is in some sense representative of a large number.

Key Verse

Dear friends, don't ignore this fact: One day with the Lord is like a thousand years, and a thousand years are like one day. The Lord isn't slow to do what he promised, as some people think. Rather, he is patient for your sake. He doesn't want to destroy anyone but wants all people to have an opportunity to turn to him and change the way they think and act. (2 Pet. 3:8–9)

Peter does not say that God's days equal a thousand years; he says that in God's perspective, a day is "like" (*bos*) a thousand years, and a thousand years like a day. God views the passing of time from a different perspective than we do. We are impatient, getting disturbed and upset by even a short delay; God is patient, willing to let centuries and even millennia go by as he works out his purposes. Peter is not telling his readers that they are wrong to believe that Christ's return is "imminent." What he is telling them is that they are wrong to be impatient when it does not come as quickly as they might like or hope.

Douglas J. Moo,
The NIV Application Commentary: 2 Peter, Jude
(Grand Rapids: Zondervan, 1996), 186–87

Three

The number *three* and groups of three occur frequently in Scripture. As the second prime number, three maintains the indivisibility of the number *one* and introduces a concept of a more-than-one number that is not easily divisible. In the area of relationships, three expands the possibilities greatly. Between A and B is one relationship. Between A, B, and C there are at least seven relationships (AB, AC, BC; A-BC, B-AC, C-AB, ABC).

Patterns of Repetition

The number *three* allows the possibility of a pattern. One time is unique, twice might be a coincidence, but a third repetition begins to look like something intentional. *Three* often conveys God's persistence in the Bible. The Lord's visit to Samuel came about as a threefold call in the night that the young man at first did not understand (1 Sam. 3). When Balaam journeyed to curse Israel in Numbers 22, God put an angel in front of Balaam's donkey that only the animal could see. Three times the animal balked at going on and received a severe beating. Then the donkey spoke and reprimanded Balaam severely on God's behalf!

In the New Testament, after denying three times that he knew Jesus, Peter was stunned into shame by a rooster's call (Matt. 26:69–75; Mark 14:66–72; Luke 22:54–62; John 18:15–27). Days later, Jesus three times asked Peter about his love and commanded the fragile disciple to "feed my sheep" (John 21:15–19). A little later, in Acts 10, Peter had to expand his understanding of who Jesus meant by sheep when three times on a rooftop in Joppa God sent down a large linen sheet filled with animals (some of them considered unclean) and invited Peter to eat. In 2 Corinthians 12:6–10, Paul described the way he prayed three times about a recurring problem he had, until God settled the matter for him: "But he told me: 'My kindness is all you need. My power is strongest when you are weak.' So I will brag even more about my weaknesses in order that Christ's power will live in me" (v. 9).

As is the case with much of literature, the repetition of three creates emphasis. Ezekiel records God's words: "Ruins! Ruins! I will turn this place into ruins! It will not be restored until its rightful owner comes. Then I will give it to him" (21:27). When Jonah refused to go to Nineveh with God's message, he spent three days in the belly of a large fish changing his attitude. Jesus used that event to point to the three days he would spend in the grave after the crucifixion. When Isaiah was given a vision of the throne room in which God's presence dwells, he heard an angelic chorus speaking repeatedly: "They

A cord of three strands is not easily broken—when God is in the center of a marriage the relationship will have lasting strength.

called to each other and said, 'Holy, holy, holy is the LORD of Armies! The whole earth is filled with his glory'" (Isa. 6:3).

The Trinity

While the term *Trinity* is not found in the Bible, clearly God has revealed himself to his creation as three-in-one. He is both the divine One and the divine Three: Father, Son, and Holy Spirit. They are fully one, yet they are revealed as three distinct persons as they impact humanity. The Trinity is made explicit in John 14–16, where we see that the Father directs and serves the Son, the Son serves and obeys the Father, and the Holy Spirit points to the Son. These persons are distinct; they are also one in essence. The great and only God, Maker of heaven and earth, displays himself quite comfortably and effectively as three persons in absolute unity who bring about what we could never accomplish for ourselves: salvation and eternal life.

Key Verse

Three times a year all your men must come into the presence of the Master, the LORD God of Israel. (Exod. 34:23)

The use of threefold occurrences in ceremonies appears in the Bible where it emphasizes the completion and perfection of obedience: the three feasts each year that require attendance (Exod. 23:14, 17; 34:23–24); Balaam's threefold blessing on Israel (Num. 24:10); David's threefold bow before his friend (1 Sam. 20:14); Solomon's offerings three times each year (1 Kings 9:25); and Elijah's threefold stretching of himself across the child brought back from the dead (1 Kings 17:21). There is also the larger rhetorical and literary usage of threefold repetition in poetry and literature to drive home important points.

Richard S. Hess, "Leviticus," in *The Expositor's Bible Commentary*, vol. 1, ed. Tremper Longman III and David Garland (Grand Rapids: Zondervan, 2008), 703

Top, when Scripture describes something in a set of three it implies intentionality; twice might be a coincidence, but three is an unmistakable pattern. Peter's threefold denial of Jesus is one example.

Threshing Floor

The harvest and preparation of grain for use as food requires the separation of the kernels from the stalks on which they grow. Because most harvesting today is done mechanically, the significance of a threshing floor and its usefulness as a symbol is somewhat lost to us. A threshing floor was a large, open, hard surface. Access to a steady wind was a preferred feature, so threshing floors were often located on hilltops. After bundles of stalks were laid on the surface of the floor, oxen were repeatedly led over the piles until the dried plants were broken up. Then the wind was used to separate the heavier kernels from the chaff by tossing the mixture in the air, an action called *winnowing*.

The threshing floor formed a backdrop to the love story of Boaz and Ruth in the book of Ruth. This was a departure from its frequent association with sexual promiscuity (Hosea 9:1). Another famous threshing floor in the Old Testament is the threshing floor of Araunah the Jebusite (who is also called Ornan in 1 Chron. 21), which became the location of Solomon's temple (2 Sam. 24).

After observing people, the psalm writer used the process of threshing as a symbol to demonstrate that, while differences may not always be obvious, the winds of adversity in life will separate people with substance from those who have no true connection with God. "Wicked people are not like that. Instead, they are like husks that the wind blows away" (Ps. 1:4).

Abundance or Judgment

A busy threshing floor was a symbol of a plentiful harvest; a bare one indicated famine, and perhaps God's judgment. Joel 2:24 speaks of that abundance as a sign of God's blessing if the people repent: "The threshing floors will be filled with grain. The vats will overflow with new wine and olive oil." And in 2 Kings 6:27, the king in Israel laments that he is helpless to supply food to his starving people: "If the LORD doesn't help you, how can I help you? I can't give you something from the threshing floor or the winepress." He is using the presence of food as a symbol of God's providential care.

The Old Testament includes a number of instances where threshing is specifically used to describe the results of conflict between nations, sometimes carrying out the ultimate judgment of God. Isaiah 21:10 says, "You, my people, have been threshed and winnowed. I make known to you what I heard from the LORD of Armies, the God of Israel," as the prophet describes in symbolic terms the fall of Babylon. And Amos 1:3 anticipates God's retribution against Syria: "This is what the LORD says: Because Damascus has committed three crimes, and now a fourth crime, I will not change my plans. The Arameans have crushed the people of Gilead with iron-spiked threshing sledges." Those who cruelly treat others will themselves be judged harshly.

The New Testament age opens with John the Baptist applying this threshing floor picture to God's plan for humanity. When he announces the coming Messiah, John pictures him as a farmer who is about to finalize his harvest: "His winnowing shovel is in his hand, and he will clean up his threshing floor. He will gather his wheat into a barn, but he will burn the husks in a fire that can never be put out" (Matt. 3:12).

Threshing is often used as a symbol for God's judgment; trials separate those who truly believe in him and those who do not.

Muzzling the Ox

Later, in explaining the value of financially supporting those whose calling makes them ministers and teachers within the church, Paul appeals to the simple principle God spelled out in Deuteronomy 25:4 about allowing the oxen who were harnessed on the threshing floor to remain unmuzzled, so they might eat part of the grain they were helping produce. Paul notes, "Moses' Teachings say, 'Never muzzle an ox when it is threshing grain.' God's concern isn't for oxen. Isn't he speaking entirely for our benefit? This was written for our benefit so that the person who plows or threshes should expect to receive a share of the crop. If we have planted the spiritual seed that has been of benefit to you, is it too much if we receive part of the harvest from your earthly goods?" (1 Cor. 9:9–11). Although the original command in Deuteronomy applied to animals, Paul pointed out its symbolic application to preachers, who should be financially compensated for their work.

Key Verse

His winnowing shovel is in his hand to clean up his threshing floor. He will gather the wheat into his barn, but he will burn the husks in a fire that can never be put out. (Luke 3:17)

Seen from the viewpoint of a grain plant, the processing that occurred on the threshing floor was a violent and painful affair. Isaiah likens the experience of God's people in exile to that of a grain plant on the threshing floor when he addresses them with these words: "O my people, crushed on the threshing floor" (Isa. 21:10). . . . The personified threshing floor feels the pain of the threshing process. The Daughter of Babylon is said to be "like a threshing floor at the time it is trampled" (Jer. 51:33).

"Threshing," in *The Zondervan Dictionary of Biblical Imagery*, ed. John Beck (Grand Rapids: Zondervan, 2011)

Top, the process of threshing separates the grain from the chaff.

243

Throne

In the ancient world thrones served the same purpose they serve today: they were the elevated, often ornate seats upon which a person of authority—usually a king—would sit to rule and utter judgments. Thrones served as the symbol for the monarchy itself (Gen. 41:40 NIV; 2 Sam. 3:10; 1 Kings 1:46). The only throne with a detailed description in the Bible is Solomon's throne (2 Chron. 9:17–19; 1 Kings 10:18–20), a carved chair made of ivory overlaid with gold and situated on a platform six steps up from the ground. On each side of the throne and on each side of the six steps were statues of lions—the Near Eastern symbol for royal power and authority. Thrones in the ancient world each had a footstool accompanying them.

Earthly kings and rulers are under God's sovereign control, so we are to respect their leadership.

The Mercy Seat

The first throne mentioned in Scripture is the throne of mercy, also called the *mercy seat*, which was the symbolic throne of God on top of the ark of the covenant (Exod. 25:17–22; Num. 7:89). The glory of the Lord filled the tabernacle like it filled the throne room of heaven (Isa. 6:1), but the intense focus of God's presence was the space between the angelic likenesses on the ark. This throne/space represented to the people the holiness and authority of God. At this time God was the king of Israel, so he alone possessed the throne.

Later, when Israel asked for a king like the other nations, God gave them an earthly king with the promise that one day the Messiah would rule on his throne (2 Sam. 7:13–16; 1 Kings 2:4; 1 Chron. 17:12–14; Isa. 9:7). The earthly kings who possessed Israel's throne were poor and flawed representatives of the true King of Israel—God himself—and they served the purpose of showing the nation that no human king was worthy of the throne. Jesus came, therefore, as the God-man to unite the earthly throne of Israel with the heavenly one.

The Throne of God

God's throne first of all symbolizes his authority and majesty. This truth is represented by the metaphor of heaven as his throne. In Isaiah 66 God declares, "Heaven is my throne. The earth is my footstool" (v. 1; see also Ps. 11:4). Other passages discuss God's throne as symbolic of his omnipotent sovereignty over human events and human governments (Pss. 47:8; 103:19; Acts 7:49). God's throne is regal, made of gold and gemstones and surrounded by a rainbow (Rev. 4:3), lesser thrones (4:4), a sea of glass (4:6),

and a myriad of angels (5:11). In short, it is dazzling, inspiring awe in those who see it in a way that earthly thrones can only begin to do (Ezek. 1:26; Dan. 7:9; Rev. 4:5; 20:11). God's throne is an eternal representation of his authority (Ps. 93:2; Lam. 5:19; Ezek. 43:7; Rev. 5:13).

The throne of God is also a symbol for judgment. Psalm 9:4 says, "You have defended my just cause: You sat down on your throne as a fair judge." God is pictured as sitting on his throne to execute judgments. When people die, they appear before the throne of God to be judged for their actions (Matt. 25:31–32; Rom. 14:10; 2 Cor. 5:10). God's throne as a symbol of his judgment is closely related to its use as a symbol for his authority, for his supreme authority gives him the right to be the Supreme Judge.

God's throne also points to his presence among his people even today. Psalm 22:3 indicates that genuine worship by God's people provides a special place for God to display himself: "Yet, you are holy, enthroned on the praises of Israel." When we gather to enjoy and proclaim the greatness of God, he makes his throne among us in those moments.

Key Verse

After these things I saw a large crowd from every nation, tribe, people, and language. No one was able to count how many people there were. They were standing in front of the throne and the lamb. They were wearing white robes, holding palm branches in their hands, and crying out in a loud voice, "Salvation belongs to our God, who sits on the throne, and to the lamb!" (Rev. 7:9–10)

In the Old Testament, the tabernacle and temple were actual locations where God symbolically established the throne of his majesty. Today the church, which is made up of believers, represents the throne of God. In the millennial kingdom, Christ, ruling on the throne of David in Jerusalem, will represent the presence of God. In heaven, the throne (Rev. 4–5) will represent him. But any symbol of him is never the prison of his essence.

John MacArthur, *Our Awesome God*
(Wheaton: Crossway, 1993), 62

Tower

In the ancient world, towers were built to protect crops, roads, and cities. They were used both domestically to watch over a landowner's fields and militarily in the defense of a city. Watchmen stood in towers, armed and ready to sound the alarm if enemies threatened their territory. The more towers a city had, the stronger it was thought to be (see Ps. 48:12–14). The tower at the center of a city would have also served as a storehouse. Towers were constant visual reminders that someone was watching out for citizens' safety as they went about their work. They evoked in people feelings of security, and people could flee to them when danger came.

Protection and Safety

Most mentions of towers in the Bible refer to a literal tower, but they were also used figuratively as a symbol for protection and provision. God is our tower, as evidenced by verses such as these: "You have been my refuge, a tower of strength against the enemy" (Ps. 61:3) and "The name of the LORD is a strong tower. A righteous person runs to it and is safe" (Prov. 18:10). The original hearers of these verses would have had an immediate mental picture of safety and security. God protects us against the dangers of the world and the attacks of Satan, and those who take refuge in him have nothing to fear.

Intelligent Design

In his search for comparisons to highlight the features of the woman he loves, the writer of Song of Solomon admits that her neck reminds him of "David's beautifully-designed tower" (4:4) and "an ivory tower" (7:4). Her nose even bears a lovely resemblance to "a Lebanese tower facing Damascus" (7:4). She is clearly not offended by these architectural comparisons and describes herself in 8:10 as "a wall, and my breasts are like towers." There is more than visual similarity going on here, since the tower conveys the idea of completion, care, design, and even peace. When Solomon's lover accepts the tower-like compliments, she adds, "So he considers me to be one who has found peace" (8:10).

A tower is used in the book of Luke as a symbol of careful planning: "Suppose you want to build a tower. You would first sit down and figure out what it costs. Then you would see if you have enough money to finish it" (14:28). Jesus was using it to illustrate the importance of counting the cost of discipleship. We should not build our lives on the rock of Christ without first being sure we are willing to give him our all.

Occasionally towers are used in the Bible as an image of arrogance. In Isaiah 2:12–18 God judges against "all who are arrogant and conceited . . . against every high tower" (vv. 12, 15). The Tower of Babel (Gen. 11) is probably the most memorable instance of a tower being associated with inappropriate human pride. A similar incident is the parable Jesus told about the man who built bigger and bigger barns rather than sharing with those in need (Luke 12:16–21). The man's foolish greed did not pay off in the end.

If a strong tower elicits feelings of security, falling towers would have been terrifying. We are told that on the day of judgment "towers will fall" (Isa. 30:25). This happened numerous times in ancient history, including in the city of Tyre in Ezekiel 26 and with the tower of Siloam in Luke 13. People who have placed their trust in anything other than the strong tower, God himself, will be helpless when the day of trouble comes. We can take great comfort in being able to look up to a tower in our lives that will never fall. God

The book of Proverbs says, "The name of the Lord is a strong tower: the righteous runneth into it, and is safe" (18:10). In other words, the righteous have a place into which to retreat. When the enemy is attacking powerfully outside, and God's people feel their defenses are being penetrated, and they are tending to lose ground, they are all right, there is no panic. Here is this tower—"a strong tower"—that is impregnable, and "the righteous runneth into it, and is safe." He enters into his fortress, and he knows that no enemy can ever penetrate it.

D. Martyn Lloyd-Jones, *Living Water: Studies in John 4* (Wheaton: Crossway, 2009), 722

is our ever-present security, just like towers in the ancient world served as constant reminders that someone was watching over the city.

Key Verse

The name of the Lord is a strong tower.
A righteous person runs to it and is safe.
(Prov. 18:10)

Top, a tower offered protection and security to the people living nearby; God is our strong tower.

247

Tree

Before they are symbols for us, trees are examples to us. The psalm writers looked at trees and recognized that their pattern of growth and life was an expression of praise to their Creator. Psalm 96:12 declares, "Let the fields and everything in them rejoice. Then all the trees in the forest will sing joyfully." And Isaiah 55:12 says, "All the trees will clap their hands." Trees reach upward. Even when planted crooked or sideways, a tree will bend its trunk to vertical—an amazing picture of their purpose to remind us of our own purpose to praise God always.

The Tree of Life

One of the amazing trees of the Bible appears briefly in the beginning and shows up again at the end, in eternity—the Tree of Life. Introduced in chapter 2 of Genesis, we are told very little about this tree: "The LORD God planted a garden in Eden, in the east. That's where he put the man whom he had formed. The LORD God made all the trees grow out of the ground. These trees were nice to look at, and their fruit was good to eat. The tree of life and the tree of the knowledge of good and evil grew in the middle of the garden" (Gen. 2:8–9). The Tree of Life sustained everlasting life. When Adam and Eve were expelled from the garden, they were denied access to it: "Then the LORD God said, 'The man has become like one of us, since he knows good and evil. He must not reach out and take the fruit from the tree of life and eat. Then he would live forever'" (Gen. 3:22).

Proverbs uses the expression "tree of life" to describe the effects of wisdom, but this is a figure of speech based on the earlier life-giving tree. For example, "Wisdom is a tree of life for those who take firm hold of it. Those who cling

to it are blessed" (3:18; see also 11:30; 13:12; 15:4). The Tree of Life makes its return in the book of Revelation (2:7; 22:2, 14, 19). This life-giving tree with its varied fruit is available to all who have gained access to the New Jerusalem by the blood of Christ.

The passage from Genesis 2 that introduces the Tree of Life also mentions the ominous Tree of the Knowledge of Good and Evil that ended up supplying the fruit that Adam and Eve tasted in the fall. It presented the first two humans with the only really meaningful choice they had in the garden. The choice about which of any other fruit to eat didn't matter; but each time they saw the forbidden tree and decided not to eat from it, they were exercising obedience. Then they ate the fruit, and the tragedy called the fall occurred and changed human history.

Trees Planted by Water

In the landscape of Bible symbols, one of the most beautiful trees is one we are to emulate. Psalm 1 describes a certain person as being "like a tree planted beside streams—a tree that produces fruit in season and whose leaves do not wither. He succeeds in everything he does" (v. 3; see also Jer. 17:8). According to this psalm, what makes a person such a tree is that he or she "delights in the teachings of the LORD and reflects on his teachings day and night" (v. 2). Isaiah later uses a particular tree to represent the kind of people God seeks: "They will be called Oaks of Righteousness, the Plantings of the LORD, so that he might display his glory" (Isa. 61:3).

Trees That Are Cut Down

In some places the image of a tree being cut down symbolizes the felling of a leader (Judg.

9:7–21; Ezek. 31:1–14). In this case we have the dual symbolism of a tree not drawing from the life available in Christ and the cutting short of mortal life as a form of judgment. In the life of a believer this might be simple pruning—the discipline of a loving Gardener. But for others it is a symbol of judgment as the life of the tree ends.

In the New Testament, Jesus used a tree symbol in his Sermon on the Mount to describe the difference between lives that bear good fruit and those that bear bad fruit (Matt. 7:17–19). As trees were the source of timbers for crosses, crucifixion was sometimes referred to as "death on a tree" (see Acts 5:30; Gal. 3:13, quoting Deut. 21:22–23 [all ESV], where those executed by stoning or other means would have their bodies hung from trees).

Trees, our steady, longsuffering, and dependable companions throughout life, are present in all their usual roles in Scripture. They remain symbolic sentinels, urging us to have their kind of deeply rooted lives, drawing up nourishment, planted in Christ (Col. 2:7).

Key Verse

He delights in the teachings of the Lord
and reflects on his teachings day
and night.
He is like a tree planted beside streams—
a tree that produces fruit in season
and whose leaves do not wither.
He succeeds in everything he does.
(Ps. 1:2–3)

Just like a tree is nourished by the constant supply of water—without which, under the blistering sun, the tree would surely die—so the life that is rooted in the Word of God will also be established and it will be strong. Your stability comes from God's Word. A fruit tree that is planted by the banks of a river suggests stability. The tree is firmly rooted in the soil so that it can resist the storm. . . . When you put your roots down deep into his Word, you will become a person of great stability.

David Jeremiah, *Sanctuary: Finding Moments of Refuge in the Presence of God* (Nashville: Thomas Nelson, 2002), 13

Trumpet/ Shofar

(See also Horn)

Trumpets in Bible times were made of metal or bone and formed into an instrument at least two feet long. They had a high sound that could be regulated to some degree, but they were used more for signaling than for making music. Rams' horns, also called *shofars*, were signaling instruments used to assemble the army (Judg. 3:27; 1 Sam. 13:3) or sound an alarm (Job 39:24–25; Jer. 6:1; Amos 3:6). They are the most commonly mentioned instrument in the Bible, with seventy-two references.

Sounds of Joy

References to horns have a particular connection with health, joy, prestige, and strength. When Hannah dedicated the miracle child Samuel to God she began her prayer, "My heart finds joy in the LORD. My head is lifted to the LORD. My mouth mocks my enemies. I rejoice because you saved me" (1 Sam. 2:1). Her phrase "my head is lifted" literally means "my horn is exalted." She was praising the strength and honor that God had bestowed on her. Later, when

David wanted to express the prestige he had graciously received from God, he exclaimed, "But you make me as strong as a wild bull, and soothing lotion is poured on me" (Ps. 92:10), which literally means, "you have lifted my horn."

Tool of Government

The trumpet was used to call the Hebrew nation to assembly. It was most commonly used as a warning of and summons to war (Judg. 3:27; 1 Cor. 14:8). This association was so strong that in Jeremiah 4:21 the ram's horn is used as a symbol for war itself: "How long must I see the battle flag and hear the sound of rams' horns?" Sometimes trumpets announced danger (Amos 3:6). It was an alarming noise that would have gotten the attention of every Israelite.

When the people of Israel entered the Promised Land, their first obstacle was the mighty walled city of Jericho. God told them to take the city by marching around it while blowing rams' horns. On the seventh day, as the rams' horns echoed from the massive walls, the walls collapsed, and the city was taken (Josh. 6:1–21).

The mere sound of the horn was a symbol of God's power. He was the true King of Israel, more powerful than any earthly king, so his trumpet call is able to conquer obstacles and remove kings.

The sound of the trumpet also alerted the people to come to the Tent of Meeting and await instruction (Num. 10:2–8). Certain

Priests blew horns in praise and celebration.

signals told them to break camp or to assemble for religious occasions. The trumpet was used to announce the moving of the ark of the covenant and the beginnings of Sabbaths and religious festivals (2 Chron. 29:28). (See also Horn.)

Heavenly Trumpets

When a new king was announced, the shofar spread the news (2 Sam. 15:10; 1 Kings 1:34; 2 Kings 9:13). This use combined the symbolism of warfare and religious events because the king was considered God's leader for the nation. In the last days a trumpet will announce the true King, Jesus, returning in glory at the second coming. "It will happen in an instant, in a split second at the sound of the last trumpet. Indeed, that trumpet will sound, and then the dead will come back to life. They will be changed so that they can live forever" (1 Cor. 15:52; see also 1 Thess. 4:16). The sound of the trumpet will get the attention of God's people and signal the beginning of a new era in the kingdom of God.

Even now trumpets are in heaven—John said that he "heard a loud voice behind me like a trumpet" (Rev. 1:10) when he was ushered into heaven. In Revelation 8, a trumpet announces each new event in the end times. No better auditory symbol for these end times events could there be than the trumpet, which was used throughout the history of Israel as an alarm of danger and a summons to action.

Key Verse

The Lord will come from heaven with a command, with the voice of the archangel, and with the trumpet call of God. First, the dead who believed in Christ will come back to life. Then, together with them, we who are still alive will be taken in the clouds to meet the Lord in the air. In this way we will always be with the Lord. (1 Thess. 4:16–17)

When a trumpet blasted in Old Testament times, it sounded an alarm, giving a warning to the people of Israel. The people in ancient Israel needed to be periodically awakened from the apathy and careless attitude toward God so they could prepare to welcome his presence into their lives. God appointed the Festival of Trumpets to blast them out of their spiritual laziness (Leviticus 23:24–25) and call them to repentance before God as the Day of Atonement approached.

Similarly, speaking of the day when the Messiah would come, the prophet Isaiah said, "In that day the trumpet will sound" (27:13). Just as the trumpets that sounded during the Festival of Trumpets called God's people out of their apathy to look for him to act, so the trumpet call of Christ awakens all who slumber spiritually when he comes to earth the second time.

Nancy Guthrie, *The One Year Book of Discovering Jesus in the Old Testament* (Wheaton: Tyndale, 2010), May 18 entry

Top, at the end of time, the trumpet of the Lord will signal the final resurrection.

251

Twelve

Outside the Bible, the recognition of twelve months in the lunar calendar made the number *twelve* an important symbol for the annual cycles of life. In the Bible, this number usually symbolizes completeness, especially with regard to the people of God. Once the twelve tribes of Israel were established, uses of the number *twelve* became a symbol pointing to the entire people of God.

The Sons of Jacob

In the Old Testament, the number *twelve* immediately points to the twelve sons of Jacob and the twelve tribes or clans that descended from them that became the nation of Israel. When Jacob was dying, the blessings he bestowed on each of his sons foresaw not only their character but the history of those who would be born in their lineage: "These are the 12 tribes of Israel and what their father said to them when he gave each of them his special blessing" (Gen. 49:28). The number of the tribes determined many of the symbolic actions in the unfolding story of the people of Israel.

During the time at Mount Sinai, Moses built an altar before the Lord out of twelve stones, one for each of the tribes he had led from Egypt (Exod. 24:4). As the people prepared to enter the Promised Land for the first time, a representative of each tribe was chosen to scout the land, resulting in the twelve spies who brought back a mixed report on the land and the possibilities of conquering it. The majority report by ten incited the people to rebel against God and set in motion a forty-year detour into the wilderness (Num. 13:1–16). Four decades later, when Joshua led Israel across the paused Jordan River, he instructed men from each tribe to pick up twelve stones to create a lasting memorial of the historic crossing (Josh. 3–4).

Another instance of this memorial use of *twelve* was put into practice by Elijah when he had his showdown with the priests of Baal on Mount Carmel. First Kings 18:31–32 describes the prophet's deliberate actions, a startling contrast to the frantic efforts the pagan priests had been exercising all day. He built an altar of twelve stones representing the twelve tribes of Israel. Instead of optimizing his chances for success, he made them worse by dousing the entire offering repeatedly with water. And when everything was soaked, he invited God to demonstrate his power. The offering, stone altar, and water were consumed by fire from heaven. The God who had brought Israel into being and promised to be her God stood by his promises that day.

Twelve Disciples

In the New Testament, the number *twelve* almost always refers to the men Jesus chose. "He appointed twelve whom he called apostles. They were to accompany him and to be sent out by him to spread the Good News" (Mark 3:14). In a number of places the disciples are simply called "the Twelve" (Matt. 26:14; Mark 9:35; 11:11; Luke 8:1, all NIV). Although Jesus' disciples were not chosen from specific tribes of Israel, their number was significant. He even promised his disciples, "When the Son of Man sits on his glorious throne in the world to come, you, my followers, will also sit on twelve thrones, judging the twelve tribes of Israel" (Matt. 19:28).

In addition, twelve baskets of food were left after the feeding of the five thousand, symbolic of the restoration of Israel that Jesus was ushering in (Mark 6:43; 8:19). James referred to "the 'twelve tribes'—Jewish believers scattered abroad" in a similar symbolic reference to Jesus' redemption of Israel (James 1:1 NLT).

Twelve in Prophecy

The number *twelve* is featured prominently in the book of Revelation, bringing back the significance of the tribes of Israel as part of God's eternal plan. John is told in his vision (7:5–8) that 144,000 persons, 12,000 from each of the tribes of Israel, will be "sealed" for God, along with "a large crowd from every nation, tribe, people, and language. No one was able to count how many there were" (7:9). When the New Jerusalem appears, "coming down from God out of heaven" (21:2), many of its features come in twelves: twelve gates featuring the names of the twelve tribes and twelve guardian angels at the gates. The measurements of the city are multiples of twelve. The words of Jesus to the disciples echo in the description of the foundation of the New Jerusalem: "The wall of the city had 12 foundations. The 12 names of the 12 apostles of the lamb were written on them" (21:14). And in a final picture that reminds us of the Garden of Eden, John sees, "Between the street of the city and the river there was a tree of life visible from both sides. It produced 12 kinds of fruit. Each month had its own fruit. The leaves of the tree will heal the nations" (22:2).

The number *twelve* is a continual symbol in Scripture that points to God's covenant promises to the twelve tribes of Israel. Every time we see the number *twelve*, we are reminded of God's redemption of his people.

Key Verse

He showed me the holy city, Jerusalem, coming down from God out of heaven. It had the glory of God. Its light was like a valuable gem, like gray quartz, as clear as crystal. It had a large, high wall with 12 gates. Twelve angels were at the gates. The names of the 12 tribes of Israel were written on the gates. There were three gates on the east, three gates on the north, three gates on the south, and three gates on the west. The wall of the city had 12 foundations. The 12 names of the 12 apostles of the lamb were written on them. (Rev. 21:10–14)

The number twelve symbolizes the ongoing community of faith in whose history God's salvation is worked out; the history of the twelve tribes (cf. Hebrews 11:10) continues in the history of the twelve apostles, who represent the true church. . . . The apostles did not bear witness to a "brand new" thing, as though God revealed one thing to Israel and another thing to the church; God is one God. . . . The wall surrounding new Jerusalem symbolizes the fulfillment of Israel's hope for God's shalom and locates its final realization in the community of overcomers.

Robert W. Wall, *Revelation*, Understanding the Bible Commentary Series (Grand Rapids: Baker Books, 1991), 252–53

Two

As one might expect, the number *two* is second only to the number *one* in usage in the Bible. Perhaps the most significant explanation of *two* is the prevalence of pairs in Scripture. Sometimes these are complementary pairs (husband and wife) and sometimes these are contrasting or even conflicting pairs (good and evil; darkness and light). But note that the Bible doesn't make a pair out of God and another being or object. So, for example, God and Satan do not make a contrasting pair as if they are in any way equal in status; nor are Jesus and Satan a duo of opponents. This is important because it stands in contrast to other religions of the world that are built on a dualism between equal forces of good and evil. Christianity has a clear superior—the good and perfect God. Satan is one of the angelic beings created by God, and, along with other fallen angels, he presents a rebellious contrast to the legions of obedient angels at God's command. He may be God's sworn enemy, but he is not God's equal.

Two in Relationship

The basis of *two* is relationship: two people, one relationship. The Bible is filled with the stories of people who are presented to us in sibling or other paired relationships: Cain and Abel, Isaac and Ishmael, Jacob and Esau, Leah and Rebekah, Priscilla and Aquila, Mary and Martha—these pairs show the dynamics of relationships, good and bad. Solomon offers a wonderful glimpse of the power in relationships that exceeds what individuals can accomplish: "Two people are better than one because together they have a good reward for their hard work. If one falls, the other can help his friend get up. But how tragic it is for the one who is all alone when he falls. There is no one to help him get up" (Eccles. 4:9–10).

When Jesus was asked about the single greatest commandment, he responded immediately with an intertwined pair: "The most important is, 'Listen, Israel, the Lord our God is the only Lord. So love the Lord your God with all your heart, with all your soul, with all your mind, and with all your strength.' The second most important commandment is this: 'Love your neighbor as you love yourself.' No other commandment is greater than these" (Mark 12:29–31).

Two Choices

The concept of *two* is also crucial to the possibility of choice. The two options usually symbolize opposites, frequently good and evil or right and wrong. This tension was built into the created order by God himself when he placed Adam in a bountiful garden filled with trees from which he could enjoy many fruits along with one tree from which he was commanded not to eat. The fact and necessity of choice is included throughout Scripture, with life presenting always two or more options that require a decision. In order for obedience to be meaningful, disobedience must be a real possibility. Moses ended his final sermon to the people of Israel with this ringing invitation: "Today I offer you life and prosperity or death

Marriage is a picture of two people becoming one flesh in a way that reflects the image of God.

and destruction. . . . I call on heaven and earth as witnesses today that I have offered you life or death, blessings or curses. Choose life so that you and your descendants will live" (Deut. 30:15, 19). These contrasting pairs symbolized two life paths. Joshua echoed that great challenge at the end of his life: "But if you don't want to serve the LORD, then choose today whom you will serve. Even if you choose the gods your ancestors served on the other side of the Euphrates or the gods of the Amorites in whose land you live, my family and I will still serve the LORD" (Josh. 24:15).

Later, Jesus clarified that the choice before us ultimately matters for eternity, not just our experience here on earth. "Enter through the narrow gate because the gate and road that lead to destruction are wide. Many enter through the wide gate. But the narrow gate and the road that lead to life are full of trouble. Only a few people find the narrow gate" (Matt. 7:13–14). Two options are always before us: whether they appear as a pair or as a mind-boggling multitude of routes, they will always come down to a choice between what God wants and anything else. God informs us in his Word about the consequences of our choices and then invites us to make the right ones.

Key Verse

The LORD knows the way of righteous people,
but the way of wicked people will end.
(Ps. 1:6)

D. A. Carson offers a summary of how the wisdom literature of the Bible utilizes two contrasting images or choices to show two ways to live, using Psalm 1:6 as a starting point:

The final contrast [of Psalm 1], strictly speaking, is not between the righteous and the wicked but between the *way* of the righteous and the *way* of the wicked. . . . That is the first psalm: two ways to live, and there is no third. There are a lot of psalms like that. They are sometimes called "wisdom psalms." These psalms and wisdom literature sometimes get tied together because in wisdom literature the way of wisdom is cast against the way of folly in a simple and absolute polarity. Wisdom literature regularly offers you a choice between two ways.

D. A. Carson, *The God Who Is There: Finding Your Place in God's Story* (Grand Rapids: Baker Books, 2010), 89–90

Top, Scripture repeatedly offers two paths—the narrow path that leads to life and the broad road that leads to destruction.

Unleavened Bread/Yeast

In scientific terms, *yeast* is a fungus that ferments carbohydrates and makes dough rise. It is a key ingredient in the making of bread, beer, wine, and spirits. Leavened bread is present in most cultures from prehistoric times onward, including that of the Israelites. That is why Moses' instruction to leave yeast out of their bread in preparation for the exodus seemed notable and became part of the remembrance celebration of the Passover.

Bread in the Old Testament

During Passover, leavened bread could not be eaten or stored in the houses of the Israelites for seven days (Exod. 12:15–20). This act was a symbolic remembrance of the first Passover, when God saved the firstborn of the Israelites who had put blood over their doors, but killed the firstborn of the Egyptians so that Pharaoh would let the people go. Omitting the leaven made the bread faster to prepare and easier to transport as the Israelites hurried out of Egypt. What began as a practical consideration became a symbol of the event.

Later on, when the Israelites were established with the laws given by God, bread took on new meaning. Leavened bread was presented as a peace offering (Lev. 7:13). It was also included in the sacrifice of the firstfruits (Lev. 23:17). In these uses, bread signified the provision of God. It was the most basic of foods, the one for which Jews gave thanks as they acknowledged that their needs were met by Jehovah. Jesus continued this image of bread as provision when he told us, in the Lord's Prayer, to be thankful for our daily bread (Matt. 6:11). These daily uses of leavened bread made the symbolism of unleavened bread all the more poignant as the wafers at Passover were reserved for a celebration of remembrance and reflection.

Yeast as Influence

The physical properties of yeast that make it multiply and cause dough to rise provide an image of the influence that permeates a population, either positively or negatively. Jesus' parable about the growth of the kingdom of heaven illustrates how the good news of the gospel will permeate the world: "The kingdom of heaven is like yeast that a woman mixed into a large amount of flour until the yeast worked its way through all the dough" (Matt. 13:33; see also Luke 13:20–21). Individual believers will affect their sphere of influence, multiplying believers. Then, by working together, they will transform entire nations.

On the other hand, Jesus also instructs us to *beware* of the leaven of the Pharisees, Sadducees, and Herod (Matt. 16:6, 11; Mark 8:15). Their negative influence can spread like yeast throughout a population and gradually poison it. Paul offers a similar warning, saying that ignoring sin in the congregation can affect a church body in the same way yeast makes its way through all the dough.

> Don't you know that a little yeast spreads through the whole batch of dough? Remove the old yeast of sin so that you may be a new batch of dough, since you don't actually have the yeast of sin. Christ, our Passover lamb, has been sacrificed. So we must not celebrate

our festival with the old yeast of sin or with the yeast of vice and wickedness. Instead, we must celebrate it with the bread of purity and truth that has no yeast. (1 Cor. 5:6–8; see also Gal. 5:9)

The Corinthians needed a new batch of bread dough to rid themselves of the false teaching that had spread through the congregation.

As we look back at the Old Testament's forbidding of yeast during the Passover and then look forward to the New Testament's use of yeast as a symbol for a person's influence for good or evil, we see a similar emphasis on the need for purity in the body of Christ. The Passover was a tangible, historical event in which God's people had to be set apart and made ready for their journey to an earthly kingdom. Unleavened bread was a crucial part of their preparation. In the New Testament, the preparations Christians make are spiritual and they are for a future spiritual kingdom. But keeping the leavening pure in the body of Christ is just as important as the physical elimination of yeast during the Passover. The encouragement to spread the kingdom in people's hearts and the warnings to avoid false teachings and sin that invade the body of Christ hearken back to the preparation of God's people to enter the Promised Land.

Key Verse

Never eat leavened bread with the meat from this sacrifice. Instead, for seven days you must eat unleavened bread at this festival. (It is the bread of misery because you left Egypt in a hurry.) Eat this bread so that, as long as you live, you will remember the day you left Egypt. (Deut. 16:3)

Bread served as a reminder of Israel's deliverance from Egypt not by human planning and preparation but by the strength of the Lord's hand (Exod. 13:3). The fact that this bread contained no leaven emphasized the unprecedented character of this event. . . . The absence of leaven commemorates a hurried escape from the hand of the Egyptians. Lacking time and preparation at the imminent flight from Egypt, it was not Israel that shared its bread with God—it was God who offered bread to the Israelites. The bread of affliction, as it is called in Deuteronomy, served as a reminder of Israel's lack and God's provision. The feast of unleavened bread is a pilgrimage festival that commemorates Israel's dependence on God and celebrates God's unexpected companionship with a people in need.

Wolfgang Vondey, *People of Bread: Rediscovering Ecclesiology* (Mahwah, NJ: Paulist Press, 2008), 62

Top, yeast is a symbol for people who influence a larger group, either positively or negatively.

Veil/Curtain

Veils and curtains take many forms. A woman in white waits with anticipation to reveal her glory to her husband. A woman in black hides her tears behind her veil as she mourns the passing of her lover. Veils are the walls we put up to separate one thing from another, and we often find them at the extremes of life. A prison, for example, is a set of walls that keeps bad people in. Gated communities use a fence to keep the rough neighborhood out. We hide important things behind walls, veils, and curtains, and we carefully give certain people access to what's inside, while keeping other people out. This is what makes the message of Jesus so radical; he tore down the curtain that separated us from God.

Veils can be metaphors for the emotional masks that keep others from seeing what we are thinking or feeling.

Veils of Separation

The veil and the curtain appear frequently in both the Old and New Testaments. In the book of Exodus, Moses met with God in the Tent of Meeting. After meeting with God, his face radiated. What that looked like is difficult to imagine, but even today such a sight would be terrifying. Moses covered his face with a veil so the Israelites wouldn't be afraid (Exod. 34:33).

Song of Solomon gives another reference to a veil. In the fourth chapter a young woman, who is to be married to her lover, is veiled (vv. 1, 3). Through her veil we see rosy, pomegranate-like temples; her face is alluring behind the simple barrier. She is set apart, much like the Jewish temple sets apart a dwelling place for God.

The books of Leviticus and Hebrews describe tabernacle structure that was replicated in the temple in Jerusalem. The original temple of the Lord had a holy place that enclosed a *most* holy place. The two were separated by a heavy curtain or veil used to set apart the dwelling place of God. Only the high priest was permitted past this barrier, and in order to enter the most holy place, he had to offer a blood sacrifice for his sins and the sins of others.

> But only the chief priest went into the second part of the tent. Once a year he entered and brought blood that he offered for himself and for the things that the people did wrong unintentionally. The Holy Spirit used this to show that the way into the most holy place was not open while the tent was still in use. (Heb. 9:7–8)

The curtain was a symbol of God's otherness and holiness. It served not as a covering and protection for his presence but as a wall of safety for those anywhere near the Holy of Holies. God wasn't hiding behind a curtain; he was ensuring his holy presence didn't destroy those approaching to worship.

The Veil Torn

The centuries of priestly atonement behind the curtain in the tabernacle and temple turned out to be the sign for one final great act of priestly work done by Jesus on the cross. At the moment of Jesus' death, this curtain was torn from top to bottom, making visible and accessible the most holy place of the temple and signaling an end to the old system. Jesus, through his death and

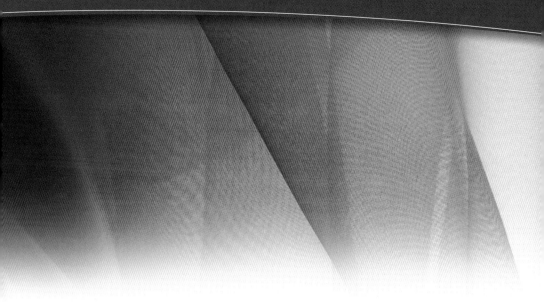

perfect blood sacrifice, removed the veil that separated the most holy of places from all of humanity as a symbol that all people now had accessibility to God. The physical separation between God's presence and God's people, and the work of the human high priest to mediate between the two, were now unnecessary.

Through Jesus' death, the veil that Moses wore was also no longer needed. Using the veil of Moses as a symbol for spiritual understanding, Paul assures us that because of Christ's death we all have access to the Holy Spirit's illumination:

> We are not like Moses. He kept covering his face with a veil. He didn't want the people of Israel to see the glory fading away. However, their minds became closed. In fact, to this day the same veil is still there when they read the Old Testament. It isn't removed, because only Christ can remove it. Yet, even today, when they read the books of Moses, a veil covers their minds. But whenever a person turns to the Lord, the veil is taken away. (2 Cor. 3:13–16)

We find veils at funerals and weddings, occasions that commemorate death and life. Amazingly, here at the cross—at the intersection of death and life—Jesus tore down the veil that separated the two. Jesus makes funerals more like wedding celebrations, where the veil separating the groom and the bride is taken away.

Christ willingly offered his life as a blood sacrifice for all people so that the barrier between us and heaven would be removed.

Key Verse

As all of us reflect the Lord's glory with faces that are not covered with veils, we are being changed into his image with ever-increasing glory. This comes from the Lord, who is the Spirit. (2 Cor. 3:18)

Israel knew that God was in the midst of them, but the High Priest was able to go in with blood and look upon God's face only once a year, and then come back out and pull back a heavy veil. It took some men to push it aside. That veil was there to shut out the unqualified from that holy face. Then, when Jesus our Lord died, . . . the veil of the temple was torn from the top to the bottom. God himself rent it with his finger, . . . and it was forever removed. . . . God was telling the entire world, "My Son, my eternal Son, by the rending of his flesh and the tearing of the veil has opened the way for you to enter. Now there is nothing to keep you out of the holy of holies, where only a priest could go before; now, all of God's people can go."

A. W. Tozer, *Experiencing the Presence of God: Teachings from the Book of Hebrews* (Ventura, CA: Regal, 2010), 140

Top, the curtain in the temple separated the people from God's presence, but Jesus' death tore the curtain and gave us full access to God.

259

Vine

Israel was a land of vineyards. Grapes were used for food and for producing wine, so they were symbolic of provision and celebration. Vineyards were typically surrounded by a protective hedge or fence, and at harvest time someone would sit in the watchtower to guard the crop from thieves. Vinedressers pruned and tended the plants to ensure a bountiful harvest, and the treading of the grapes to make wine was cause for celebration.

Israel the Vine

The vine became a symbol for the people of Israel. Psalm 80:8–9 illustrates this point: "You brought a vine from Egypt. You forced out the nations and planted it. You cleared the ground for it so that it took root and filled the land." God prepared the land, planted the seed of Israel, and tenderly cared for it. He did these things in expectation of a fruitful harvest. Unfortunately, in the metaphor of Israel the vine, we learn that God's people turned away from him and produced bad fruit. Isaiah 5 tells about God planting and caring for the vineyard; then we read, "What more could have been done for my vineyard than what I have already done for it? When I waited for it to produce good grapes, why did it produce only sour, wild grapes?" (v. 4). Despite God's tender care and protection, Israel turned away from him. The image of Israel the fruitful vine was replaced by the image of Israel the rotten, unproductive plant. It was not fulfilling the purpose for which it had been created.

God's Judgment

In time, God will judge the unfruitful vine. Isaiah 5 goes on to describe the removal of the hedge around Israel and the subsequent trampling and death of the vine. Jeremiah 6:9 gives us the image of the vine being plucked clean: "Thoroughly pick through the faithful few of Israel like someone picks through a grapevine." The vine has become a symbol of God's judgment. Ironically, the place that should be full of celebration and fruitful harvest—the vineyard—becomes a place of weeping (see Isa. 16:10; Amos 5:17). In the book of Revelation we again see the vineyard as an image of God's judgment: "The angel swung his sickle on the earth and gathered the grapes from the vine of the earth. He threw them into the winepress of God's anger" (14:19).

The use of a vineyard as a symbol of God's judgment is also found throughout Scripture in descriptions of people planting vineyards but not being able to enjoy the fruit of their labor. In Deuteronomy 28:30 we are told that those who break God's law "will plant a vineyard, but . . . won't enjoy the grapes." When God restores his people, however, the vineyards will once again be healthy, and God's people will enjoy their fruit. "Once again you will plant vineyards on the mountains of Samaria. Those who plant them will enjoy the fruit" (Jer. 31:5). The ability to enjoy a productive vineyard was evidence of God's blessing. This is further illustrated by the fact that security and peace were apparent in Solomon's day: "As long as Solomon lived, Judah and Israel (from Dan to Beersheba) lived securely, everyone under his own vine and fig tree" (1 Kings 4:25). When a person has a vine and fig tree, he or she has ready access to the good things in life.

Jesus the Vine

In John 15, Jesus further expanded on the image with himself as the vine, his people as the vine's "branches," and God as the vinedresser. He said,

"I am the true vine, and my Father takes care of the vineyard. He removes every one of my branches that doesn't produce fruit. He also prunes every branch that does produce fruit to make it produce more fruit" (vv. 1–2). The key difference between this description of Israel the vine and the vine image in the Old Testament is that here Jesus himself is our life source, the vine. We are the branches of the vine, and when we remain connected to him, drawing our energy and sustenance from him, we are productive and fruitful. We don't have to do anything, only remain in Christ. If we fail to produce fruit as we should, God the gardener will prune and discipline us to make us more productive.

The development of the vine symbolism in the Old Testament—Israel being tenderly cared for but then judged if they are unfruitful—into this image of Christ as the vine illustrates the unfolding of God's redemptive plan throughout Scripture. Rather than only caring for us as a gardener, Jesus has connected himself to us and become our life source. Our spiritual health and productivity are no longer dependent on our own actions but on our connection to Christ.

Key Verse

I am the vine. You are the branches. Those who live in me while I live in them will produce a lot of fruit. But you can't produce anything without me. Whoever doesn't live in me is thrown away like a branch and dries up. Branches like this are gathered, thrown into a fire, and burned. (John 15:5–6)

In the Old Testament passages and in the parables, God is the owner of the vineyard. Here [in John 15] he is the Keeper, the Farmer, the One who takes care of the vineyard. Jesus is the genuine Vine, and the Father takes care of him. In the Old Testament it is prophesied that the Lord Jesus would grow up before him as a tender plant and as a root out of the dry ground. Think how often the Father intervened to save Jesus from the devil who wished to slay him. The Father is the One who cared for the Vine, and he will care for the branches, too.

J. Vernon McGee, *John Chapters 11–21*, Thru the Bible Commentary Series: The Gospels, vol. 39 (Nashville: Thomas Nelson, 1995), 90–91

Top, Jesus promised that if we abide in him, we will bear fruit.

Water

Humans can exist for days without food, but water is absolutely essential for life. Besides quenching thirst, water is also an important component of daily living. We use water to keep ourselves and our possessions clean, grow our crops, and cool ourselves down. In the desert and semiarid regions depicted in the Old and New Testaments, water was considered a precious commodity, and life was oriented around access to water sources.

Water is also characterized as a deep and chaotic primal force. Psalmists used it as a symbol of death in verses such as 18:16: "He reached down from high above and took hold of me. He pulled me out of the raging water." Time and again God demonstrated his power over water as a symbol of his role as Creator and his sovereignty over all the created order. Old Testament passages depicting God's control over the waters (Gen. 1:2; Exod. 14:21–22; Job 38:11; Ps. 93:4) mirror similar accounts in the New Testament when Christ calmed the seas. In response to Jesus' demonstration of power, the disciples declared, "Who is this man? He gives orders to the wind and the water, and they obey him!" (Luke 8:25).

Baptism

One of the most significant uses of water imagery in the Bible surrounds baptism. The use of water during baptism symbolizes both a spiritual cleansing and a passage from death to new life (Col. 2:12). Undoubtedly part of this symbolism harks back to the ancient thought of water as the abyss, a symbol of death (see SEA OF GALILEE). More than that, it symbolizes cleansing from sin and resurrection to eternal life. John the Baptist, Jesus' cousin, compared his ministry of water baptism to that of Jesus who baptizes with the Holy Spirit (John 1:33; Acts 1:5; 8:38; 10:47; 11:16). Christ's sacrificial love relationship with the church is also characterized by a cleansing water (Eph. 5:26; Heb. 10:22).

Living Water

Since water is an essential element to life, its meaning throughout Scripture often illustrates eternal life given by God. In a hymn of praise, the prophet Isaiah records, "With joy you will draw water from the springs of salvation" (12:3). Jesus dramatically expanded this image of saving water while talking to the Samaritan woman beside the well. Explaining the difference between normal well water and "living water," Jesus told the woman, "Everyone who drinks this water will become thirsty again. But those who drink the water that I will give them will never become thirsty again. In fact, the water I will give them will become in them a spring that gushes up to eternal life" (John 4:13–14).

Jesus called himself "living water," a reference both to the refreshing springs of water that were highly prized in arid Israel and to

Baptism represents plunging into the abyss—dying to self—and rising to new life.

Jeremiah's prophecy: "My people have done two things wrong. They have abandoned me, the fountain of life-giving water. They have also dug their own cisterns, broken cisterns that can't hold water" (2:13). Water is symbolic of the spiritual growth and satisfaction that comes from following God. Those who are led by the Lord "become like a watered garden and like a spring whose water does not stop flowing" (Isa. 58:11). For all those who are spiritually thirsty, God offers the Holy Spirit as the "water of life" that will spring up within the believer and flow out to others (John 4:13–15; 7:37–38; Rev. 21:6; 22:1, 17). Jesus announced the same truth and declared himself to be the Messiah: "On the last and most important day of the festival, Jesus was standing in the temple courtyard. He said loudly, 'Whoever is thirsty must come to me to drink. As Scripture says, "Streams of living water will flow from deep within the person who believes in me"'" (John 7:37–38).

Some of the most powerful water imagery appears in John's vision of the end times. In the pages of Revelation, Jesus is at last pictured in his full glory, having a voice "like the sound of raging waters" (1:15). During these final days, John reveals, the Good Shepherd will lead believers to "springs filled with the water of life, and God will wipe every tear from their eyes" (Rev. 7:17). The symbolic connection of water with eternal life carries through to the final words of the Bible,

which triumphantly declare, "Let those who are thirsty come! Let those who want the water of life take it as a gift" (Rev. 22:17).

Key Verse

Jesus answered her, "Everyone who drinks this water will become thirsty again. But those who drink the water that I will give them will never become thirsty again. In fact, the water I will give them will become in them a spring that gushes up to eternal life." (John 4:13–14)

Jesus encourages a healthy thirst. "If anyone is thirsty, let him come to me and drink. Whoever believes in me, as the Scripture has said, streams of living water will flow from within him." This invitation is open to anyone who thirsts. To receive this divine gift is spiritual health. To hunger and thirst for the water that Christ gives is hunger and thirst for righteousness. . . . Jesus is saying that the part of us that is never satisfied, the part of us that craves so much, becomes, when we receive this water, the part that is satisfied. Our unfulfilled desires can become fully satisfied by virtue of the indwelling Spirit of Christ in our lives.

R. Kent Hughes, *John: That You May Believe*, Preaching the Word (Wheaton: Crossway, 1999), 216–17

Top, Jesus is the water of life, the one who satisfies our longings.

263

White

One word in Hebrew (*laban*) and one in Greek (*leukos*) are usually translated "white" in English Bibles. Whereas black absorbs light and clear objects refract light or allow it through, objects that are white reflect light; and the whiter they are, the more light creates a bright glow rather than a color. So, for example, when Jesus was transfigured in front of his disciples, his clothes became beyond white. "Jesus' appearance changed in front of them. His face became as bright as the sun and his clothes as white as light" (Matt. 17:2). And when angels took up a post outside Jesus' empty tomb after his resurrection, their appearance was remarkable: "As they went into the tomb, they saw a young man. He was dressed in a white robe and sat on the right side. They were panic-stricken. The young man said to them, 'Don't panic! You're looking for Jesus from Nazareth, who was crucified. He has been brought back to life. He's not here. Look at the place where they laid him' " (Mark 16:5–6).

Purity, Righteousness, and Joy

White indicates purity, righteousness, and joy. Speaking out of a repentant heart, David could write, "Purify me from sin with hyssop, and I will be clean. Wash me, and I will be whiter than snow" (Ps. 51:7). And God tells Isaiah, " 'Come on now, let's discuss this!' says the LORD. 'Though your sins are bright red, they will become as white as snow. Though they are dark red, they will become as white as wool' " (Isa. 1:18). The whiteness of both snow and wool give an indication of the sense of purity that forgiveness and cleansing bring about in a person's life.

Leviticus 13 has more uses of the term *white* than any chapter in the Bible. There the color is used to diagnose the severity of skin diseases. Throughout the chapter, the presence of white skin in the affected area is not necessarily bad but always a reason to give that part of the body special attention over time.

White is also associated with royalty. The rich ride on white donkeys (Judg. 5:10 NIV). The home of Ahasuerus had white curtains (Esther 1:6). The writer of Ecclesiastes tells us to show joy by our white garments: "Always be clothed in white, and always anoint your head with oil" (9:8 NIV).

The Color of Transcendence

Revelation repeatedly uses the color white in describing what John saw in his vision of the end of history, bringing together its symbolism of purity, righteousness, and joy. Jesus sat on a white throne (Rev. 20:11) and he had a white appearance:

There was someone like the Son of Man among the lamp stands. He was wearing a robe that reached his feet. He wore a gold belt around his waist. His head and his hair were white like wool—like snow. (Rev. 1:13–14)

Jesus was the perfect sacrificial Lamb, without spot or blemish of any kind.

In his comments to the church at Sardis, Jesus describes what he will do for those who remain faithful to him in this life:

> But you have a few people in Sardis who have kept their clothes clean. They will walk with me in white clothes because they deserve it.
> Everyone who wins the victory this way will wear white clothes. I will never erase their names from the Book of Life. I will acknowledge them in the presence of my Father and his angels. (Rev. 3:4–5)

The purity and righteousness of white also comes through in the garments of those who have been martyred for their faith and in the gathered bride of Christ, the church. Revelation 6:11 describes the former: "Each of the souls was given a white robe. They were told to rest a little longer until all their coworkers, the other Christians, would be killed as they had been killed." And Revelation 19:7–8 gives us a picture of the church: "His bride has made herself ready. She has been given the privilege of wearing dazzling, pure linen. This fine linen represents the things that God's holy people do that have his approval."

Not only does Jesus show up on a white horse to put a final end to Satan's schemes, but those who come with Jesus are also in white: "The armies of heaven, wearing pure, white linen, follow him on white horses" (Rev. 19:14). And then the culmination of judgment comes: "I saw a large, white throne and the one who was sitting on it. The earth and the sky fled from his presence, but no place was found for them" (Rev. 20:11). In the end of history, God will bring about true purity and victory for those who will spend eternity with him in the New Jerusalem.

Key Verse

I saw a large, white throne and the one who was sitting on it. The earth and the sky fled from his presence, but no place was found for them. (Rev. 20:11)

In speaking of the great white throne of Revelation 20, Charles Haddon Spurgeon said,

Possibly it is called a white throne because of its being such a convincing contrast to all the colors of this sinful human life. There stand the crowd, and there is the great white throne. What can make them see their blackness more thoroughly than to stand there in contrast with the perfections of the law, and the Judge before whom they are standing? Perhaps that throne, all glistening, will reflect each man's character.

Charles H. Spurgeon, *Sermons on the Last Days* (Peabody, MA: Hendrickson, 2009), 34

Wilderness

The wilderness of the Near East is a desolate, dry land consisting mostly of rock and sand, and is unfit for casual habitation. Life in the wilderness takes constant attention. Moses spent forty years in the wilderness, learning its ways. Into this setting God led the Israelites after rescuing them from Egypt. Living conditions were poor, and the Israelites faced serpents, scorpions, and drought (Deut. 8:15). The land became an object lesson in trusting God through difficult circumstances as well as a test of Israel's obedience. When the Israelites complained and rebelled against God, they were forced to wander in the wilderness for forty years until all that entire generation of adults had died (Num. 14:32–33). This time of wilderness wandering is referred to throughout the Bible, including in Job (12:24), Psalms (106:26), and Hebrews (3:8–11).

A Place Apart

Perhaps because of the inherent difficulties of living there, the wilderness became a symbol for isolation and exposure to evil. It was thought of as a place of judgment. The scapegoat, the animal that bore the sin of the people, was sent into the wilderness (Lev. 16:22). A possessed man was driven into the wilderness by a demon in Luke 8.

The wilderness is also a place of testing. Without the benefit of food and shelter, one is forced to either rely on God or turn from him. All our easy crutches are stripped away when we face the raw forces of nature. The Israelites had to be tested and humbled in the wilderness before they could enter the Promised Land (Deut. 8:2). Paul faced trials and difficulties in the wilderness (2 Cor. 11:26). Most notably, Jesus was driven into the wilderness to be tempted (Matt. 4:1–11). In these cases, the dangers of the wilderness became an outward symbol for the inner turmoil caused by the temptations of evil.

Desolate Wilderness to Fertile Field

God also shows his providential care over people in the wilderness. He redeems the desolation and danger of the wilderness and makes it a place of refuge and security. After Jesus was tempted in the wilderness, angels came and cared for him. Elijah escaped to the wilderness, and God provided him with a brook from which to drink and ravens to deliver food to him (1 Kings 17:1–6). The Israelites experienced God's miraculous provision in the wilderness, including daily manna, quail to eat, and water from a rock (Deut. 2:7). In fact, the Feast of Tabernacles is a remembrance of God's provision in the wilderness

The wilderness, with its natural challenges, is often a place of testing and meeting God.

(Lev. 23:34–36). In the end times, the woman who represents Israel in the Apocalypse will flee to the wilderness and be saved from the dragon (Rev. 12:6, 14).

The culmination of God's redemptive plan for humankind is symbolized by the desolate and dangerous wilderness becoming a place of refreshment and abundance. This began with the work of John the Baptist, who lived in the wilderness, received the word of God there (Luke 1:80; 3:2), and then carried out his ministry of preaching and baptism there (Mark 1:3–5). Jesus performed many miracles in the wilderness, showing his authority over the evil found there. Philip's meeting with the Ethiopian eunuch took place in the desert (Acts 8). Isaiah explains that when the Spirit comes, "the wilderness will be turned into a fertile field, and the fertile field will be considered a forest. Then justice will live in the wilderness, and righteousness will be at home in the fertile field" (Isa. 32:15–16). Furthermore, "the desert and the dry land will be glad, and the wilderness will rejoice and blossom.... Water will gush out into the desert, and streams will gush out into the wilderness" (Isa. 35:1, 6). This reversal of fortunes is a common theme in Scripture as God brings justice to the world,

bringing low what was exalted by the world and exalting what was made low by the evil forces in the world.

Key Verse

Then those who are lame will leap like deer,
*   and those who cannot speak will shout*
*   for joy.*
Water will gush out into the desert,
*   and streams will gush out into the*
*   wilderness. (Isa. 35:6)*

> The wilderness in Scripture represents not only a place of testing but also a place of judgment. Jesus as the new Adam experienced in the desert the curse brought about by the first Adam. Jesus as the new Israel labored for forty days under the wandering imposed on the old Israel for their idolatry and grumbling against God. Jesus as the new king wandered in a wasteland of exile, with no people there over whom to reign.
>
> Russell D. Moore,
> *Tempted and Tried: Temptation*
> *and the Triumph of Christ*
> (Wheaton: Crossway, 2011), 52–53

Top, the Israelites spent forty years wandering in the wilderness, learning to trust God.

267

Wind

From the delicate breeze to the terrifying hurricane, wind is a force of nature. We can't see the wind, but we know it is there. Throughout time, humans have learned to harness the wind to fill sails and run wind turbines. We also struggle to limit the destruction caused by wind as the major cause of erosion on earth. Due to its unpredictability and raw power, wind holds both positive and negative connotations throughout the Bible.

Wind as a Negative Symbol

In the Old Testament, wind is often used as a picture of temporality or futility. The length of a human life is frequently imagined as a "whisper in the wind" (Pss. 39:5, 11; 62:9; 78:33). "It's like trying to catch the wind" is the common refrain of Ecclesiastes to show pointless or meaningless actions (1:14, 17; 2:11, 17, 26; 4:4, 16; 6:9). Isaiah tells us that the people of God went through labor but gave birth only to wind, symbolizing the futility of their actions (Isa. 26:18). They went through the motions to bring forth life but did not bring salvation to the earth. Troublemakers are said to "[inherit] only wind" (Prov. 11:29), indicating the futility of their lives.

Wind also negatively signifies doubtfulness or uncertainty. In his letter to the Ephesians, Paul speaks about believers who develop spiritual maturity as opposed to those who are "tossed and carried about by all kinds of teachings that change like the wind" (4:14). James 1:6 states, "A person who has doubts is like a wave that is blown by the wind and tossed by the sea."

Due to its potential to destroy things with its sweeping strength, wind is employed as an image of God's judgment. Throughout the Old Testament, God's influence in the lives of evildoers is pictured as a "scorching wind" (Isa. 11:15; Hosea 13:15), "like a hailstorm, a destructive wind" (Isa. 28:2), and a "driving wind" (Jer. 30:23). Scripture warns that the lives of the wicked are like husks that the wind blows away (Pss. 1:4; 35:5; 83:13). The implication is that God is the Judge who provides the wind. Wind symbolizes adversity in Jesus' promise that it will not prevail against a house (a life) built on a solid foundation (Matt. 7:27).

Wind as a Positive Symbol

Wind in the Bible is also positively connected with God's breath and his ultimate authority over the world. In Hebrew, the word for "breath" (*ruah*) can also mean "wind." God created with his breath (Gen. 2:7). We see the play with these words in Ezekiel 37:9:

Wind is often a demonstration of God's awesome power.

"Then the Lord said to me, . . . 'Come from the four winds, Breath, and breathe on these people who were killed so that they will live.' " Specifically, the collected image of the "four winds" (east, west, north, and south) signals the comprehensiveness of God's power (Dan. 7:2; 8:8; Zech. 2:6). "I'll bring the four winds from the four corners of heaven against Elam and scatter its people in every direction" (Jer. 49:36). Revelation 7:1 pictures the angels holding back the "four winds of the earth." Throughout the New Testament, Jesus demonstrates control over the wind (Matt. 8:26; Mark 4:39–41). This is yet another proof of his identity as the Son of God.

The most famous use of wind as a symbol is to represent the Holy Spirit. John states, "The wind blows wherever it pleases. You hear its sound, but you don't know where it comes from or where it's going. That's the way it is with everyone born of the Spirit" (John 3:8). A further connection between the Holy Spirit and wind is seen at Pentecost, when the coming of the Spirit was accompanied by "a sound like a violently blowing wind" (Acts 2:2).

Just as we cannot see wind but notice its sometimes very powerful effects, so it is with the Holy Spirit. The Spirit's role is to glorify the Father and the Son and to indwell believers— both tasks make him unseen and yet highly noticeable. Further, the Holy Spirit works in unpredictable ways; we can't control or manipulate him to do our bidding, nor can we anticipate what he will do next. The Holy Spirit is also like the wind in that he breathes life into a believer at the moment of conversion. He convicts the believer of sin in the same way the wind of the Old Testament was often a sign of judgment.

Key Verse

Flesh and blood give birth to flesh and blood, but the Spirit gives birth to things that are spiritual. Don't be surprised when I tell you that all of you must be born from above. The wind blows wherever it pleases. You hear its sound, but you don't know where the wind comes from or where it's going. That's the way it is with everyone born of the Spirit. (John 3:6–8)

> Wind is well suited to be a type or symbol of the Holy Spirit in that the characteristics of wind are similar to those of the Holy Spirit in many respects. The power, invisibleness, immaterial nature, and sovereign purpose of wind in creation have their counterpart in the person and work of the Spirit.
>
> John F. Walvoord, *The Holy Spirit: A Comprehensive Study of the Person and Work of the Holy Spirit* (Grand Rapids: Zondervan, 1965), 24

Top, wind is an image for the Holy Spirit—we cannot see it, but its effects are unmistakable.

Wine

In the ancient world water was a precious commodity, not as accessible as it is today but crucial for human life. In the absence of plentiful water, wine, or fermented grape juice, became an important part of daily life. It was produced by Noah after the flood (Gen. 9:21) and was brought to Egypt before 3000 BC. Wine was a daily beverage that was viewed by the Hebrews as a gift from the Lord to cheer their hearts (Judg. 9:13; Ps. 104:15). Grapes were gathered in baskets and trampled in a winepress to produce juice, then bottled for fermentation. Wine was stored either in clay jars or in wineskins made out of the skin of goats. Wineskins could not be reused because the fermentation process would cause old skins to burst (Matt. 9:17). Once it was bottled, wine became a significant trade item in places like Palestine (2 Chron. 2:10, 15) and Damascus (Ezek. 27:18).

The Blessings of Wine

Wine was the drink offering used throughout the Old Testament (Exod. 29:40; Lev. 23:13). It accompanied most offerings, including the daily offering, the offering of firstfruits, the burnt offering, and the freewill offering. Its use as a staple of daily life and its association with celebration made it an important element of sacrifice. The importance of wine in worship in the Old Testament made it a fitting symbol for Christ's blood at the Lord's Table in the New Testament. Jesus said as he served the Passover wine at the Last Supper, "This cup that is poured out for you is the new promise made with my blood" (Luke 22:20).

Wine is also used in the Bible as an image of celebration, much as it is thought of today. It was a key part in wedding festivities, as we see in the account of the wedding at Cana (John 2). The teacher in Ecclesiastes says, "Go, enjoy eating your food, and drink your wine cheerfully, because God has already accepted what you've done" (9:7). At the same time, moderation is mandated so that the celebration does not get out of hand (Deut. 21:20–21; Isa. 28:1–8; Eph. 5:18; 1 Pet. 4:3; 1 Tim. 3:3).

Because wine was so crucial to life, it became associated, together with grain and oil, with the covenant blessings promised by God in exchange for Israel's obedience. One of the consequences listed if Israel were to break the covenant is clearly stated: "You will plant vineyards and take care of them, but you won't drink any wine or gather any grapes, because worms will eat them" (Deut. 28:39). The daily provisions of life—produce and wine—would be freely available as long as the Israelites kept God's covenant but would be withheld if they broke it. These items thus became a symbol of God's blessing on the nation.

Wine in the End Times

Not surprisingly, wine also figures prominently in the new heaven and the new earth: "On that

Jesus' first miracle was turning water into wine at a wedding feast in Cana.

day new wine will cover the mountains" (Joel 3:18). Here wine is an image of abundance and the full blessing of God. The covenant is now fulfilled, and the promised wine is available to all. In Jewish thought an abundant supply of wine accompanied the messianic age (Gen. 49:11–12; Jer. 31:12). This sign of wine is made explicit when we read that the coming marriage supper of the Lamb will also feature wine: "On this mountain the LORD of Armies will prepare for all people a feast with the best foods, a banquet with aged wines, with the best foods and the finest wines" (Isa. 25:6). At the Last Supper, Jesus spoke of this future banquet of blessing: "Then he took a cup and spoke a prayer of thanksgiving. He said, 'Take this, and share it. I can guarantee that from now on I won't drink this wine until the kingdom of God comes'" (Luke 22:17–18).

A contrasting use of wine is as a symbol of God's judgment. The cup is filled with the wine of God's wrath, and evildoers are forced to drink that wine of wrath: "This is what the LORD God of Israel said to me: Take from my hand this cup filled with the wine of my fury, and make all the nations to whom I'm sending you drink from it" (Jer. 25:15; see also Isa. 63:6). In Revelation we read that "whoever worships the beast or its statue, whoever is branded on his forehead or his hand, will drink the wine of God's fury, which has been poured unmixed into the cup of God's anger" (Rev. 14:9–10). The image evokes thoughts of anger let loose, no longer held in check to await

the people's repentance. God will unleash his fury on the day of judgment.

Key Verse

Jesus told the servers, "Fill the jars with water." The servers filled the jars to the brim. Jesus said to them, "Pour some, and take it to the person in charge." The servers did as they were told.

The person in charge tasted the water that had become wine. He didn't know where it had come from, although the servers who had poured the water knew. . . . Cana in Galilee was the place where Jesus began to perform miracles. He made his glory public there, and his disciples believed in him. (John 2:7–9, 11)

John's account of Jesus' conversion of such a large quantity of water into wine at a wedding feast is one way of announcing that the kingdom of God, the eschatological time of salvation, has arrived in the presence of the long-awaited Messiah. Jesus shows himself to be the Son of God come down from heaven bringing the blessing of the eschatological age symbolized by abundant wine. The miracle of Cana allowed Jesus to manifest his glory to his disciples and evoke their belief.

Duane F. Watson, "Wine," in *Dictionary of Jesus and the Gospels*, ed. Joel B. Green, Scot McKnight, and I. Howard Marshall (Downers Grove, IL: InterVarsity, 1992), 873

Xerxes the Great
(and Other Significant Rulers)

The Bible is a historical book as well as a spiritual one. As such, it contains many important historical leaders and describes their impact on the nation of Israel. These people are not often used as symbols in the Bible, but their influence on the history of God's people carries symbolic importance because of the particular interactions they had. The Jews look back on these leaders as people who operated under the sovereign will of God either to help them as an instrument of mercy or to test and punish them as an executor of his just wrath.

Xerxes was the king during the time of the events written about in the book of Esther. He ruled Persia from 486–465 BC. He imposed anti-Semitic laws at the advice of his highest official, Haman (Esther 3:8, 12–14), but through the influence of Esther he later enabled the Jews to forcefully resist assaults against them (8:10–14). Esther's actions are celebrated at the feast of Purim, observed by Jews throughout the centuries in a joyous festival. Xerxes is a portrait of a leader who changed his mind due to God's leading. (See also Purim.)

Nebuchadnezzar was the king of the Neo-Babylonian Empire from 605–562 BC. He captured Jerusalem, destroying the temple as he did so, and took the people of Judah into captivity in Babylon. He was the hand of God that had been warned about in Jeremiah 21–52 and elsewhere. The book of Daniel tells about what happened while the Jews were in Babylon under his rule and portrays seven years when he lost his sanity and lived among cattle as punishment for his prideful boasts (Dan. 4:32). Nebuchadnezzar is an example of a leader who enacted judgment on God's people but was still under the control of God even as he abused the nation of Israel.

Cyrus was king of Persia from 559–530 BC. He allowed the Jewish captives to return to Jerusalem and rebuild the temple (2 Chron. 36:22–23; Ezra 1:1–4). Indeed, Cyrus and his successor, Darius, helped them gather materials and protected them as they worked (Ezra 6:1–12). Daniel was a member of his court as well as Nebuchadnezzar's (Dan. 1:21; 6:28; 10:1). Cyrus is remembered as a wise and just leader who was able to bring together various ethnic and religious groups. Isaiah called him "shepherd" and "anointed one" (Isa. 44:28; 45:1).

Herod the Great was the Roman ruler in Palestine from 37–4 BC. He took actions that pleased the Jews, such as protecting the temple from being defiled by invading Romans. After the birth of Jesus, however, he tried to ensure his position by killing all male babies in the region of Bethlehem who could threaten his rule. This is known as the "slaughter of the innocents." He also murdered his wife Mariamne, and when two of his sons discovered this, he murdered them as well. Herod the Great is remembered by Christians as

Ancient rulers often persecuted the Jews.

the king at the time of Jesus' birth, whose cruel murder of infant boys forced Mary and Joseph to escape by fleeing to Egypt (Matt. 2:13–15). He was a paranoid and despicable ruler.

Herod Antipas, son of Herod the Great, ruled during the life and ministry of Jesus. He is the one who married Herodias, the wife of his half-brother. He came to respect John the Baptist, who spoke boldly against this action, but later had him beheaded (Matt. 14:6–12; Mark 6:21–29). For a time Antipas thought that Jesus was John the Baptist raised from the dead. Jesus' popularity was a threat to Antipas, so Antipas sought to kill him (Luke 13:31). Jesus called him a "fox," indicating his cunning and deceit (Luke 13:32), and appeared before him at his trial (Luke 23:6–12). Herod Antipas seemed to be curious about Jesus but could find no wrong in him, so he returned Jesus to Pilate. We can think of Herod Antipas as a leader who was exposed to the truth on numerous occasions yet refused to accept it.

Pontius Pilate was Roman prefect of Judea from AD 26–36. He is best known for sentencing Jesus to death by crucifixion (Matt. 27; Mark 15; Luke 23; John 18–19). He was never popular with the Jews, because he did not support their religious practices; but whenever they rebelled, he backed down from his policies. That weakness was what led him to act as he did at Jesus' trial—attempting to appease the crowd by beating Jesus, shirking his responsibility by handing Jesus over to Herod Antipas, and eventually sentencing Jesus to death but washing his hands of the whole thing in front of the crowd. Pilate is the supreme biblical example of a person who will do anything to meet his own selfish goals. He knew Jesus was innocent, and he had the power to release him, but Pilate gave in to the demands of the crowd to save his own career.

Key Verse

On that very day, when the enemies of the Jews expected to overpower them, the exact opposite happened: The Jews overpowered those who hated them.

The Jews assembled in their cities throughout all the provinces of King Xerxes to kill those who were planning to harm them. No one could stand up against them, because all the people were terrified of them. (Esther 9:1–2)

> Christians should give thanks for government as an institution of God; we should pray regularly for our leaders (cf. 1 Timothy 2:1–2); and we should be prepared to follow the orders of our government. But we should also refuse to give to government any absolute rights and should evaluate all its demands in light of the gospel.
>
> Douglas J. Moo, *The Epistle to the Romans*,
> The New International Commentary on the New Testament
> (Grand Rapids: Eerdmans, 1996), 810

Top, despite the flaws of our earthly rulers, believers are told to obey those in authority.

273

Yoke

A *yoke* is a wooden harness that connects a pair of animals to a plow or cart. Oxen were most often used for these tasks, and a pair of oxen was called a "yoke of oxen" (1 Sam. 11:7 NASB; Luke 14:19 NIV). These animals had to work together, so it was best if they were of a similar size. Literal mentions of yokes in the Bible include using unyoked animals for sacrifices (Num. 19:2; Deut. 21:1–9) and not yoking different animals together (Deut. 22:10). The yoke was used in several different ways to represent a burden to which a person must submit.

Bondage or Duty

The yoke is frequently used as a symbol of slavery to a foreign king. One of the punishments listed for breaking the covenant is "you will serve the enemies the LORD sends against you. He will put an iron yoke on your neck until he has destroyed you" (Deut. 28:48 NIV). This image was even used in connection with oppressive Israelite kings. Evil King Rehoboam told his people, "My father made your yoke heavy; I will make it even heavier" (1 Kings 12:14 NIV).

Animals that are yoked together are closely joined, so it is important that they be well matched.

Being treated like yoked oxen is a fitting symbol for slavery and oppression.

Sin is also portrayed as a yoke of bondage. Jeremiah wrote, "My rebellious acts are a heavy burden for me. They were tied together by God's own hands. They were tied around my neck. He has weakened me with them. The Lord has handed me over to people I cannot oppose" (Lam. 1:14). The image is of a yoke being put on him. Likewise, Paul called the Jewish ceremonial laws a "yoke that neither we nor our ancestors have been able to bear" (Acts 15:10 NIV). As such, he held that Gentile believers should not be placed under its rigorous regulations.

Alliance or Union

Animals that are yoked together are closely joined and forced to move together, so a yoke is also used as a symbol for an alliance or union. Believers have to be careful in making associations with others, either in friendship or in business. When Israel participated in pagan rituals it was said to have "yoked" itself with Baal (Num. 25:3, 5 NIV). Paul warns us, "Do not be unequally yoked with unbelievers. For what partnership has righteousness with lawlessness? Or what fellowship has light with darkness?" (2 Cor. 6:14 ESV). Here he calls to mind the Old Testament prohibition against yoking oxen with donkeys: "Never plow with an ox and a donkey harnessed together" (Deut. 22:10). This prohibition was most likely made either for the mercy of the animal, because an ox would be stronger than a donkey and thus would have to pull more than its fair share of the weight, or to avoid joining a ceremonially clean animal with an unclean animal. The implication for Paul's warning, then, is that a nonbeliever might pull a believer into sin, particularly in matters of conscience.

The Yoke of Christ

The most famous use of a yoke as a symbol is in Jesus' promise, "Place my yoke over your shoulders, and learn from me, because I am gentle and humble. Then you will find rest for yourselves because my yoke is easy and my burden is light" (Matt. 11:29–30). In contrast with the oppressive regulations placed on the Jews by the Pharisees, Jesus offered a simple life of love and devotion to a kind heavenly Father. The laws to which we should submit are for our own good. The burden of suffering he gives us is filtered through his loving hands. He is the kind of master whose yoke it is easy to submit to.

Key Verse

Place my yoke over your shoulders, and learn from me, because I am gentle and humble. Then you will find rest for yourselves because my yoke is easy and my burden is light. (Matt. 11:29–30)

The Jews used the phrase *the yoke* for *entering into submission to*. They spoke of the yoke of the law, the yoke of the commandments, the yoke of the kingdom and the yoke of God. But it may well be that Jesus took the words of his invitation from something much nearer home than that. He says: "My yoke is *easy*." The word *easy* is in Greek *chrēstos*, which can mean *well-fitting*. In Palestine, ox-yokes were made of wood; the ox was brought, and measurements were taken. . . . The yoke was carefully adjusted, so that it would fit well, and not chafe the neck of the patient animal. . . . Jesus says, "My yoke fits well." What he means is: "The life I give you is not a burden to cause you pain; your task is made to measure to fit you." Whatever God sends us is made to fit our needs and our abilities exactly.

William Barclay, *The New Daily Study Bible: The Gospel of Matthew* (Louisville: Westminster John Knox, 2001), 20

Zion / Jerusalem

Before becoming David's capital city and the center of Israelite life, Jerusalem—also called the City of David or by its symbolic name, Zion—was a city of the Jebusites (2 Sam. 5:6–10). And long before that, Jerusalem was simply Salem, the city where Abraham met King Melchizedek and offered up a tithe offering because Melchizedek somehow represented the same God under whose direction Abraham was living (Gen. 14:17–20). A long-standing tradition says Jerusalem was the site of Mount Moriah, the place where Abraham took Isaac to sacrifice him before God provided a sacrificial animal to meet the requirements (see also MOUNT MORIAH). Given its central role, it is not surprising that Jerusalem eventually became symbolic of Israel itself. The fate of the city was the fate of the nation. The faith of the city represented the faith of the nation (Isa. 2:2; Amos 2:5; Mic. 4:1). With David's founding of his kingdom in Jerusalem, a long and painful history of God's great blessings and a people's persistent apostasy began.

The City of Promise and Punishment

Jerusalem was considered the royal city for two reasons: it hosted the throne of the house of King David, and it held the grand temple built by Solomon to house the ark of the covenant symbolizing God's presence among his people as the ultimate King. As such, the city became a symbol of God's promises to Israel, and a popular assumption held that the city could never fall nor the temple be touched by foreign invaders. At various times the inhabitants of Jerusalem blatantly ignored God's clear condition that the safety of the city was dependent on their faithfulness to God. Morally bankrupt from within, Jerusalem suffered attacks, sieges, and destruction from without. In 586 BC, the Babylonians destroyed Jerusalem and the temple, exiling much of the population (as God's punishment for her apostasy—see Jer. 19).

Yet even after his most severe judgments, God held out hope for a remnant that would preserve Jerusalem. Over and over again he promised that his people would return and restore the city. And indeed they did. Seventy years after Jerusalem was devastated, the king of Persia allowed exiles to return and begin to rebuild the city and the temple (2 Chron. 36:22–23).

With the coming of Christ, Jerusalem became a symbol for the religious establishment— God's chosen people who rejected him—ushering in the age when God's chosen people would come from all nations, not just Israel. Perhaps no sadder words were ever pronounced over a city than Jesus' cry when Jerusalem came into view during what became known as his triumphal entry:

> When he came closer and saw the city, he began to cry. He said, "If you had only known today what would bring you peace! But now it is hidden, so you cannot see it. The time will come when enemy armies will build a wall to surround you and close you in on every side. They will level you to the ground and kill your people. One stone will not be left on top of another, because you didn't recognize the time when God came to help you." (Luke 19:41–44; see also Matt. 24:15–25; Luke 21:1–24)

Jerusalem had the chance to welcome her once and future king; yet in that crucial moment, the city rejected and put her sovereign to death.

Mount Zion

Throughout the New Testament, Zion takes on the double identity of a city that doesn't measure up to its potential and a city that will be renewed by God in order to serve its ultimate purpose. Paul said, "Hagar is Mount Sinai in Arabia. She is like Jerusalem today because she and her children are slaves. But the Jerusalem that is above is free, and she is our mother" (Gal. 4:25–26). And the writer of Hebrews contrasted the anticipation that pilgrims always felt after a long journey toward Jerusalem with the anticipation of our arrival in the kingdom of God: "Instead, you have come to Mount Zion, to the city of the living God, to the heavenly Jerusalem. You have come to tens of thousands of angels joyfully gathered together" (12:22).

The New Jerusalem

John, in Revelation, gave us the picture of a New Jerusalem shaped by God. This city is the centerpiece of the new heaven and the new earth. Everything that the old Jerusalem had hoped to be is fulfilled in the New Jerusalem. And this new city doesn't need a renovated magnificent temple of Solomon because "the Lord God Almighty and the lamb are its temple" (21:22). All has been restored to perfection in Zion.

Key Verse

Instead, you have come to Mount Zion, to the city of the living God, to the heavenly Jerusalem. You have come to tens of thousands of angels joyfully gathered together. (Heb. 12:22)

Cities come to figure prominently in the Bible as the expression of human wickedness. Babel, Sodom and Gomorrah, the cities of Egypt and Canaan, and finally Babylon and Rome all represent concentrations of human godlessness. . . . There is a city of God, Jerusalem or Zion, but it becomes the city in which the Son of God is condemned to death. Only the heavenly Jerusalem, whose builder and maker is God, brings human society into perfect relationship with the rule of God.

Graeme Goldsworthy, *According to Plan: The Unfolding Revelation of God in the Bible* (Downers Grove, IL: InterVarsity, 1991), 108

Top, Jesus was the promised King of Zion who would save the people from their sins, yet they rejected and killed him.

277

Image Credits

Lower image on page 17 © Dorling Kindersley/Thinkstock.

Upper image on page 17 © iStockphoto/Thinkstock.

Image on page 18 © iStockphoto/Thinkstock.

Image on page 19 © iStockphoto/Thinkstock.

Right image on page 20 © iStockphoto/Thinkstock.

Left image on page 20 © Adam Gault/Thinkstock.

Image on page 21 © Disgital Vision/Thinkstock.

Image on page 23 © iStockphoto/Thinkstock.

Image on page 24 © Dorling Kindersley/Thinkstock.

Image on page 25 © iStockphoto/Thinkstock.

Image on page 26 © Photos.com/Photos.com.

Image on page 27 © iStockphoto/Thinkstock.

Left image on page 28 © iStockphoto/Thinkstock.

Right image on page 28 © iStockphoto/Thinkstock.

Image on page 29 © iStockphoto/Thinkstock.

Image on page 31 © iStockphoto/Thinkstock.

Image on page 32 © Olena Zhuchkova/Photos.com.

Image on page 33 © Zsolt Farkas/Photos.com.

Image on page 35 © iStockphoto/Thinkstock.

Image on page 37 © Ingrid H.S./Photos.com.

Image on page 39 © Design Pics/Thinkstock.

Image on page 41 © iStockphoto/Thinkstock.

Image on page 42 © iStockphoto/Thinkstock.

Image on page 43 © iStockphoto/Thinkstock.

Image on page 44 © Ingram Publishing/Thinkstock.

Image on page 45 © iStockphoto/Thinkstock.

Image on page 46 © F1online/Thinkstock.

Image on page 47 © iStockphoto/Thinkstock.

Image on page 48 © Image Source/Thinkstock.

Image on page 49 © Hemera/Thinkstock.

Image on page 50 © iStockphoto/Thinkstock.

Image on page 51 © iStockphoto/Thinkstock.

Image on page 52 © iStockphoto/Thinkstock.

Image on page 53 © iStockphoto/Thinkstock.

Image on page 54 © iStockphoto/Thinkstock.

Image on page 55 © iStockphoto/Thinkstock.

Image on page 56 © Hemera/Thinkstock.

Image on page 57 © iStockphoto/Thinkstock.

Image on page 59 © iStockphoto/Thinkstock.

Image on page 60 © Denny Thurston/Photos.com.

Image on page 61 © Oksun70/Photos.com.

Image on page 62 © Pawel Aniszewski/Photos.com.

Upper image on page 63 © iStockphoto/Thinkstock.

Lower image on page 63 © Olga Khoroshunova/Photos.com.

Image on page 65 © Hemera Technologies/Photos.com.

Image on page 66 © iStockphoto/Thinkstock.

Upper image on page 67 © iStockphoto/Thinkstock.

Lower image on page 67 © iStockphoto/Thinkstock.

Image on page 68 © iStockphoto/Thinkstock.

Image on page 69 © iStockphoto/Thinkstock.

Image on page 70 © Hemera Tech./Thinkstock.

Image on page 71 © Fuse/Thinkstock.

Image on page 72 © Mihtiander/Photos.com.

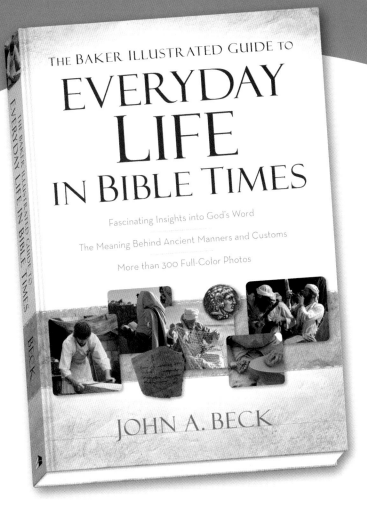

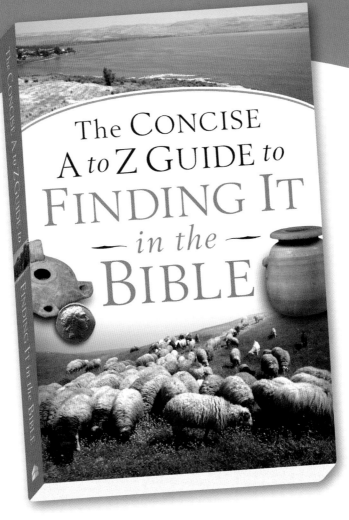

ESSENTIAL BIBLICAL REFERENCE BOOKS FOR EVERY CHRISTIAN HOME

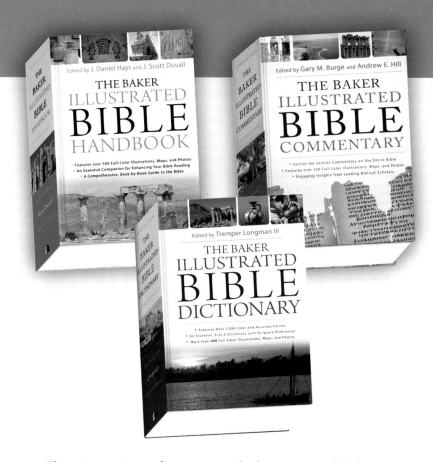

These innovative, information-packed resources will help you gain a deeper understanding of the Bible in your own personal study or in preparation for teaching.

FEATURING

- *Engaging Insights from Leading Evangelical Scholars*
- *Full-Color Illustrations, Maps, and Photos*
- *Essential Resources to Enhance Your Bible Reading*

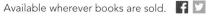